MADISON'S HAND

MADISON'S HAND

Revising the
Constitutional Convention

Mary Sarah Bilder

Harvard University Press

Cambridge, Massachusetts
London, England

First Harvard University Press paperback edition, 2017
First printing

Library of Congress Cataloging-in-Publication Data

Bilder, Mary Sarah, author.
  Madison's hand : revising the Constitutional Convention /
Mary Sarah Bilder.
       pages cm
  Includes bibliographical references and index.
     ISBN 978-0-674-05527-8 (hardcover : alkaline paper)
     ISBN 978-0-674-97974-1 (pbk.)
1. United States. Constitutional Convention (1787) Journal of the
Federal Convention.   2. Constitutional history—United States—
Sources.   3. Madison, James, 1751–1836.   I. Title.
  KF4510.B55 2015
  342.7302'92—dc23
                                                    2015009815

CONTENTS

IV

ABANDONING THE NOTES

V

COMPLETING THE NOTES

Illustrations follow page 138

ABOUT MADISON'S NOTES

This book uses simple numerical references for Madison's Notes. The absence of page numbers in the manuscript long has caused difficulties. In the 1790s, when John Wayles Eppes was copying the manuscript for Thomas Jefferson, a sheet containing part of the September proceedings appeared to be missing. Eppes wrote "there appears to be wanting in this place part of a days debate." But the absence of page numbers left Eppes uncertain.

I refer to the manuscript as if Madison numbered every folded sheet of paper. Madison later referred to his pages as "sheets." He folded a large sheet (a paper size called post, approximately 9 inches high and 15 inches wide). The fold created four writable pages. After using a sharp point to rule margin lines, Madison placed the fold on the left. He began writing on that first page. He then opened the sheet, wrote down the left and then right side. He closed the sheet and finished writing on the back. While many sheets remain intact, a number have been torn at the center margin and are in two pieces. On others, the inside margin is adhered together at the fold—likely the result of hinges used by earlier archivists.

Although specialists refer to sheets as *bifolia,* for greater accessibility to a general reader, *sheet* is employed in the text. The manuscript references, however, have been numbered as *bifolia.* The manuscript consists of 136½ bifolia. The first sheet of the manuscript is b.1. The last bifolium of the Convention proper is b.132. Each page of the sheet is referred to in the order in which it was written. The first sheet has four pages: b.1-1, 1-2, 1-3, 1-4. As an example, the first May 14 entry appears on b.1-1; the last sentence of the September 17 entry appears on b.132-4. A slip of paper added by Madison to the manuscript is referred to by the page on which it was attached. Slips are numbered in order of their sequence on the page.

For example, Madison inserted the list of delegates on slip 1, b.1-1. As part of the manuscript, the sheets containing Madison's copies of Hamilton's plan and Randolph's July plan are included. The catalogue in the Evidence section lists the bifolia and slips. Adding 10 to these numbers will produce the current Library of Congress numbering system with two exceptions: the first two sheets and two sheets currently out of order.

Most specific references are to the manuscript or the transcript in *The Documentary History of the Constitution*. I have provided citations for specific information; general facts evident from any edition of the Notes are not cited. Sentence-terminating ellipses have been omitted. Letters have been silently capitalized or de-capitalized to read in accord with the surrounding sentences.

"... when men put a machine into motion it is impossible for them to stop it exactly where they would choose ..."

—*George Washington as recorded by Thomas Jefferson (1793)*

INTRODUCTION

James Madison's record of the Constitutional Convention in Philadelphia in the summer of 1787 is the single most important source for the Convention. Politicians, judges, and scholars rely on the record, which was printed posthumously in 1840. The Library of Congress classifies the manuscript as a "Top Treasure" among the written documents it holds "in trust for the American people." This record—Madison's Notes—has acquired iconic status. But, in the process, the Notes have become misunderstood. This book is the story of the making of the Notes. It is a biography of the Notes. It is inevitably also a history of James Madison's mind, of the politics of the Constitutional Convention, and of the gradual emergence of the Constitution.[1]

Madison's Notes are the most complete and detailed description of the Constitutional Convention. An official record of the Convention was compiled by its secretary, William Jackson. In addition, notes survive from over ten other delegates. Madison's Notes, however, are the only ones that cover every day of the Convention, beginning on May 14 and ending on September 17, 1787. No other notes are as long. The manuscript is comprised of 136½ sheets of paper, folded in half with four pages of writing—over five hundred pages. In one modern printed edition, the Notes cover over 550 pages. Even a recent, significantly abridged version comes close to 150 pages. And no other notes depict the Convention as Madison's Notes do: as a political drama, with compelling characters, lengthy discourses on political theories, crushing disappointments, and seemingly miraculous successes.[2]

To a remarkable degree, Madison's Notes created the narrative we inherit of the Convention. Over a century ago, Gaillard Hunt, the editor of the first modern scholarly edition of Madison's writings, proclaimed that Madison's record "outranks in importance all other writings of the founders of the American Republic." Another noted editor, Max Farrand, concurred. When the Notes appeared, "at once all other records paled into insignificance." As a leading expert on ratification, John Kaminski, commented, "More than any other source, Madison's notes of the debates have remained . . . the standard authority for what happened in the Constitutional Convention." Two relatively recent reprints confirm this status.[3]

As a reliable source, however, Madison's Notes are a problem. They were revised; indeed, this book will suggest, revised to an even greater extent than has been recognized. Yet revision has long been intertwined with the Notes. The first printed edition described the Notes as having been revised. In the initial edition in 1840, the editor included a letter from Dolley Madison explaining that Madison had "them transcribed and revised by himself." A doctored reproduction of a partial page with revisions was reprinted in that edition. In the 1890s, the government published a lengthy transcript showing the visible revisions. In 1911, the influential publication, *The Records of the Federal Convention of 1787*, included selected revisions. In the 1930s, after discovering Madison's copy of the official journal of the Convention, Yale professors Roy Keller and George Pierson declared, "the *Debates* were pretty extensively revised within a few years after the Convention closed."[4]

Scholars have shied away from exploring the significance of the revisions. Their reluctance may arise from an anxiety about being perceived to accuse James Madison of manipulating the Notes. As James Hutson explained, "there has been an undercurrent of skepticism about their accuracy" ever since the 1840s, when Alexander Hamilton's son, John C. Hamilton, alleged that Madison inaccurately portrayed his father's positions. More provocatively, in the mid-1950s, William Crosskey, a law professor at the University of Chicago, argued that Madison had forged pages in the 1820s. Madison biographer Irving Brant and James Hutson, chief of the Library of Congress's Manuscript Division, rejected the forgery claim based on watermark and paper evidence. The existence of revisions has been known but nonetheless largely unexamined.[5]

The revisions do not detract from the manuscript's significance; they enhance it. The story of Madison's composition of the Notes emphasizes his inability—and that of his fellow delegates—to perceive the extraordinary document that the Constitution would become. Tracing Madison's decade-long composition of the Notes guides us back to a moment when the substance and fate of the Constitution remained uncertain.

Madison did not take his notes because he wanted to have a record of the proceedings of the Convention that wrote *the* Constitution. This implicit assumption that his audience must have been us appears in accounts of the Convention and of the Notes. As a recent introduction explains, "Inspired by a keen sense of history-in-the-making, he decided to keep detailed notes of the entire proceedings." But Madison did not know that they were going to write *the* Constitution. The delegates were writing a constitution a decade after an earlier effort at a constitutional document, the Articles of Confederation, had been drafted. Madison knew that the meeting was important—he wanted to keep notes—but he was not taking notes in the summer of 1787 in anticipation that those notes would be read 225 years later as the founding narrative of our Constitution. One purpose of history is to remind us that those in the past could not see the future. Historian Bernard Bailyn has written that what "impresses" the historian "are the latent limitations within which everyone involved was obliged to act; the inescapable boundaries of action; the blindness of the actors." Madison's Notes recorded one man's view of the writing of a constitution in which the politics and process of drafting the document deferred comprehension of the Constitution as a unified text. Madison's Notes, in the form they existed in the summer of 1787, revealed this indeterminacy.[6]

I suggest that Madison took his Notes first for himself, but also with the belief that the Notes would be read by Thomas Jefferson. To focus on Madison and Jefferson as readers does not mean that Madison was unaware of the possibility of a future, public audience. But the Notes were not taken *for* the public. They belonged initially to a genre of legislative diaries, kept by political figures in the era before official reporters and recorders kept accounts of the speeches and strategies of legislative proceedings. Madison kept such notes when he served in Congress in the early 1780s. Jefferson read those notes and praised Madison for them. During the summer of 1787, Madison wrote to Jefferson, who had been in Paris since 1784, that he had taken lengthy notes. Madison began composing the Notes because he had previously taken notes, and with the awareness that Jefferson would be a likely reader. Indeed, only with Jefferson's impending return to the United States in 1789 did Madison feel the need to complete the Notes. In famously referring to the relationship between Jefferson and Madison as "the great collaboration," historian Adrienne Koch focused on the period after the Convention. The story of the Notes suggests that Jefferson's absence from the Convention, Madison's notetaking, Madison's revisions, and Jefferson's reading of the Notes were a foundational aspect of their later collaboration and influenced Jefferson's interpretation of the Constitution.[7]

Madison's Notes were not originally an attempt at an objective record. As Hutson emphasizes, "they are far from a verbatim record of what was said in the Convention." Prior scholars have warned of two obvious limits. First, with the delegates meeting often for six hours a day, Madison's record was highly selective. In 1905, the reporter for the House of Representatives, Frederic Irland, speculated that Madison copied "no more than one-tenth of all that was said." Second, as Hutson also notes, "Madison could not speak and record at the same time." Madison rarely kept notes for his own speeches and did not speak from a prepared text. The notes created a record of what Madison stated in the Convention. As historian Richard Beeman appropriately observes, "Madison's diligence was in some measure self-serving." Madison's record of his speeches inevitably diverged from the versions that others heard. In the Notes, Madison created his own version of his comments and those of others.[8]

As Madison wrote the first original pages of the Notes, he was shaping his understanding of the Convention. Madison's eventual title emphasized that they were by *James Madison, a member.* He was always a participant. As he continued his entries, the pages reflected different distances: in some instances, Madison wrote his entry a few hours after the event; for other entries, it was days; and in some places, it was years. After the first weeks, Madison composed the Notes by rewriting and revising rough notes taken with his personal style of abbreviations. How much of substance did Madison alter even in his initial version? Did he omit things said by himself or others? Did he slightly shift or shade others? Did he reorder discussions? Did he change motivations and reasons? The Notes were never a neutral record of the Convention. I have come to believe that Madison understood his revisions as repeated efforts to create a record—his record—of what he saw as significant in the Convention. Yet each revision increased the distance between Madison's Notes and the actual Convention.

This book explores this distance through three questions. First, how did Madison originally write the Notes and what story did they tell? Second, how and why did he revise the Notes in subsequent years? Third, how does recognition of the original Notes and their revision alter our understanding of the Convention and the Constitution? Because a complete answer would require a variorum edition and a tome on constitutional interpretation, the book seeks to sketch answers by following Madison as he wrote and revised his notes. The narrative focuses on the first two questions. Madison revised the manuscript far more extensively than has been realized. Evidence suggests that Madison wrote most of the first two-thirds of the manuscript over the summer of 1787; however, he did not finish it until sometime after the fall of 1789. Eventually, he completed the post–August 21 section and substituted a small number of new sheets containing his own speeches. The manuscript was likely complete by the time that Thomas Jefferson became vice-president in 1797, and Madison's revisions after that point are visible. I leave the final question— the significance for modern constitutional interpretation—largely to the reader. For myself, I believe that the Notes indicate the impossibility of the delegates' fully comprehending the final text of the Constitution in its entirety in September 1787 and the degree to which the understandings of the significance of the Constitution, apart even from its multiple meanings, developed in the years after 1787.

Madison's practice of writing the Notes shaped his understanding of the decisions, controversies, and strategies. The book is a story about how Madison composed the Notes and also about the way in which the Notes reveal Madison's shifting understandings. This view raises questions about aspects of the traditional narrative of the Convention. In recounting Madison's composition of the Notes in the summer of 1787, this book addresses questions that interested me. To what degree did the small states care about state sovereignty? The Notes indicate more concern about large state political dominance than an ideology of state sovereignty. What role did Pinckney's alternative plan play? The Notes suggest the plan may have remained a strategic counterproposal throughout June and July. Was Hamilton serious about his suggestions concerning an executive on good behavior? The Notes hint that Hamilton's speech was, in significant part, a political strategy to make the Virginia plan appear moderate. Were the particular compromises reached over slavery inevitable? The Notes suggest Madison's troubling role in creating the dynamic that permitted constitutional protection for slavery. What influence did Pinckney's proposal for rights have on Madison? The Notes raise the possibility that Madison's initial succinct rendering of rights may be the source of the distinctively broad and simple eventual language.

The purpose of the book, however, is not to advance these interpretations as independent theses, but to show the importance of reading a primary document such as the Notes with consideration of context, genre,
audience, and subsequent provenance. Madison's original Notes and
revisions reopen many debates in constitutional history. The Notes deserve their place as a foundational text once we appreciate that they are
both text and artifact.

A biography of the Notes is inevitably a biography of James Madison.
The process of reconstructing the original Notes from the summer of
1787 introduced me to a James Madison slightly different from the moderate, unemotional man often depicted. In the original Notes, particular
adjectives, brief characterizations, even the rhythm of composition made
Madison appear on occasion catty, aggravated, frustrated, annoyed, and
even furious. Madison's revisions, by altering or excising these words
and comments, obscured this aspect of the Notes. Read as a legislative
diary, the Notes illuminate a private side of his personality at the Convention; read as the revised debates, the Notes confirm a public persona
of dispassionate, analytical demeanor. What a text suggests about an author's psychological state is open to many interpretations. History and
biography can never recover a true self from the paper remnants of a
person's life. Although I do not share historian Lance Banning's view of
Madison, he perceptively noted that "our interpretive container simply
would not hold the founder's understanding of himself." Madison's understanding of himself was itself an intellectual and literary construction.[9]

The biography of the Notes intersects also with Madison's intellectual
exploration of American federalism. Here again, I tell a story drawn from
the Notes that differs in some respects from prior accounts. The founding
generation sought to reconcile practical politics that favored republican
government with theoretical and historical understandings about the
struggles faced by such a government. In an era in which prominent
political thinkers suggested that only a small republic could prosper,
Madison became identified with the prediction that an extensive American republic could thrive. Indeed, in modern political science and law,
Madison is almost synonymous with the idea that the large size of the
republic cures majoritarian government's inherent tendency to empower
certain interests and oppress other legitimate minority interests. Although
this idea appears in Federalist 10, an essay written during the ratification
debates over the Constitution, the origins of the idea has been traced to
other Madison notes made before the Convention, and also his June 6

Convention speech. In reconstructing the Notes, I have come to believe that Madison did not have this idea clearly delineated prior to the Convention and that the process of writing down his speeches and recording other speakers was essential to its development. In the spring and summer of 1787, Madison seems to have wanted a specific structural solution rather than an assertion that the problem simply would not arise. Later revisions to the Notes rearranged the chronology. This story may help explain the puzzling observation of certain scholars that Madison's supposed famous theory seemed to have little influence at the Convention. Scholars in history, law, and political science, more well-versed than I about modern theories of political science and federalism, may disagree with the way I align the dots. Regardless of the details, however, I hope to persuade that Madison was not the intellectual father of the Constitution; instead, his constitutional ideas were nurtured through participation in Convention discussions and the endeavor of taking and revising the Notes.[10]

One political narrative emerged more strongly than any other in the original Notes: Madison's quest to establish a national government with proportional representation in both houses. Over the last two centuries, certain terms—"national," "state," "federal"—have become increasingly politically contested. Terms such as "national" and "state" were inherently entangled with the realities of political power. The Notes depict Madison's advocacy of a government that was expansively national in power and theoretically committed to proportional representation rather than state suffrage—and yet, nonetheless potentially politically dominated by one state, Virginia. The Notes emphasize Madison's dismissal of smaller state delegates' anxieties about Virginia's future power and conversely his willingness to promote slave state delegates' desires to protect slavery in his quest for bicameral proportional representation.

Virginia's possible dominance in future national politics came from size and slavery. The Convention delegates used rough estimates of population. There were three large states: Virginia, Pennsylvania, and Massachusetts. Of the three, only Virginia had a significant enslaved population. The later 1790 census offers useful comparative figures: 454,983 nonslave inhabitants in Virginia; 430,636 in Pennsylvania; 475,327 in Massachusetts. Virginia was the location of an additional 292,627 enslaved people. In fact, nearly half of the enslaved population in the United States was in Virginia. Virginia's potential future political power rested on incorporating enslaved people into the representation calculation by some means.

Debates over political representation necessarily related to the future legitimacy of slavery. If enslaved people—despite being denied freedom, legal autonomy, voting, and political rights—were counted, Virginia would be the single largest political power in national politics. Every other state would have to build a coalition even to equal Virginia's votes. On issues that affected Virginia's interests, the state's representatives might exert undue influence over United States politics. And the issues that the Virginians might be relatively unified on ranged from slavery to navigation of the Mississippi to the location of the national capital. This possibility haunted the decisions at the Convention.[11]

In exploring this story, I have been indebted to a vast body of scholarship on Madison, the Convention, and the early republic. Archivists and editors have worked to compile and elucidate the documentary record of the Convention and of the Notes. The indispensable *Papers* of the central figures and early Congresses have collected and made understandable the larger context. Historians and political scientists have explored the relationship of the Convention to the social, economic, and political culture. Legal scholars and legal historians have explored how the framing generation thought about the interpretation of the Constitution. Narrative accounts of the Convention have conveyed the complexity of the proceedings and its underlying politics. Recent years, in particular, have seen an outpouring of writing on James Madison and his colleagues. With specific respect to the revisions, this book builds on insights by Irving Brant, Max Farrand, James Hutson, Gaillard Hunt, John Franklin Jameson, Roy Keller, George Pierson, Leonard Rapport, and the editors of the Madison and Jefferson papers. In particular, this book agrees with prior work proving that some revisions incorporated material from a copy by Madison of the official Convention journals and the published notes of Robert Yates. Lastly, this book is animated by history of the book scholarship's consideration of the creation, storage, and transmission of the text as a physical artifact.[12]

In the prior scholarship on Madison's Notes, understandable errors occurred. Earlier studies sought to date the manuscript by examining watermarks in the Notes and Madison's correspondence. In the process, some watermarks were misinterpreted, and differences among them were overlooked. Some verification in Madison's correspondence was mistaken. Comparisons were made to Jefferson's copy of the Notes but the extent of its missing sections was miscalculated. Of equal importance, the implications of Madison's 1789 copy of the official journals (identified first in 1930) was obscured by continued scholarly reliance on the 1911 edition of Farrand's *Records*. The cumulative effect of these assumptions has placed the Notes outside of the ordinary practice of repeated reinterpretation of historical texts.

A variety of relatively inexpensive new technologies have made this book possible. For much of the past century, the need to protect and preserve the manuscript complicated efforts to study it. Throughout the twentieth century, the pages of the manuscript were attached by hinges in large volumes. By the twenty-first century, the Notes had been disassembled. The pages are now stored separately, flat in mylar sleeves. Disassembly has had a significant benefit for this study. For the first time, the sheets can be compared side by side. Microfilm, digitized microfilm, and digital photography allow the comparison of sources at different institutions. Pages can be digitally enlarged and compared. Light tables and digital technologies provide rapid, inexpensive images of watermarks. For my endeavor, the Library of Congress and other repositories generously provided images of the watermarks and helpful access to the various manuscripts.[13]

Technological advancements and future research will continue to expand information about aspects of the Notes, such as additional watermarks and illegible passages. Perhaps new documents will be found: Madison's rough notes from the Convention; his original sheets before he made substitutions; or missing pages from Jefferson's copy. Perhaps information from the publication of the retirement series of the Papers of James Madison will cast further light. Perhaps other notes will be discovered or reinterpreted. Efforts to produce high-quality digital images, to check watermarks, and to trace provenances will continue to add to our understanding.

To facilitate further historical scholarship in this area and, inevitably, reinterpretations, I have attempted to be transparent about the underlying evidence. In instances of more speculative suggestions, I have sought to describe evidentiary limits. A section entitled "Evidence" follows the book chapters and offers a detailed discussion of the six manuscripts and a catalogue of each sheet with available watermark information.[14]

The arc of the Notes spans nearly a half century. In 1787, Madison started the Notes as a thirty-six-year-old Virginian with passionate commitments to reconfigure the power of the state legislatures in order to establish a functional national government. He had no certain income or profession; the health of both parents stood between him and the inheritance of Montpelier. He was unmarried. He tended to become sick. Unlike Jefferson, he was not an antiquarian or collector. More than anything, he loved politics. The Revolution had ended officially only four years earlier, and the first effort at writing a constitution, the Articles of Confederation, had proved a moderate disaster. Washington and Franklin had established their fame; for Madison, reputation proved elusive. He struggled with a desire for credit, an often unacknowledged jealousy of others, and a preference for results. As a Virginian, Madison perceived himself responsible in large part for the effort to alter the Articles. But at the end of the Convention, he was dismayed, particularly by the apparent remaining power of the state legislatures. As historian Pauline Maier notes, Madison left Philadelphia "pessimistic" and "not altogether happy" with the result. Madison was uncertain of the Convention's success and anxious about ratification.[15]

In 1836—the year Madison died—at eighty-five years of age, he had outlived every other member of the Convention. He was, as historian Drew McCoy aptly termed him, the "Last of the Fathers." He had authored various essays of the *Federalist Papers*—although precisely which ones were in dispute. He had introduced the amendments that we know as the Bill of Rights. During the 1790s, a group of one-time allies, if not quite friends, divided as Madison and Jefferson on one side and Hamilton and Adams on the other came to believe that their opponents' success would destroy the republic. Madison had joined Jefferson in the creation of a powerful opposition Republican party. He had served as secretary of state and eventually president. He had guided the nation through another war with Great Britain. He had stood on both sides of certain issues (the national bank and states' rights); indeed, increasingly he found himself at odds with young southern politicians. He had been called the "Father of the Constitution" and for years fielded requests for accounts and explanations of the event and the document. He had acquired control of his letters and carefully prepared his papers. As historian Jack Rakove nicely puts it, in "his own way, he sought to enhance the heroic aura that already surrounded the Convention." Yet Madison could not bring himself to publish his Notes in his lifetime. His decision reflected an ambivalence about the Notes that had grown deeper as he aged.[16]

In writing this book, I grappled with the inherent challenge of multiple strands of narrative. The story unfolds in chronological order, focusing on different aspects of the construction and revision of the Notes, while also suggesting connections to larger interpretive issues. In the first eight chapters, I discuss the Notes as they likely appeared in the summer of 1787; readers familiar with conventional texts of the Notes that incorporate Madison's subsequent revisions may on occasion wonder whether a familiar quote or speech was original or likely a revision. In most cases, the visible revisions appear as small type in the transcript of the Notes printed in the *Documentary History of the Constitution,* volume 3. Major Madison speeches on replaced sheets can be located through the Catalogue in the Evidence section.

I tell the story of Madison's Notes in five parts. Part One begins before the Constitutional Convention with two examples of Madison's notetaking practice: his prior experience with a legislative diary; and his use of working notes, here notes for a possible opening address to introduce the Virginians' constitutional plan. Part Two follows Madison as he learns to keep a diary of the Convention, exploring his record of the opening days and his struggle to record the early speeches. Part Three examines the sustained section of Notes from mid-June to mid-August in which Madison delineated his political strategies, confronted failure in mid-July, and then gradually found a new role arising out of his notetaking. Part Four describes Madison's abandonment of the Notes in late August as illness, committee service, and the complexity of drafting the Constitution overwhelmed him, and his stance on the Notes as a result of the changing relevance of the Convention between 1787 and 1789. Part Five describes Madison's effort to complete the Notes for Jefferson's return from France, the levels and types of revisions, Jefferson's relationship to the Notes, and Madison's eventual rejection of Jefferson's request to publish. The Conclusion traces Madison's effort to transform the Notes from a diary into debates in the decades before his death and reconsiders the meaning of Madison's famous account of writing the Notes.

The Political Events of 1786–1796

The events of this book occurred during the pivotal decade between 1786 and 1796, when the political structure of the United States gradually shifted. For some readers, these events are well known. For others, they may lie dimly among facts acquired in school. This brief overview is aimed at providing sufficient background to understand the situation in which James Madison found himself.

Prior to the American Revolution, the American colonies had been part of a transatlantic British imperial governance structure. Each colony had a local legislature and a governor. In eight of the thirteen colonies that declared independence in 1776, the governor was appointed by the crown. Similarly, the laws passed by most colonial legislatures were subject to review in England by the Privy Council. Only Rhode Island and Connecticut held colonial charters from the crown that left them largely independent of this control. Cases from colonial courts could also be appealed to the Privy Council. Although the colonies were not permitted to send representatives to the British Parliament, colonial law remained bounded by British political authority.

With the Revolution, the American colonies developed new governing authorities, the most significant of which was Congress, usually referred to as the Continental Congress. The first Continental Congress assembled in Philadelphia in September 1774. The second Continental Congress met the next spring and became the governing authority for the colonies. The Declaration of Independence was drafted by this Congress. This Congress also drafted the Articles of Confederation in 1776 and 1777. The Articles established a new constitutional structure for the united states. Under the Articles, a unicameral Congress was created in which each state had an equal vote. There was no separate executive or judicial branch. The Articles required nine of the thirteen states to agree on many important matters. Amendment of the Articles was only possible with unanimous consent of every state. In March 1781, the Articles were finally ratified.

Throughout the period, Congress continued to meet. To signal the new constitutional authority, Congress after the Articles' adoption is usually referred to by historians as the Confederation Congress. In September 1783, the Revolutionary War officially ended with the signing of the Treaty of Paris. Congress and the states faced numerous challenges: for example, financial (significant domestic and foreign loans from the war); economic (disagreements over interstate and foreign trade); diplomatic (ongoing negotiations over commercial and other foreign relations and perceived lack of respect from European nations); and political (state legislative disregard of Congress). Although Congress needed revenue, the Articles provided no taxing power except the power to request funds from the states. In 1783, Congress recommended a revenue plan, including a proposal that apportioned the economic burden by population (with the enslaved population being incorporated at a calculation of three-fifths of the white population). The 1783 revenue plan met resistance, and an effort to amend the Articles failed.

In September 1786, the Annapolis Convention met. The Convention was comprised of men sent by state legislatures to Annapolis, Maryland, to focus on commercial and trade concerns. Although nine states elected delegates, the Convention began with members from only five states present. The Convention quickly decided to write a report recommending that a new Convention be convened in Philadelphia in May 1787. In February 1787, Congress followed this approach, agreeing that the states should send delegates to a Convention to revise the Articles and "render the federal constitution adequate to the exigencies of Government & the preservation of the Union." With the exception of Rhode Island, twelve states eventually elected and sent delegations to Philadelphia.

In May 1787, the Convention began in Philadelphia. Between May 25 and September 17, the delegates drafted the document that we refer to as the Constitution. The Convention proceeded in stages. After establishing rules and electing officers, the Convention met on May 30 as a committee of the whole house to debate a set of proposed resolutions. Although resolutions were submitted by Edmund Randolph and Charles Pinckney, the Committee proceeded by considering Randolph's resolutions, usually referred to as the Virginia Plan. On June 13, the Committee of the Whole House agreed to report a set of amended resolutions to the Convention. Between June 14 and June 19, the submission of the report was postponed. The Committee considered an alternative plan proposed by William Paterson, the so-called New Jersey plan. On June 19, the Committee submitted the June 13 report. From June 19 to July 26, the Convention debated, altered, and amended these resolutions. A five-man committee of detail was appointed to report a constitution conformable with the resolutions. On August 6, this committee submitted a printed report, in essence, a draft of the Constitution. From August 7 to September 10, the Convention reviewed this draft, again altering and amending, often by using committees to redraft language or recommend solutions. A new five-man committee was appointed to revise the style and arrangement of the amended articles in the draft. On September 12, this committee submitted a printed report. From September 12 to September 15, the Convention reviewed this report and agreed to it. On September 17, 1787, the engrossed Constitution was read and signed by thirty-nine of the forty-two delegates still present. The Constitution was then sent to the Confederation Congress.

After some debate, Congress agreed to send the Constitution to the states for ratification. Beginning with Delaware's ratification on December 7, 1787, state conventions considered whether to ratify the Constitution. With New Hampshire's ratification on June 21, 1788, the required nine states had ratified the Constitution. Of the four remaining states, ratification by Virginia and New York was essential for the new government's effective existence. Virginia ratified shortly after New Hampshire. New York did so in late July. North Carolina ratified in November 1789 and Rhode Island in May 1790. Although various conventions recommended amendments to Congress, ratification was not conditioned on the adoption of amendments.

In March 1789, representatives and senators met in New York City as members of the first Congress under the Constitution. This Congress created the early structure of the government. It established the departments, devised the procedures of government, and organized the judiciary. It also began to address the many divisive problems facing the nation: among them, national revenue, slavery, and the location of the capital. In early June 1789, as a member of the House of Representatives, James Madison recommended amending the Constitution. Eventually Congress would settle on twelve amendments to be inserted at the end of the Constitution. By December 15, 1791, the third through twelfth had been ratified. The original first amendment, relating to congressional apportionment, was never ratified. The original second amendment, relating to congressional pay raises, became the Twenty-Seventh Amendment. We refer to the third through twelfth ratified amendments as the Bill of Rights.

In the fall of 1789, Thomas Jefferson returned to the United States. Earlier that year, George Washington had been elected president. John Adams had been elected vice-president. Alexander Hamilton was appointed secretary of the treasury. In March 1790, Jefferson joined the Washington administration as secretary of state. Jefferson served as secretary of state until he resigned at the end of December 1793. By the time of Jefferson's resignation, he had come to believe that Alexander Hamilton's policies were antithetical to Jefferson's vision of the United States. Hamilton resigned in December 1795. In September 1796, Washington declared his intention to retire at the end of his second term. Two political parties had come to dominate Congress: the Federalists and the Republicans. Under the Constitution, the winner of the electoral balloting was to be president, the runner-up, vice president. John Adams, a Federalist, beat Thomas Jefferson, a Democratic-Republican, by three electoral votes. In March 1797, the two men became president and vice-president. For the prior eight years, since the beginning of the new government in March 1789, Madison had served as a representative in Congress. As Jefferson became vice president, Madison retired from national politics and, with his wife, Dolley Madison, returned to Montpelier, the family plantation outside Orange, Virginia.

The revisions to the Notes matter. Even the smallest revisions altered the depiction of the Convention and the Constitution. Consider the original first sentence of the manuscript:

> Monday May 14 was the day fixed for the meeting of the deputies in Convention for revising the federal Constitution.

Today, we refer to the men at Philadelphia as delegates or representatives, not "deputies." We describe *The* Convention, not a "convention" as a type of parliamentary proceeding. We assume they were revising the Articles of Confederation, not a pre-1787 government described as "the federal Constitution." We call the 1787 Constitution the first constitution, not a possible second constitution. The original language of the first sentence of the Notes betrayed the distance between the world of the summer of 1787 and that of the later reader.[17]

Madison's subsequent revisions minimized the distance. As with so many concepts debated that summer, words had subtly shifted to acquire new meanings. The document written in Philadelphia in the summer of 1787 and ratified the following year was the "federal Constitution." The prior description of the Articles' government as a "federal constitution" was confusing. Eventually—likely decades later—Madison scratched out "Constitution" and rewrote the phrase as "federal system of government." He did not need to change the archaic references to "deputies" or "in Convention"—a reader would interpret those words with a post-1787 spin.

In the published version of Madison's Notes, the first sentence is subtly but significantly different:

> Monday May 14th 1787 was the day fixed for the meeting of the deputies in Convention for revising the federal system of Government.

The revised first sentence emphasized the significance of the meeting and asserted a dramatic transformation in American political history. By replacing one word, ironically the word, "Constitution," Madison altered the meaning of the Convention. No longer was there a gradual and ambiguous shift from a government under a federal Constitution to one under a new Constitution of a yet-to-be determined nature. Madison's narrative instead neatly split American history into two periods. In 1787, the Convention had revised a "system of Government" into a "Constitution."[18]

Nonetheless, over the half century that Madison fiddled with the text, he left a word unchanged. He never altered "revising." That word, part of the original congressional charge to the Convention, remained as accurate to the eighty-five-year-old author as it had been when he had first written it in the summer of 1787. The significance of the Convention and of Madison's Notes—perhaps of every word in the Constitution—lay in the inherent ambiguity of *revising*.

I

NOTES BEFORE THE CONSTITUTIONAL CONVENTION

THE GENRE OF LEGISLATIVE DIARIES

The Notes of the Constitutional Convention were not initially written for posterity. They were composed for Madison's use with the intent to be shared with Thomas Jefferson. Madison's prior practice of keeping a congressional diary and his habit of sharing intelligence provided the foundation for the Notes. The genre of printed debates of American political assemblies was just beginning in the mid-1780s, and printed debates largely postdated the Convention. Instead, the 1780s was a world of closed political proceedings. In this world, personal accounts of political intelligence held considerable value. While in the Confederation Congress, Madison kept a congressional diary. This diary was shared with Jefferson and probably also with Virginia political colleagues. This congressional diary and the Notes belong to the same genre of manuscripts that this book will describe as legislative diaries, using "legislative" in the expansive meaning of relating to law making.

In these years before the Convention, Madison kept a particular style of legislative diary. Writing was a way of thinking for Madison. His diary focused on his political commitments, strategies, and conflicts. Over time, the diary came to include additional matters relating to Jefferson's interests. The diary focused on political divisions within the Virginia delegation in Congress. A consistent theme was the opposition of certain Virginians and the support of allied delegates. The entries emphasized Madison's desire for a national government and his frustration over Virginia's recalcitrance. The entries also recorded his perception of responsibility for the development of the three-fifths ratio to calculate the revenue contributions of the respective states. His apparent comfort with this compromise over slavery may have begun to become entwined with his self-identity. These substantive commitments would continue to motivate his

19

ideas in Philadelphia. Madison's legislative diary provides the starting point to reconsider the Notes.

Over a decade before the Philadelphia Convention on the eve of Revolution, Madison expressed impatience with closed political proceedings. In the fall of 1774, his college friend William Bradford wrote Madison about the Continental Congress in Philadelphia: The "proceedings are a profound secret & the doors open to no one." In 1774, the colonists took their very first steps of sorting out the nature of American—as opposed to colonial, transatlantic, imperial, and British—representative politics. The new institution—a congress—was meeting in Philadelphia. Delegates had been sent from colonial legislatures and conventions to consider the appropriate response to parliamentary legislation that appeared to limit traditional colonial rights and charters. Madison wanted to know what transpired.[1]

Madison assumed that newspapers would carry news of the proceedings. He even wondered whether the members might follow the relatively new English practice of grudgingly allowing newspaper writers to take notes of the debates. He explained, "Indeed I could wish their Debates were to be published which might greatly illuminate the minds of the thinking people among us and I would hope there would be sufficient abilities displayed." He knew that whatever appeared in print would be a partial account. He asked Bradford to send "a brief account of whatever is singular and important in their proceedings that can not [sic] be gathered from the public papers." Madison wanted political intelligence.[2]

The new Continental Congress had closed its doors. On Monday, September 5, 1774, the delegates assembled. On Tuesday, they established rules barring the public: "That the door be kept shut during the time of business." Recognizing that closed doors only kept information from the public during the meeting, they added "that the members consider themselves under the strongest obligations of honour, to keep the proceedings secret, until the majority shall direct them to be made public." Members were not supposed to share information with correspondents.[3]

Congressional information fell along a spectrum of confidentiality. The official records reflected this spectrum. An official journal of proceedings was published by the Continental Congress. Although the journal repeatedly referred to time spent deliberating and debating, the actual debates were not included. The journal included only formal orders, resolutions, and official votes. Other congressional journals remained in manuscript as "secret" journals and were not published. The "More Secret Journal," for example, contained materials relating to peace negotiations with Great Britain between 1781 and 1782.[4]

Even with respect to the printed journal, the particular information that appeared reflected political strategies. The record of individual votes was particularly controversial. Each delegation possessed one total vote; the delegation's vote was determined by the majority vote of the individual members. In the Continental Congress, each colony had a vote; in the Confederation Congress, each state had a vote. Throughout the period, Congress permitted voting to be recorded by name if requested by a member—a practice known as the ayes (or yeas) and the nays. The individual votes within the delegations were thus recorded. Nonetheless, Congress also permitted the removal of the ayes and nays from the record. On controversial votes, members debated whether the substantive vote would appear in the printed journal and whether individual names would be included. Members similarly debated whether votes should be recorded in the regular journals or the secret journals. An individual member's position was only publicly known if the ayes and nays were printed in the journal.[5]

Compared to British parliamentary proceedings, the Continental Congress was more confidential. Parliamentary proceedings were closed to nonmembers—referred to as "strangers"—but, as a practical matter, observers were permitted in the public gallery for uncontroversial discussions. A single member, however, could clear the gallery by declaring, "Mr. Speaker, I spy strangers." This practice continued into the late nineteenth century and, as a formal matter, not until 1875 did the House of Commons finally abandon the rule that one member could bar public observation. Americans were familiar with closed parliamentary proceedings because the House of Commons closed its doors in 1774 when discussing the American political situation. On both sides of the Atlantic, closed doors were accepted.[6]

Closed political proceedings made political intelligence more valuable. Indeed, in 1775, Madison wanted to discover what went on behind the closed doors. He had read two congressional publications, a "Declaration of the Causes & necessity of taking up arms" and an "Address to the inhabitants of Great Britain." He asked, "Is it discoverable who were the original Authors of them?" Madison thought "the traces of Livingstons pen" were visible. He was wrong. Among the drafters were his fellow Virginians, Thomas Jefferson and Richard Henry Lee. But the admonition of secrecy made tantalizing any hint of intelligence.[7]

When Madison entered the Continental Congress in March 1780, he joined a world in which political allies shared intelligence about the closed proceedings. The word "intelligence" is ubiquitous in political correspondence. The president of Congress, Elias Boudinot, wrote General George Washington with "the Intelligence of Congress" and included "private intelligence but of undoubted Authority." Intelligence was often confusing. Edmund Pendleton complained that accounts he had been given were "well authenticated, but so jumbled together" and seemingly divergent that he could not develop "the Intelligence Satisfactorily." Some members even advocated broad sharing of intelligence. David Howell, a delegate from Rhode Island, commented, "Should you think the intelligence in this Letter of sufficient consequence you may permit a good writer to copy it & hand that copy to any of your friends."[8]

Madison shared intelligence with a small circle of colleagues in Virginia. Throughout the 1780s, letter after letter sent by Madison promised intelligence or complained of the lack of intelligence. Four correspondents received particularly detailed information. Edmund Pendleton explained that prior delegates had "handed me all the important intelligence which was allowed to be made public." Madison assured him: "I shall endeavor to drop you a line by every post, or at least as often as any thing material occurs." Joseph Jones, a fellow delegate who had returned to Virginia, was sent the journals and "such information of the proceedings from time to time as you may think necessary." Edmund Randolph and Jefferson also received details of congressional deliberations and "other congressional intelligence." Concerns about unintentional additional readers led Madison to use code to hide disparaging comments, political predictions, and gossip, particularly about other Virginians or delegates.[9]

Madison was not alone in his desire to share congressional intelligence. The editor of the congressional delegates' letters, Edmund Burnett, noted, "Few delegates there were who did not develop a facility in leaping over the bar or crawling under it." Aware that the proceedings were confidential, the delegates nonetheless told trusted allies. One member, Arthur St. Clair, sent an abstract of congressional debates with the comment that he was not "insensible of the impropriety of divulging the Substance to [of?] Debates where Secrecy is enjoined." The sensibility did not stop him. Secrecy and confidentiality were not absolute bars but admonitions.[10]

Political intelligence mattered because American legislative debates were not printed in this period. In England, since the seventeenth century, re- porting of parliamentary proceedings had been a breach of privilege and punishable by contempt. "Debates"—printed reports of proceedings— nonetheless appeared despite the technically "illegal" nature of the prac- tice. To avoid sanction, mid-eighteenth century publishers resorted to quasi-fictional names. The most famous debates were written anony- mously by Samuel Johnson for a London political magazine with many speeches thought to be "products of Johnson's mind alone." The Johnson debates and other speeches were reprinted in *A Collection of the Parlia- mentary Debates in England from the Year 1668 to the Present Time* by John Torbuck. In 1774, John Almon began another publication, the *Parliamentary Register,* to compile debates. American colonial newspa- pers reprinted parliamentary speeches. Madison's proposed booklist for the congressional library included various *Parliamentary Debates* and *The Parliamentary Register.* Jefferson's library included additional col- lections. As historian Patrick Bullard notes, "Printed debates were desir- able texts, but they continued to occupy an eccentric, marginal place in the literary world, mixed in with the trashiest journalism." Verbatim speeches were never the aspiration and the debates were the product of illicit notes, memory, bribery, and a considerable liberality of composition.[11]

Over a decade later, when Madison went to Philadelphia for the Con- vention, American printed debates were just beginning to develop. In August 1785, Mathew Carey, an Irish printer and newspaper publisher, began to publish debates of the Pennsylvania Assembly. He noted that published debates were "here quite a novelty." In 1786, he published *De- bates and Proceedings of the General Assembly of Pennsylvania,* focusing on the controversial debate over the bank charter. The success of Carey's venture led to competitive reports on the Pennsylvania Legislature and eventually the Pennsylvania Convention by Thomas Lloyd. Nevertheless, in 1787, debates of Congress were not reported. An established genre of American printed legislative debates post-dated the Philadelphia Convention.[12]

Printed debates required creative license. Available symbolic systems of shorthand did not allow reporters to capture verbatim text. Carey explained that he did "not understand short hand, without which it is utterly impossible to keep pace with a speaker, unless he delivers himself very leisurely." He thought, however, that "very few of the material arguments on either side, have escaped him." A later set of shorthand records by Lloyd demonstrate the degree of creative interpolation. Lloyd recorded the speeches using symbolic shorthand. The transcribed symbols for one speech were:

> Bland in n lwring fl s mc f ncsty f rsing rvn and vry frt gt t b t tt b wn the mns gt t tk sm t sbvrt thmslvs consdr bfr w dpt

In print, Lloyd expanded the brief passage with considerable more detail. The skeleton argument with phrases and words became a coherent speech.

> Mr. BLAND. I join with the gentlemen who are disposed to lower the duties, although I feel the necessity we are under of raising revenue as much as any other gentleman possibly can, yet I think we ought to deliberate fully upon the means before we adopt them.

Even a trained shorthand expert needed an excellent memory and a flair for creative composition.[13]

In the absence of printed debates, Madison, like other congressional members, kept a diary. American historians have never adopted a name for such notes, referring to them as notes, diaries, or journals. British historians employ the term "parliamentary diary" to describe private diaries taken by members of Parliament about proceedings and political strategies. Parliamentary diaries, congressional diaries, and the Notes belong to the same genre. The differences in institutional power among the pre-1787 Congress, the Convention, and the post-1787 Congress, complicate the choice of an appropriate adjective for diaries. For want of an established term, this book will use "legislative diary." "Legislative" is used thus broadly to signal the general law-making focus of these diaries regardless of the type of law or the political authority possessed by the convened assembly.

On the other side of the Atlantic, parliamentary diaries provided the diarist with an independent source of information, a "personal *aide mem-*

oire." Some diaries were written to be shared with political leaders and associates; they were not intended for publication. Some were likely taken for reasons of "personal vanity." Many diarists kept rough notes and later created a fair copy of the notes after the legislative meeting. Diaries that were taken during the proceedings are marked by "marks of spontaneity," to use historian Maija Jansson's phrase, such as inconsistent handwriting, "erratic pagination," little punctuation, and poor "grammatical structure." Parliamentary diaries reflected the diarist. Some cast themselves in the "leading role," while others were too involved to take notes on matters of significant involvement. As English historian Geoffrey Elton notes about an earlier period, "Speeches are a notorious problem." Parliamentary diaries were not objective or unbiased.[14]

Although most parliamentary diaries remained unpublished, the practice was formally transmitted across the Atlantic through the publication of two English parliamentary diaries in the 1760s. In 1763, Anchitell Grey's diary of the House of Commons was published in ten volumes, *Debates of the House of Commons*. Grey had died in 1702, and the diary dated from the seventeenth century. The publication was a foundation narrative demonstrating the "Re-establishment of the Constitution" after the Glorious Revolution in the late seventeenth-century. Soon thereafter, Sir James Caldwell published his more contemporary notes of the Irish parliament as *Debates relative to the Affairs of Ireland*. The edition similarly sought to establish the legitimacy of the Irish legislature. Both editions sought to reassure readers about the authenticity of the material. The editor of Grey's *Debates* explained that Grey had taken notes "only for his own Use or Amusement" and not in "the Service of a Party" or for planned publication. Caldwell similarly emphasized his careful attendance at the sessions, even admitting he had been one day "confined by Indisposition." To explain the lengthy speeches, he referred to his process of writing from "Memory, before it should be mixed with other Ideas." Caldwell acknowledged inevitable inaccuracy. He had tried "nearly to imitate the Colouring, and always to preserve the *Contour*" of the speeches. The publication created a model for members' private diaries; indeed, Jefferson owned both sets.[15]

Many legislative diaries exist from the Continental and Confederation Congresses. Some cover a few days, a few weeks, a few months, or even a year or two. Some diaries are in a diary format, whereas others are "scattered memoranda." Diarists took notes in varying styles. Congressional delegate Arthur Middleton, for example, had learned shorthand at the Middle Temple in London, and he used that method. Others used a personal system of abbreviations or even wrote longhand. The diaries were often later fair copies of rough notes. The notes reflected momentous events such as the Declaration of Independence as well as the petty disputes, divergent interests, and political maneuvering of members. No congressional delegates had published notes; not one delegate did so at the time.[16]

A variety of recording techniques were used. In John Adams's legislative diary, one 1775 entry attempted to convey the dialogue:

> Gadsden. I am against the Extensiveness of the Rhode Island Plan, but it is absolutely necessary that some Plan of Defence by Sea should be adopted.

> J. Rutledge. I shall not form a conclusive opinion till I hear the Arguments. I want to know how many Ships are to be built and what they will cost.

> S. Adams. The Committee cant make an Estimate untill they know how many Ships are to be built.

> Zubly. Rhode Island has taken the lead. I move that the Delegates of R.I. prepare a Plan, give us their opinion.

A subsequent entry provided simply a general summary: "Zubly, Rutledge, Paine, Gadsden, lightly skirmishing." Adams recorded himself but usually in the third person: "J. Adams. The Motion is entirely out of order." The technique created distance between the diarist as speaker and notetaker.[17]

Like Adams, Jefferson kept some notes, although he did not have the diarist inclination. In June 1783, he sent Madison a fair copy of notes he possessed on the drafting of the Declaration of Independence. He summarized certain proceedings and in other places recorded speeches of considerable length. Jefferson relatively consistently introduced the speakers with descriptive action phrases: "Mr. Chase moved," "Mr. John Adams observed," "Mr. Harrison proposed," "Mr. Wilson said." As was typical of private notes, the record implicitly focused on Jefferson's participation and interests. The notes summarized the opinions for and against Virginia's resolution on independence. Jefferson then wrote, "the committee for drawing the declaration of Independence desire me to <prepare> it. <I did so.> it was accordingly done and being approved by them, I reported it to the house." The remaining notes described changes and arguments over Jefferson's draft and the debates over the Articles of Confederation relating to slavery and state suffrage. Creating a record for oneself and sharing intelligence with close colleagues were the central purpose of legislative diaries.[18]

Madison began to keep a legislative diary only after he had been in the Confederation Congress for two and a half years. The immediate purpose for the diary was likely to share with political confidantes—initially, Jones and Randolph. In November 1782, Madison briefly lost voting power when he became the only Virginia delegate in Congress. Votes were tallied by state and two members had to be present to vote for the state's vote to be counted. Jones was sick and "a prisoner" of his room. Edmund Randolph was in Virginia. Madison likely took the notes to apprise Jones of the proceedings. His letters to Randolph often closely tracked the diary entries. In a late November letter, Madison wrote Randolph that, for "want of something more interesting, I will epitomize for you the proceedings of Congress on Friday last."[19]

Nearly from the outset of Madison's practice of keeping a legislative diary, Jefferson was a likely future audience for the information and, eventually, the diary itself. Shortly after Madison began taking notes in late November, he learned that Jefferson would pass "some days" in Philadelphia gathering "information." Madison planned to provide "the communication of characters and the intelligence." Whether Madison intended to orally relay the information or share the diary is unknown. When Jefferson was in Virginia, Madison likely used the diary to recount proceedings for his letters. In May 1783, Madison explained to Jefferson that his "absence from Congs. the past week disables me from giving you the exact information of their latest proceedings." Jefferson knew of the diary and considered it reliable. When elected to the Confederation Congress in 1783, Jefferson wrote asking for "a perusal of your Congressional notes with leave to take notes from them, as they will better than any thing else possess me of the business I am to enter on." Madison's notes and his perception of congressional politics seemed essential.[20]

Madison recorded matters of interest to Jefferson. In May 1782, Jefferson's wife, Martha Wayles Jefferson, died. Madison maneuvered behind the scenes to have Jefferson sent to France as a member of the peace negotiating team. In the diary, Madison recorded a private conversation about Jefferson as secretary of foreign affairs. He included discussions relating to the release of British prisoner, Captain Charles Asgill. (Asgill had been chosen by lot to be executed in retaliation for the murder of Joshua Huddy—who himself had been hanged in retaliation for the alleged murder of Philip White.) Madison described issues related to the peace treaty and France; indeed, a comment in one entry on the peace negotiations was much later rendered unreadable, perhaps because it inappropriately breached the higher level of secrecy. Even after Jefferson's planned journey was made irrelevant by news of the likely completion of negotiations, Madison continued to include matters of likely interest to Jefferson. Once Jefferson decided to serve in the Confederation Congress, Madison focused the diary on the Virginia delegation's internal disputes over revenue plans. He included a long footnote enumerating the states' positions on a revenue bill and then copied the information into a memorandum to be sent to Jefferson.[21]

The legislative diary solved the concern about sharing confidential intelligence. In November 1782 New England newspapers published a letter by David Howell, a Rhode Island delegate, containing congressional information about foreign affairs. In Congress, Howell insisted that there was no power to "call any member of their body to account for any information which he may think proper to communicate to his constituents (the secrets only of Congress excepted)." A committee was appointed on rules for "keeping the information received by Congress or the proceedings of Congress secret." The resulting proposal involved a mandatory declaration not to reveal secrets. The proposal, however, failed. Madison criticized aspects as "very indistinct and objectionable." The discussion emphasized the advantages of communicating confidential intelligence by diary, and Madison's legislative diary began that same month.[22]

Madison's legislative diary did not attempt to record the proceedings as a third-party reporter might have. Indeed, as the editors of the Madison Papers comment with respect to one entry, "the printed journal of Congress . . . bears no resemblance to what JM recorded for that day." The diary focused mostly on Madison. The selective coverage disproportionately included items on which he had made a motion or comment; on occasion, these were very minor matters. The diary also included his involvement in congressional committee matters outside of the sessions. Madison also used the diary to offer interpretations. On a controversial vote, he noted that the yeas and nays "standing singly on the Journal, w[oul]d not express the true ideas of the yeas, and might even subject them to contrary interpretations." The diary recorded Madison's interest and ideas.[23]

With respect to Madison's role in unfortunate outcomes, the entries could tend towards circumlocution. He was inadvertently involved in the failure of an effort to fix revenue issues under the Articles. To pay for the war, a proposed amendment placed a 5 percent duty or impost on imported goods. The Articles required unanimous ratification, and eleven states agreed by July 1782. Virginia made its ratification conditional on the other states' ratification. A delegation was sent to Rhode Island to argue for ratification. They turned back after learning that Virginia had apparently repealed its conditional ratification and was unconditionally opposed. In the diary, Madison commented, "The most intelligent members were deeply affected & prognosticated a failure of the Impost scheme, & the most pernicious effects [to] the character, the duration, & the interests of the confederacy." The rumor of Virginia's repeal came from a private letter to Madison, shared by him with one of the Rhode Islanders. Madison described the circumstance in the entry but avoided the implication that, but for the letter, the congressional delegation might have continued onward, perhaps to success.[24]

The debates focused on the Virginia delegation. Madison kept track of disagreements, recording split votes and dissenting votes. He favored a general revenue to reestablish public credit and to pay war creditors. In Congress, Madison was outvoted by the other Virginia delegates, Arthur Lee and Theodorick Bland, who were bolstered by a powerful group in the Virginia legislature. Over multiple days, Madison recorded speakers on the revenue, particularly those who agreed with him. He believed that, if his "Constituents" had the "same knowledge of facts," they would also agree with him. The "Virg[ini]a. Delegates as concur" in supporting the revenue were "in a delicate situation" in Congress. Madison kept careful track of Bland and Lee. He mentioned that Bland and "still more" Lee "smiled" and noted privately an imprudent comment made by Hamilton. He included other delegates' criticism of the two—for example, Gorham's observation that Bland "would leave our army to starve." When John Francis Mercer, the new Virginia delegate arrived, Madison indicated the successful reestablishment of control over the Virginia vote: "Va. no: Mr. Bland ay. Mr. Lee silent." In fact, Mercer plunged into the discussion with such speed that one wonders if he had read the diary.[25]

The diary recorded Madison's speeches supporting the establishment of a permanent revenue for the government. One speech declared that, under the "true doctrine of the confederation," such a revenue would not be "inconsistent with the principles of liberty & the spirit of the Constitution." In another speech, he justified his disagreement with Virginia constituents. He believed that a delegate "owed a fidelity to the collective interests of the whole." A representative "ought to hazard personal consequences" to follow "his clear conviction" as to the "true interests of the whole." As historian Geoffrey Elton cautions, when a diarist records his own speech, one cannot be certain "that the speech represents what was delivered—or indeed whether the speech was ever delivered at all." Madison's speeches represented the best arguments for his positions.[26]

One particular concern relating to the revenue issue loomed large in the diary: the development of a three-fifth ratio to address slavery. The diary portrayed the ratio as Madison's solution. The Confederation Congress had debated how to consider enslaved people in calculations to raise revenue. In late March, Madison recorded that some members were "for rating slaves high" because "the expense of feeding & cloathing them was far below that incident to freemen, as their industry & ingenuity were below those of freemen." One representative, Hugh Williamson, however, was "principled ag[ain]st slavery; & that he thought slaves an incumbrance to Society, instead of increasing its ability to pay taxes." Amidst divergent opinions, Madison offered a recommendation. As he put it, his "professions of liberality" suggested, "Slaves should be rated as 5 to 3." This three-fifths ratio—calculating revenue contributions by equating five enslaved persons to three free persons—became part of the proposed revenue plan. When Madison drafted the "Address to the States by Congress" to justify the plan, he asserted the three-fifths clause was the "only material difficulty." He characterized it as the "proper difference between the labor and industry of free inhabitants, and all other inhabitants."[27]

Although Madison characterized the ratio as the product of "mutual concessions," it accorded with his attitude about slavery. Madison was the son of a Virginian plantation owner with approximately 100 enslaved people. Madison believed that slavery violated the principles of the Revolution and nonetheless participated in the perpetuation of the institution. When Madison left Philadelphia in fall 1783 to return to Virginia, he left behind Billey, an enslaved man, because he "judged it most prudent not to force Billey back to Va. even if it could be done." Madison first wrote as a slaveholder: "I am persuaded his mind is too thoroughly tainted to be a fit companion for fellow slaves." A sale would not recover "near the worth of him." Madison then added that he could not "think of punishing him by transportation merely for coveting that liberty for which we have paid the price of so much blood, and proclaimed so often to be the right, & worthy the pursuit, of every human being." Madison perceived Billey as property and as a human being coveting liberty. The three-fifths ratio reflected his underlying personal compromise to accept slavery—one that did not alter fundamentally during his life.[28]

After the revenue plan was sent to the states for consideration, Madison lost interest in the diary. Madison later acknowledged to Jefferson that his notes had "been much briefer and more interrupted." By April, the entries were short. By May, Madison was often writing a sentence, "See Journal," or "No Congress." Madison's last entries recorded the abrupt removal of the Confederation Congress to Princeton in June 1783. On June 19, Congress had grown concerned about discharged soldiers in Philadelphia. In the diary, Madison mocked the delegates' anxiety. In his opinion, there was little "danger from premeditated violence" other than soldiers "occasionally uttering offensive words and wantonly pointing their muskets to the Windows of the Hall of Congress." Moreover, Madison found Princeton annoying. He complained that the "situation here for writing" was quite "incommodious." The room "scarcely admits the use of any of my limbs." Between June 30 and November 1, Madison attended less than half the sessions. He abandoned the diary. As much as Madison found the legislative diary useful, it was the product of comfortable circumstances and ample time.[29]

Over the summer, Madison returned to writing lengthy letters about Congress to Jefferson, Jones, and Randolph. Madison was pursuing a relationship with Kitty Floyd, the sixteen-year-old daughter of a fellow congressional delegate. But by midsummer, the relationship had ended without a marriage. He continued to share congressional information. An October 1783 letter to Randolph included the votes, divisions, and names of voters on the permanent location for Congress. As Jefferson prepared for Congress, he asked for "perusal of your Congressional notes with leave to take notes from them." Madison explained that he could not "obey your wishes with regard to the notes I have on hand." He did, however, compose a lengthy summary of the debate over the permanent seat of Congress. Jefferson had remarked that Madison's notes offered insight into contemporary congressional politics "better than any thing else." Madison's failure to keep the diary through 1783 may have been a disappointment to Jefferson. Five years later, Madison may have not wanted to admit that he again had stopped recording the proceedings for Jefferson.[30]

Several years later, when Madison returned to the Confederation Congress, he sporadically returned to his practice of keeping a legislative diary. The entries cover approximately seventeen days between February 19 and April 26, 1787. They reflected the delegates' inability to conduct business. Repeatedly Madison wrote, "Nothing of consequence done"; "Nothing noted." Indeed, as one delegate noted, only for one week had the requisite nine states been represented. There was "little prospect of any thing being done in Congress."[31]

Again, the legislative diary served as a source for correspondence to Virginia. Eleven entries were written on a Tuesday or a Wednesday, coinciding with the day on which Madison often wrote letters. The entries continued to inform his letters. When the diary described the Confederation Congress's response to the Annapolis Convention Report, the topic appeared in letters to Pendleton, Monroe, and Randolph that weekend. His notes for early April were reflected in a letter to Randolph.[32]

Jefferson was in Paris but remained an important audience for the diary. Madison recorded matters likely to interest Jefferson. Matters omitted from the official congressional journal or likely recorded in the secret journals were recorded. For example, in the Confederation Congress, discussions over control of the Mississippi and treaty negotiations with Spain were matters of considerable confidentiality. In Madison's diary, many entries address the Virginians' concern about the navigation of the Mississippi and issues involving Spain. The diary included two lengthy entries describing private or semiprivate discussions with the Spanish emissary, Don Diego de Gardoqui, over navigation on the Mississippi. Similarly, the record of Madison's April 25, 1787 speech argued over whether seven states could authorize suspension of the use of the Mississippi. For the Virginians who desired open navigation of the river above and beyond other national concerns, the political issue of the Mississippi was ever present.[33]

As a future reader, Jefferson shaped the diary entries. In late March, Madison recorded the debate over the salary of the secretary of foreign affairs, a position that he hoped that Jefferson would take. Some members wanted to reduce the salary from $4000 to $3000. Madison argued for $4000. A motion to reduce the salary failed, with the ayes and nays to be recorded in the journal. The opponents then advanced a reduction to $3500 as a "Compromise." Six states favored the measure, with the Virginia delegation split. Madison voted aye. But to Madison's dismay, the original "yeas & nays" were withdrawn from the record. The only vote remaining was the salary reduction. Madison's entries proved his vote for the high salary. He explained his decision to give "up his opinion to so great a majority." The only reason to record the minor dispute was to make apparent to Jefferson that Madison had thought the higher salary appropriate.[34]

Like the earlier diary, these entries focused on Madison. A speech in March on the treaties reflected his interest in the distinction between the authority of ordinary laws and that of constitutions paramount to state legislative authority. Late April entries focused on the Mississippi, which Madison viewed as crucial to Virginia and southern states' economic survival. He remained occasionally misleading about his role. The Confederation Congress voted to suspend enlistment of troops, and the members debated whether to record the vote. Charles Pinckney wanted a record to "justify himself to his constituents." Others wanted the vote recorded in the secret journals, in essence, off the public record. In the end, Madison explained, "The expedient of a temporary concealment was proposed as answering all purposes." The passive voice—"was proposed"—hid the fact that the two-month injunction of secrecy was Madison's proposal. Madison may have worried about Jefferson's reaction or simply struggled with his own desire for credit.[35]

This distancing tendency appears in a phrase near the end of the diary. Madison recorded the debate over an unexpected effort to remove the Confederation Congress to Philadelphia so that the Convention and Congress would meet in the same place. Madison wanted Congress eventually to move south of New York, but not until after the Convention. Madison and his adversary Rufus King of Massachusetts engaged in a complicated procedural dance. King eventually succeeded in preventing removal. King's correspondence outlined Madison's political machinations. Madison left little trace in his diary. Indeed, he used the phrase, "the opinion of myself," as if he was writing about someone else.[36]

The reference—"myself"—was unusual. Throughout the 1783 and 1787 entries, Madison left a blank after *Mr.* or wrote *M* when referring to himself. Although the practice made writing faster, it also created a certain disassociation. Only years later when he revised the diary for eventual publication did Madison add his name.

Madison did use "I" in his diary on April 26, 1787. The last sentence on the last entry in the diary stated: "Nothing further was done . . . till Wednesday May 2. when I left N. York for. . . ." Madison crossed out the original final word—but it may have been "Philadelphia." Later, he would revise the concluding sentence to state that he left for "the Convention to be held in Philadelphia." The significance of the Convention was only obvious in retrospect. But attendance at Philadelphia was a rare decision for which Madison was willing to assert responsibility.[37]

2

THE PRACTICE OF WORKING NOTES

Madison went to the Philadelphia Convention prepared to keep a legislative diary and with a set of working notes outlining national problems. The Philadelphia Convention was his second national convention in recent years. Almost a year earlier, he had attended the Annapolis Convention. Although the Virginia legislature formally issued the initial call for the Annapolis meeting, for Madison the convention may have offered an opportunity to advocate for even broader national authority without the direct opposition of certain Virginia politicians. Conventions might make possible a different combination of political concerns. At the recommendation of the unsuccessful Annapolis Convention, the Confederation Congress authorized a second convention to "render the federal constitution adequate to the exigencies of government and the preservation of the Union."[1]

The brief Annapolis Convention did not result in the creation of a new legislative diary; instead, in the aftermath, Madison used working notes to record his political theories and insights. Like his legislative diaries, Madison shared his notes with close colleagues. In the year before the Convention, his notes blamed the state legislatures for the failure of the government under the Articles of Confederation. The notes recorded Madison's development of four strategic goals and a series of recommendations for a new government. The national government was to have due supremacy; the states were to have subordinate utility. To prove the necessity of minimizing state power, Madison prepared an outline of problems facing the nation—his famous "Vices of the Political System" manuscript. He may have intended it to be the substance of an opening speech at the Convention. Madison, however, did not give the opening speech. Nonetheless, he kept the notes, awaiting another opportunity to

use them. This practice of reusing and revising working notes—of turning them to new purposes—would come to be one of Madison's great
strengths.

In 1786, the Annapolis Convention marked the return of Madison to an
official role in national politics. The Articles of Confederation barred a
congressional delegate from serving for more than three years in any
six-year period. At the end of Madison's term in the fall of 1783, he returned to Virginia to his parents' house, Montpelier. In the 1780s, his
father and mother were alive. Indeed, his father would live until 1801;
his mother died in 1829 at the age of ninety-eight. Born on March 16,
1751, Madison was the eldest in a large family. At twenty, he graduated
from the College of New Jersey (now Princeton) and stayed on an extra
year for additional studies. Afterward, he had focused on politics. At
twenty-five years of age, he was elected to the Virginia legislature; three
years later, he was elected to the Confederation Congress. In 1783,
Madison was considering law as a possible profession. He began to study,
borrowing law books from Jefferson's library at Monticello. In notes
taken during his law reading, Madison seemed particularly drawn to the
way in which law wrestled with the inherent ambiguities in language. This
interest would remain, but a legal career was put to the side, and he never
took steps to become a member of the bar. Madison instead followed a
political career, aspiring to offices with reimbursed expenses or salaries.[2]
  In 1784, Madison joined the Virginia state legislature as an astute observer of legislative politics. A December 1784 letter to his father described an array of strategic considerations. A bill needed to be adapted
to the "many latent objections of a selfish & private nature to which every
innovation is liable." A year later, Madison described how motions and
"other dilatory artifices" could be used for delay. It was often better to
accept an amendment that "somewhat defaced the composition" but not
the substance of a bill than "run further risks." Success could come when
opponents had not "known their strength in time." Legislative machinations fascinated him.[3]
  Even away from the Confederation Congress, Madison continued to
receive congressional intelligence. Before departing for France in 1784,
Jefferson sent confidential facts and derisive comments about individuals
in code. James Monroe likewise sent Madison encoded letters with names,
characterizations, and political gossip. When William Grayson joined the

Virginia congressional delegation, Madison struck up another correspondence. The assumption that intelligence was to be sent to Madison became sufficiently well known that the new Virginia delegate in 1786, Henry Lee, wrote Madison by "way of introduction of a correspondence" and enclosed a congressional report.[4]

Interpretive questions under the Articles of Confederation intrigued Madison. He thought about questions under the Articles as constitutional questions. During these years, the meaning of "constitution" shifted from a description of the entire political system of government toward a specific written document establishing the frame of government. Under the Articles, a state was required to deliver to another state "any person guilty of or charged with treason, felony, or other high misdemeanor." Madison and Randolph exchanged letters discussing the "difficult point" about the words, "Treason &c." Did the word, "treason," refer to British legal definitions or should it be defined as whatever activities to which the various states had "annex[ed] the same titles and penalties?" For Madison, the text of the Articles did "not clear the ambiguity." He concluded: "The truth perhaps in this as in many other instances, is, that if the Compilers of the text had severally declared their meanings, these would have been as diverse as the comments which will be made upon it."[5]

The history of the Articles also interested Madison. While in the Confederation Congress, he copied materials from the journal related to the drafting process. Jefferson sent him additional notes on "the debates in Congress on the subjects of Independance [sic], Voting in Congress, & Quotas of money to be required from the states." Madison wanted more materials. Jefferson asked George Wythe, another Virginia delegate, for "notes on the Confederation." Madison's purpose is unknown. The material would have made sense for a speech or essay on the Articles. It also would have supported an argument that the Articles authorized broader powers in the Confederation Congress.[6]

By the mid-1780s, Madison advocated more extensive national authority, particularly over commerce. Other Virginians disagreed. Madison complained that even if national measures passed, "a few members" of the Virginia legislature could sink it. He commented, "Congress have kept the Vessel from sinking, but it has been standing constantly at the pump, not by stopping the leaks which have endangered her." Madison was not alone. George Washington wrote: "We are either a United people, or we are not." Washington wanted "a nation" with "national objects to promote, and a national character to support." In March 1785 at Mount Vernon,

Washington hosted a group of commissioners from Maryland and Virginia with hopes of addressing jurisdictional and trading concerns. Madison had been appointed to the Virginia commission but did not attend because Governor Patrick Henry never informed him or Randolph of the time and place.[7]

Madison increasingly believed that the foundational arrangement under the Articles needed to be altered. He compiled a set of notes on the problems of government based on confederated political structures. The notes compared "Ancient & Modern Confederacies," a popular form of political analysis. Montesquieu had used models of ancient and modern governments in *The Spirit of the Laws*. In 1782, the Académie Royale in Paris even sponsored a contest with the winning essay comparing the Achaean, Helvetic, and Belgic Confederacies. Madison selected similar confederacies, many of which had the advantage of appearing in two encyclopedic works sent by Jefferson. For the confederacies, Madison summarized the structure of "Foederal Authority" and described the "Vices of the Constitution." Madison excelled at paraphrasing. For example, Montesquieu's original text stated: "In Lycia, the judges and town magistrates were elected by the common council." Madison concisely simplified it: "The Judges and Town magistrates were elected by the general authority." The paraphrase demonstrates another Madison trait. He translated ideas into his political vocabulary, replacing "common council" with the concept of "the general authority." As Madison wrote, he was reformulating the original text into his own conceptual vocabulary.[8]

The Confederacies notes emphasized the impossibility of using a confederation structure for national purposes. Washington read and copied the manuscript. The notes repeatedly emphasized the lack of effective authority in confederated political structures. Madison summarized and Washington copied: "Jealousy of the Imperial authority seems to have been a great cement of the confederacy." Jealousy, however, was a shaky foundation for a nation. In 1786, both men hoped that an upcoming "Continental Convention" would propose a method to "correct the vices of the Confederation."[9]

In August 1786, Madison traveled north for the Annapolis Convention. John Adams was told the meeting likely "originated in Virginia and with Mr. Madison." Some historians believe he was responsible for the Convention; others argue that it was not his "brainchild." Regardless of responsibility, Madison considered the Convention "a remedial experiment." Even if "nothing can be done," that recognition would "be worth the trouble."[10]

On the journey north, he stopped in Philadelphia, likely at the establishment run by Mary House—which Madison referred to as a "hotel" and we might consider a guest house. During his earlier years in Congress, Madison had stayed with the Houses. Madison was close to House's widowed daughter, Eliza House Trist, although the relationship remains obscure.[11]

Although historians know of no notes kept by Madison at Annapolis, he seems to have acquired by then the paper on which he later recorded the Philadelphia Convention. On the journey to Annapolis, Madison had purchased various imported items using money from tobacco sales. Perhaps en route, Madison bought the fine English paper by James Whatman that he later used for the Convention Notes. His two letters on September 8 and 11, 1786, about the Annapolis Convention match the paper in the early Notes.[12]

The Annapolis commissioners were a small but impressive gathering. New York sent Alexander Hamilton and Attorney General Egbert Benson. Virginia sent Madison, Edmund Randolph, and St. George Tucker. Delaware and New Jersey also sent strong delegations. John Dickinson, principal drafter of the Articles of Confederation, was in attendance.[13]

Madison's aspirations were ambitious. In a letter to Jefferson, Madison described the eight states that had appointed deputies and the reasons for other absences. He hoped the meeting would end up being "subservient to a Plenipotentiary Convention for amending the Confederation." Regardless of that possibility, he expected "Commercial Reform." Such reform was no small thing. Rufus King noted that Madison's proposed commercial reform would "necessarily be extensive." It would require "full powers" for Congress over commerce and a "federal Judicial" structure. It would "run deep into the authorities of the individual States." Yet Madison was also uncertain. After he arrived, he wrote to his brother that the meeting might be "prolonged" or "shortened."[14]

On Monday, September 11, the Convention convened. The credentials were read describing the authority delegated by the state legislatures. Some states focused on commerce, while New Jersey gave authority to permit consideration of "a uniform system in their commercial regulations and other important matters." The Convention appointed a committee to draft a report and then adjourned until Wednesday. Madison had a slim hope of "the sudden attendance of a much more respectable number." On Wednesday, the Convention decided to wait one more day but on Thursday no news of additional commissioners was received. In the end, the Convention agreed to a report, which recommended a second Convention in May in Philadelphia.[15]

The report finessed possible disagreements. Madison wanted to explain "the expediency of extending the plan to other defects of the Confederation." The report admitted "important defects in the system of the Foederal Government." Adroitly, it avoided any "enumeration" of defects, claiming they were well known and the "subject of public discussion." Each state could interpret "defects" as it chose. The purpose of the successive convention was similarly ambiguous: to "devise such further provisions as shall appear to them necessary to render the constitution of the Foederal Government adequate to the exigencies of the Union." The "constitution of the Foederal Government" could be interpreted as mere amendment of the Articles of Confederation, or it could mean extensive restructuring of the political structure to promote the Union.[16]

Annapolis taught the delegates present important lessons about requirements for a more successful proceeding. Philadelphia, the former location of the Confederation Congress, would improve attendance. The Pennsylvania delegation—represented only by Tench Coxe at Annapolis—would be hard pressed not to appear. A low quorum requirement would permit business to begin—the Philadelphia Convention required only seven of the thirteen states. The Delaware delegation learned a different lesson about the need to ensure no alterations to equal state suffrage. The same three men at Annapolis (Read, Dickinson, and Bassett) returned to Philadelphia with specific credentials. Although they could cooperate with Virginia and other states on amendments to the Articles, they could not agree to alter Article Five, "which declares that 'In determining Questions in the United States in Congress assembled each State shall have one Vote.'" The specificity and commitment to the instruction would ultimately sidetrack Madison's greatest aspiration in Philadelphia. The discussions at Annapolis may have been influential on the large group of men who appeared at both conventions. In addition to the three Delaware delegates, other men returned, most importantly, Madison, Edmund Randolph, and Alexander Hamilton. For Madison—as for others—Philadelphia was a second try.[17]

After Annapolis, Madison spent several weeks in Philadelphia at the House hotel. In October, Henry Lee wrote Madison that the "long time . . . gives eye to various suggestions all tending to prove you are in full gallop to the blessed yoke." Madison biography Gaillard Hunt believed Lee; biographer Irving Brant dismissed the comment as a "myth of a mysterious romance." The widowed Eliza House Trist—Madison's long-time correspondent—is one obvious possibility. James Monroe asked Madison to pass along his "best respects to Mrs. Trist & the family." But whatever relationship Madison had with Mrs. Trist, or another woman, never materialized in a marriage. Eliza Trist, indeed, never remarried. Instead, in mid-October, Madison left Philadelphia for the Virginia legislative assembly session, no doubt hoping to return to Philadelphia. He traveled south with James Monroe and his wife, stopping on the way to visit General George Washington at Mount Vernon.[18]

In the absence of certainty about the success of the forthcoming convention, Madison continued to advocate for significant reform under the Articles. A page of notes on discussions in the Virginia legislature argued that national commercial regulation to prevent "dissolution of the Confederacy" was "within reason of federal constitution" and "[e]ssential to preserve fed[era]l. Constitution." If the Philadelphia Convention had not occurred, Madison would likely have pushed for broader legislative powers under the Articles. He later saw, however, these discussions in light of future events and added the subtitle: "In Virg[ini]a. Legislature previous to Convention of 1787." He drafted the bill to appoint the Convention delegates and, in December, was appointed a deputy for the "purpose of revising the federal Constitution."[19]

Madison had also been appointed a member of Virginia's delegation to the Confederation Congress in New York. In February 1787, he traveled to New York. The Virginia delegation was perilously small. He and William Grayson alone were present—and Grayson had been notoriously ill. Only near the end of March did another delegate, Edward Carrington, arrive; only in late April did a fourth, Henry Lee, appear. Madison returned to his habit of acquiring and receiving political intelligence. He wrote Pendleton to "revive my claim to a correspondence" relating to the congressional proceedings. Jefferson wrote with a "just estimate of certain public characters" to assist Madison as he "returned into Congress." Various diplomats, starting with John Adams, were described in code with an array of unflattering adjectives.[20]

Other congressional delegates planned to attend the Convention. Nathaniel Gorham and Rufus King (Massachusetts), William Samuel

Johnson (Connecticut), Pierce Butler (South Carolina), William Pierce (Georgia), and eventually William Blount (North Carolina) would leave the Confederation Congress to travel to the Convention. They were to be joined by others who had been elected to Congress but had not yet attended: Charles Pinckney (South Carolina), James Wilson (Pennsylvania), Abraham Baldwin and William Houstoun (Georgia), John Lansing, Jr. (New York), Nicholas Gilman and John Langdon (New Hampshire), and Alexander Martin and Hugh Williamson (North Carolina). The significant overlap meant that, by April, the focus in Congress had shifted towards the Convention. A future Convention delegate noted that "the season being near at hand for the meeting of the Convention little else is talked of." People had "great expectations."[21]

Madison, however, had worries. One related to the Virginia delegation. If the Convention followed congressional voting rules—one vote per state—Madison needed a majority of the delegation in agreement with him. The Virginia delegation was to include Washington and Randolph, as well as Patrick Henry, John Blair, George Wythe, and George Mason. By March, Randolph assured his attendance and two other likely allies for Madison. Randolph would employ a "state boat" to convey Wythe and Blair so that the "badness of their cavalry" did not prevent their attendance. Fortunately, Patrick Henry—an oppositional vote for Madison—resigned. He was replaced with another Madison ally, Dr. James McClurg. By April, George Washington had been persuaded to attend. Madison had qualms about Mason but was reassured that he planned to "take an active part in the amendment" of the confederation.[22]

An additional concern related to the "partial views and interests" of delegates. Madison worried about two scenarios. One was a "propensity towards Monarchy." Barely a decade since the American Revolution, the commitment to the new idea of republican government was still tenuous. The other was "a partition of the Union into three more practicable and energetic Governments." The two possibilities reflected concern about republican government. Contemporary political theories suggested that republic political structures worked only over small territories. The strength needed to govern an extensive and expansive country like the United States was thought to require the authority of an executive analogous to a monarch. The possibility of division appears to have been a serious concern. John Dawson feared "an end to the General confederacy." William Pierce asked, "shall we be three confederated Republics or not?" Madison explained, "I hope the danger of it will rouse all the real friends" to favor "such an organization of the Confederacy, as will perpetuate the Union." He worried about the possible "partition of the Empire into rival & hostile confederacies." The unease about monarchy and permanent division would shadow the Convention.[23]

In the meantime, the three Virginians—Washington, Madison, and Randolph—prepared. Randolph suggested they draft "some general propositions" to feel "the pulse of the convention." Washington advocated linking current problems to new solutions. The Convention should "adopt no temporizing expedient, but probe the defects of the Constitution to the bottom, and provide radical cures, whether they are agreed to or not." Madison had long aspired to a "thorough reform of the existing system." Indeed, to Jefferson in mid-March, Madison described "leading ideas" that he viewed as "necessary" but others would see as "improper" to address the "mortal diseases of the existing constitution."[24]

By mid-April, Madison circulated "*some* outlines of a new system" that restructured—indeed, basically abandoned—the confederated governmental structure. In letters to Randolph and Washington, Madison argued that "individual independence" of the states was "utterly irreconcileable" with the "idea of aggregate sovereignty." Madison did not reject the theoretical possibility of complete consolidation of the states, but he thought it practically infeasible. He proposed "a due supremacy of the national authority," leaving "local authorities so far as they can be subordinately useful." Four proposals sought to attain this balance of due supremacy and subordinate utility:

1. Alter the principles of representation to end equality of suffrage of the states in a bicameral national legislature.
2. Enlarge the powers of the national government to "positive and compleat authority in all cases which require uniformity."
3. Place a negative in all cases over state laws in the national legislature.
4. Ensure that the constitution was paramount to state legislatures by ratification of the people of the states.

"National supremacy" extended to the creation of a "national Executive" and "Judiciary departments." Madison acknowledged that the ideas—promoting national supremacy and diminishing state legislative authority—"strike so deeply at the old Confederation."[25]

In particular, Madison was captivated by a national negative over state laws. The positive power of expanded national legislative authority needed to be supported by a reciprocal negative authority over state legislation. The negative (a word whose meaning has since vanished) was a mechanism to disallow a law, often before it went into effect. The negative's origins lay in the constitutional limits on the colonial legislatures. Over most colonies, the British Privy Council had the authority to negative colonial legislation. Although most colonies had been governed by such a negative, by the Revolution it had grown controversial, and for the past decade no such mechanism had existed at the national level. Madison saw it as a solution for "the aggressions of interested majorities on the right of minorities and of individuals." The national authority could use the negative as a "dispassionate umpire in disputes between different passions & interests in the State." Madison implied the mechanism was the "great desideratum" for "Republican Governments." William Grayson commented, however, "Figure to yourself how the States will relish the idea of a negative on their laws &c &c &c."[26]

In addition to drafting general propositions, Randolph recommended the preparation of an "an address to accompany the new constitution." That spring, Madison recorded his ideas in a manuscript, known to historians as the "Vices of the Political system of the United States." The manuscript has been traditionally interpreted simply as Madison's working notes. Madison's commentary, however, is written under a centered heading, "Observations"—the purpose was "Observations on the Vices of the Political system of the United States." The manuscript listed twelve vices of political system under the Articles. The first eleven vices were explained; the twelfth vice has no explanation under the heading. The structure permitted it to have served as the basis for an opening address at the Convention.[27]

The surviving manuscript does not resemble material for an opening address because of a lengthy discussion under the eleventh vice. This extended section analyzed the problem of societal interests and factions. The discussion speculated that the extensive size of the future country would ameliorate the ability of various interests to control the majority. This idea appears in similar form in Madison's famous Federalist 10 essay after the Convention.[28]

The extended discussion of the eleventh vice may have been added at a later time to the manuscript. Textual evidence hints that the extended discussion may be an anomaly. As the Madison Papers editors point out, it does not align with constitutional and political ideas advanced contemporaneously by Madison. Moreover, the pages on which it appears are on a different paper—paper that appears visually to match the paper used during the Convention. The extended discussion cannot yet be definitively shown to predate the Convention.[29]

With the extended discussion omitted, the vices were explicated through brief observations. Madison used "we," "us," and "our"—all words that made sense in an address—and included rhetorical questions as if addressing an audience. The structure and style resembled an opening address on the defects of the current system. The vices were divided into three groups of four. The first four vices related to the federal authority. The words—*failure, encroachments, violations,* and *trespasses*—were strong, condemnatory synonyms.

1. Failure of the States to comply with the Constitutional requisitions
2. Encroachments by the States on federal authority
3. Violations of the laws of nations and of treaties
4. Trespasses of the States on the rights of each other

The second four vices were described as *wants of*—with the uniform phrase unifying the somewhat awkward framing.

5. Want of concert in matters where common interest requires it
6. Want of Guaranty to the States of their Constitutions & laws against internal violence
7. Want of sanction to the laws, and of coercion in the Government of the Confederacy
8. Want of ratification by the people of the articles of Confederation

The last four vices involved the *laws of the States.* Madison elsewhere summarized the "internal vicisitudes [*sic*] of State policy." He expanded the idea to four vices; the symbolically evocative twelve vices was an improvement over nine for an opening address. Madison bothered with a stylistic flourish: *multiplicity* with *mutability* and *injustice* with *impotence.*

  9. Multiplicity of laws in the several States

10. Mutability of the laws of the States

11. Injustice of the laws of the States

12. Impotence of the laws of the States

As literary scholar Eric Slauter notes, *impotence* was a word favored by Madison's contemporaries. The implicit sexual connotation to a Convention of men may have been an irresistible ending.[30]

As an opening address, the Vices promoted Madison's fundamental commitments: due supremacy of the national authority and the subordinate utility of local authorities. The eighth vice (want of ratification by the people) emphasized the need to ensure that the constitution would be superior to state laws. The twelve vices supported Madison's proposals about a new government structure. In particular, the last four vices— emphasizing the problems of state laws—emphasized the need for a broad negative on state laws. The address was Madison's demonstration of the "existing embarrassments and *mortal* diseases of the Confederacy."[31]

If Madison planned to give an opening address, his plan never came to fruition. Edmund Randolph introduced the propositions from Virginia. Madison may have shared the Vices with Randolph but, in the end, Randolph used his own notes for the speech—notes that Madison several years later sought to obtain. Madison would record in his notes only a brief summary of Randolph's address—perhaps because it mirrored in certain respects Madison's ideas, perhaps because he thought his own version superior. The manuscript, however, was not discarded. Madison would rearrange the ideas for a speech in mid-June defending the plan. As these notes demonstrate, Madison's talent lay in his remarkable facility to revise his analyses to support new political ends.

II

LEARNING TO KEEP A
CONVENTIONAL DIARY

3

THE SUCCESS OF THE OPENING DAYS

The opening days of Madison's Notes of the Philadelphia Convention were a legislative diary. The initial entries were casual and perhaps intended to be drawn on for correspondence. With the imposition of confidentiality for the duration of the Convention, the entries grew longer. During the first week, Madison stopped writing the Notes from memory. He began to keep rough notes during the session, afterwards transcribing them into readable entries. A consistent narrative voice began to appear with an opening summary sentence for each speaker, uniform terminology, and modulated emotion.

The entries recorded the significant events for Madison—and also for Jefferson as a future audience. Madison's perception of significance—and insignificance—reflected his views in early June 1787. The original Notes hint at emotions not usually associated with Madison: annoyance at a suspiciously similar plan by Charles Pinckney; exasperation at Edmund Randolph's refusal to go along with a single executive; apparent frustration at the revolutionary-era political opinions of the aging Benjamin Franklin. Madison skipped rules, motions, and entire topics. The Virginians were the leading figures; the other delegates were either allies or critics. The first week of the Notes from Friday, May 25, to Saturday, June 2, focused largely on one issue. Madison was determined to replace the equal representation of the states under the Articles of Confederation's unicameral Congress with proportional representation in both Houses of a new bicameral national legislature. Stripped of later revisions, the opening days of the Notes reveal Madison's conviction that he would succeed.

A month before the Convention began, uncertainty about the outcome was pervasive. Madison, Randolph, and Washington headed to the Convention with only cautious aspirations of success. Other politically astute Virginians, however, predicted a different outcome. Virginia congressional delegate Edward Carrington wrote Jefferson that the sounding of "an alarm" was the most likely outcome. The system under the Articles was "very imperfect" but Carrington believed the problems were not related to "defectiveness in the constructure [*sic*]." The other Virginia congressional delegate, William Grayson, was convinced that the Convention would either "effect nothing" or the "States will not confirm." Since the Revolution, the Confederation had been beset with problems. A continuation of the same frustrations was an equally plausible outcome. In the summer of 1787, Madison and the other delegates did not know they would be successful in drafting a new constitution.[1]

On May 5, Madison arrived in Philadelphia. He immediately moved into his old quarters at the House hotel. Washington planned to stay at the House establishment but was persuaded by Robert Morris to reside in his mansion. Randolph and McClurg would eventually join Madison, but they had not yet arrived.[2]

On May 14, the second Monday of May, the Convention was supposed to begin. Only eight members attended, however, all from the Pennsylvania or Virginia delegations. Randolph arrived the next day. Washington kept track in his diary as members trickled in. The delay served to "sour the temper of the punctual members"—likely referring to the Virginians. By Saturday, May 19, only four delegations had the necessary two members to cast votes: Virginia, Pennsylvania, South Carolina, and New York.[3]

While awaiting a quorum, the Virginians strategized. The delegation met every day for two to three hours to "form a proper correspondence of sentiments." George Mason outlined the plan to his correspondents. A two-branch "national council or parliament" would be based on "equal proportionate representation." The legislature would have "full legislative powers upon all the subjects of the Union" and a negative over state laws "contrary to the interest of the federal Union." The negative—analogous to a legislative veto—would ensure that state legislatures were "subordinate to the national." An executive and judiciary were included. Mason was optimistic. Conversations suggested "greater unanimity and less opposition" than he had expected. Mason noted only one likely group of dissenters: "the little States."[4]

The little states would be understandably dismayed with the Virginians' plan. It abandoned equal state suffrage. In the Confederation Congress, each state had one vote. A decade earlier, when the Articles had been drafted, the Virginia delegates had objected to the equal state suffrage. Madison was convinced that it remained the underlying cause of current problems. In April, he predicted the "change in the principle of representation will be relished by a majority of the States, and those too of most influence." The "Northern States" would agree because of the "*actual* superiority" of their populations and the "Southern" states because of their "*expected* superiority."[5]

Virginia would benefit from a shift to proportional representation. It was the largest state, encompassing present-day West Virginia and the area that would soon become Kentucky. The largest population of people held in slavery lived in Virginia. Under proportional representation, if the population held in slavery was even partly included, Virginia could exert a dominating influence. The change to proportional representation had another advantage. An individual delegate's vote would likely be made independent from the other members of the state's delegation. Madison believed that abandoning equal state suffrage would liberate delegates from the ill-considered views of the state legislatures and their fellow delegates. He knew the small states would disagree; however, he was convinced that they would "ultimately yield to the predominant Will."[6]

The Virginians' plan was not the only circulating plan that "lesser States" would dislike. The Delaware delegates acquired a "copied draft," apparently by South Carolina's Charles Pinckney. Pinckney was a fellow guest at the House hotel. Pinckney's plan also shifted power toward large-state inhabitants. Members were to be elected based on number of inhabitants: specifically numbers of white inhabitants plus three-fifths of all others, including enslaved people. A senate would be elected from "four great districts," requiring the theoretical grouping of smaller states. A president would serve for seven years. The Delaware delegates believed the plan reflected a "proposed Consolidation of States." George Read calculated that Delaware would have only one of the approximately eighty representatives. He predicted that the "larger States" would "probably combine to swallow up the smaller ones by addition, division, or impoverishment." To the delegates from the smallest states, proportional representation in both houses meant more than diminished governmental power; it seemed to lead to the eventual extinction of the smallest states.[7]

Other state delegations worried about possible consequences. Rufus King of Massachusetts was "mortified" to be "alone" from New England. On May 24, King urged Connecticut's Jeremiah Wadsworth to "hurry on your Delegates" and put aside "personal Sacrifices." For smaller New

England states, King declared that the "Backwardness may prove unfortunate." Pennsylvania, Virginia, New York, North Carolina, and South Carolina had delegations. Maryland and Georgia were expected soon. The smallest states would participate in the Convention with diminished power. Delaware was present at the outset; Connecticut and New Jersey gradually arrived. New Hampshire's delegates, however, appeared only in late July. Rhode Island never sent a delegation. If Madison could create a coalition of five or six states, he would control the Convention.[8]

For Madison the slow start was the salient initial fact about the Convention. His Notes emphasized the delay. He began with the official day set by Congress:

> Monday May 14th was the day fixed for the meeting of the deputies in Convention for revising the federal Constitution. On that day a small number only had assembled. Seven states were not convened till,

After the comma, Madison left the rest of the line blank. He placed "Friday 25 of May"—the first day of proceedings—on the next line. The space visually indicated the aggravating delay.[9]

The opening sentence reflected Madison's interpretation of the Convention's purpose. The lengthy congressional charge was summarized. The charge described "the sole and express purpose of revising the Articles of Confederation and reporting to Congress and the several legislatures such alterations and provisions therein as shall when agreed to in Congress and confirmed by the states render the federal constitution adequate to the exigencies of government and the preservation of the Union." Madison, however, wrote the succinct phrase, "revising the federal Constitution." The tension between solely revising the Articles and rendering the constitution adequate for Union was erased. In substituting the more general description (federal Constitution) for the specific document (the Articles), Madison indicated little concern about alleged limits to the Convention's authority. In his mind, the purpose all along was to revise the federal Constitution.[10]

On Friday, May 25, the Convention mustered a quorum for the first time. That Sunday, May 27, Madison wrote letters to his father, Edmund Pendleton, and Joseph Jones. He noted, "I have put off from day to day writing to my friends from this place in hopes of being able to say something of the Convention." He optimistically explained, "the members seem to accord in viewing our situation as peculiarly critical and in being averse to temporising expedients." He carefully folded the letter, addressed it, and marked it with his name and "Free"—his franking privilege as a member of the Virginia delegation.[11]

Unlike letters he sent the previous week, Madison wrote these letters—like the subsequent letters that he would send from Philadelphia that summer—on paper made by the English papermaker James Whatman. Madison may not have used this paper since sending his letters from the Annapolis Convention. The Whatman paper had slightly visible evenly spaced chain lines that helped to keep handwriting neat and straight. For the Notes, Madison folded each sheet in half. On the left side of the first page, he scored a margin to keep his writing aligned.[12]

Madison's first entry in the Notes was a page-long political analysis. The tone was short and chatty. It was likely written from memory and is so similar to his Sunday letters that it is difficult to guess which were written first.

Friday 25 of May

M^r. Robert Morris informed the members assembled that by the instruction & in behalf, of the deputation of Pen^a. he proposed ~~the~~ George Washington Esqr. ~~should~~ late Commander in chief ~~should~~ for president of the Convention. M^r. Jno. Rutlidge seconded the motion; expressing his confidence that the choice would be unanimous, and observing that the presence of Genl. Washington forbade any observations on the occasion which might otherwise have been proper.

The General was accordingly unanimously elected by ballot, and conducted to the chair by M^r. R. Morris and M^r. Rutlidge; from which he thanked in very emphatical manner the Convention for the honor they had conferred on him, reminded them of the novelty of the scene of business in which he was to act, lamented his want of the requisites for it, and claimed the indulgence of the House towards the involuntary errors which his inexperience might occasion.

The nomination came with particular grace from Pennā, as Doc^r. Franklin alone could have been thought of President [illegible words] of obtaining the [illegible word] of Genl. Washington. The Doc^r. was himself to have made the nomination of the Genl. but the season of of the rain did not permit him to venture to the Convention chamber.

Mr Wilson moved that a Secretary should be appointed, and nominated M^r. Temple Franklin.

Col Hamilton nominated Major Jackson.

On the ballot Maj^r. Jackson had 5 votes & M^r. Franklin 2 votes.

The appointment of a Committee, consisting of Messrs. Wythe, Hamilton & Pinkney, on the motion of M^r. Pinkney, to prepare rules was the only remaining step of this day[.]

Madison focused on the waning of Franklin's influence. He delineated the obviously choreographed nomination of Washington by the wealthy and powerful Robert Morris of Pennsylvania, with the second made by John Rutledge of South Carolina, perhaps the most prominent member of the southern delegations. Morris's nomination at the "instruction" of the Pennsylvania delegation underscored the lack of support for Franklin within his own state. Although Franklin apparently was to have made the nomination, he did not. Madison's comment—"the season of the rain did not permit him to venture" to the chamber—implied almost cattily that Franklin had chosen not to appear. The Pennsylvania delegation had nominated Franklin's grandson, Temple Franklin, as secretary. But instead of the consolation prize, William Jackson of Virginia, was elected. Madison carefully noted the votes: Jackson had received five votes; Franklin only two.[13]

The entry presumed a reader who shared Madison's exasperations. Washington's acceptance speech was recounted with a sense of frustration at the repeated self-deprecating comments. The spelling of Charles Pinckney's name may have contained a similar private message. Two Pinckneys attended the Convention: Charles and his cousin, Charles Cotesworth. Madison usually referred to C.C. as "General." The younger Charles Pinckney annoyed Madison. He was staying at the same hotel and had served in Congress with Madison. He was approximately six years younger with a confident personality. In the days before the Convention, Pinckney had been circulating his own plan. Throughout the original Notes, Madison consistently misspelled his name as "Pinkney." Madison may have simply cared little about names. Indeed, in late eighteenth-century correspondence, names are often misspelled. Pinckney is not alone; Madison spelled other names incorrectly—for example, *Rutlidge* for *Rutledge* and *Franklyn* for *Franklin*. But perhaps, the misspelled Pinkney—suspiciously emphasizing the *Pink* and thus resulting in *Pinkknee*—reflected a prior shared joke with Jefferson.[14]

The first day was recorded as in a legislative diary—now, perhaps more appropriately referred to as a conventional diary. Like the earlier congressional diaries, Madison began the Convention with the assumption that he would use his diary for letters and then later Jefferson would likely read it on his return from France. On Sunday, Madison wrote to his father: "It is impossible as yet to form a judgment of the result of this experiment." As reflected, however, in the diary, Madison had already formed judgments of the progress of the first day.[15]

Madison expected to be able to write to his correspondents about the Convention. In mid-April, John Dawson wrote that he planned to come to Philadelphia during the Convention. He was not a delegate, but he wanted "to gain information of many political points." He hoped that "if it can be done with propriety," he could hear the debates. If not, he assumed that Madison would "give me any information in your power." To the same end, Virginia congressional member Edward Carrington ensured that the Convention's members could send and receive letters free of postage. Carrington wrote Jefferson that the "Convention will be productive of things worth communicating to you." He promised to write "after its commencement." The assumption seemed to be that the Convention proceedings would be closed but that delegates would continue to communicate confidentially with trusted correspondents.[16]

The Convention closed its doors and, to some surprise, barred even confidential communications. The initial rules considered by the Convention on Monday, May 28, did not address communications. On Tuesday, an additional new rule prevented the copying of "any entry on the journal" without permission of the delegates. A second new rule explicitly stated that "nothing spoken in the House be printed, or otherwise published, or communicated without leave." The Secretary explained that it was to prevent "licentious publication of their proceedings"—a member giving material to a newspaper. The explicitness of the two rules shifted the Convention away from the casual confidentiality of Congress.[17]

The members explained to correspondents that they were not supposed to indulge even in "confidential communications" until the Convention ended. Richard Spaight wrote to the North Carolina governor that he was not "at Liberty to Communicate anything that passes." Washington wrote to his nephew, George Augustine Washington, "I have nothing more to communicate than what you will find in the Papers." Madison described to Jefferson the "rules of caution which will for no short time restrain even a confidential communication of our proceedings." "Anything," "nothing," "even"—underscored the inability to send confidential communications.[18]

Nevertheless, political intelligence leaked—likely more than we recognize. Mason wrote to his son: "All communications of the proceedings are forbidden," but also discussed the reception of the "idea I formerly mentioned to you, before the Convention," and added it was "still the prevalent one." Nathan Dane wrote Rufus King that he agreed with the "propriety" restraining members from communicating but felt "a strong desire and curiosity to know how it proceeds." He noted that "one of your members" was in New York and did not seem to "fully understand the true meaning" of the restraint. Manasseh Cutler related an incident in which Franklin had been about "to forget that everything in Convention was to be kept a profound secret." Monroe heard about an alleged decision of the Convention via John Beckley who had been staying with Randolph.[19]

The people likely to be told confidential information were those reliable about keeping secrets. Virginia congressional delegate Edward Carrington wrote Jefferson that the proceedings were in "profound secrecy" but then described "schemes" reflecting the plans in circulation. Louis-Guillaume Otto, the French chargé d'affaires, similarly wrote French officials a relatively good description about the Virginia plan. Correspondence may have been destroyed containing information about the Convention. For example, Madison sent at least two letters to Joseph Jones during May and June. Neither letter has been found. Similarly, two letters are not extant from Madison to Virginia delegate McClurg after the latter left the Convention. Madison may have divulged details that led to a decision by the recipient or Madison to destroy the letters.[20]

Moreover, members did not have to violate confidentiality too much for politically astute observers to guess significant decisions. In June and July, the controversial issues involved general principles. On June 3, Nathaniel Gorham wrote Nathan Dane. Although, he did not know that he was "at liberty to mention in any manner what the Convention has done," he continued "in confidence" that the members had agreed unanimously on a "National Legislative Executive & Judiciary." That information indicated that the Convention had abandoned the Articles. A month later, Washington wrote David Stuart that "independent sovereignty" and "separate interests" would need to "yield to a more enlarged scale of politicks." Stuart now knew that Washington and others were attempting to diminish the role of the states.[21]

As the Convention progressed, concerns about strict confidentiality may have waned. When Nicholas Gilman arrived in late July, he wrote that "secrecy is not otherwise enjoined than as prudence may dictate to each individual." He gave "a hint" to his brother and a few others "who will not make it public" about the general principles. On August 29, Gorham wrote a letter mentioning the eighteenth article of the draft. On September 6—a week and a half before the Convention ended—Madison wrote a long letter to Jefferson detailing the structural decisions made by the Convention.[22]

Of equal importance, no member appears to have believed that the bar on confidential communications would last beyond the Convention. Most members, in fact, emphasized that communications were barred only until the conclusion. Washington wrote Lafayette that he would write a "long letter" when the members "are at liberty to communicate the proceedings more freely." He similarly wrote George Augustine Washington, "As the proceedings . . . are not intended to be made known till the business is finished I can give you no information." William Samuel Johnson wrote to his son that "for the present our deliberations shall be kept secret." Mason wrote that the proceedings were not to be communicated "during their sitting." Indeed, he assumed in the Virginia legislature, the "whole weight of explanation" would eventually fall on him. The members accepted that the proceedings were closed and confidential—and even a bit secret—but only for the short term.[23]

This strict confidentiality altered the purpose of Madison's conventional diary. The entries could not be used as a source for correspondence. On June 6, Madison sent the names of the delegates to Jefferson. Madison did not bother to include the names in the Notes. He added that "this list of names . . . exhausted all the means which I can make use of for gratifying your curiosity." Only in the future could the Notes gratify Jefferson's curiosity.[24]

The Convention's decision about confidentiality was of little interest to Madison. He did not copy most of the rules into his Notes. They were similar to rules for Congress. They would be recorded in the official journal kept by the secretary. Madison may have assumed that the official journal would be published after the Convention. He focused on the debate over whether the secretary should be supervised. Charles Pinckney wanted a committee to "superintend" the minutes. Gouverneur Morris objected. A committee would have an "interest & bias in moulding the entry according to their opinions and wishes." The vote was close: four states favored a committee; five states did not. The proposal lost, and the secretary would keep the official journal. No explicit decision was made about future publication. It would be in legislative diaries like Madison's that delegates could mold the narrative of the Convention according to their wishes and understanding.[25]

The discussion over voting was the only other rule recorded by Madison. The initial proposed rules recommended the congressional practice of allowing a member to call for the "yeas & nays and have them recorded on the minutes." The yeas and nays created a record of individual votes. Objectors worried about political reputations and the inevitable complexity of the drafting process. The record, if "promulgated," would provide "handles to the adversaries" after the Convention. The minutes would be filled "with contradictions" as members changed their positions. The yeas and nays were rejected. Only the votes of each state would be recorded in the journal. With this decision, legislative diaries acquired additional importance. They became the only place to indicate individual opinions. Madison's record of the delegates' comments and speeches became a device for tracking and counting individual votes.[26]

For the first two or three days, Madison wrote the Notes from memory. The first day (Friday, May 25) read like a letter. The second day (Monday, May 28) briefly discussed the debate over the rules. The third day (Tuesday, May 29) noted the losing vote over the minutes and summarized Edmund Randolph's opening speech on a new governmental structure. Each relatively short entry began at the top of a page emphasizing the discrete events of that day.[27]

The description of Randolph's "long speech" occupied three and a half lines. Other notetakers—James McHenry, William Paterson, Gunning Bedford—recorded the speech; Madison did not bother. He merely summarized the main ideas:

> the various defects in the federal system, the necessity of transforming it into a national efficient Government, and the extreme danger of delaying this great work. . . .

The words—federal system to national Government—emphasized the intended transformation.[28]

Randolph proposed specific resolutions. Madison referred to them as "sundry propositions." Historians often referred to them as Randolph's Plan or the Virginia Plan, the latter term emphasizing group authorship. The propositions were designed to focus debate and achieve agreement. Madison initially did not copy them into the Notes. He left the bottom of the page and the following page blank, apparently intending to copy them into the space in what would have required very small writing. He eventually instead copied them on a separate sheet under the title, "Resolutions proposed by Mr. Randolph in Convention." The title, ample spacing, and care of the copy suggest that Madison may have made it slightly later, perhaps as late as June 13 when he made a similar copy of the Committee Report on the resolutions, or even later. As coauthor, Madison knew that the propositions and a neat copy for a future reader could wait.[29]

Throughout the early Notes, Madison was casual about the text of the resolutions. He referred to the resolutions using quotations; however, the quoted words were summaries of the purpose, not the actual text. For example, one resolution proposed broad congressional authority: "the national legislature ought to be empowered . . . [t]o legislate in all cases, to which the separate States are incompetent." Madison wrote using quotations, "Legislative power in all cases to which the State Legislatures were individually incompetent." The description emphasized the significant breadth of authority, rather than the precise words. This similar focus on the underlying purpose of the propositions appeared in his description of a vote on the negative. He did not even mention it specifically but simply noted a favorable vote on "the other clauses giving powers necessary to preserve harmony among the States and so forth." Madison thought about the resolutions as propositions about significant purposes and powers of the government.[30]

Madison omitted mention in the Notes for Tuesday of an alternative plan introduced by Charles Pinckney. The existence of Pinckney's plan is not doubted, although the details remain a matter of debate. The draft shared certain similarities with the Virginia resolutions. Indeed, according to Lansing, Pinckney "confessed" that his plan "was grounded on Principles similar." The two plans had a number of similar components: a bicameral legislature with proportional representation; a council of revision; a broad legislative negative over state laws; an executive; a judiciary. The Virginians had decided on some of these ideas prior to arrival in Philadelphia, and Madison may have been exasperated at Pinckney's presumption in including them.[31]

The omission of Pinckney's draft also avoided acknowledging important differences. Pinckney had included titles: Congress, House of Delegates, Senate, and President. Pinckney proposed a single president with a
council composed from the heads of the great departments, in contrast
to the ambiguous executive in the Virginia resolutions. Pinckney employed an enumeration of specific legislative powers, instead of broadly
worded legislative authority (for the "harmony of the United States")
under the Virginia resolutions. In addition, he explicitly based representation on slavery and theoretical state consolidation. The House was to
have one member for a to-be-determined "thousand Inhabitants 3/5 of
Blacks included"; the Senate was to be drawn from "four Districts." The
Virginians had sought to sidestep the first issue by proportioning suffrage
to "Quotas of contribution, or to the number of free inhabitants." They
ignored the problem of how to form a small second branch from the thirteen unequal states. Pinckney's draft offered an important alternative
structure, and various delegates seem to have repeatedly referred to its
ideas in subsequent weeks. The Notes, however, made these suggestions
seem to be original recommendations. Madison's omission misleadingly
left the Virginians alone in the leading role.[32]

By the fourth day, as the delegates began to debate the Virginia resolutions, writing the diary from memory became unsatisfactory. The Convention had converted itself into a Committee of the Whole House to
consider Randolph's resolutions and Pinckney's draft. The Committee
was the group of delegates, freed from procedural rules such as lim-
iting the number of times a member could speak. The product of the
discussion would be a committee report, which would then be debated
again in the Convention. These proceedings could no longer be summarized on a single page and Wednesday, May 30, occupied four pages of
a sheet.[33]

Madison was struggling to sort out an appropriate style. He used summaries ("verbal criticisms"; "by several it was observed") and tried to
capture some speeches. The entry began in debate-style with each speaker
delineated but ended with a long paragraph describing a debate. Madison's frustration appeared. George Read of Delaware wanted to postpone
debate over abandoning equal state suffrage. He argued that the delegation's instructions required them to "retire from the Convention" if the
suffrage rule was altered. Madison's goal was to end equal state suffrage;
the claim by Delaware that the issue could not be discussed thwarted the
plan. Madison's paragraph explained his effort to obtain agreement and

Read's obstinacy. Nonetheless, Madison ended the entry with an optimistic comment that the change from equal state suffrage would "certainly be agreed to" as there was "no objection or difficulty . . . from any
other quarter." The Notes reflected Madison's belief that Delaware represented, at most, an annoying interruption.[34]

Madison's selective recording emphasized political strategies. Madison
recorded speeches as an aide de mémoire for individual strategic positions. The Notes tracked dissent within the state delegations. Counting
dissenters mattered because the majority controlled the state's vote; an
evenly divided vote resulted in no vote being cast for the state. The first
significant vote on Wednesday demonstrates the pattern. By an over-
whelmingly favorable vote (six of the eight states), the delegates agreed
to the Virginia plan's "national Government" with a "supreme Legislative Executive & Judiciary." The Notes nonetheless carefully explicated
Connecticut's negative vote. Roger Sherman appeared to be the cause. He
had taken "his seat" that day and agreed with "additional powers" but, to
ensure ratification, seemed not disposed to "Make too great inroads on
the existing system." Madison also described the divided New York delegation: "Col. Hamilton ay M[r]. Yates no." With two delegates, New York
could vote, but, until a third delegate arrived, the state's vote was uncertain. Even within the six affirmative votes, Madison sensed disagreement.
He worried about the South Carolina delegation. Charles Pinckney was
cast as a troublemaker, asking whether the plan would "abolish the
State Govern[ts]. altogether." Madison described Pierce Butler as "rather
cautious." Butler's affirmative vote might be open to being altered as he
"had not made up his mind." General Pinckney had concerns over the
legality of discussing departures from the "federal Constitution." Within
the Massachusetts delegation, Madison noted that Elbridge Gerry "seemed
to entertain the same doubt" as General Pinckney. Madison also carefully
recorded two strong supporters of a national, supreme government:
Gouverneur Morris of Pennsylvania and, reassuringly for Madison, George
Mason. Madison was not a stenographer but a political cartographer.
The speeches focused on divisions and were fundamentally biased towards areas of disagreement.[35]

By midweek, Madison may have begun to take rough notes during the
proceedings. The entries became longer and more detailed. Many of the
characteristics of these entries remained throughout the Convention.

Some stylistic tendencies arose from the method of composition; others were the product of Madison's personality.

The Notes were probably written biweekly. Twice a week, Madison wrote letters, usually once on the weekend and on either Tuesday or Wednesday, apparently timed with the mail delivery to Virginia. He appears to have written the Notes for the most part on the same days. This writing pattern is visible on several occasions where the entries refer to a decision made several days later. The biweekly habit affected the Notes. Only on one day each week during the Convention—usually Wednesday, occasionally Tuesday—did Madison write about events that had just occurred. For most entries, he wrote several days after the fact with knowledge of the subsequent decisions and debates. He inevitably revised his understanding of which discussions were significant and which could be omitted. Saturday's entries had a particular advantage. They were written likely on Sunday, relatively close in time, and Madison had the leisure of added time for composition because of the absence of Sunday proceedings. The Notes reflected a pattern established by this schedule of composition.[36]

The Notes were transcribed from his rough notes. Madison presumably took the rough notes using abbreviations. Trained shorthand writers often used symbolic shorthand, but no example of Madison's use of symbolic shorthand has been located. Madison's use of abbreviations does survive in a few documents. His technique relied on the use of familiar eighteenth-century superscripts, the thorn ("y") for "th," the omission of many vowels, and the notation of a few letters of a word. Rough notes from the Convention have not been found. Madison may have destroyed them as he transcribed. One piece of paper summarizing the committee report of July 9, 1787, may be one part of the rough notes. It offers a relatively easy to read example of abbreviations:

> The Com^e to w^m. w^s ref^d. y^e. 1st. clause of y^e. 1st. propos. reported from ye grand Com^e. beg leave to report
>   That in the 1st meeting of y^e. Legis^l. the 1st. b. thereof consist of 56 m^{bers}. of wch. n^o. . . . .

Madison abbreviated *States* as Sts; *inhabitants* as inh^{ts}; *wealth* as w^{lth}; *Representatives* as Rep^s. In lengthier passages, the abbreviations became difficult to decipher. For example, a lengthy partial copy of a letter to Jefferson in October 1787 relied on abbreviations. Although Madison copied nearly word for word, the extract is almost impossible to transcribe despite knowing the text. For example, one sentence to which commentators accord great significance was rendered:

y^r· w^l· b. rch & p^r· crd^r· & db$^{r··}$ a land$^{d·}$ int$^{st·}$, a mon$^{d·}$ α ^{d} a mercanth α ^{d} a manf^{tg} α ^{d}

This line is the sentence: "There will be rich and poor; creditors and debtors; a landed interest, a monied interest, a mercantile interest, a manufacturing interest." At the Convention, the speed of speakers meant Madison recorded words and phrases, and likely only on rare occasions a complete sentence.[37]

The technique demanded creativity. Madison deciphered the abbreviations often several days later. Singular and plurals words would have been difficult to distinguish. It would have been tricky to determine words with a common base, such as representative and representation, or judicial and judiciary. Deciphering the abbreviation itself was difficult. The superscripts may have been so small as to be occasionally illegible. The dots under the superscript may have been confused with periods and commas. Determining the beginning and end of sentences would have been challenging. Madison necessarily had to rely on his memory and use a certain license of composition.

In transcribing the rough notes, Madison imposed a consistent, detached style on the speakers. Other note takers left speeches in the first person. In their notes, speeches are often disjointed, written as run-on sentences separated by commas or ideas separated by dashes. In contrast, Madison imposed order. Using a consistent third-person narrative voice, the name of the delegate was followed by a verb ("Mr.___ insisted . . ."). Madison included coherent punctuation. He placed the ideas into full sentences. Perhaps most significantly, Madison summarized the point of the speech at the outset. Although few people begin to talk by stating the conclusion, Madison created a first sentence to summarize the position of the speaker or the proposal. The summary allowed Madison to follow with whatever sentences he recorded. So consistent is this topic sentence style, that the Notes can be followed by reading the first sentence of each speech.[38]

Madison toned down the emotional tenor of speakers. Other note takers record strong emotions. King heard Dickinson declare, "We cannot have a limited monarchy." Madison's version was more passive, "A limited

monarchy however was out of the question." Madison turned impera-
tives like "must" into desirable outcomes such as "should" and "ought."
He omitted emphasis. Madison cast over almost every speech a veil of
measured reasonableness. King recorded Dickinson's comment as "A
vig[orous]s executive with checks &c can not be republican, it is peculiar to monarchy." Madison created an attenuated sentence: "such an
Executive as some seemed to have in contemplation was not consistant
[sic] with a republic; that a firm Executive could only exist in a limited
monarchy." The Convention appears moderate and reasonable in the
Notes because Madison recorded it as such—not necessarily because it
was calm and considerate as originally stated. And, when Madison recorded anger and emotion, it was likely so extreme that even he could
not avoid it.[39]

Madison translated the speakers' political concepts and ideas into his
own terminology. Other note takers recorded an inconsistent variety of
political concepts and vocabularies; the delegates do not always seem to
be speaking about the same idea or in the same political language. In the
Notes, however, speakers used uniform terms. Dickinson in King's version says "Repub[lic]s are for a while industrious but finally destroy
[the]mselves—they were badly constituted—I dread Consolidation of the
states." Madison phrased Dickinson's remarks in terms so familiar that
it sounded almost like Madison: "If antient republics have been found
to flourish for a moment only & then vanish forever, it only proves that
they were badly constituted; and that we ought to seek for every remedy
for their diseases." In the entries, speakers disagree about whether the
concepts are good or bad, but they appear to be talking about the same
idea. This convergence may have often been the product of Madison's
mind.[40]

Order was imposed on disorder. Pierce's notes for Thursday, May 31,
reflected a disorganized debate over how to discuss election of the legislative branches. Madison was frustrated at "wandering from one thing to
another without seeming to be settled in any one principle." Spaight
thought the manner of Senate appointment was "necessary previous to
the decision" on the first branch. King, however, declared the question
"premature, and out of order" and added, "unless we go on regularly
from one principle to the other" the proceedings will be of "endless
length." In contrast, Madison's Notes indicate little disorganization.
Motions designed to redirect were omitted. Madison sorted the speakers
into two groups. On one side were those who distrusted the people: they

were "constantly liable to be misled" (Sherman), "dupes of the demagogues" and "misled into the most baneful measures and opinions by the reports circulated by designing men" (Gerry). On the other side were speakers who saw the people as the "grand depository of the democratic principle" (Mason), and believed in the "confidence of the people" (Wilson) and "necessary sympathy" between the people and "their rulers" (Madison). Madison portrayed a calm debate over principles instead of frustration over interrelated principles.[41]

A future reader of the Notes—presumably Jefferson—was assumed to be capable of grasping the political undercurrents from subtle signals. Madison focused on Randolph's adamant insistence on a three-person executive. (As other note takers' notes make apparent, Madison supported a single executive.) Under the Articles, there was no executive; a committee of Congress handled matters. As written, Randolph's proposed resolutions were ambiguous about the executive, using the pronoun "it"—not "he"—to permit the executive to be comprised of more than one person. The Notes described the moment where the delegates confronted the issue. On Friday, June 1, Wilson and Pinckney proposed a single executive, advocating a "vigorous Executive," not "a Monarchy, of the worst kind, towit [sic] an elective one." A single executive with broad powers raised concerns about an elective monarchy. The Notes conveyed the delegates' reluctance to speak. Madison described a "considerable pause" before the chairman, Nathaniel Gorham, asked if he should "put the question." Franklin asked the delegates to deliver their "sentiments." Rutledge criticized the delegates' "shyness." The Notes seemed to hint that the silence was in deference to Randolph's opposition. At last, Randolph spoke and "strenuo[u]sly opposed" the single executive as the "foetus of monarchy." He advocated an executive composed of three members. In the face of Randolph's opposition, the delegates were "unprepared for any decision." On June 2, Madison again recorded Randolph speaking with "great earnestness." He would oppose a single executive "as long as he lived." The Notes established Randolph's responsibility for the resolutions' ambiguity and also implied that others— likely most others—favored a single executive. They also reflected concerns that comments favoring a single executive could be misconstrued as favoring monarchy.[42]

Concerns about misinterpretation pervaded the Notes. Madison paused on occasion to explain that statements were not to be misconstrued. One example occurred as the delegates debated whether ratification would require unanimity among the thirteen states or a lesser number. Wilson favored ratification based on "partial union, with the door open for accession of the rest." He explained that the "inconsiderate or selfish opposition" of a few states should not stop a "plurality of States" from confederating. Which were the selfish states? Virginia had been known for its initial failure to support amendments to the Articles. Madison, however, added a comment in the body of the Notes to prevent that interpretation: "This hint was probably meant in terrorem to the smaller States of N. Jersey & Delaware." Conjuring up stony-faced silence, Madison added, "Nothing was said in reply to it." The largest states—Pennsylvania and Virginia—were willing to write a constitution that a few states (the smallest states) would be reluctant to ratify.[43]

Speeches were a challenge to record. For the first several days of the Notes, the speeches amounted to an introductory sentence summarizing the major point and at most another sentence or two. By mid-week, they became a paragraph—in Madison's small handwriting, often over a hundred words. The only speech of significant length in the first week was that of Delaware's John Dickinson on Saturday, June 2. It was a "discourse of some length" and Madison recorded it as a little over a page. The length was in part the consequence of being given on a Saturday—which meant Madison had time the next day to compose it. In part, the length also indicated the topic's importance to Madison.[44]

Speakers mattered to Madison when they criticized his ideas. Nonetheless, he had difficulty recording the criticism as explicitly as it was given. Dickinson accused "some" of appearing "desirous to abolish altogether" the states. He argued that the "accidental lucky division" into states was a "source of stability." The "different sizes" of the states would lead to disagreement over proportional representation in both houses. Dickinson predicted that the issue "must probably end in mutual concession." The phrase was awkward and seemed to combine forceful words from Dickinson—"must end"—with Madison's need to downplay the claim with the caveat, "probably." As he transcribed and composed speeches from his rough notes, Madison inevitably revised.[45]

The absence of other lengthy speeches in the first week was made less apparent by Madison's later insertion of Franklin's June 2 speech, copied from Franklin. Franklin claimed "ambition and avarice" were the "true sources" of divisive "factions." His proposed remedy, however, was that the executive and men serving in the executive department receive no salary. Salaries would encourage the "natural inclination in mankind to Kingly Government." They would promote those with "indefatigable activity in their selfish pursuits." Although Madison worried about selfish interests, he also believed in government salaries. Franklin's idea may have struck Madison as an idealistic proposal from an earlier revolutionary age. Madison described the delivery in an almost mocking manner. Wilson had read the speech because Franklin was "very sensible of the effect of age on his memory." Madison originally used the spelling, "Franklyn," favored by Jefferson. Madison recounted the delegates' tepid response.

> The motion was seconded by Col. Hamilton with the view he said merely of bringing so respectable a proposition before the Committee, and which was besides enforced by arguments that had a certain weight. No debate ensued, and the motion was postponed for the consideration of the members. It was treated with great respect, but rather from respect for the author of it, than any apparent conviction of its expediency or practicability.

Madison's own voice appears in the final sentence. A curious tone of possible condescension appeared ten days later (after Franklin outmaneuvered Madison on the phrasing of a standard for compensation). Madison wrote that "Doctr Franklyn" had "very pleasantly," but apparently somewhat irrelevantly, surveyed history from the Apostles to the papal system. Franklin might have been the oldest delegate but the Notes displayed Madison's rather impatient view towards his opinion.[46]

Madison was an unreliable narrator about himself. His use of the third-person—Mr. M.—created an illusion that the writer was accurately recording the speaker. Pierce, for example, used the first person in his notes: "I was myself of opinion"; "it appeared clear to me." Through the third-person voice, Madison could write about himself as if he were a stranger. For example, he included the awkward sentence referring to himself: "What his opinion might ultimately be he could not yet tell."[47]

The Madison of the Notes could be more tentative than other note takers recorded. In the early debate over enumeration of national legislative powers, Pierce described Madison's rejection of the idea: "at present he was convinced it could not be done." In the Notes, Madison phrased his position as expressing "some doubts about the practicability" of an enumeration but insisted that he "could not yet tell" his ultimate opinion. In a debate over judicial selection, Pierce wrote, "Mr. Madison was for appointing the Judges by the Senate." Madison instead used the phrases that he had "hinted . . . only" and been "rather inclined" towards the idea. Madison wanted to appear more open-minded in the Notes than he may have been in reality.[48]

In fact, positions taken by Madison were omitted from the Notes. On the controversial matter of the single executive, King and Pierce recorded Madison's advocacy: "the best plan will be a single Executive of long duration" (King); "an Executive formed of one Man" (Pierce). Madison, however, included no such comment by himself. Even the explanation of Virginia's vote favoring the single executive diminished Madison's responsibility. The vote within the delegation was 3–2, with Madison the apparent tie-breaker. (Randolph and Blair had voted against; Madison, McClurg, and Washington had voted yes.). Madison did not explain his own vote but tried to create legitimacy for the affirmative vote by claiming that George Wythe, who had left the Convention, favored the single executive. The Notes obscured Madison's open support for the single executive.[49]

The Notes were far from those of an impartial observer on matters that Madison cared about deeply. Similar to the executive composition, the Virginia resolutions were ambiguous on the precise calculation of proportional representation. It suggested two possibilities: "Quotas of contribution, or to the number of free inhabitants, as the one or the other rule may seem best in different cases." "Quotas of contribution" implied the three-fifths ratio of the congressional revenue plan—an approach Madison had taken responsibility for in his congressional notes. Lansing succinctly wrote, "in Proportion of Numbers or Property."[50]

The official journal recorded that, on Wednesday, May 30, Hamilton pushed for free inhabitants. His motion, however, was postponed. Randolph successfully suggested that the delegates agree to suffrage "not according to the present system." Madison then attempted to sidestep any debate over free inhabitants by proposing that an "equitable ratio of representation" be substituted. The motion, however, was postponed and the delegates adjourned.[51]

Madison's portrayal of the day was decidedly different and cast himself as the successful political strategist. He made himself as the first speaker, omitting Hamilton's motion. He thus appeared to be responding to no one but preempting the issue by observing that "the words *free inhabitants* might occasion debates which would divert the Committee from the general question whether the equality of votes should be changed." Madison similarly skipped Randolph's motion. He explained that he "at length" proposed new language to abandon the old rule and substitute "an equitable ratio of representation." Madison declared his substitution "generally acceptable" and "would have been agreed to." Although it was postponed, Madison predicted future success: "change of representation would certainly be agreed to." The Notes portrayed Madison's belief that he had sunk equality of suffrage.[52]

Nevertheless, in describing the "quarter" of opposition, the entry betrayed Madison's failure to recognize the strength of countervailing coalitions. He attempted to downplay the problem of the Delaware delegation. Madison visually depicted his annoyance with an awkward line break:

> . . . This was generally acceptable ~~Dela~~ and would have been agreed to
> when
> Mr. Reed moved that the whole clause relating to the point of Representation might be postponed . . . .

On the final page, Madison recorded frustration, using no paragraphs and switching abruptly from speaker to speaker. He insisted that "equality of suffrage" was incoherent in a "national Governm[en]t." He noted that "several" speakers "observed that no just construction" of the Delaware instructions "could require or even justify a secession of her deputies." His proposed procedural "expedient" to record the "sense of the members" on the issue was rejected. Madison sarcastically noted that it "did not appear to satisfy Mr. Read." Although the Notes seemed written to demonstrate the stubbornness of one man—George Read—in foiling a majority of votes for proportional representation, from a more distant perspective, the entry suggested that Madison strategically erred by underestimating the opposition of certain delegates from small states.[53]

4

STRUGGLING WITH SPEECHES

Not until the second week of the Convention did Madison record a major speech of his own. The Notes revealed the challenges he faced as he tried to include his speeches. In writing the speeches up after the fact, Madison often likely adopted a somewhat improved version of the one he orally delivered. For example, he did not record his June 4 significant speech because of an underlying procedural error; instead, he incorporated the speech into the June 6 entry. In recording other delegates' speeches, Madison was similarly selective. The Notes were not an objective record of discussions but reflected Madison's inevitable distortions.

Madison's speeches defended controversial aspects of the Virginia plan: a national Council of revision, a small second branch not based on equal state suffrage, a national legislative negative over state laws, and a bicameral Congress based on proportional representation. With the exception of the negative, Madison met considerable opposition. For delegates from New Jersey and Delaware, the proposals threatened to create a political system in which Virginia could exert disproportionate influence. As the Notes indicate, Madison considered their concern insignificant in comparison to the political coherence of proportional representation and the need to control the state legislatures. He recorded accusations that he was supporting abolition of states; however, he omitted a different criticism—that the proposed system promoted slavery. Despite the controversies, on June 13, Madison's copy of the Committee Report of the Whole House on the Virginia Resolutions suggested that he perceived significant success.

On Monday, June 4, Madison delivered his first major speech—a speech that he never recorded. Other note takers recorded the significant speech.

William Pierce described a "very able and ingenious Speech." The speech advocated the Council of revision—the "propriety of incorporating the Judicial with the Executive in the revision of the Laws"—as a structural solution to unjust majoritarian legislation advanced by particular interests. No such speech, however, was recorded in the Notes. Even as the entries grew lengthier, the Notes remained a diary without perfect fidelity to the proceedings.[1]

The Council of revision offered a mechanism for reviewing national legislation. The Virginia plan's eighth resolution described a Council composed of the executive and a "convenient" number of the national judiciary. It was to "examine every act of the National Legislature" prior to operation. If the Council dissented, the act was rejected unless overridden by the legislature. By June 4, the Council had become controversial, particularly in light of the likelihood of a single executive. The resolution was postponed. In lieu of the Council, the executive was given the power to negative national legislation, now known as the veto. Madison and Wilson were unhappy. On June 4, they tried to restore the Council of revision by moving to insert the words, "a convenient number of the national judiciary," after the "national Executive" in the new veto power.[2]

According to other note takers, Madison's June 4 speech in support of their motion portrayed the Council as a structural mechanism to solve a fundamental problem of republican government. The speech likely had the following structure:

1. Historical survey of ancient republics
2. Diversity of interests a fundamental problem for republican government
3. Same problem will arise with American government
4. Checks on interested majority needed to protect minority
5. The Council of revision as the solution

Pierce implied that the first part was too long. Madison "ran through the *whole* Scheme of Government" and "*all* the beauties and defects of ancient Republics." According to King, the history demonstrated the problem of republican governments: the "diversity of Interest" among the "Rich & poor," the debtor and creditor, the "followers of different Demagogues," and the "diversity of religious Sects." Republican government permitted these interests to become oppressive by empowering majorities. The "Effects of these parties are obvious" in the ancient republics and "the same causes will operate with us." Pierce also found this part excessive. Madison had compared the situation of other republics to "ours wherever it appeared to bear any anology" [*sic*].[3]

For Madison, the Council was a superior check on unjust majoritarian legislation. It would ensure the "safety of a minority in Danger of oppression from an unjust and interested majority." King recorded Madison as stating a "check or negative" on legislation would "destroy the measures of an interested majority." The "Judges and the Supreme Executive Magistrate" would have the strength to reject such laws. Madison insisted that the combination was "strictly proper" and "would by no means interfere with that indepen[den]ce so much to be approved and distinguished in the several departments." In Madison's mind, the inevitable oppression of the minority justified, indeed necessitated, the modification of independence of other branches.[4]

Madison's speech not only failed to persuade but the underlying motion was also ruled out of order. In the discussion after the speech, Hamilton made an "objection of order." The rules barred members from immediately reconsidering an issue that had been determined by a majority without unanimous consent. The motion was too similar to the vote postponing the Council of revision. No one was sympathetic. Although Wilson and Madison asked for their motion to be reconsidered on Tuesday, reconsideration was set for Wednesday, June 6. On Wednesday, the Council of revision failed. Although Virginia voted in favor, joined by New York and Connecticut, the eight other states rejected the idea.[5]

On Wednesday evening, when Madison likely sat down to write the Notes for Monday to Wednesday, he faced a dilemma of composition. If he included the speech on Monday, he also would have to include the procedural mis-step—the fact that he had given a long speech on a motion, only to be told that it was out of order. Alternatively, he could insert the material from the speech on Wednesday, June 6, when the matter was reconsidered. Perhaps not surprisingly, Madison seems to have chosen the latter course. In the June 4 entry, Madison focused on arguments favoring the veto because the judiciary already had the power to void laws for "Constitutionality." He included the postponement motion but made no mention of the motion by Wilson and him to add the judges, his speech, or Hamilton's objection. On June 4 in the Notes, it appeared that Madison had never argued for the Council and had never discussed it as the solution to interests.[6]

The original entry in the Notes for June 6, however, is a puzzle. Madison's original June 6 entry is likely missing, eventually replaced by Madison with two new sheets. On the new sheets, ideas apparently drawn from the June 4 speech appear; however, the ideas are used to justify election of the first branch of the legislature, not the Council. This new first branch election speech is considered by scholars to be one of Madison's most important speeches. It suggested that the problem of oppressive majority interests would not arise in a large, extended republic because the size would prevent the interests from becoming a powerful majority. Curiously, the other note takers did not record such a speech and scholars have been troubled by discrepancies. Later in this book, I suggest that the version of the June 6 speech in the Notes was likely composed after the Convention, possibly between the fall of 1789 and the spring of 1790, and was in place by 1791.[7]

The notes of other members suggest that Madison gave two speeches on June 6—but neither seems to have involved repetition of a strong argument about interests. One speech related to who should elect the first branch; the other advocated for the judiciary's addition to the executive negative (the Council idea). The first speech discounted concerns that "corrupt and unworthy men" would manipulate the people. Madison declared that the people could "safely" elect if "you enlarge the Sphere of Election." The second speech argued the executive would be too weak to veto a unanimous legislature. Joining the judiciary would "prevent encroachments by the Legislature on the Executive, the Judicial, or on private Rights." If Madison repeated his June 4 argument about interests in either speech or suggested that interests would not combine dangerously in a large republic, the note takers did not record it in any detail.[8]

Although Madison seems unlikely to have presented these ideas in the Convention on June 6, the Notes contributed to the development of his insights. By shifting the June 4 speech to June 6, Madison may have begun to realize that his analysis of the diversity of interests related to other structural mechanisms. When Madison originally wrote his entry for June 6, he probably incorporated the June 4 material relating to diversity of interests and the need for checks on interested majorities because the Notes offered an opportunity for preserving his thoughts. Although the most obvious location was the speech on the Council of revision (and Madison might have written it so), Madison instead might have incorporated the material into his speech on election of the first branch. Regardless, Madison seems not to have reached the conclusion that an extended republic itself solved the problem. In speeches later that week, Madison worried about the need to develop checks so that interests did not produce bad results. Only after the Convention does Madison seem to have been willing to suggest that an extensive republic alone—without structural mechanisms—would solve interest oppression.[9]

Although the puzzle of the June 6 speech complicates the standard account of the emergence of Madison's political theory, it also reveals his significant talent for intellectual revision and creative thinking. The Notes reflected Madison's thought processes. In writing the entries, Madison revised his ideas. The fact that by June 6, the Notes reflected Madison's mind, not necessarily the precise words stated, may have made subsequent changes to the Notes easier. In a sense, the Notes were an intellectual diary—one which bore a somewhat attenuated relationship to Madison's precise statements in the Convention.

The loss of the Council of revision left Madison disappointed. He sought to add a Council of revision into late July, when the idea was voted down for a final time. His letters on Wednesday expressed his concern. To William Short, he wrote, "No hope is entertained from the existing Confederacy" but there were "real or imaginary difficulties, within or without doors." To Jefferson, he predicted that the "result will in some way or other have a powerful effect on our destiny." Madison was unsure whether the future held promise or the reality of political collapse.[10]

On Thursday, June 7 and Friday, June 8, Madison again met little success. On Thursday, the delegates unanimously voted for election of the second branch by the state legislatures. Madison wanted election by the first branch of the national legislature. He gave two speeches relating to the second branch. On Friday, Madison lost an effort to broaden the jurisdiction of the national legislature's negative over state laws. He also offered two speeches on this topic. Two of the four speeches were eventually replaced by Madison; one on the second branch and one speech on the negative. Although little evidence indicates how Madison originally recorded himself, his original speeches likely emphasized his frustrated effort to reduce the influence of the state legislatures.[11]

In writing the Notes, Madison interestingly moderated his comments, framing them as concerned with the deliberative function of the second branch as opposed to who would hold political power. On June 7, his commitment to proportional representation was under attack. Dickinson suggested a second branch, possibly with 80 members appointed by the state legislatures, and resembling the British House of Lords. Madison portrayed himself as responding by drawing on Roman history and arguing that a small second branch was necessary to avoid replicating factions and to ensure that it deliberated with "more coolness" and "more wisdom" than the first branch. Other note takers, however, recorded a Madison speech with controversial implications. Lansing heard Madison reject state sovereignty: "If each State retained its Sovereignty an Equality of Suffrage would be proper, but not so now." King heard Madison similarly reject "Ideas founded alone in the plan of confed[eratio]n." The speech suggested that Madison might favor consolidation of the states. Similarly, King heard a claim about political power: the second branch "ought to come from, & represent, the Wealth of the nation." Delegated power had "the most weight & consequence in the hands of the few." Wealth hinted at representation based on land value and calculations of enslaved people. But where others heard a speech about political power, Madison composed a speech about political process.[12]

Just as Madison recast his speeches, he also minimized criticism of himself. Dickinson opposed Madison's effort to end equal state suffrage. He offered a striking depiction of the government as the planetary system. The note takers captured the idea: "Let our Gov[ernmen]t be like that of the solar System: let the Gen[era]l. Gov[ernmen]t. be the Sun and the States the Planets repelled yet attracted." Madison wanted to extinguish the planets—as Dickinson put it: "abolish the States and consolidate them into one Gov[ernment]." Dickinson offered three criticisms. First, Madison's approach was an "attempt to unite distinct Interests," whereas "Safety may flow from this variety of Interests." Second, Madison was wrong that "power delegated to a few will be a better & more weighty check to the Democ[rac]y." Third, Madison's reliance on Roman history "proves too much." In the Notes, Madison skipped the first two important, substantive criticisms. He recorded only the last complaint about the reliance on historical precedents: "If the reasoning of Mr. [Madison] was good it would prove that the no. of the Senate ought to be reduced below ten, the highest no. of the Tribunitial corps." In writing the Notes, Madison seemed incapable of including meaningful criticism of himself on certain topics.[13]

An additional criticism of Madison involved his support for large districts, and he appears to have eventually replaced his speech favoring the idea. The large district idea apparently involved the unification of several states for purposes of elective representation in the second branch. In brief, in the second branch, not only would the states not be represented individually but each state would not necessarily have unique individual representation. The idea of large districts for elections for the second branch was in the Pinckney plan on May 29, hinted at by Wilson on May 31, and proposed on June 7 by Wilson and Morris. By electing the second branch from large districts—districts that merged smaller states—the second branch would remain small. According to Madison, Wilson argued that "election by the people in large districts" would "be most likely to obtain men of intelligence & uprightness." Lansing recorded that Madison was of the "same Opinion" as Wilson. Paterson wrote a note on Saturday that stated: "Mr. Madison—Districts." The speech that Madison originally recorded for himself in the Notes probably discussed large districts because Madison left in place successive comments related to districts. Sherman opposed districts; Pinckney suggested a scheme of classes based on size. But Madison omitted from the Notes the critique of large districts leading to diminishment of small states. Dickinson argued that large districts would be "unfair" because such districts might require "parts of distinct States united," and, if so, "the small States will never have a member." The idea hinted at eventual small state consolidation. The district idea lost, with only Pennsylvania voting in favor. If Madison originally recorded a speech hinting at his support for large districts, now, no trace remains.[14]

Madison's original Notes also likely made more apparent his efforts to achieve due supremacy of the national government with subordinate utility of the states. On Friday, June 8, Madison and Pinckney sought to broaden the negative over state laws to "all laws" which appeared "improper" to the national legislature. Four note takers recorded Madison's speech defending this broad negative. The negative would be a "check to the centrifugal Force" operating in the states to "force them off a common Centre, or a national point" (King's notes). The negative was necessary because "[n]o line can be drawn between the State Governments and the General Government" (Butler's notes). The Lansing and Yates version linked these points. It was "totally impracticable" to draw a "precise Line" because state judiciaries would be "compelled to expound the Laws so as to give those of the individual State an Operation" (Lansing's notes). Madison wished that a "line of jurisprudence" between state and national jurisdiction could be drawn, but it was "impossible." State judges would favor state laws even if they "abridge[d] the rights of the national government." The national negative was "the only attractive principle which will retain its centrifugal force, and without this the planets will fly from their orbits." For Madison, a broad national negative was the linchpin of the new system.[15]

Again Madison replaced his original version of the speech. He continued to insist on the importance of a negative in "all cases." The speech still defended the "indefinite power to negative legislative acts of the States as absolutely necessary to a perfect system." But the replaced version omitted two important points heard by the other note takers. First, it said nothing about state judiciaries being required to favor state laws. Second, it skipped the impossibility of drawing a line between the state and general governments. The replaced speech promoted the negative and complained about the state legislatures but did not connect these ideas to a sense that certain understandings of the states were theoretically incompatible with the proposed national system.[16]

Madison's comfort with reducing state power was evident in a second speech on the negative that remains as originally composed. He recommended placing the power of the negative in the "senate alone." He suggested adopting the British model in royal colonies of permitting temporary assent over urgent state laws. He threatened opponents with a choice: either accept reduced state power with proportional suffrage or face inevitable political collapse of the nation. He asked, "What would be the consequence of a dissolution of the States w[hi]ch seemed likely to happen if no effectual substitute was made for the defective system existing."[17]

By June 8, Madison faced dissension within the Virginia delegation. The broader negative lost. Only the largest states voted in favor: Massachusetts, Pennsylvania, and Virginia. The Virginia delegation was not in agreement. Madison noted the individual votes. Madison, Doctor McClurg, and Blair had voted aye. Randolph and Mason had voted no. Washington had been "not consulted"—the curious phrase suggesting a politically cautious decision by Washington or Madison. The Notes were also tracking Madison's growing disagreement with Randolph and Mason.[18]

Although many of the Virginia resolutions advanced, Madison's proposals lost. He was insistent on proportional representation in both houses. He desperately wanted national control over the state legislatures. He desired a small—probably very small—second branch. He believed in checks in the form of negatives—a council of revision combining the executive and judiciary to control the national legislature; an expansive negative in the second branch to control the states. He did not believe a line could be drawn between matters appropriate for the national legislature and the states, suggesting a theoretical shift toward a national government. He was willing to consider large districts to elect the second branch. He was aligning himself with those delegates willing to entertain consolidation of the smaller states for purposes of the second branch. Thus when Madison supported a small second branch, some members heard erasure of the smallest states' boundaries. When he supported the broad negative, some delegates heard inevitable control of the smallest state legislation by large states such as Virginia. When he hinted at the inability to draw a line, some delegates heard the end to traditional state jurisdictions.

The Notes suggest that Madison failed to understand the growing perception of other delegates. He saw himself as an outsider in Virginia politics with the Virginia legislature as his nemesis. Within the Convention, he was acutely aware of growing disagreement from Randolph and Mason. Madison wanted to save the nation from Virginians, but he could not see that, for others, his proposals raised the threat of governance by Virginians. The role of Jefferson as a future reader may have also influenced these entries. Whether he would align himself with Madison or with Randolph could not be known. Uncertain of Jefferson's views, Madison may have moderated some of his speeches in the Notes and, in other instances, perhaps recorded a stronger version than offered in the Convention. Unfortunately, this original voice was obscured by his later replacements. But Madison's original depiction of himself in the Notes may have tilted more decisively toward greater diminishment of the states. The voice that others heard in the Convention may have sounded even more emphatic.

As Madison settled into a writing routine, a speech's length became a partial proxy for significance. Most speeches occupied less than half a manuscript page. There were a few exceptions. A long Franklin speech was included, but it had been copied from a paper read by Wilson. The placement of the speech—after the vote as if it had not been of any influence—suggested that the serendipity of Madison's ability to copy the actual text accounted for the length. The nearly page-long speeches by Wilson and Mason debated whether a single executive could be reconciled with republican government. But one speech—that of Paterson—stood out for its unusual length.[19]

Paterson's speech on Saturday, June 9, was the longest speech of another delegate recorded by Madison in the early Notes. In part, the two-page record was a product of timing. Sunday offered a respite from Convention proceedings and provided ample time for Madison to transcribe his rough notes with leisure. Moreover, composing the Notes only one day later made it easier to fill in the gaps and expand the missing sections of the rough notes. But in large part, the speech reflected Madison's concern about Paterson's accusation that the Virginians were creating a national government in which Virginia would dominate.[20]

The speech arose amidst a long debate over the rule of suffrage in the national legislature. David Brearley of New Jersey had been explicit. Madison recorded: "Virg[ini]a with her sixteen votes will be a solid column indeed, a formidable phalanx." King heard Brearley describe Virginia's sixteen members as "united." Madison did not use the word, perhaps incapable of writing what he believed to be an improbability. Brearley calculated the likely distribution of representatives. Madison did not record the figures but others did: Virginia, sixteen representatives; Massachusetts, fourteen; Pennsylvania, twelve; Connecticut and New York, eight each; the Carolinas and Maryland, six each; New Jersey, five; New Hampshire, three; Rhode Island, two; the smallest states, Georgia and Delaware, one each. The calculations delineated the future power imbalance. The little states would have no "weight at all."[21]

Brearley proposed a radical solution of geographic equalization. As King recorded, "I shall be willing to take the map of the U S. and divide it into 13 equal parts." Madison's account of the proposal was similar: "One [remedy] only, that a map of the U.S. be spread out, that all existing boundaries be erased, and that a new partition of the whole be made into 13 equal parts." Brearley may, or may not, have been serious. But his creative suggestion pinpointed the problem with proportional representation on existing state boundaries.[22]

Paterson's supporting speech exasperated Madison. As the summary opening sentence noted, Paterson described proportional representation as "striking at the existence of the lesser States." Writing as if Paterson were still speaking, Madison repeatedly wrote "we ought" and "we must"—and crossed out sporadic "we must's." Madison did not minimize Paterson's complaint. Proportional representation gave the large states "an influence in proportion to their magnitude." Paterson asked "why a rich State should have more votes than a small one than that a rich individual citizen should have more than an indigent ´one." Relying on an analogy from inheritance law, the nation should be thrown into a "hotchpot" from which "an equal division" should be made. If "we are to be considered as a nation, all State distinctions must be abolished." Only "when an equal division is made," will there be "fairly an equal representation." Madison included the final threat. Just as Wilson had earlier threatened that the large states were willing to confederate without the smallest, so too the smallest would contemplate an alternative path if necessary. If the plan resulted in the largest states' dominance, Paterson would "do everything in his power to defeat" it. He would rather "submit to a monarch, to a despot, than to such a fate."[23]

In the Convention, Madison remained silent. But in the Notes, he placed two final speakers as apparent substitutes for his opinion. Wilson declared that a "new partition of the States" was "desireable, but evidently & totally impracticable." Partition would make proportional representation more theoretically coherent, but it was not the solution. New Jersey should instead "part with her Sovereignty." Madison gave the last spoken word to Williamson, a delegate only occasionally appearing in the Notes. Williamson suggested a different way to think about the states. In counties of different sizes, proportional representation was "admitted to be just." If the states were analogized to a subordinate type of sovereignty—as, for example, counties—proportional representation might be similarly perceived to be just. In recording the comment—one that no other note taker recorded—Madison revealed his interest in reimagining the states as something less than sovereign. The issue over the best description for the states had been placed on the table. Were they sovereign entities? Were they basically counties? Was there another concept that could be employed to resolve the difficulty? Madison did not try to resolve it. He noted simply that, as "so much depended" on representation, the suffrage debate was postponed until Monday. The Notes indicated that Paterson and Brearley had finally described their concern in a way that even Madison considered a serious threat.[24]

Just as the written record of speakers reflected Madison's mind, so too did his omissions. He did not record everyone or everything that was said. His failure to include various motions betrayed his lack of interest. His decision to omit certain speakers underscored that inclusion served his purposes. With motions and votes, the secretary's official journals provide a record for comparison. With speeches, if no other note taker recorded a speech, it is as if it was never spoken. The silences in the Notes are as significant as the speeches.

Madison focused on successful proposals. Recording motions and proposals that went nowhere held little interest. For example, he omitted a series of motions on the judiciary in favor of summarizing. He stated that the sections "relating to the jurisdiction of the Nati[ona]l tribunals" was deleted to "leave full room for their organization." He summarized the debate on another matter that became irrelevant: "several members did not see the necessity of the clause at all, nor the propriety of making the consent . . . unnecessary." Madison was similarly bored by votes on which he knew the outcome. In a list of nine questions, he recorded only a description of the clause without discussion and gave the vote: "Question on the clause . . ." or "On a question for. . . ." He ignored the growing number of motions for reconsideration of issues. Madison repeatedly skipped over votes that lay outside his political commitments.[25]

Perhaps the most significant omission during the first weeks involved Elbridge Gerry's speech on slavery. On Monday, June 11, the delegates returned to debate how representation in the first branch should be proportioned. Wilson moved the introduction of the three-fifths ratio. Four note takers recorded Gerry's speech against the ratio. Madison did not. Indeed, his brief notes implied that there had been no debate.

Madison alluded to the three-fifths ratio in a brief paragraph. He summarized the Wilson motion: "fix the equitable ratio of representation in the 1st. branch by referring to the act of Congs. agreed to by Eleven States, which proposes that the quotas of the States should be apportioned to their number of inhabitants, rating 5 slaves as equal to 3 freemen." The approach taken in the Confederation Congress's revenue act was being advanced as the calculation for representation. Significantly, the ratio applied to political representation markedly benefited Virginia, which possessed the largest number of enslaved people. The ratio passed with only New Jersey and Delaware dissenting. Madison reported the favorable vote but described no discussion.[26]

A debate, however, had occurred, and it had involved Madison. Four note takers thought it worthy of record. Gerry spoke against the ratio. Madison responded. All four note takers recorded Gerry's speech.

Gerry as recorded by Paterson (NJ):

Rule of Taxation not the Rule of Representation—4 might then have more Voices than ten—Slaves not to be put upon the Footing as freemen—Freemen of Massts. not to be put upon a Footing with the Slaves of other States—Horses and Cattle ought to have the Right of Representat[io]n Negroes—Mules—

The Taxes must be drawn by the nat[iona]l Governm[en]t immediately from the People; otherwise will never be collected—

Gerry as recorded by Butler (SC):

Are we to enter into a Compact with Slaves. No! Are the Men of Massachusetts to put their hands in our purses. No! The Gentleman makes a Calculation of the possibility of four out voting 6. Are not the four bound by the same law. Well if you take the Blacks out of the Question in One way surely they ought in another. This Country will not pay in proportion to its wealth. The Gentleman says 3 10th pray is not that a Compact. The Gentleman says no Acct. of Blacks pray of what Acc[oun]t are the Number of White Inhabitants of Massachusetts to the southern states if they cant be brought therein to defend it.

Gerry as recorded by Lansing (NY):

If Negroes represented why not Horses and Cows—Slaves not to be taken in under any Idea of Representation.

Gerry as recorded by Yates (NY):

The idea of property ought not to be the rule of representation. Blacks are property, and are used to the southward as horses and cattle to the northward; and why should their representation be increased to the southward on account of the number of slaves, than horses or oxen to the north?

Interesting discrepancies occurred among the note takers, for example, the use of different words to describe enslaved persons: *slaves, negroes,* and *blacks*. Nonetheless, all four heard Gerry attack the use of the ratio as a rule for political representation. All four heard his sarcastic suggestion that if people held as property were to be counted for representation, then horses and cows should be also included. And, everyone save for Lansing recorded a regional division between Massachusetts and the southern states.[27]

Madison's omission obscured more than the reality of an objection. It avoided acknowledging an additional challenge to his desire for proportional representation in both houses. A bicameral legislature based on proportional representation with the ratio favored the slaveholding states and, once again, favored Virginia most of all. In Massachusetts, slavery had been abolished. Other northern states were considering gradual emancipation and abolition. A three-fifths clause, however, gave political power to states with slavery. Although Gerry did not criticize slavery, the ratio inevitably depended on a judgment about slavery.[28]

In skipping Gerry's speech, Madison omitted his role in the discussion. Madison may have been the only person to respond to Gerry. According to Paterson and Yates, Madison spoke and ended the discussion. Paterson heard him suggest that "the particular rule for the present" be left. Yates recorded Madison's recommendation that "the detail be the business of a subcommittee." Although in the Notes, Madison created the illusion of near consensus, no discussion, and personal disinterest, the reality was the opposite. The omission suggested a discomforting willingness to obscure his responsibility.[29]

With the three-fifths clause adopted, the delegates from the smaller states lost their struggle for an "equal vote" in Congress. The Virginia delegation held a coalition of larger states (Virginia, Massachusetts, and Pennsylvania) and southern slaveholding states (North Carolina, South Carolina, and Georgia). Thus, on Monday, June 11, proportional representation with the three-fifths ratio was applied to the first branch of Congress (9–2). Then, by a narrower vote (6–5), this six-state coalition extended the three-fifths ratio to the second branch. Proportional representation accompanied by the three-fifths ratio promised power to the largest states and to those with enslaved people. Virginia benefitted most of all. The smallest states' delegates had failed. The Virginians—and Madison, in particular—appeared to have won.[30]

On Wednesday, June 13, the report of the Committee of the Whole House emphasized Madison's success in achieving proportional representation in both houses. The manner in which Madison copied the Committee Report conveys the impression that he was pleased. He squished prior comments by General Pinckney and Williamson so he could place the Report on a separate sheet. (Williamson's speech was written in such small handwriting that it was missed entirely in Jefferson's copy of the Notes.) Madison's handwriting was large, careful, neat, and clear. Despite criticism from the outset, two and a half weeks into the Convention, Madison believed he had succeeded.[31]

His confidence spilled over into the Notes for Tuesday and Wednesday. Madison recorded six comments that he made on those days; indeed, the only debates that he bothered to record were those in which he participated. The other speakers merely set up or responded to Madison. The entries cataloged his opinions. He preferred elections every three years for the first branch. "Instability is the great vice of our republics." He declared—no doubt to the annoyance of other delegates—that they "consider what was right & necessary" and not what their constituents would think. He entered into a small spat over the proper standard for compensation. He advocated a seven-year term for the second branch to give "stability" to balance the "popular branch." He suggested judicial appointments be given to the Senate because ordinary legislators were "too much influenced by their partialities." He insisted that the Senate would be composed of "generally a more capable sett [sic] of men" and they should participate in "money bills" (funding legislation). Each speech contained a little thought on government. Read together, they were rather self-congratulatory.[32]

Madison had not succeeded in every respect. The Council of revision was gone. Although the numbers of both branches were based on proportional representation, the selection of the second branch had been given to the state legislatures. The negative on state laws was specific rather than broad. Smaller issues had been lost. But the Report remained remarkably similar to the government Madison had wanted earlier that spring.

The Report's nineteen resolutions established a "National Governm[en]t." In contrast to the Articles of Confederation, the resolutions were "Articles of Union." In the bicameral "National Legislature," the first branch was elected by the people, serving three years; the second branch was chosen by the state legislatures, serving for seven years. For both branches, the "rights of suffrage" were "according to some equitable ratio of representation": specifically, "white & other free citizens & inhabitants" and three-fifths of other persons. In addition to the powers of the Confederation Congress, the National Legislature had extensive new authority: the power to legislate "in all cases to which the separate States are incompetent; or in which the harmony of the U.S. may be interrupted by the exercise of individual legislation." The Legislature had the authority to negative state laws contravening the Articles of Union or treaties. A single "National Executive" would serve a single, seven-year term, chosen by the National Legislature. The Executive had a right to negative national legislative acts but with a legislative override. A "Nat[iona]l Judiciary," appointed by the second branch, had jurisdiction over collection of revenue, impeachments, and "questions which involve the national peace & harmony." State legislatures, executives, and judiciaries were to be "bound by oath to support" the Articles of Union. A republican constitution and laws were guaranteed to each state, new states could be formed and admitted, and amendments made.[33]

For Madison, the Committee Report completed the first stage of the Convention. In the Notes, he emphasized the separation. The Report occupied three pages. The final page of the sheet was blank. In the years that followed, Madison never wrote on this page. As far as Madison was concerned, Wednesday, June 13 brought to a close a critical phase of the Convention. Never again would his vision and that of the apparent majority of delegates align so closely.[34]

Only one thing marred his apparent triumph. Consideration of the Report was postponed until Thursday. Madison added in the tiniest of squished words at the absolute bottom of a page, the delay was to "give an opportunity for other plans to be proposed." Perhaps some foreboding led him to write his brother that same day: "I think the Session will be of considerable length." Madison may have been capable of certain self-delusion but he nevertheless remained politically astute.[35]

RECORDING THE
CONSTITUTIONAL CONVENTION

5

AN ACCOUNT OF FAILED STRATEGIES

In the wake of the Report of the Committee of the Whole House, Madison began to record the Convention in greater depth. A month later, he would write Jefferson that he had "taken lengthy notes of every thing that has yet passed." For Madison, the process of writing the Notes also became a process of revising his ideas. The version of his speeches in the Notes diverged from their oral delivery. On June 19, for example, other note takers heard Madison make a disorganized defense of the Report. Madison, however, recorded an organized, revised version of his never-delivered opening address, as outlined in the "Vices of the Political System." Conversely, in other instances, Madison may have recorded ideas that he had not yet even stated in the Convention. From Thursday, June 14, to Tuesday, July 17, the Notes focused on Madison's struggle to ensure minimal control by the state legislatures in the national system. It was a diary of his political ambitions.[1]

Over these five weeks, Madison recorded speeches criticizing and defending the Report of June 13. He included seven significant speeches of his own. His speeches originally portrayed his relentless pursuit of proportional representation in both houses. Rebutting state representation, he came close to openly advocating that the states should be considered as corporations and that the Senate should represent wealth and property. How explicitly he made these claims is uncertain because four speeches were subsequently replaced. As certain delegates pushed for compromise over representation, Madison refused to accept equal state suffrage. Instead, on July 9 he strategically raised the future protection of slavery to win votes. The decision to use the slavery issue to win proportional representation likely confirmed for some delegates their suspicions about Madison's Virginia sympathies. Madison continued to misperceive concern about proportional representation as focused on state sovereignty rather than large-state power. Despite his efforts, as his core commitments lost one by one, the Notes recorded his increasing frustration. On Tuesday, July 17, after a controversial vote to support an executive with a tenure of good behavior, Madison's Notes reached a nadir.

For Thursday, June 14, Madison started a new sheet, carefully spacing his words. Comfortably adopting the diarist voice, Madison wrote a brief paragraph explaining that the New Jersey delegation was developing a plan "contradistinguished" from the Report. He then began Friday's entry with a diarist's description of the presentation of Paterson's plan. Madison then wrote an analysis, which he marked "N.B."—nota bene. The centrality of this strategic analysis is overlooked in modern editions of the Notes because Madison eventually relocated it to a footnote.[2]

The point that Madison wanted the reader to note well involved the fragility of the opposing coalition. He emphasized the division among the delegates from Connecticut, New York, New Jersey, and Delaware. The latter two states opposed a national government because of proportional representation in both branches. Connecticut and New York, on the other hand, wanted to "add a few new powers" to Congress rather than "to substitute, a National Gov[ernmen]t." Madison dismissively added that Maryland's Luther Martin "made a common cause on different principles," leaving unclear what those principles were. The analysis implied that New York and Connecticut did not care as much about equal state suffrage. If the Report could be portrayed as creating something other than a substitution of "National" government, they might alter their votes.[3]

Madison concluded his analysis with a striking comment, possibly made privately. Dickinson warned, "you see the consequence of pushing things too far." Dickinson continued,

> Some of the members from the small States wish for two branches in the General Legislature, and are friends to a good National Government; but we would sooner to submit to France or any other foreign power than submit to be deprived of an equality of suffrage, in both branches of the legislature, and thereby be thrown under the domination of the large States.

Dickinson suggested that the desire for equal state suffrage was a concern about political power rather than a theoretical belief in state sovereignty. The small-state delegates wanted a national government that would be, in their minds, national. They feared a national government that was for all practical purposes controlled by Virginia. Madison, however, refused to believe *he* was pushing things too far. He wrote down Dickinson's caution—and then completely dismissed the advice.[4]

Only after undercutting political support for Paterson's plan, did Madison copy the plan for the "federal Constitution." The plan offered solutions to known problems under the Articles of Confederation. It added powers to the existing unicameral Congress over commerce and authorized revenue collection by duties. It specified that requisitions would use a three-fifths clause. Congress was to elect a "federal Executive," who was to appoint a "federal Judiciary." Congressional laws and treaties were made the supreme law binding on the states. Naturalization rules were made uniform across the states. The plan suggested that current problems could be solved and a stronger government created under equal state suffrage. In view of Dickinson's comment to Madison about favoring two branches, the plan was a bargaining position rather than the desired outcome.[5]

The Notes indicate that Madison had little concern about the plan. The initial debate took place on Saturday, giving him time on Sunday to write up the lengthy speeches. He gave the entry a header emphasizing the two positions: "Mr. P & Mr. R." He devoted six pages to the delegates favoring (Lansing and Paterson) and opposing (Wilson and Randolph). He remained interested in aesthetics and ensured that Monday, June 18, would begin on a new page.[6]

Recording a lengthy speech was still a struggle for Madison. He muddled the tenses and points of view. Paterson's speech began in the third person *(he),* shifted to the first person singular *(I),* to the first person plural *(we),* then to third person ("[he] reads the 5th article of Confederation"). Madison alternated between summaries and apparent quotation. He summarized Randolph's speech: "He painted in strong colours, the imbecility of the existing confederacy, & the danger of delaying a substantial reform." The lengthy speeches tended to disintegrate near the conclusions. Paterson's speech shifted to questions: "Why? For the purpose of a check." Several sentences later, Madison wrote: "Do the people at large complain of Cong[res]s? No." Wilson's speech remained a bare outline: "2. Representation of the people at large is at the basis of the one—the State Legislatures the pillars of the other." As the speech continued, it became more succinct: "9. Revision of the laws—no such check." Madison grew impatient with the task of creating speeches from rough notes.[7]

The emotion of the speakers was moderated. Lansing, for example, dramatically characterized the Report's consequences for the states. Lansing's own notes described the national system of the Report as involving "a total Subversion of State sovereignties." Other note takers recorded Lansing's strong statement:

> *Paterson's version:* "will absorb the State-Governm[en]ts."
> *King's version:* "Will absorb the State sovereignties & leave them mere Corporations, & Electors of the nat[iona]l Senate."
> *Hamilton's version:* "proposes to preserve the state Sovereignties . . . Ind[ividual] States cannot be supposed to be willing to annihilate the States"
> *Yates's version:* "which latter must ultimately destroy or annihilate the state governments."
> *Madison's version:* "The plan of M[r]. R in short absorbs all power except what may be exercised even in the little local matters of the States which are not objects worthy of the supreme cognizance."

In contrast to the others, Madison constructed an elaborate sentence. Words such as "sovereignty" and "annihilate" were eliminated. "Absorb" was included, but the object shifted to the more ambiguous idea of "power" instead of "sovereignty." The states were to have authority over "little local matters," but they were not explicitly called "corporations." The attenuated structure muted the impact.[8]

Madison devoted far more space—eight cramped pages—to Hamilton's speech sketching an alternative on Monday, June 18. As if to emphasize that Hamilton's speech was intended to cast light on the choice between the Report and the plan, Madison titled the day, "on the propositions of M[r]. Patterson & M[r]. Randolph." The purpose of the speech is ambiguous. Hamilton described a far more national plan than the Report. The speech may have reflected Hamilton's beliefs or it may have been a strategy to make the Virginia plan appear to be centrist. Hamilton never moved to introduce the plan.[9]

Madison heard Hamilton offer two significant ideas. First, Hamilton took the beliefs that interested Madison (the states "constantly pursue internal interests" and the relevance of past confederacies) to the logical end. The general government should have "a compleat sovereignty." No plan that left "the States in possession of their sovereignty could possibly answer the purpose." The states should be replaced with "[s]ubordinate authorities": "district tribunals" and "little corporations for local purposes." Hamilton thus provided an alternative concept of the states reduced to local courts and corporations. Indeed, the next day, Madison recorded Hamilton's insistence that he "had not been understood yesterday." As "no boundary could be drawn" between national and state legislatures and the subversive "rivalship of the States," the national legislature should have "indefinite authority." "As States," the states "ought to be abolished." Hamilton thought they should be construed as "Corporations"—and even then, the "extent of" the largest "would be formidable." The corporation concept left the states with limited local authority.[10]

Second, Hamilton addressed another problem that intrigued Madison: the "extent of the Country to be governed" and the "separate interests" arising from "debtors, Creditors &c." Hamilton doubted that power was ever safe: "Give all power to the many, they will oppress the few. Give all power to the few they will oppress the many." Nonetheless, Hamilton recommended ensuring that the senate and executive had "firmness" to control the interests motivating the first branch of the legislature. He recommended the senators and executive serve on good behavior; that is, they were to be elected without a term limit but removable for misconduct. Hamilton insisted that the executive was not a "monarch." Madison heard Hamilton rather quietly praise the British Government, "In his private opinion he had no scruple in declaring . . . that the British Gov[ernmen]t was the best in the world."[11]

Madison included a "sketch" of Hamilton's plan. Although Madison used somewhat fancy roman numerals, the sketch was informal. The dashes, repetitive "to be," and explanations ("in order to do this . . .") suggested that Madison or Hamilton was summarizing the sketch. The divergence from the Virginia resolutions was apparent. Absolute followed absolute: "All laws of the particular States contrary to the Constitution or laws of the United State to be utterly void."; "The Senate to have the sole power of declaring war." On a spectrum of possible republican governments, the Virginia plan appeared relatively moderate in comparison.[12]

As originally recorded, the Notes made clear that Hamilton's ideas were not formally introduced. Hamilton "did not mean to offer the paper" as propositions. Instead, it was to give "a more correct view of his ideas" and suggest possible future amendments. What Madison may have heard in Hamilton's speech was repeated reinforcement of ideas about the fundamental problems. Madison inserted no comment rejecting it, and his speech the following day made no effort to criticize it. Nonetheless, in the 1790s Hamilton's speech would become the most controversial aspect of the Convention. The states as corporations and an executive on good behavior became linked suspiciously to sympathy for an elective version of British monarchy. The Notes would play a role in the reinterpretation of the speech.[13]

After writing Hamilton's speech, Madison ensured that his contribution to the debate appeared similarly thoughtful. On Tuesday, June 19, Madison gave a lengthy speech. Although other note takers recorded it as somewhat meandering, in the Notes the speech was a well-organized six-page disquisition. Madison incorporated his two sets of pre-Convention notes. He "reviewed the Amphyctrionic & Achæan confederacies . . . and the Helvetic, Germanic & Belgic among the moderns, tracing their analogy to the U. States." But Madison did not bother to write out this section; he simply wrote at the end of the sentence, "see paper B." Paper B was presumably the confederacies notes (leaving unclear why it was described as "Paper B"). The purpose was to record the insights he had, not the precise manner in which he had offered them. Madison may have intended to attach the notes as an insert or appendix.[14]

In this speech, Madison finally was able to reuse and revise his earlier notes on the Vices. He broke up the previous arrangement and focused on his theory that the government should be based on the people, not the states. He omitted irrelevant vices: Vice 1 (on state failures to comply with requisitions) and Vice 5 (on areas where national power would be preferred). Certain sections were copied more or less directly from the Vices notes. The reorganization can be seen below:

[A.] Convention not limited to a "federal" plan in which government exercises power on people collectively and derives appointments from states

[B.] Articles of Confederation can be dissolved without unanimous consent because one party's breach absolves others of obligations [Vice 8]

[C.] Paterson's plan will not preserve Union and remedy evils:
1. Will not prevent violations of law of nations and treaties [Vice 3]

2. Will not prevent encroachments on federal authority [Vice 2]
    [a.] Review of state violations [Vice 2]
    [b.] Review of ancient and modern confederacies ["see paper B": Notes on ancient and modern confederacies"]
    [c.] Patterson plan defective because no ratification by people [Vices 7 & 8] and no federal trial courts
3. Will not prevent trespasses of states on each other [Vice 4]
4. Will not secure internal tranquility of states [Vice 6]
5. Will not secure good internal legislation: 1. multiplicity of laws passed by states; 2. mutability of laws; 3. Injustice of laws; 4. Impotence of laws [Vices 9–12]
6. Will not secure the Union against the influence of foreign powers over members [Vice 3]
7. Begs small states to consider burden on the small states of Patterson plan
8. Consequence of dissolution if no plan

[D.] Difficulty of "the affair of Representation"—impracticable to repartition states because of different property rules and manners; better for small states to voluntarily join together; new western states with equal vote will be a danger to all

In ending with partition, Madison acknowledged validity to the concerns about the extent of Virginia's vote. His solution was pragmatic. If New Jersey and Delaware were worried, the Constitution should permit them to voluntarily join a neighboring state. Madison's reasoning for the original Virginia plan—now the Committee Report—at last found a place in the Notes.[15]

The proceedings of Monday and Tuesday—the long speeches by Hamilton and Madison—were presented in the Notes as set pieces. At the conclusion of his speech, Madison skipped a procedural motion and only reported a motion on whether "M^r. Randolphs propositions be re-reported without alteration." With evident delight, Madison added, it "was in fact a question whether M^r. R's should be adhered to as preferable to those of M^r. Patterson." For the astute reader, the vote division was significant. Madison catalogued seven states in favor, three opposed (New York, New Jersey, and Delaware), and the divided vote of Maryland. In the week since June 14, Connecticut shifted to support the Report. Moreover, the New York negative vote was fragile and required both Yates and Lansing to be present to outvote Hamilton and prevent a divided vote. New Jersey and Delaware apparently had failed.[16]

Although the delegates began a new phase of the Convention, Madison perceived continuity. On the line after the final vote in the Committee of the Whole House, Madison wrote the heading: "M^r. Randolph's plan as reported from the Com[m]ittee before the House." The heading implied the Committee Report remained essentially the original Virginia plan. Madison did not copy the amended Report into his Notes. If he had a copy, it has not been located. Madison did not start a new sheet or even a page when the delegates began to debate the Committee Report as a Convention. Although he introduced the discussion with a line describing the first proposition being taken up, the summary sentence for the first speech resembled the previous debate. Wilson stated that "by a Nat[iona]l Gov[ernmen]t he did not mean one that would swallow up the State Gov[ernmen]ts as seemed to be wished by some gentlemen." Hamilton and King similarly emphasized that the Report would not annihilate the states but take "much of their power." On Wednesday, June 20, Connecticut's Oliver Ellsworth finessed the disagreement by replacing the term, "national government," with the neatly ambiguous "government of the United States." Madison's prediction about Connecticut's position had been accurate. As the Convention turned to review the Report, Madison's Notes suggested that he expected eventual success. In his mind, his plan was moving forward. Proportional representation in both houses and a negative over state laws would structure the future government.[17]

As the Convention proceeded to debate the Report, Madison focused the Notes on political strategy. Even as the longer speeches began to bear a resemblance to those found in the published debates of Parliament, the Notes substantively served as a record of shifting political positions and potential votes. The Notes also remained a diary in which Madison could write and revise his developing ideas. It was a place to work out problems. In late June, one particular problem dominated Madison's thoughts: the conception of the states. Madison gave three related speeches. He eventually replaced the two speeches he gave on June 21 and June 29; in contrast, his lengthy speech of June 28 remains on the original sheets. In the course of the three speeches, Madison shifted into alliance with delegates contemplating the corporation as the appropriate structure for the states. The Notes likely originally reflected this shift.[18]

Madison appreciated that underlying intentions could be difficult to discern. For example, in a vote over whether the national or state governments should pay representatives' salaries, Massachusetts voted to delete the words referring to the national treasury. Immediately after the vote, Madison wrote "Note." He explained that it was "not because they thought the State Treas[ur]y ought to be substituted; but because they thought nothing should be said on the subject." The Massachusetts delegates believed that, without an explicit decision, the obligation would "silently devolve" on the national treasury. Madison offered another explanation after a vote on salaries diverged from what might have been expected of him by a future reader such as Jefferson. After noting the vote had been unanimous, he added that "friends" of fixed stipends were "willing that the practicability of fixing the compensation" would be worked out later in "forming the details." In both instances, the Notes indicated that intentions were not always evident in the visible record.[19]

The knowledge that the future reader was an astute politician underlay accounts of procedural strategies. The Notes highlighted the successful use of adjournments to counter a controversial proposal by Franklin. On Thursday, June 28, Franklin suggested that a clergyman be hired to conduct prayers. Madison may have planned to insert specific language relating to the proposal later because he left a small blank space after "He therefore proposed." Madison relatively briefly summarized Franklin's speech: the "diversity of opinions" in the Convention; the "groping . . . in the dark"; the idea of "applying for light to that powerful friend who alone can supply it"; the claim to becoming "more & more convinced, that God ruled in the affairs of men." Madison then devoted nearly as much space to the objections, all of which sought to sink the proposal for technical reasons. "Mr Hamilton & several others" raised concerns that the idea would send a signal of failure to the public. Williamson noted there were "no funds." Randolph proposed an alternative, delaying any morning prayer until after July 4. Others made "several unsuccessful attempts for silently postponing the matter by adjournment." Eventually, the adjournment "at length carried," and the delegates avoided voting on the motion. The Notes suggested that the proposal had been sunk without anyone having to reject or even explicitly oppose prayers. Moreover, the proposal seemed apparently sufficiently defeated as to be never raised again. Indeed, the procedural adjournment meant no official record even was kept of the motion. Franklin might have wanted a clergyman—but the Notes suggested few others did.[20]

Above all, the issue that fascinated Madison involved the appropriate conception of the states. The delegates struggled to describe what a *state* should be. In King's notes, Connecticut's William Johnson suggested fundamental consensus. Almost everyone agreed that "the national" or general government should "be more powerful—& the State Gov[ernmen]ts less so." Johnson argued that, if the Report's proponents offered reassurance that the "State Gov[ernmen]ts will be secure" from the general government, then "we may all agree." The challenge lay in finding a "less" powerful, but secure, conception of the states.[21]

The Notes recorded the efforts of Madison's allies to find an appropriate analogy for their conception of the states. Hamilton and King appear to have suggested the corporation. By corporation, they did not mean the modern business corporation but a political authority that held delegated political power. On June 19, Madison recorded Hamilton suggesting that the states be considered as "subordinate jurisdictions" analogous to "corporations." That same day, King apparently argued, or at least contemplated arguing, that the "States are now subordinate corporations or Societies and not Sovereigns." A state should be given "the right of regulating its private & internal affairs in the manner of a subordinate corporation." Configuring the states as corporations did not obliterate the states and yet clarified that they were subordinate. Indeed, because many of the colonies had been initially established as corporations (e.g., Massachusetts and Virginia), the analogy had a historical pedigree.[22]

In favoring a limited jurisdiction for the states, Madison seems to have flirted with the corporation analogy. On Thursday, June 21, King heard Madison explain that history proved "that there never has existed a danger of the destruction of the State Gov[ernmen]ts by encroachments of the Gen[era]l Gov[ernmen]ts" Madison argued that the people wanted to protect the aspect of the states that served useful functions such as to "punish offenders." In Lansing's notes, Madison hinted that the states might be seen as corporations: "Legislatures of States have not shewn Disposition to deprive Corporations of Priviledges—Why should they here." In Yates's notes, Madison asked if "any state governments ever encroached on the corporate rights of cities?" He repeated Hamilton's argument that the "line between the two"—national and state governments—cannot be drawn. He was "inclined for a general government." On June 21, no one recorded Madison stating that the states should be corporations, but his arguments came very close.[23]

When Madison wrote this June 21 speech into the Notes, did he hint more explicitly at his comfort with the corporation conception? The speech was likely eventually replaced. The replaced speech asked a hypothetical question: "let it be supposed for a moment that indefinite power should be given to the Gen[era]l Legislature, and the States reduced to corporations dependent on the Gen[era]l Legislature." Madison's answer was that, if the states performed convenient functions, the people would protect those functions. A second question asked, "Supposing therefore a tendency in the Gen[era]l Government to absorb the State Gov[ernmen]ts." The answer given was blunt: "no fatal consequence would result." Even the replaced speech suggested Madison's sympathy to the idea that no harm would come from reducing the states to corporations or absorbing the state governments. In the original Notes, he may have written the speech to openly favor that possibility or perhaps added a comment at the end indicating his shift in that direction to the reader. One sentence—even a few words—was sufficient to indicate his inclination.[24]

A week later, Madison searched for a conception of the states that would prove the equal suffrage argument was founded on a "fallacy." On June 28, Madison recorded his long speech that once again wandered through the history of other confederacies. He suggested approximating the states to "the conditions of Counties." They would be "mere counties of the same one entire republic, subject to one common law." On the spectrum between "perfect independence" of the thirteen states and "perfect incorporation," Madison leaned toward incorporation. His response to the smallest states' anxiety was to suggest that "equalization, which is wished for by the small States, now but can never be accomplished at once" might be obtained by voluntary and gradual "partitions of the large & junctions of the small." The speech included short, choppy sentences typical of rough notes—almost as if he had perhaps relied on another delegate's notes (Yates's notes, for example, contain somewhat similar sections). Madison's dissatisfaction with his attempt to reconstruct the speech appeared in word changes and grammatical corrections riddling the pages. Because the description of the states as counties and recommending voluntary partition never became controversial after the Convention, Madison never replaced this speech.[25]

The following day, however, Madison explicitly argued that the states were corporations. Not surprisingly, he eventually replaced this Friday, June 29, speech. King recorded that Johnson declared the fundamental problem to be the definition and conception of the state. He suggested "compromise—let both parties be gratified—let one House or Branch be formed by one Rule && [*sic*] the other by another[.]" Madison rejected compromise. According to other note takers, Madison described the states as corporations. According to King, Madison said the states "are not sovereign." He analyzed sovereignty as a continuum from "the lowest Corporation" to the "most perf[ec]t Sovereignty." The States were "Corporations with power of Bye Laws" and "not in that high degree Sovereign." Paterson similarly summarized Madison's desire to "have the States considered as so many great Corporations, and not otherwise." In short, King and Paterson heard Madison suggest that the states and state law-making authority be treated as subordinate political authorities with delegated power.[26]

If the Notes originally included Madison's declaration of the states as corporations, he eventually removed it. In the replaced speech, Madison left the continuum from the "smallest corporation" to the "most perfect sovereignty" of an empire. But he omitted where the states fell. In late June 1787, the states as corporations fit his theory of proportional representation in both houses. It made coherent his commitment to a national government that operated on individuals. He was not alone in holding the position. The Notes suggested that others, such as King and Hamilton, agreed. In late June, when the Notes remained a legislative diary, Madison had no reason to disguise his willingness to configure the states as corporations.[27]

The original speeches of June 21 and 29 cannot be reconstructed, but the pattern of the replaced speeches is tantalizing. In both speeches, the structure of original analysis remained, but the subsequently controversial conclusion or comment seems to have been omitted. In the absence of the conclusion, the replaced speeches resembled speculation. With the conclusions, the original speeches likely read as a declaration of Madison's underlying intentions and alliances.

The persistent disagreements over proportional representation in both houses and the conception of the states had slowed progress. By Saturday, June 30, the delegates had only reached the seventh resolution of the Report. They debated a resolution requesting that Washington write the governor of New Hampshire to urge the delegates to travel to Philadelphia. For some, another very small state—and one that may have been understood to have abolished slavery—was a desirable addition. For others, among them Madison, it threatened to make agreement more difficult. No letter was sent. By the time, the New Hampshire delegation arrived in the third week of July, Madison had crossed into utter frustration.[28]

In addition to worrying about the concept of the states, Madison gave three speeches on the conception of the second branch and political office. Again, he later replaced two of these three speeches (June 23 and June 26). His speech on June 30 is on its original sheet. Originally, the Notes likely suggested his support for a small second branch with members serving lengthy terms, eligible to other national offices, and representing property holders. Some delegates perceived this vision to be uncomfortably close to an elective version of the British House of Lords.[29]

On Saturday, June 23, Madison argued that political offices should be seen as an incentive for government service. The new national government would create salaried government positions. Madison wanted representatives to be eligible for other national offices after legislative service. The debate focused on whether legislators should be ineligible for other national offices for a certain period. Arguments varied from the cynical (officeholders would simply be shuffled to create space) to the suspicious (sons and brothers would be appointed instead) to the laudatory (there was nothing wrong with a career in government offices). Madison stated that eligibility to "other offices" would serve as "an encouragm[en]t to the Legislative service." He proposed reducing limits on ineligibility to only one year. He lost, outvoted even within the Virginia delegation.[30]

Once again, Madison's replaced speech diverges from what other note takers heard on one controversial idea. The less-than-reliable Lansing and Yates heard a defense by Madison that suggested salary or perks of future national government offices would motivate men. According to Lansing, Madison argued that it was "necessary to hold out Inducements to Men of first Fortune to become Members." According to Yates, Madison claimed that "patriotism" was insufficient and "we must hold out allurements." The implication in both versions was that there were economic and status benefits to national office. Madison's replaced speech is similar to these versions except that it omits any claim that national offices will serve as inducements. The speech emphasized the need to attract the "most capable citizens" to serve in political office but did not explain why eligibility after only one year would be motivational. The explanation heard by Lansing and Yates—that offices would be an inducement—did not appear. If the original version made the claim, Madison eventually omitted it.[31]

The inducement idea was not the only part of the original Notes that vanished. Madison's summary of Charles Pinckney's plan for the Senate also eventually disappeared. On Monday, June 25, Pinckney gave a lengthy speech supporting proportional representation in the second branch. He presented a plan that divided the country into senatorial districts. Lansing described it as an arrangement of the states into "five Classes—to have from one to five Votes." Madison may have originally included the plan. When Pinckney made the same recommendation a week later (Monday, July 2), Madison wrote, "see it Monday June 25." Madison later copied Pinckney's speech on two separate sheets using a copy given to him by Pinckney. The speech began with the words "The people of the U. States are perhaps the most singular of any we are acquainted with." Later, Madison wrote a new beginning to the speech on the replaced prior sheet. Presumably, the original sheet introduced or summarized the Pinckney speech. If Madison originally included a description of the district idea, a brief summary of Pinckney's speech, or a comment on it on the original page, it vanished with the replacement.[32]

If Madison offered an opinion on the speech, it would have been fascinating. In a critique of Madison and Hamilton, Pinckney argued that models based on the British Constitution and the "Helvetic or Belgic confederacies" were inappropriate. Pinckney declared "equality" the "leading feature" of America. He argued: "None will be excluded by birth, & few by fortune" from voting. He disagreed that there were divergent interests. Professional men, commercial men, and the landed interest shared "one interest." Ignoring slavery and enslaved people, Pinckney stated that the "vast extent of unpeopled territory" would be "the means of preserving that equality of condition which so eminently distinguishes us." In the draft, Pinckney referred to "a new extensive, country." If Madison originally summarized the speech, he might have indicated his opinion on Pinckney's claim of equality as the essential feature of the United States.[33]

In the Convention, Madison disagreed with Pinckney. Three note takers (Butler, Lansing, and Yates) described Madison's June 26 speech. According to them, he claimed that "distinctions" from an "Inequality of Property" would characterize the nation. There were divergent interests of debtors and creditors. Although the "landed Interest" was supreme, "the commercial may prevail" in the future. Government was needed for "Balance" and to "protect one Order of Men from the predominating Influence of the other." Madison therefore advocated a Senate that represented the property-holding minority. Butler recorded: "Property ought to be defended against the will of even the Majority." Lansing recorded: "The Senate ought to represent the opulent Minority." Madison wanted protection for property holders.[34]

This speech also was replaced. Did Madison originally suggest a Senate for the "opulent minority"? Did he suggest that a small group of senators serving lengthy terms could protect "property"—particularly types of "property" that majorities might disagree with such as property in enslaved people? In the replaced speech, Madison's analysis about different interests—debtors and creditors, rich and poor—remained. He still predicted that those who "labour under all the hardships in life" will "outnumber" those "placed above the feelings of indigence." He even continued to ask, "How is the danger in all cases of interested co-alitions to oppress the minority to be guarded ag[ain]st?" But, as with the other sheets, his complete answer is missing. He implied it was a Senate on lengthy terms but omitted the idea of a Senate based on property representation—a Senate that, to some delegates, may have had awkward parallels to the House of Lords. Indeed, the Notes recorded delegates responding to this argument. Hamilton declared, "He [Madison] was right in saying that nothing like an equality of property existed." Gerry referred to "the position of Mr. [Madison] that the majority will generally violate justice when they have an interest in so doing." Mason summarized an "important object" of the Senate as "to secure the rights of property." The minority that Madison seemed to care about involved property.[35]

Madison's vision of the Senate clung to the belief that an elite group could be selected. He wanted the Senate to be "the impartial umpires & Guardians of the justice and general Good." They were to "give stability" as a "firm, wise, and impartial body." They were not to be "mere Agents & Advocates of State interests & views." The senators should not represent the states, and they should not represent a popular majority. The number of senators was to be few. They were to serve lengthy terms. And yet, with respect to the second branch, Madison was losing ground. The seven-year term lost, and he eventually rendered illegible his description of General Pinckney's argument for a four-year term. By an overwhelming vote (9–2), senatorial selection was given to the state legislatures. Only Pennsylvania voted with Virginia. All that remained was suffrage: would proportional representation remain? How Madison could protect his vision was not yet apparent.[36]

The Notes reflected Madison's frustration as proportional representation in both houses began to slip away. Between Friday, June 29, and Tuesday, July 10, the Notes shifted from moderated emotion to outright anger. Madison continued to comment in diary style on proposals to achieve compromise—undercutting them all. He copied a compromise plan developed by Randolph but never proposed. He was unwilling to accept the compromises that were based in any way on equal state political power.

On Friday, June 29, Madison recorded a proposed "compromise" by Ellsworth. "We were partly national, partly federal," Ellsworth stated. Therefore proportional representation should exist in one house; equal state suffrage in the other. King heard Madison reject the idea: "we are in utmost Danger" if the states had "equal, influence, and votes in the Senate." Madison, however, recorded no comment that day by him. Instead, the following day, he recorded his speech aggressively criticizing Ellsworth. He insisted the "reasoning of Mr. E at different times did not well . . ."—eventually revising the sentence to obscure the final word. Four times in the speech, Madison disagreed explicitly with "Mr. E."[37]

Although the emotional tenor was rising, Madison continued to dampen it in the Notes. On Saturday, the delegates continued to debate whether the states should have "an equal vote" in the second branch. They again adjourned without decision. Gunning Bedford of Delaware threatened that the small states would find a foreign ally if there was no compromise. The Notes retained the speech's spontaneous character with short sentences, repeated insistence ("we must"), and rhetorical questions. But Madison moderated the emotion. Instead, he included others' description of emotion. King condemned its "intemperance" and "vehemence unprecedented." Randolph referred to the "warm & rash language of Mr. Bedford on Saturday." But, almost as if Madison could not accept anger, he did not record it in the Notes.[38]

Madison's distress, however, was apparent. On Monday, July 2, before adjourning for the July 4 anniversary, the delegates had formed a committee to attempt a compromise, or, as Sherman suggested, to "hit on some expedient." An earlier deadlocked vote (5–5–1) that day, suggested Madison was losing his coalition. Only five states favored proportional representation in the Senate: the large states (Virginia, Pennsylvania, Mas-

sachusetts) and two southern states (North Carolina, and South Carolina). The coalition supporting equal state suffrage included Connecticut, New York, New Jersey, Delaware, and Maryland. No doubt to
Madison's annoyance, Georgia was divided. Charles Pinckney had raised
the three southern states' "peculiar interest" and again proposed his district plan, but it had no outward effect. Madison did not think a committee would help. Although he lost, the Notes catalogued his objections. A committee caused "delay," and any "scheme of compromise"
could be proposed as "easily" in the House.[39]

To the astute reader, the committee's membership revealed the
underlying dynamics and the reason for Madison's concern. The
committee was comprised of delegates who disagreed with Madison:
Ellsworth, Paterson, Bedford, Martin, Gerry, and Franklin. From Virginia,
it was Mason—not Madison—who was elected. The southern members
were William Davie, John Rutledge, Abraham Baldwin—delegates who
had made little appearance in the Notes. The Committee contained no
advocates in Madison's mind for bicameral proportional representation.
He lacked votes in the Convention; he lacked votes to achieve a more
favorable committee.[40]

Although Madison disliked the committee, his decision to record at
length one particular speech in support of it indicated fascination with
the underlying ideas. Gouverneur Morris returned to the Convention
shortly after Hamilton left it. Somewhat similar to Hamilton's earlier
speech, Morris proposed a second branch composed of men of property
serving for life and no pay, appointed by the executive. Morris's reason,
however, was the opposite of Madison's theory for favoring a Senate
based on property holders. Morris wanted a branch of property holders
to limit their power. The rich would "do wrong"—they "will strive to
establish their dominion & enslave the rest." If they mixed with "the
poor," they would "establish an Oligarchy." By separating, the "aristocratic interest," it could be checked. Repeatedly, Madison described Morris's theory of balancing opposed interests. The branches must check
each other. Each "interest must be opposed to another interest." Vices
"must be turned ag[ain]st each other." As Madison composed the Notes,
Morris's insistence on a "mutual check and mutual security" among opposing interests may have burrowed deep within his mind.[41]

The committee's report on July 5 was everything Madison feared. The
Notes made apparent his dismissal of the report. The report put forward
a three-part compromise: (1) in the first branch, every 40,000 inhabitants

(calculated using the three-fifths ratio) had one representative, with at least one member for each state; (2) in the second branch, each state had an equal vote; (3) control over bills for "raising or appropriating money" and fixing government salaries was placed in the first branch. Madison included a footnote to undercut the report. A source on the committee apparently informed Madison that the compromise had been advanced by Franklin—that likely diminished it as far as Madison was concerned. It had been "barely acquiesced" in by opposing members. Unfortunately, the bare acquiescence had been interpreted by the "other side" as "a gaining of their point." Madison also recorded a comment by Gerry that the report had been agreed to "merely in order that some ground of accommodation might be proposed." The opponents considered themselves under no "obligation to support the Report" in the Convention. The Notes portrayed the report as a temporary political strategy rather than a permanent political accommodation.[42]

In the speech by Madison that followed in the Notes, he made no effort to moderate his words. He rejected money bills as a meaningless concession. He wrote that "the Convention was reduced to the delusion of either departing from justice in order to please conciliate the smaller States, and the minority of the people of the U.S. or of displeasing these by doing justice to them by gratifying the larger states and the majority." Condemning Bedford's earlier threat as a "rash policy of courting foreign support," Madison argued that Delaware and New Jersey would not leave the union even if they lost equal state suffrage. If "the principal States comprehending a majority of the people . . . should concur," he hoped the other states "would by degrees accede to it." He insisted that the majority of people would support proportional representation in both houses. In a final ambiguous sentence—perhaps part of the speech, perhaps a comment to the future reader—Madison added, "These observations w[oul]d show that he was not only fixed in his opposition to the Report of the Com[itte]e but was prepared for any want that might follow a negative of it."[43]

For once, Madison sporadically reflected the delegates' anger in the Notes. In the Notes for July 5, Paterson complained of the "manner in which M^r. M & M^r. Govr. Morris had treated the small States." Morris proclaimed, "We cannot annihilate the States but we may perhaps take out the teeth of the serpents." Mason declared that, as much as he missed his home, "he would bury his bones" in Philadelphia rather than dissolve the Convention "without any thing being done." In the Notes for July 7,

Table 5.1. Distribution of Members: June Estimates and July 9 Report

	VA	MA	PA	MD	CT	NY	NC	SC	NJ	NH	RI	DE	GA
Brearley's June estimate (90 members)	16	14	12¾	8¾	8	8	6¾	6	5	3¼	2	1¼	1
July 9 report (56 members)	9	7	8	4	4	5	5	5	3	2	1	1	2

Morris declared that the states "were originally nothing more than colonial corporations." He asked, "What if all the Charters & Constitutions of the States were thrown into the fire, and all their demagogues into the ocean?" Unmediated, likely unaltered, Madison recorded Morris's sarcasm: "Good God, Sir, is it possible they can so delude themselves."[44]

Madison continued to write the Notes as if equal suffrage would fail. When Virginia, Pennsylvania, and South Carolina were outvoted on the committee report's recommendation of equal state suffrage (6–3, with 2 states divided), Madison insisted in the Notes that the vote was temporary. He wrote a "Note" after the vote: "several votes were given here in the affirmative" without concern because another vote would be taken on the entire report. On July 9, after a new committee of five men reported on the size of the lower house, Madison undercut it. He noted the admission of its chair, Morris, that the "Report is little more than a guess." The method of calculation was unclear. Paterson complained that "the Combined rule of numbers and wealth" was "too vague." The report dropped the number of representatives in the first branch to fifty-six. The reduced number given to the three larger states was smaller than in earlier June estimates. The inconsistency and speculation in the numbers underscored the sense of a need to compromise.[45]

Madison recorded an alternative compromise—never introduced. He copied a plan by Randolph, dated July 10, with the title, "an accommodating proposition to small states." In modern editions, the plan is usually omitted; in the 1820s, Madison placed it in the appendix. Randolph's plan was clever. It proposed a second branch, incorporating both proportional representation and equal state suffrage. Equal state suffrage was required for specific enumerated matters: for example, ports, duties, and river navigation; state citizen rights in another state; guarantees of territory, war, or rebellion; regulation of coin and the post office; new state admission; militia and army; executive appointment; and the seat of government. Slavery was not on the list. The plan explicitly dealt with conflicting state and national laws, and provided an appeal to the national judiciary to void laws contrary to "the principles of equity and justice." In proposing the plan, Randolph perceived that concerns over proportional representation arose from anxieties about future political problems, not a theoretical commitment to state sovereignty. Randolph, however, did not introduce the plan—perhaps because Madison may have discouraged him. Madison still believed that proportional representation in both houses could be achieved without any such compromises.[46]

By July 9, Madison decided to use a different, divisive strategy to achieve proportional representation in both houses. He argued the two branches should reflect the division over slavery between northern and southern states. He sought to persuade the three southern states to vote with the three largest states in order to guarantee a future with slavery. Defeating equal state suffrage remained Madison's concern. The Notes recorded Madison's shift towards a slavery coalition.

As the Notes reveal, the slavery strategy was developing in Madison's mind in late June. On Saturday, June 30, Madison ended a speech by describing a regional difference between "having or not having slaves." The "great division of interests" lay "between the Northern & Southern" and required that "security" be provided against "the encroachments of the other." Then Madison added—and he may have no longer been recording spoken words but writing his developing thoughts—"He was so strongly impressed with this important truth he had thought of any expedient that would answer the purpose." The expedient was to give the "Southern Scale" the "advantage" in one house and the "Northern in the other." Therefore, one branch would reflect "the number of free inhabitants only" and the other, the entire population, "counting the slaves as free." Madison wrote that he had been "restrained from making this expedient" because of his concern about emphasizing the sectional division. No one recorded Madison proposing the compromise, and the sentences may reflect that the idea was still only a thought as of the end of June.[47]

Ten days later, Madison openly proposed his idea as the "proper ground of compromise." On July 9, he argued that, in the first branch, "the States should be represented according to their number of free inhabitants" and, in the second branch, "according to the whole number, including slaves."

Table 5.2. Distribution of Members: July 10 Report

	VA	MA	PA	MD	CT	NY	NC	SC	NJ	NH	RI	DE	GA
July 9 report (56 members)	9	7	8	4	4	5	5	5	3	2	1	1	2
July 10 report (65 members)	10	8	8	6	5	6	5	5	4	3	1	1	3

Madison had no illusion about the purpose in giving the states representation for enslaved people not permitted to vote. One of the "primary objects" of the second branch was the "guardianship of the rights of property." The second branch would represent property—including property in people.[48]

The Notes reflected Madison's perception of support for his proposal. Butler agreed "warmly." King implied that he was willing to accept such a compromise. As he put it according to Madison, the Southern States had to have "some respect . . . paid to their superior wealth." In fact, when yet another committee was elected to recalculate the representation, Madison was elected for the first time. Perhaps not surprisingly, King was also elected. On July 10, this committee increased the representation in the first branch to 65 members. Virginia continued to have the largest number of representatives.[49]

Over the following week, the Notes focused on the sectional divide over slavery. Madison struggled with whether to claim credit. He initially began to record King's explanation that he was "fully impressed with the idea" of a regional divide—words that suggested credit was due to the person who had proposed the idea—Madison. But Madison struck the words and instead recorded King merely stating that he was "fully convinced" about the fact of a "difference of interests" between North and South instead of large and small states. The Notes suggest that Madison was ambivalent about whether to accept individual responsibility as the catalyst for the slavery strategy.[50]

Over the next several days, the debate focused on sectional division and congressional power over slavery. Some disagreement related to the line of division between the regions. General Pinckney "considered" Virginia "a Southern State." Dayton thought the "dividing State" was Pennsylvania. Other concerns emphasized the need to guarantee slavery from national government power. General Pinckney insisted that "property in slaves should not be exposed to danger under a Gov[ernmen]t instituted for the protection of property." Even Randolph, who "lamented that such a species of property existed," stated that "as it did exist[,] the holders of it would require this security." North Carolina's Davie declared that "it was high time now to speak out" because "some gentlemen [meant] to deprive the Southern States of any share of Representation for their blacks." On July 13, Madison repeated his theory while recommending more members for North and South Carolina, as too many had been "allotted" to the Northern states.[51]

Although Madison's proposal to base bicameralism on slavery did not advance, the future power of the southern states became a new focus in the Notes. He tracked the prominent northern delegates' support—albeit reluctant—for the three-fifths ratio's inclusion in proportional representation. In the Notes, the Massachusetts delegation loomed large. Gorham seemed to accept the three-fifths clause. Madison seemed worried about King. By the end of July 11, the Notes recorded King making a convoluted claim about the inclusion of enslaved people: "He had never said as to any particular point that he would in no event acquiesce in & support it." Nonetheless, a day later, King apparently reached a pragmatic conclusion. When "the Southern states shall be more numerous than the Northern, they can & will hold a language that will force" their result— Madison then immediately decided "force" was too strong, crossed it out, and wrote "awe." On the Pennsylvania delegation, Wilson acknowledged that the three-fifths clause made absolutely no sense but agreed that such "difficulties" had to be "overruled by the necessity of compromise." The Notes accurately reflected a division within Massachusetts. The delegation divided on the July 12 vote to approve the three-fifths clause. Recording speeches was Madison's method of tracking individual positions within the two large, northern states.[52]

Only one delegate in the Notes objected to the strategy of encouraging sectional division. Over three days, Madison recorded Morris's passionate criticism. On Wednesday, July 11, Morris described "the dilemma of doing injustice to the Southern States or to human nature." He preferred injustice to the South. He did not want to "give such encouragement to the slave trade," and he "did not believe that those States would ever confederate on terms that would deprive them of that trade." On Thursday, Morris repeated that it was "high time to speak out." He insisted that Pennsylvania "will never agree to the representation of Negroes"— meaning representation based on ownership in slaves. On Friday, he accused Madison of instigating the sectional divide. Morris explained, "A distinction had been set up & urged, between N[orther]n & South[er]n

States." He had "hitherto considered this doctrine heretical" and still believed it "groundless." But the distinction "persisted." Morris predicted, "the South[er]n Gentlemen will not be satisfied unless they see the way open to their gaining a majority in the public Councils." Madison completely agreed. In recording Morris's complaints, the Notes ironically acknowledged the success of Madison's strategy.[53]

Madison included Morris's attempt to use Madison's strategy against him. Morris declared that he would be "obliged" to vote for the "vicious principles of equality" in the second branch to protect the northern states. Morris recommended that the "Middle States"—large and small—side with the northern states. If the southern states got "power into their hands," they would join with "the interior Country" and "inevitably bring on a war with Spain for the Mississippi." Morris dared Madison to take back the sectional distinction. If it were "fictitious let it be dismissed." If real, "let us at once take a friendly leave of each other." Madison apparently stayed silent.[54]

On Saturday, July 14, Madison composed a dramatic speech tying equal state suffrage to northern dominance. A plan for proportional representation in the second branch was advanced by Pinckney. The Notes commented, "M[r]. [Madison] concurred in this motion as a reasonable compromise." The speech argued for proportional representation as the only "proper foundation" for the government. Madison could not find "a single instance" in which the proposed government would not be operating on the "people individually." To permit equal state suffrage was to empower a minority. Madison chose strong verbs: a few states would "negative the will of the majority of the people," "extort" special legislation, and "obtrude" measures. There was no moderation in his words. Over time, the "evil" would grow. Madison insisted, "The institution of slavery & its consequences formed the line of discrimination." Equality would give "perpetuity . . . to the N[or]rth[er]n ag[ain]st the South[er]n Scale." Proportional representation in both branches promised a future with southern slavery.[55]

To Madison's dismay, the proposal for proportional representation in the second branch failed. The Notes underscored the unanticipated reason: Massachusetts had voted no. Madison explicated the Massachusetts negative vote: "M[r]. King ay. M[r]. Ghorum absent." On Sunday, King wrote a memorandum summarizing the "twelve days" of debates over representation. The proportional representation in the second branch was "lost," King wrote, "to my mortification by the Vote of Mass[achusetts]." When Madison wrote the Notes for Saturday, July 14, he knew this outcome. The Notes focused disproportionately on the Massachusetts delegation. A change in the Massachusetts vote would have left a bare majority for equal state suffrage (4–5–1), perhaps too close to have been interpreted as decisive. The delegation's shift, however, had created the division (4–6) against proportional representation in the second branch. The Notes recorded the failed effort to achieve, what Madison regarded as the only correct result.[56]

On Monday, July 16, Madison used the Notes to allocate blame. The first sentence described the final affirmative vote on the report, "including the equality of votes in the 2d branch." Madison listed the four members of the Massachusetts delegation by name: Gerry and Strong had voted aye; King and Gorham had voted no. Gorham's reappearance, however, came too late to do anything but divide the delegation. The four-state coalition, two large (Virginia and Pennsylvania) and the two southern (South Carolina and Georgia), lost. Madison did not bother to copy the report into the Notes.[57]

The Notes recounted the failed effort to alter the result. Randolph proposed an adjournment so that "the large States might consider" the proper steps and the "small States might also deliberate on the means of conciliation." He emphasized that the government's powers—already discussed by the delegates—were founded on "the supposition that a Proportional representation was to prevail in both branches." The Notes then reflected others' anger over this implicit refusal to accept the vote. Paterson claimed Randolph's request was for adjournment sine die—an adjournment without any promise to return—an adjournment to suspend or end the Convention. Madison included Randolph's comment that he had been "so readily & strangely misinterpreted." After a contested debate and divided vote on adjournment, the Convention at last adjourned.[58]

After leaving a significant blank space, Madison wrote entirely in diary style about the next morning before the Convention. The next day, delegates from the large states met before the Convention "for the purpose of consulting on the proper steps." Unfortunately, the opinions "varied much." Madison complained: "The time was wasted in vague conversation on the subject, without any specific proposition or agreement." Nothing was accomplished. In fact, Madison ended by noting sarcastically that the lack of agreement proved to the smaller state delegates who had attended that they had "nothing to apprehend." There would be no "Union of the larger" in "any plan whatever ag[ain]st the equality of votes" in the second branch.[59]

Madison explained how far he wanted to push the matter. He wanted a "firm opposition." He described one side—his side—as representing "the principal States, and the majority of the people of America." These were the members who believed "no good Governm[en]t" could be founded on equal state suffrage. They wanted a "separate recommendation, if eventually necessary." The idea of a minority report, however, was not adopted. Madison mocked the delegates who disagreed. They preferred to "concur" in a report "imperfect & exceptionable" that was agreed to by a "bare majority of States and by a minority of the people of the U[nited] States." As far as Madison was concerned, the compromise over the branches was theoretically incoherent and due to the weak resolve of others. He was furious and in no mood for conciliation.[60]

Madison's Notes for Tuesday, July 17—written of course afterwards—expressed frustration at every turn. The solutions Madison had initially introduced had been abandoned one by one. Dismay was pervasive. An effort by Morris to sidestep the second branch vote was "probably approved" by some (perhaps even Madison), but they "despaired of success or were apprehensive that the attempt would inflame the jealousies of the smaller States." He recorded briefly and half-heartedly the debate over whether to attempt to draw a line between general and state powers. Sherman read an "enumeration of powers" for Congress. Madison did not bother to record specifics. He summarized the speakers in one or two sentences. He focused only on Morris's pointed comment that Sherman had omitted a power for direct taxes. The delegates resoundingly dismissed Sherman's suggestion.[61]

Desperation to thwart the states was written into Madison's speech attempting to preserve the legislative negative on the states. It was riddled with dislike of the states. The states would "pursue their particular interests in opposition to the general interest." Without a negative, the states' laws will "accomplish their injurious objects." State tribunals were not adequate guardians "of National authority and interest." Madison seemed to go out of his way to praise the "British System." The crown's use of the negative "stifles in the birth every Act of every part tending to discord or encroachment." Madison struggled to downplay concern about the historical realities of the British practice. Three times he wrote *sometimes:* "It is true the prerogative is sometimes sometimes sometimes or a preference to one particular part yᵉ. empire." The "salutary power of the negative" over state laws was Madison's ultimate limit on the states. But here again, he lost. The Convention voted against it.[62]

As the entire structure of government was shifting from Madison's initial vision, he refused to budge. Other delegates decided that the judiciary represented a superior limit on state laws than the congressional negative. Morris explained that the "Judiciary departm[en]t" would "set aside" the state law or, as a final resort, a national law could repeal it. Sherman argued that the structure of the new constitutional system limited state laws. They would not be "valid & operative" if "contrary to the articles of the Union." Madison seemed to care little about this underlying theory. The introductory summary sentences for both speeches linked them to opposition to the negative. Indeed, Madison only briefly summarized the unanimously approved motion to add a supremacy clause, although it explicitly stated that state courts would be bound to follow national law notwithstanding state legislation. Madison was intellectually stuck.[63]

A final losing vote on July 17 betrayed Madison's frustration over his failure to limit the state legislatures. On July 17, the executive branch remained largely unformed. Madison's interest focused on who would control the executive—whatever it ended up being. The delegates rejected popular election of the executive and the use of electors. Unanimously, they agreed to the Committee of the Whole House Report's recommendation of an executive "chosen by the National Legislature." Although the Report recommended a single seven-year term, the delegates postponed consideration of the length but decided to permit eligibility for a second term. A second term raised concerns in Madison and others about the executive's dependence on the legislature (particularly given equal state suffrage in the second branch). A motion recommended that the executive serve on "good behavior." Although the motion lost, an unusual coalition of four states voted in favor: Virginia, Pennsylvania, New Jersey, and Delaware.[64]

The vote on an executive tenure of good behavior, despite losing, became controversial in the aftermath of the Convention. The original discussion is unknown. Madison replaced the original sheet containing the motion by Madison's colleague, Dr. James McClurg, the vote, and any explanation of Madison's position. No other note taker recorded the proceedings. Given Madison's tendency in the Notes to explain strategy, the original sheet may have described the motivation for the vote and the Virginia vote in favor. Madison may have decided to support, if necessary, an elected executive on good behavior if it would promise control over the state legislatures. Two days later in the Notes, on an original sheet, Madison argued that the executive should be "held by some tenure" or by a mode of appointment that would give him "free agency" from the legislature. Over time, Madison repeatedly revised the replaced sheet with the vote, seeking to create a distinction between those who supported the motion for strategic reasons and those who substantively favored an executive on good behavior. Such a distinction, if it existed on July 17, may have been largely irrelevant to Madison. His strategies to limit the state legislatures had failed. Neither the largest state coalition nor the southern slavery coalition had worked. Although he had favored an elective tenure for the executive in the Virginia plan, his anxiety about an executive dependent on a legislature controlled by small states may have been overwhelming. The motion and vote may have been an attempt to once again emphasize the consequences of state control.[65]

By the end of July 17, the Notes recorded profound disappointment. For weeks, Madison wrote under the assumption that he could defeat the equal state suffrage position and create a national government operating on individuals. To his dismay, he never persuasively rebutted the perception that proportional representation in both branches gave too much political power in particular to Virginia. He argued for the incoherence of the states in a national system—perhaps as corporations—but was unpersuasive. He was equally unpersuasive in suggesting the second branch should protect property. Finally, he implicated slavery. He successfully persuaded delegates of a sectional divide and encouraged the southern states to prioritize protection of slavery. But Madison never gained a solid majority against equal state suffrage. Instead, the three-fifths clause was approved, southern delegates coalesced around slavery, and important northern delegates declared willingness to compromise over slavery. Madison encouraged the dynamic that would end with constitutional protections for slaveholders—but nothing more.

In June, Dickinson warned Madison of the consequences of pushing things too far. Madison never heeded the advice. The replaced sheets obscured how far Madison had pushed by altering speeches on the states as corporations, a Senate for property holders, and, if even for only one vote, an executive on good behavior. Significantly, however, Madison never attempted to disguise his willingness to embed slavery into the national government.

6

ACQUIRING A NEW ROLE

On Wednesday, July 18, Madison apologized to Jefferson for not having written recently: "As soon as I am at liberty I will endeavor to make amends for my silence." He explained, "I am still under the mortification of being restrained from disclosing any part of their proceedings." He added, "I . . . mean to go on with the drudgery, if no indisposition obliges me to discontinue it." Drudgery did not alter the perspective of the Notes; they remained a diary of Madison's interests. As the delegates finished consideration of the Committee of the Whole House Report, the Notes focused on shifting votes, political strategies, and Madison's theories. By late July, Madison was positioned outside of the delegates' evolving direction. Randolph, not Madison, was placed on the committee of detail to compose the draft of the Constitution based on the Report. In August, however, as the delegates debated the draft, Madison gradually became an important and constructive participant and, indeed, was chosen to be on the most important committees. In large part, his new role arose from his practice of composing the Notes.[1]

The Committee of Detail draft of August 6 marked a turning point in the Notes. Until then, the Notes recorded successes and failures measured against Madison's initial political commitments. By the end of July, failures dominated his thoughts. After the lengthy adjournment, Madison copied the draft into the Notes. While other delegates simply read the draft, the process of copying gave Madison an intimate understanding of the structure and language. An interest in the difficulties of drafting appeared in the Notes. Madison worried about contemporary cavilers and future misinterpretations of votes and, in particular, about the different ways in which language could be interpreted. Madison continued to track shifting voting coalitions and individual positions. He continued to minimize competitors—in particular, Charles Pinckney. But the Notes suggest that the drafting debate played to Madison's strengths, and his private record of proceedings gave him references that others lacked. By the third week in August, Madison had become so involved in the process of revising the draft that the Notes completely collapsed.

The final days between Wednesday, July 18, and Thursday, July 26, were filled with decisions as the delegates debated the ten remaining resolutions in the Committee Report. They settled on a method to elect the executive, addressed remaining questions about the executive, figured out how to appoint judges, agreed to an amendment process, and decided on the number of senators. Madison recorded these decisions at some length, but his selection and coverage remained the product of his particular interests.

In writing the Notes, Madison absorbed the ideas of other delegates. While writing, he was thinking. Throughout the Notes, he recorded other delegates making arguments that resonated with ideas that scholars have long associated with Madison. Did Madison record these delegates when or because their speeches mirrored his ideas? Or did he record other delegates' ideas and, in the process of recording, revise and absorb them as his own? The Notes leave the relationship ambiguous. One important, arguably critical example is the link between the extensive size of the country and interests. On July 19, Madison recorded at length Morris's discussion of the "maxim in Political Science that Republican Government is not adapted to a large extent of Country." The executive was a check on "Legislative tyranny" and the "guardian" and "great protector" of the people. Nonetheless, there was concern that the executive could be "the tool of a faction, of some leading demagogue in the Legislature." Morris believed, however, that popular election was possible because the "extent of the Country" would prevent the influence of the "factions & discontents of particular States" and "those little combinations and those momentary lies." This idea that extensive size altered the influence of factions appears in Madison's famous essay, Federalist 10. If Madison had not previously formulated his theory, the process of recording the speech advanced the process.[2]

Madison's lack of interest in certain parts of the government, notably the judiciary, continued. He merged two votes establishing a "national tribunal" consisting of "one supreme tribunal." He omitted votes approving tenure on good behavior and fixed salaries. He cursorily summarized the debate over inferior tribunals. He noted "criticisms" on the "definition" of the judiciary's jurisdiction but did not enumerate them. Included instead was his successful motion that ensured the courts would operate akin to the negative: "the jurisdiction shall extend to all cases arising under the Nat[iona]l laws." Similarly, he recorded his effort to implicate the sectional politics of judicial nominations. Madison warned that if the Senate appointed, the decisions could be thrown "entirely into the hands of N[or]thern States." His record on the judiciary focused only on areas where the judiciary intersected his broader interests.[3]

The practice of skipping over issues appears in any comparison of the Notes to the official journal. On Monday, July 23, Madison focused on the ratification process. Although the delegates agreed unanimously to provide for amendments, Madison recorded no comments. He only briefly recorded comments on the issue of state oaths to support the "articles of Union." He summarized the debates over whether two or three members should serve in the Senate (the delegates decided on two) and whether the members should vote per capita or by state (the delegates decided on per capita). Although the two New Hampshire delegates finally arrived, Madison made no mention of them except abruptly including the state in his vote tally.[4]

Conversely, minor matters were recorded if Madison was involved. The delegates rejected a provision that the Confederation Congress would continue until a "given day" after the adoption of the constitution. Nonetheless, Madison recorded the discussion between Morris (who thought the provision unnecessary) and himself (who considered it an important principle against "interregnum"). Similarly, Madison included his initial clumsy wording for the national government's protection: "the Constitutional authority of the States shall be guarantied to them respectively ag[ain]st domestic as well as foreign violence." He withdrew it after Wilson's "better expression of the idea." The Notes were above all about Madison.[5]

His speeches advanced his favorite theories. He promoted ratification conventions. The state legislatures were "incompetent" to ratify because the new constitution would make "essential inroads on the State Constitutions." A constitution differed from a "league and treaty." He accepted judicial power as a legislative limit. Madison wrote, a "law violating a constitution established by the people themselves would be considered by the Judges as null & void." Another speech promoted executive electors. Madison worried that the "Southern States" would "have no influence" in a popular election. Southern property requirements limited the right of suffrage to fewer white male inhabitants and "the Negroes" could not vote. After electors were rejected, Madison recorded another lengthy speech critiquing the remaining modes of executive selection. Although Madison claimed to like "best" popular election, the speech seemed equally designed to create a coalition for electors. Madison employed his sectional argument. Popular election required a "sacrifice" from the South and as an "individual from the S. States," Madison was willing to sacrifice for the "general interest." The implication, however, was that other southern delegates might reach a different conclusion. Electors promoted southern voting interests.[6]

The Notes provided a space for issues that Madison had already lost. He tried to restore the revisionary council. A revisionary power would give the judiciary an additional method of "defending itself ag[ain]st Legislative encroachments." The legislature was the "real source of danger to the American Constitutions." The "Theory" of separated powers or a limit "on paper" would not limit the legislature. A "defensive power" was needed to "maintain the Theory in practice." A "balance of power and interests" was required to "guarantee the provisions on paper." In a revisionary council, Madison saw no "violation of the maxim which requires the great departments of power to be kept separate." Madison lost, although the Notes included supporting speeches by Mason, Wilson, and Morris, as if to show that others of considerable political acumen agreed with him.[7]

Madison appreciated comments that conveyed strategic signals; he assumed his reader would also. When he described the election of the committee to prepare the draft of the Constitution, he likely knew the composition. He recorded comments designed to influence the voting. On Monday, July 23, General Pinckney "reminded the Convention" that he might be "bound by duty to his State" to vote against the draft "if the Committee should fail to insert some security to the Southern States ag[ain]st an emancipation of slaves, and taxes on exports." The reminder of implied national power described what was at stake. Madison took care to record the votes over the committee size. The first suggestion—a delegate from each state—failed as "the States were no. except Delaware." The second suggestion—a seven-member committee—also lost. Madison's inclusion of Pinckney's comment suggests he believed the southern states were calculating control. In the end, five members were unanimously agreed to. The selection, however, was postponed until the following day. The delay allowed strategic maneuvering.[8]

On the next day, Madison made certain the Notes explained additional concerns about who was chosen for the committee. Before the vote, Daniel Carroll "took occasion to observe" that he might oppose the draft if it retained the clause linking direct taxation to representation. In a comment marked "N.B.," Madison explained that the "object was to lessen the eagerness on one side & the opposition on the other, to the share of Representation claimed by the S. States on account of the Negroes." The suggestion that the committee could remove the link between taxation and representation emphasized the committee's apparent discretion.[9]

Madison ordered the committee names in the same manner as the secretary, suggesting that it reflected number of votes. The first name, South Carolina's Rutledge, reflected the strength of the southern slavery states. Randolph's election—not Madison's—emphasized that Madison was associated with minority positions. Like Randolph, Gorham and the final man, Wilson, were the most electable members of the largest states. Ellsworth was the likely consensus choice of the smallest states.[10]

Madison was irritated with Randolph. On July 26, Madison emphasized the division within the Virginia delegation. After the committee's election, the delegates had spent two days finishing the executive. Election of the seven-year single-term executive remained with the national legislature. Madison was unhappy. On the vote to refer the executive clause to the committee, Virginia was divided with Madison and Washington against, and Mason and Blair in favor. Madison seemingly snidely wrote, "Randolph happened to be out of the House." The Massachusetts delegation also was not "on floor." The three small northern states and the three southern states voted in favor. The three middle states voted against. With the votes of Virginia and Massachusetts uncertain, the Notes suggested the apparent agreement was tenuous.[11]

Randolph was not the only Virginia delegate annoying Madison. Mason was a problem. Madison recorded Mason's speech favoring "election by the Nat[iona]l Legislature as originally proposed." Mason successfully reinstated the seven-year single term. To Madison's equal aggravation, Mason moved to give the committee two additional clauses. One required executive, judiciary, and legislative members to hold landed property, United States citizenship, and prevent legislative members from having "unsettled accounts" with the United States. Madison twice spoke against aspects of the proposal. The other was a motion on the seat of government. Madison was silent. He cared deeply about the issue but may not have wanted specific regulation in the constitution. The Notes conveyed Mason's independent political agenda.[12]

The Notes for July 26 ended in the present tense: "Adjourned till Monday. Aug[u]st 6, that Com[mitte]e of detail may have time to prepare & report the Constitution." Although the secretary noted that Pinckney's May plan and Paterson's plan were also referred to the committee, Madison omitted that information from the Notes. Despite everything, the Notes remained the story of the original Virginia plan.[13]

In the weeks to come, the Notes gave Madison a significant advantage over other delegates. Before adjournment, the delegates took two votes relating to records of the proceedings. First, the delegates agreed to furnish committee members "copies of the proceedings." Second, ordinary members would not be permitted to "take copies of the resolutions which have been agreed to." The Virginians voted in favor, but the motion lost (5–6). Most delegates were left to their memories or their personal notes. Madison curiously did not include this vote in the Notes. The Notes provided Madison with information that most delegates lacked. As the Convention entered a new phase, the Notes—albeit selective, self-oriented, and imprecise—gave him a record of earlier debates.[14]

When the delegates reconvened on Monday, August 6, Madison copied the draft—the Report of the Committee of Detail—into the Notes. He followed the seven-page printed copy given to each member. The copy was printed on one side of the sheets with a large left margin to permit emendation. Madison devoted considerable space to his manuscript copy, using more than three entire sheets. He made the copy resemble the printed draft. He altered his handwriting to mimic the type used for the preamble ("We the people of the states . . .") and the article numbers. The legislative powers were placed in a list. He even imitated the inverted quotation marks of the printed copy. Madison kept his handwriting so neat that he broke words with hyphens rather than squishing them on the line. Madison nonetheless followed his idiosyncratic approach to capitalization. The Notes' copy gave Madison a pristine version, regardless of how extensively he might choose to amend the printed draft.[15]

The process of copying gave Madison an intimate familiarity with the structure, language, and substance. In copying and proofing, Madison noticed every word. Unlike the final Constitution with seven articles, the committee of detail draft contained twenty-three articles. The printer, John Dunlap, had placed "VI" above both the sixth and seventh articles, resulting in the subsequent articles being incorrectly numbered. In the Notes, Madison corrected the numbers. Madison also incorporated a small textual alteration apparently intended by the committee but not included on the printed draft.[16]

The Notes portrayed the proceedings after August 6 as a discussion over a draft rather than a freewheeling debate on political theory. Madison left spaces as visual dividers between the discussions—making the Notes easier to follow than modern reprints that omit the spacing. As the delegates followed the draft in order, he did not bother to repeat the text of the section under discussion. This focus on sections led Madison to overlook a break in his rough notes. He had been particularly interested in the issue discussed on Friday, August 10, and Saturday, August 11. He had unsuccessfully advanced a motion about secrecy for the Senate journal. The discussion had continued into the following day. In writing up the Notes, he missed the change in day. He had to go back and squeeze in small letters, "Adjourned" and "Saturday August 11." The issues raised by the draft were beginning to fascinate him.[17]

The Notes never returned to the relatively polished style of the mid-June to mid-July section. In the weeks following the August 6 draft, Madison's notetaking became increasingly disjointed and uneven. He spent less time converting his rough notes into polished text. More than ever, the format resembled his earlier legislative diaries.

On the first day of discussion, August 7, two speeches show this casual approach. Sherman gave a speech on the time of the meeting of the future Congress. Madison left the speech in the spontaneous style of rough notes.

> M^r. Sherman was decided for fixing the time, as well as for frequent meetings of the Legislative body. Disputes and difficulties will arise between the two Houses, & between both & the States, if the time be changeable— frequent meetings required at the Revolution in England as an essential article of liberty. So also in most of the American charters and constitutions. There will be business eno' to require it. The Western Country, and the great extent and varying state of our affairs in general will supply objects.

Madison composed his trademark summary sentence but did not bother to try to connect Sherman's ideas. He did not specify the details. He did not smooth out the sentences. Morris's speech did not even have a leading summary sentence:

> He had long learned not to be the dupe of words. The sound of Aristocracy therefore, had no effect upon him. It was the thing, not the name, to which he was opposed, and one of his principal objections to the Constitution as it is now before us, is that it threatens the Country with an Aristocracy. The aristocracy will grow out of the House of Representatives. Give the votes to people who have no property, and they will sell them to the rich who will be able to buy them. We should not confine our attention to the present motion.

Madison was writing up the phrases and words likely in his rough notes. He was spending less time composing.[18]

The Notes have a contemporaneous feel. Some sentences were short and choppy: "Children do not vote" (Morris); "If not don't deserve it" (Morris again). Other sentences were long, run-on sentences or began with "And." He summarized speakers, noting that a motion "was strongly opposed by Mr Ghorum and several others, as likely to produce unnecessary delay; and was negatived." Although Madison often led with a summary sentence, he tended to follow with abrupt sentences and phrases. The second sentence in Morris's speech was "Treaties he thought were no laws." Madison was not polishing sentences.[19]

The Notes were not attentive to procedural issues. They overlooked details and technicalities. Votes were combined. For example, Wilson's motion to reconsider a section to restore the three-year citizenship requirement and the decision to place the reconsideration on Monday were combined. Similarly, Madison summarized a "sect. 6 & 7" as if they were simultaneously considered when they were instead considered separately. Madison made mistakes. On Thursday, August 9, he recorded that the delegates had "ag[ree]d to" a motion presented by himself and Morris to strike language in the article regulating the times of holding elections. According to the journal, however, the motion was rejected nearly unanimously. He was not focused on procedural perfection.[20]

By the end of the week, with the delegates only on the sixth of the twenty-three articles, Madison began to summarize extensively: "M^r. Williamson supported the ideas of M^r. Spaight"; "M^r. Carrol was actuated by the same apprehension." He lost track of the textual changes to section 8 and ended with the comment that, "after some further expressions from others" and a failed motion for recommitment, the "Section was left in the shape it now bears." He skipped motions and votes, and ignored technical language. Even on significant issues—for example, the decision to have a three-quarter override vote for the veto, instead of two-thirds—Madison recorded only a brief remark by Williamson making the motion and noted that Wilson seconded the motion, "referring to and repeating the ideas of M[r]. Carroll." On August 13 and 14, he neglected matters that occurred at the end of the day's proceeding. On August 16, he ended "&c. &c." Perhaps he may have begun to leave early.[21]

Even Madison's speeches were written without elaboration or length. A speech on August 14 was only tenuously related to the motion. The issue involved whether members were to be paid by the states or the national treasury. Madison made no effort to connect his remarks to the motion. He criticized the lack of stability in the future government. He added an unconnected thought that the "enlargement of the sphere of the Government" was a "favorable" circumstance as "he had on several occasions undertaken to show." In earlier weeks, Madison would have linked the ideas into a coherent speech; instead, he simply sketched random thoughts.[22]

Increasingly Madison recorded fewer of his speeches. On Wednesday, August 15, Madison moved to require that acts be submitted to the "Executive and Judiciary Departments." He omitted his lengthy technical language. If he gave a speech in support, he omitted it. Near the end of the day, Madison made a motion to enumerate the types of legislative acts that could be negated by the executive. He did not bother to record any speeches on the motion. He simply noted that after "a short and rather confused conversation," his motion lost. On Thursday, August 16, Madison recorded a short speech to prevent the legislature from taxing exports. He recorded it as five unconnected, numbered points. He did not bother to include that he was speaking against the motion. On Friday, August 17, Madison recorded a short speech arguing, "felony at common law vague." The speech was a set of sentences linked by dashes. Although he recorded his sporadic brief comments through Tuesday, August 21, he never presented the remarks as speeches of significance.[23]

Overall, Madison was impatient and perhaps growing fatigued. On a motion to postpone, he included the irritated comments: Gorham "saw no end to these difficulties and postponements." Ellsworth added, "We grow more & more skeptical as we proceed." Rutledge "complained much of the tediousness of the proceedings." Such remarks may well have reflected Madison's own feelings. He wrote his father on August 12 that it was "not possible yet to determine the period to which the Session will be spun out." He thought it likely "some weeks" and "possibly may be computed by months." The loose debate that characterized the Committee of the Whole House and the struggle over principles in June had vanished. Amidst the tedious process of reviewing the Report, the sporadic nature of the Notes reflected Madison's inconsistent interest.[24]

The Notes continued to record speeches as a method to track shifting political positions, particularly those taken in opposition to outcomes Madison preferred. King, a supporter of the earlier slavery coalition, was wavering. He had hoped the earlier "concession" would lead to a strong general government. The Report "put an end to all these hopes." The "admission of slaves" into the calculation of representation "was a most grating circumstance to his mind." King worried about people "imported without limitation" as slaves and then included to increase representatives from those states. He declared that he might not "assent to it under any circumstance." The speech signaled King's potential dissenting vote.[25]

Nevertheless, Madison considered King's qualms too little and too late. Madison emphasized the failure of those attempting to remove slavery from the calculation. Morris unsuccessfully moved to insert "free" so that representation would be based on "free inhabitants." He rejected "upholding domestic slavery." The "nefarious institution" was "the curse of heaven." The practice violated the "laws of humanity." Not mincing words, Morris accused Georgia and South Carolina residents of traveling to the "Coast of Africa" to tear the would-be slave "away from his fellow creatures." He mockingly commented that these states would acquire more votes in a government "instituted for protection of the rights of mankind." Morris asked why the people held as slaves should not be made "Citizens & let them vote?" The northern states had made a "sacrifice of every principle of right & of every impulse of humanity." Morris threatened to withhold his assent. He preferred a "tax for paying for all the Negroes in the U. States" than "saddle posterity with such a Constitution"—implicitly hinting that slavery could be ended under national taxing power. Support for Morris and King, however, was limited to a second from the New Jersey delegate Jonathan Dayton to "mark his sentiments." Sherman and Wilson supported the original clause. Only New Jersey voted with Morris. The coalition to protect slavery, instigated by Madison, remained in control.[26]

Madison continued to provide a record of strategic reasons behind votes. He recorded the discussion of whether the congressional legislative journals would include the individual yeas and nays. Gorham complained that individual votes misled people who nonetheless "never know the reasons determining the votes." Nevertheless, the delegates did not like the suggestion that a member be permitted to record a dissent. If the "reasons" were recorded, the journals would be filled "with pleas, replications, rejoinders &c." Virginia favored the losing proposal; Madison liked records of reasons.[27]

Madison used the Notes as evidence of prior votes. In a debate over the money bill clause, Madison referred to prior votes. Some delegates wanted to strike the clause giving exclusive rights to the House to originate money bills. Madison declared it "no advantage to the large States." Randolph disagreed. Although the clause was struck, Randolph attempted to restore it as part of the original "compromise" over equal state suffrage. Madison discussed the five states that had originally voted against the equal state suffrage in the Senate (Massachusetts, Pennsylvania, Virginia, North Carolina, and South Carolina). The Notes may have helped him recall the votes, or his notetaking practice gave his recollection validity. He reviewed the subsequent shifts. Pennsylvania, Virginia, and South Carolina subsequently voted against the "proposed compensation on its own merits." Massachusetts was "divided." Only North Carolina still "set a value" on the clause. Madison concluded the clause could be removed. The Virginia delegation disagreed. Randolph and Mason voted— joined by Washington—against Madison. A majority of the delegations agreed with Madison, but his frustration at Randolph and Mason was growing.[28]

Madison did not abandon his earlier concerns. A lengthy discussion focused on eligibility to government offices after legislative service, previously a significant concern for Madison. The Notes tilted in favor of those favoring incentives for talented individuals. Madison included delegates who had not often or ever made an appearance. Mercer, for example, described in captivating terms a government "of plunder." Mercer later remarked, "It is a great mistake to support that paper we are to propose will govern." He explained, "The paper will only mark out the mode & the form- Men are the substance and must do the business."

Madison liked the ideas but omitted the technicalities of the underlying motion.[29]

The recorded Madison speeches focused on the dangerous power of the state legislatures and the process of election: suffrage qualifications for the House (August 7); citizenship qualifications for the Senate (August 9) and House (August 13); state legislative power over House elections (August 9); and property qualifications for the legislature (August 10). He gave a long speech relating to the power of the two branches over money bills (August 13). His speech on the location of the government (August 11) and the regulation of the militia (August 18) also focused on concerns about the states. Even his speech on taxing exports devolved into a discussion of sectional division (August 16) and a discussion of the appropriate use of "the Gen[era]l authority" (August 21). Madison could not abandon his suspicion of the state legislatures. When he discussed the definition of treason (August 20), he included the comment that it "w[oul]d be as safe as in the hands of State legislatures." The Notes suggest that he had altered surprisingly little on the issue.[30]

In recording these speeches, Madison portrayed himself as open-minded even when he was set on his conclusion. In his August 7 speech on voter qualifications for representatives, Madison suggested that freeholders—people who held land—would be best. In the future, he argued that the majority would not have landed property or any "sort of, property." Such people would become "the tools of opulence & ambition." He wrote, "If the authority be in their hands by the rule of suffrage, the rights of property & the public good will not he thought bid fair to be very secure." Madison, however, added that his views would "depend much on the probable reception" of a requirement. Other note takers did not hear any hesitancy about freeholders. McHenry wrote that Madison "supported similar sentiments" to Morris, who favored "confining the suffrage to *free holders*." King recorded Madison "in fav[o]r of the rig[h]t of Election being confin[e]d to Freeholders." The Notes made Madison appear more tentative with respect to controversial issues than others heard.[31]

Amidst the tedium of debating the draft, a new interest emerged. The Notes indicate Madison's fascination with the drafting process. His interest predated the Convention and drew on his earlier law studies and state and congressional legislative experience. He had a talent for working out semantic compromises that sidestepped theoretical disputes. He was thoughtful on the question of which matters belonged in a constitution and which were more appropriately left to ordinary legislative politics. He was interested in problems of terminology. He was increasingly adept at resolving a debate by suggesting a textual change or claiming that another part of the report resolved the problem. He began to have a role in the Convention other than pushing for his core political commitments—most of which had lost.[32]

A recurring pattern of debate intrigued Madison. A delegate would imagine a possibility permitted or not permitted by the draft's phrasing in the draft. Alternative language that solved that particular possibility was suggested. In turn, the new language would give rise to a new concern. The debate would then veer off into a discussion on this new issue.

Madison's tendency to intervene in these issues was reflected in the Notes. One of the first of such disputes involved each branch's negative "in all cases" of the other branch. Mason worried that "all cases" might be read to include appointments. Morris suggested substituting "legislative acts." But that phrase only raised new problems. Gorham raised concerns about not using joint ballots in elections. Mason worried about treaties. Morris responded that treaties "were not laws" and that statement—which raised other implications—threatened to sidetrack the discussion. At this point, Madison intervened. He recommended striking the words relating to "all cases." The purpose was not to resolve the underlying concern. Instead, Madison suggested that the idea was "sufficiently expressed" in the preceding article "vesting the 'legislative power' in 'distinct bodies,'" and other aspects were "more fully delineated in a subsequent article." The comment offered an interpretive argument for moving forward. The deletion was approved. Although Madison had not been involved in creating the draft, copying the draft gave him a command of the Report's provisions.[33]

A repeated drafting issue recurred in the Notes: which matters were appropriate in a constitution, and which were best left to be decided by ordinary legislation? For example, the Report stated that the "Legislature should meet on the first Monday in December." Madison spoke against "fixing a time by the Constitution." He wanted the time to "be fixed or varied by law." Congress should have discretion to alter the time of legislative meeting. The Notes described the colloquy between Madison and other delegates. Randolph cleverly ended the discussion by substituting "until altered by law"—a verbal attempt to embrace both arguments. The debate then devolved into a disagreement over May or

December. Madison "preferred May." December required travelling in "the most inconvenient seasons of the year." Wilson countered that winter was better "for business," and Ellsworth mentioned the involvement in agriculture of many legislators. May lost, and the Notes reflected Randolph's refusal to agree with Madison on this small issue; he too had preferred December.[34]

In general, Madison's comments in the Notes reflected his growing conviction that the Constitution should avoid unnecessary specifics. He opposed lengthy citizenship requirements for Senators. The draft required four years; Morris moved to lengthen it to fourteen years. Madison argued that any restriction "in the Constitution [was] unnecessary, and improper." The restriction would "give a tincture of illiberality to the Constitution." The legislature should be able to confer the "full rank of Citizens" to "meritorious strangers." Madison recorded Franklin's nearly identical declaration that he would be "very sorry to see any thing like illiberality inserted in the Constitution." Once again, Randolph's position—contrary to Madison's by being willing to raise the requirement to seven years—was included. The Convention agreed to nine years with the Virginia delegation voting in favor. Madison, however, wanted the legislature to have greater discretion.[35]

When specific terms were debated, the Notes focused on the inevitability of misconstructions. With respect to the qualifications for representatives, the Report had used the words "resident of the State." The delegates unanimously voted to substitute "inhabitant" as "less liable to misconstruction." Madison thought that both terms were "vague but the latter less liable least so in common acceptation." He explained that "[g]reat disputes had been raised" in Virginia over the "meaning of residence." The outcome was "determined more according to the affection or dislike to the man, than any fixt interpretation of the word." Madison added that "resident" would unfortunately "exclude persons absent occasionally for a considerable time on public or private business." The comment implicitly alluded to Jefferson—and the Notes thus made apparent that Madison looked after Jefferson's interests, regardless of whether Jefferson would have wanted again to serve as a legislator.[36]

Madison was most worried when his belief that language was inevitably vague combined with his distrust of state legislatures. The delegates began to worry that the Report permitted state legislatures to appoint "a Senator ag[ain]st his consent" and thereby prevent someone from serving in another national office. Madison successfully supported additional words "to prevent doubts" whether Senators could resign or refuse to accept the position. A similar anxiety arose with respect to state decisions about the time, place, and manner of elections. Madison thought the draft used "words of great latitude." No one could "foresee all the abuses that might be made of the discretionary power" in the states. He successfully supported words to empower Congress, "not only to alter the provisions" made by states, but to make "regulation in case the States should fail or refuse altogether." Through the alteration of a word here and a phrase there, Madison used his new role as a draftsman within the Convention to restrict the state legislatures. He had failed to win on the large principles; he tried to minimize the damage to the degree he could in amending the language of the Report.[37]

As Madison's interest in the drafting process expanded, the Notes became an unwanted distraction. On Thursday, August 16, the delegates reached Article VII, describing the powers of the national legislature. As Madison offered a motion or opinion on seemingly every change, his Notes became particularly rough. He tended towards paraphrasing. The "&c" was a signal for textual details. His reference to "commerce with foreign nations &c." was the Report's "commerce with foreign nations, and among the several States." Although he often placed words seemingly from the Report in quotations, they represented the concept rather than the precise text. Regulating "foreign coin" was the Report's "value of foreign coin" and "constitute inferior tribunals" was the Report's "constitute tribunals inferior to the supreme Court." Even as he worried about words, Madison continued to think about the text as conceptual principles.[38]

When Madison was most interested, his Notes seemed to become even more imprecise. For example, his Notes about the succinct power—"to make war"—reflected discussion. Madison recorded that he and Gerry moved to replace *make* with *declare* to leave "the Executive the power to repel sudden attacks." He included four delegates' brief arguments, only the first and last focused on the difference in the verb. The issue of war versus peace seemed an equally strong theme. By comparison, in McHenry's notes, the delegates "debated the difference between a power to declare war and to make war" before "substituting declare"— suggesting a detailed discussion on the verb. Madison recorded only one vote (7–2) on the question with New Hampshire and Connecticut opposed. He then commented that "Elseworth gave up his objection," but did not show another vote. The journal, however, shows two votes on the substitution: the first failing more dramatically (4–5); a "repeated" question passing (8 states in favor, New Hampshire opposed). If the journal was accurate, Madison must have recalled the vote imprecisely. His participation may have led him to stop taking rough notes and, if so, here and elsewhere, he may have been writing from memory.[39]

Increasingly, explanations seemed constructed after the fact for a future reader—most likely in Madison's mind, the absent Jefferson. One matter involved the removal of the phrases, "and emit bills on the credit of the United States," from the proposed list of Congress's explicit powers. Delegates offered contradictory reasons: one did not like paper money but could "not foresee all emergencies"; one thought the words could be struck and room would be left for some power; one worried the words would lead to use of the power; one assumed the words were superfluous because the power was inherent in the power to borrow; one seemed to think striking the words would omit the power. The comments reflected incompatible intentions but agreement over deletion. Madison offered his analysis. He "became satisfied that striking out the words would not disable the Gov[ernmen]t from the use of public notes as far as they could be safe & proper; & would only cut off the pretext for regular emissions and particularly for making them a tender either for public or private debts." The explanation interpreted the legislature's power in the absence of the explicit power and sought to exclude possible misinterpretations. Madison did not want the reader to believe that the deletion was meant to bar the legislature from all power over public notes. Subtly the Notes presented Madison's interpretation as the correct one.[40]

The Notes' promotion of Madison's interpretation appeared in the power of Congress to punish certain crimes. The Notes reflected—perhaps showed off—his knowledge of common law. In the early 1780s, Madison had read law using Jefferson's library. The original language of the Report gave Congress power:

> To declare the law and punishment of piracies and felonies committed on the high seas, and the punishment of counterfeiting the coin of the United States, and of offences against the law of nations;

Madison objected. Led by Madison, the delegates began to redraft the section. Madison successfully struck "and punishment." Morris successfully struck "declare the law" and inserted "punish." Madison moved to insert "define and." Wilson opposed the idea, arguing that "'felonies' [were] sufficiently defined by Common law." Madison, however, complained that "felony at common law [was] vague" and "defective." He countered by referring to a "defect supplied by the Stat[ute]: of Anne"—a British statutory solution—to the common law's treatment of "running away with vessels" as "breach of trust only," as opposed to a more serious crime of piracy. Madison wanted "uniformity and stability" for offenses at sea. In the end, the delegates agreed to "define and punish." Madison thought the difference crucial; whether the other delegates did is unknown.[41]

Madison had a competitor for this new role as drafter: Charles Pinckney. But Madison continued to diminish Pinckney's contributions. On Saturday, August 18, the journal recorded twenty additional suggestions of legislative powers to be referred to the August 6 drafting committee. Nine likely came from Madison; six from Pinckney; and five apparently from other delegates. The powers proposed by Madison overlapped with those proposed by Pinckney. Both men included five powers relating to national legislative power over a seat of government, granting charters of incorporation, securing copyrights, establishing universities, and encouraging rewards, prizes, and institutions to advance useful knowledge. Pinckney also included a power granting patents. Although Madison listed a patent power on the list he proposed in the Notes, the Journal does not show it. Initially, Madison may have thought the power contained within the broad wording of his power for the "advancement of useful knowledge and discoveries"—or the secretary may have overlooked it. Madison's other four powers addressed unappropriated land, new states, Indians, and forts.[42]

Pinckney's proposed powers did not appear in the Notes, and the omission hid the significant overlap. Madison mentioned dismissively that Pinckney had proposed "sev[e]ral additional powers which had occurred to him." Madison did not enumerate them. The center of Madison's list was the beginning of Pinckney's list. For some powers, the wording was remarkably similar. Pinckney suggested copyrights "to secure to authors exclusive rights for a certain time"; Madison recommended "to secure to literary authors their copy rights for a limited time." Other powers shared concepts:

> Pinckney: To establish public institutions, rewards and immunities for the promotion of agriculture, commerce, trades, and manufactures.

Madison: To encourage, by proper premiums and provisions, the advancement of useful knowledge and discoveries.

One man may have copied from the other, or the two lists may represent a prior shared discussion. The omission of Pinckney's list, however, left Madison in the Notes as possessing sole responsibility for broader congressional power.[43]

In contrast, Madison acknowledged one contribution by Pinckney: "sundry propositions" relating to rights. On August 20, Pinckney proposed a group of detailed rights and other recommendations. The Notes recorded the list of eleven suggestions. The wide-ranging list gave the legislature power to imprison, authorized advisory judicial opinions to the other branches, secured habeas corpus, preserved liberty of the press, barred troops in peacetime without legislative consent, limited the length of military expenditures, limited the quartering of soldiers, prevented national and state office holding, barred religious tests and qualifications for office, and gave the United States the rights and privileges of a "Body-corporate."[44]

Madison summarized the suggestions in simpler language. Consistently, Pinckney's complicated limits were erased, and the underlying principle was expanded. For example, Pinckney proposed that habeas corpus be "enjoyed" in the "most expeditious and ample manner" and suspended only "upon the most urgent and pressing occasions" for "limited time" with a specific time limit to be set in terms of months. In the Notes, Madison wrote "securing the benefit of habeas corpus." Madison similarly converted Pinckney's complicated description that "[n]o religious test or qualification shall ever be annexed to any oath of office" to "forbidding religious tests to Civil offices." Pinckney's suggestion that the legislature and executive have the authority to "require the opinions" of the Court "upon important questions of law, and upon solemn occasions" was converted by Madison "to require opinion of the Judges." Pinckney's detailed rights became broad principles in the Notes:

"securing the benefit of the habeas corpus"
"preserving the liberty of the press"
"guarding ag[ain]st billeting of soldiers"
"ag[st] raising troops without the consent of the Legislature"
"forbidding religious tests to Civil offices."

The summaries could have reflected Pinckney's oral descriptions. But the straightforward, strong concepts resembled Madison's approach to summarizing evident throughout the Notes. His strength lay in capturing the central point and describing it in simple language. As the list suggests, recording Pinckney's propositions appears to have made a marked impression on Madison. The descriptions resemble certain amendments he proposed in 1789 in Congress—the basis for what we know now as the Bill of Rights.[45]

The decision to record Pinckney's suggestions was unusual, and Madison skipped detailing other ideas. Morris and Pinckney submitted suggestions for "organizing the Executive department." Madison could have easily summarized the proposed "Council of State" with seven officers (secretaries of domestic affairs, commerce and finance, foreign affairs, war, marine, state, and a chief justice). Even from memory, he could have recorded the list. But he did not bother. The details of the executive department had not particularly interested him.[46]

As the delegates completed Article VII, Madison recorded comments that enlarged Congress's powers. Gorham successfully added "and support" to the clause, "raise armies." Madison similarly explained that a "more convenient definition of the power" would be to "provide & maintain a navy" instead of "to build and equip fleets." Then, Madison wrote, "'To make rules and regulation of the land & naval forces,' added from the existing Articles of Confederation." The Notes described expansion toward Congress having a broad, national military power.[47]

Even when Madison described a failed effort to add a power, the Notes reinforced broad legislative power. With typical imprecision, Madison placed quotes around Mason's desire for a congressional power "to enact sumptuary laws"—technically "to make." Madison did not like the idea. The Notes conveyed his sense that Mason (like Franklin previously) was trapped in an early revolutionary period. Morris criticized sumptuary laws as creating "a landed Nobility, by fixing in the great-landholders and their posterity their present possessions." Ellsworth argued that a more sensible power already existed. The "reasonable" "regulation of eating & drinking" was provided for by the "power of taxation." Madison used the Notes to suggest that the failure of the motion related to concerns about sumptuary laws, not broader uses of the taxing power.[48]

In the Notes, Madison worried about future cavilers narrowly misreading clauses. For example, the final clause provided: "And to make all laws that shall be necessary and proper for carrying into execution the foregoing powers, and all other powers vested, by this Constitution, in the government of the United States, or in any department or officer thereof." Madison and Pinckney thought it "liable to cavil" that "all laws" might be interpreted to not include "offices." They proposed adding, "and establish all offices." Madison did not bother to copy the individual rebuttals. He explained that Morris, Wilson, Rutledge, and Ellsworth—a group not often in agreement—"urged that the amendment could not be necessary." The motion was rejected with Virginia also voting in the negative. Madison seems to have been persuaded himself as he noted that the original language was agreed to "nem. con." The Notes indicated that, after an objection was raised, the rejection of the objection did not mean that the opposite interpretation prevailed.[49]

Madison's desire for "more latitude" for Congress also underlay the debate over the phrase "concerning Treason." Although the section was lengthy, Madison believed the "definition too narrow." It was "inconvenient" to "bar a discretion which experience might enlighten." The Notes were taken under Madison's assumption that a reader such as Jefferson understood the larger issues. Madison referred to Morris and Randolph's failed effort to substitute "the words of the British Statute," assuming that the specifics of the treason statute were known.[50]

The Notes' depiction of the treason discussion focused on the challenges of language instead of reflecting the precise textual alterations. Although Madison filled four pages with the discussion, he missed several motions, alterations of language, and votes. The journal recorded fourteen votes. Madison described eleven voted motions. The Notes reflected that, as the delegates focused on the words, problems arose. Morris thought "adhering" could be read to "not go as far as giving aid or comfort" or, contrarily, that words would be more "restrictive." Wilson thought "giving aid and comfort" was "explanatory, not operative." Dickinson thought an addition of the words was "unnecessary & improper; being too vague and extending too far." Madison suggested "and" be changed to "or." After the delegates struck out words implying to some that the states could declare treason, Madison argued that the change "has not removed the embarrassment." Later, after additional changes, Wilson declared that "the clause is ambiguous now." After another substitution, Madison decided that he "was not satisfied with the footing on which the clause now stood." A final change added "or on confession in open court"; however, Madison explained that the three negative votes were not in opposition but considered the "words superfluous." The Notes emphasized the distance between the procedural record and the multiple understandings.[51]

Conversely, an awareness of strategic silence to avoid discussing divergent understandings was apparent in Madison's account of a section relating to slavery. The original text provided: "the proportions of direct taxation shall be regulated by the whole number of white and other free citizens and inhabitants." The delegates struck "white and other." Madison described the words as "superfluous." King then asked, "what was the precise meaning of direct taxation." Madison commented, "No answ^d"—no answer or no one answered. The question and the silent response hinted that no one wanted to figure out whether shared understandings existed.[52]

By Tuesday, August 21, the Notes were rough, containing far more dashes than usual. Many speakers were given only a sentence. The date had "Friday" crossed out and "Tuesday" written over it as if Madison was using a sheet that had been ruled for another date or was writing on a Friday. A committee appointed previously on debts and militia made a report, but Madison summarized it briefly, ending with "to organize Militia &c." Madison fell back on abbreviations, writing "y^e" instead of "the," an ampersand (&) for "and," and "w^d" for "would."[53]

Madison tried to preserve future power in the national legislature. He wanted to prevent a total prohibition against a tax on exports. A tax on exports "may not be expedient at present," but it "may be so hereafter for the general good of the Union." The regulation of exports "may & probably will be necessary hereafter." An embargo "may be of absolute necessity." Facing disagreement, he eventually suggested that a two-thirds vote to tax exports would be "a lesser evil than a total prohibition." Madison lost 5–6; Virginia voted no. Madison, however, carefully recorded that "Genl Washington and JM" had voted together in favor. Mason apparently had used Madison's arguments against him, suggesting that only those who were "for reducing the States to mere corporations" should favor taxing exports and that the eight northern states have "an interest different from the five South[er]n States." Madison's final recorded position in the Notes favored "national and permanent views."[54]

The last matter recorded in the Notes responded to the claim that the three-fifths clause was dishonorable in an American constitution. The Report provided, "No tax or duty shall be laid by the Legislature . . . on the migration or importation of such persons as the several States shall think proper to admit; nor shall such migration or importation be prohibited." Luther Martin wanted to insert the word "free" before "persons," or as Madison explained, "to strike out the clause restraining a prohibition of the importation of slaves." Martin's argument appeared as numbered sentences claiming that the clause would encourage the importation of slaves and "weaken[]" the region. Martin's final reason was stark: "[I]t was inconsistent with the principles of the revolution and dishonorable to the American character to have such a feature in the Constitution."[55]

The Notes reflected Madison's belief that the political coalition supporting the slave trade would hold. Madison recorded only responses by South Carolina and Connecticut delegates. Rutledge argued, "Religion & humanity had nothing to do with this question." Pinckney declared that South Carolina would not accept the plan "if it prohibits the slave trade." The state had watched "expressly & watchfully" in "every proposed extension" of Congress's powers to prevent "meddling with the importation of negroes." Ellsworth agreed that "the morality or wisdom of slavery" belonged to the states and the "old confederation had not meddled" on importation. Madison included an awkwardly recorded final comment by Pinckney. If "left at liberty," South Carolina "may perhaps by degrees" follow Virginia and Maryland in barring the slave trade. The double uncertainty of "may perhaps" suggested Madison's doubts about the possibility.[56]

And with these comments, Madison's Notes ended on page 3 of the sheet. He left the last page blank. Only squiggly lines appear on it. The break between Tuesday, August 21, and Wednesday, August 22, was obvious to the young man who copied the manuscript for Thomas Jefferson. After copying the proceedings of August 21, John Wayles Eppes also left the remaining page blank. The Notes and Jefferson's copy indicated the break. The entry for August 21 is the last contemporaneous glimpse in the Notes of Madison's mind during the Convention.[57]

James Madison four years before the Convention, miniature painted by Charles Willson Peale (1783). Library of Congress, LC-USZC4-4097.

Thomas Jefferson in France the year before the Convention. Painted by Mather Brown (1786). National Portrait Gallery, Smithsonian Institution /Art Resource, NY. NPG 99.66.

First page of the Notes showing revisions. James Madison, Debate Notes, May 25, 1787. b.1 (DLC 10). Conservation Division, GR_142_0065. James Madison Papers, Manuscript Division, Library of Congress.

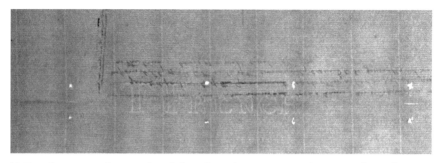

T. French watermark on replaced sheet for July 17. Notes, July 17 to July 18, b.62 (DLC 72). Conservation Division. Debate Notes, James Madison Papers, Manuscript Division, Library of Congress.

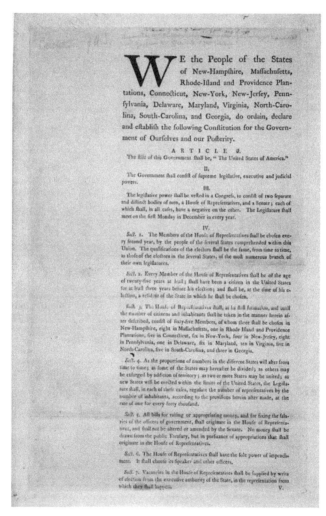

Madison's copy of the Committee of Detail report. James Madison Papers, Manuscript Division, Library of Congress.

Original August 20 description of Pinckney's rights and revision with inserted slip. Notes, Slip 2, b.95-2 (DLC 105c). Conservation Division, GR_142_0371. James Madison Papers, Manuscript Division, Library of Congress.

Madison's copy of the Committee of Style report. James Madison Papers, Manuscript Division, Library of Congress.

Whatman countermark (with short M) appearing in summer 1787 Notes on June 19. b.26 (DLC 36). Conservation Division. James Madison Papers, Manuscript Division, Library of Congress.

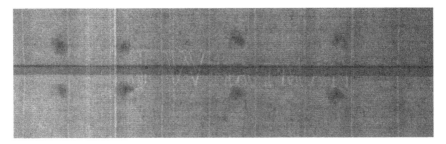

Whatman countermark (with long M) appearing in Notes on August 23. b.102 (DLC 112). Conservation Division. James Madison Papers, Manuscript Division, Library of Congress.

Copy of ~ Journal of the Federal Convention, held in
Philadelphia May 14. 1787. ~ from & after

Monday August 20. 1787.

It was moved & 2ded. to refer the following propositions to the
committee of five. ~ which passed in the affirmative ~

Each House shall be the judge of its own privileges, & shall
have authority to punish by imprisonment any person violating the
same; or who, in the place where the Legislature may be sitting
and during the time of its Session, shall threaten any of its members
for any thing said or done in the House; or who shall assault any
of them therefor ~ or who shall assault or arrest any witness or
other person ordered to attend either of the Houses in his way going
or returning; or who shall rescue any person arrested by their
order.

Each branch of the Legislature, as well as the supreme
Executive shall have authority to require the opinions of the
Supreme Judicial Court upon important questions of law, and
upon solemn occasions.

The privileges and benefits of the writ of Habeas corpus
shall be enjoyed in this Government in the most expeditious
manner; and shall not be suspended by
the Legislature except upon the most urgent & pressing occasions,
and for a limited time not exceeding   months.

The Liberty of the press shall be inviolably preserved.   No troops shall be kept up in time of peace, but
by consent of the Legislature.

The military shall always be subordinate to the
civil

Entry for 20 August 1787 in Madison's Journal Copy. Journal of the Federal
Convention of 1787, Box 1, folder 49 (in Madison's Hand), GEN MSS 271,
United States Presidents Collection. General Collection, Beinecke Rare Book and
Manuscript Library.

Slip with delegates' names, entry for May 1787. Slip 1, b.1–1. (DLC 10b).
Conservation Division, GR_142_0067. James Madison Papers, Manuscript
Division, Library of Congress.

Jefferson's son-in-law, John Wayle Eppes, 1805. Engraving by Charles Balthazar
Julien Fevret de Saint-Mémin [Washington, D.C., 1805]. Library of Congress.

Thomas Jefferson as secretary of state, painted by Charles Willson Peale (1791).
Courtesy of Independence National Historical Park, Philadelphia.

Wednesday, Aug. 22 in Convention.

Art VII. Sect. IIII. resumed.

mr Sherman was for leaving the clause as it stands. He disapproved of the slave trade: yet as the States were now possessed of the right to import slaves, as the public good did not require it to be taken from them; and as it was expedient to have as few objections as possible to the proposed scheme of Government, he thought it best to leave the matter as we find it. He observed that the abolition of slavery seemed to be going on in the United States and that the good sense of the several States would probably by degrees compleat it. He urged on the Convention the necessity of dispatching its business.

Col. Mason. This infernal trafic originated in the avarice of British merchants. The British Government ~~have certainly~~ constantly checked the attempts of Virginia to put a stop to it. The present question concerns not the importing States alone but the whole union

August 22 entry of Jefferson Copy by Eppes reflecting August 22 division of the Notes, Massachusetts Historical Society.

First page of the Press Copy of Jefferson Copy. New York Public Library.

James Madison at age eighty-two, July 1833. Engraved by T. B. Welch from a drawing by J. B. Longacre taken from life at Montpelier Va., July 1833. *The National Portrait Gallery of Distinguished Americans with Biographical Sketches* (Philadelphia: D. Rice & A. N. Hart, 1856), volume 3, frontis.

Dolley Madison. Painting by William S. Elwell (1848). National Portrait Gallery, Smithsonian Institution/Art Resource, NY.

Dolley Madison's completion of James Madison's explanation. Debate Notes, 7a. Conservation Division, GR_142_0053. James Madison Papers, Manuscript Division, Library of Congress.

IV

ABANDONING THE NOTES

7

THE COMPLEXITY OF DRAFTING

The Notes were never finished during the Convention in 1787. Following August 21, there is, to borrow a geological term, an unconformity—a missing section of time. Madison composed the Notes for the remainder of the Convention after the fall of 1789. His comments in these final weeks are thus particularly unreliable. He appears to have continued to take rough notes but had later difficulties in deciphering them. If Madison gave lengthy speeches, he kept no record. Throughout the Convention, the Notes had been necessarily written in hindsight. But the Notes for the final weeks of the Convention were drafted with the advantages of a distance of two years—an entirely different vantage point.

The unconformity somewhat ironically reflected Madison's personal success. In the final weeks of the Convention, he became a major contributor. During the first three months, Madison had been chosen for only one committee. He had pushed his deepest commitments without uniform success. In August, however, as the delegates debated the draft, he had gradually been drawn into the process of drafting and proven his value in improving language and sidestepping controversy. On Wednesday, August 22, Madison was chosen as a member of an important committee. He also became sick. The combination led to the initial collapse of the Notes. His almost continuous service on committees through the end of the Convention likely reinforced the decision to stop writing. In a deeper sense, Madison may have sensed that the Notes could not capture the complexity of the final drafting and, particularly, significant decisions that were repeatedly decided by committees. The unconformity thus also captured the delegates' inability to grasp the emerging scope and dimensions of the Constitution.

Into late August, Madison likely intended to keep taking rough notes and writing them up as a record for himself and Jefferson. But he did not. In July, he had worried that an "indisposition" might oblige him to "discontinue" the Notes. During the week of August 20, Madison indeed became sick. His letter to McClurg describing the illness unfortunately has never been located. In response, McClurg wrote that he was "not surprized to hear that you have been indisposed." Few of Madison's friends would have been surprised. Although Madison lived well into his eighties, he considered himself a person prone to illness. His close correspondents were often treated to detailed descriptions of ailments. McClurg recommended that Madison rest and focus on his health. Despite the indisposition, Madison continued to attend the proceedings.[1]

Even without illness, new committee work would have made the Notes challenging. Between August 22 and the close of the Convention, Madison served on three significant committees. With the possible exception of a few days at the end of the month, Madison was either serving on a committee or observing and participating in the report of a committee on which he had served. On September 6, Madison wrote Jefferson that it was the "first day which has been free from Committee service, both before & after the hours of the House." Between illness and committee service, Madison had little time to write up whatever rough notes he took.[2]

The unconformity reflected a larger shift towards committees in the final weeks. With a few exceptions, the important decisions were made there, not on the Convention floor. Whatever rough notes of the Convention Madison took reflected a small portion of the discussion over drafting decisions. As Madison participated in debates in committees, the Notes from the Convention may have seemed less useful. The Convention was not where important decisions were initially being made.

The delegates resorted to committees to decide the controversial and complicated issues. Six committees were created between August 18 and the end of the Convention. The original August 6 drafting committee also apparently remained active. The increase in committee work caused a change in the adjournment time from 4:00 pm to 3:00 pm, to leave time for committee meetings.[3]

Madison served on the three most important committees in the final three and a half weeks. On August 22, he was selected for an eleven-man committee dealing with three controversial sections involving slavery in Article VII. The committee offered a report, which was only partially discussed. On August 31, he was then selected for another eleven-man committee to deal with all the postponed matters, including the report of his previous committee. The committee met over the entire next week. It made three partial reports between Saturday, September 1, and Wednesday, September 5. On Saturday, September 8, the delegates still were debating aspects of these reports. That same day, Madison was selected to his third committee, the five-man committee to revise the style and arrange the articles. The committee of style prepared a final draft of the Constitution and a letter to Congress. On Wednesday, September 12, the committee made its report. On Monday, September 17, the Convention permanently adjourned. The committee work left little time to transcribe rough notes.[4]

List of Committees (Madison's committees in italics)[5]

Debts and militia committee (eleven members):
  Appointed August 18; reported August 21; debated August 22–23
Holdover Committee (August 6 Report) (five members):
  Additional matters sent on August 18 and 20; reported August 22; postponed for members to take copies; additional matter sent on August 23
Committee on slavery (4, 5, 6, sections of 7th article) (eleven members):
  Appointed August 22; reported August 24; debated August 25, 29
Committee on duties (eleven members):
  Appointed August 25; reported August 28, debated August 31
Committee on bankruptcy and full faith (five members):
  Appointed August 29; reported September 1; debated September 3
Committee on postponed matters (eleven members):
  Appointed August 31; reported September 1, 4, 5; postponed for members to take copies September 4; debated September 3, 4, 5, 6, 7, 8
Final draft committee (to revise style of and arrange articles) (five members):
  Appointed September 8; sent instruction to prepare address September 10; reported September 12 and 13; address debated September 12; debated September 13–15

Madison's service on the final drafting committee related to his service on the two prior committees. The committee included three men from the postponed matters committee who understood those recent decisions and compromises: Madison, Morris, and King. A fourth member, William Samuel Johnson, had served on the committee that addressed bankruptcy and the judiciary. Madison, Johnson, and King similarly had served on the committee addressing slavery-related issues. Hamilton alone had not served on any prior committee, having only recently returned to Philadelphia. If delegates still associated him with his mid-June speech, he brought a vision of a stronger executive and national government. As the sole New York delegate, he could not vote. Other than Madison, notably absent were members of the southern delegations. For southerners worried about protection for slavery, Madison's presence may have sufficed.[6]

Not only did committee service leave Madison with less time to write up his Notes, but it complicated the taking of extensive rough notes. It may have been difficult to separate the delegates' debates in the Convention from the committees' reasoning. The last two committees on which Madison served created many characteristics of the final Constitution. The postponed matters committee defined ineligibility of legislators, rewrote the introductory powers of Congress, addressed impeachments, created a vice-president, introduced the electoral college as the mode of electing the president, defined the requirements for president, described presidential powers, created power over the seat of government, and authorized copyright and patent protection. The final draft committee— often referred to by historians as the committee on style—significantly altered the working draft by converting the twenty-three articles adopted thus far to the final seven articles, while also altering words and punctuation. This committee created the relationships and groupings that define the final Constitution. Madison's failure to write up the Notes during these weeks suggests that Madison had become too involved in helping to revise the draft to bother with the Notes. Moreover, he may have been unable to divide his work as a committee member from his role as a delegate. The Notes as he had taken them could no longer reflect his experience of the Convention.

Madison's decision—inadvertent or deliberate—to stop writing the Notes altered their coverage. For example, if he had continued to compose the Notes, he might have included the committee report creating a Privy Council. The holdover committee received various matters, including Mason's suggestion of a council. On Wednesday, August 22, the committee presented language that created a "Privy-Council" for the president, to be comprised of the Senate president, the speaker of the house, the chief justice, and the heads of the major departments. Delegates were permitted to take copies of the report, although no copy has been located in Madison's papers. No motions related to the Privy Council appear on the journal. The committee on postponed matters likely acquired jurisdiction and sunk the recommendation. At the time, however, the demise would not have been apparent. Originally, Madison might have included the suggestion; but by the time he composed the entry, he knew that a constitutional Privy Council had been a dead end.[7]

The changes—arranged by the committees, debated by the delegates, often altered again by a subsequent committee—defied the recording ability of Madison as a note taker. Even with knowledge of the outcome and possession of the relevant reports, tracking the changes to the drafts is difficult. As aspects of the draft were revised in committee—and in turn revised again—perceiving what the entire document amounted to became increasingly difficult. Only on September 12, was the complete final draft of the Constitution apparent. At that point, the delegates made markedly few changes before finally adjourning. The most observant and involved member could not stand apart and observe the final drafting.[8]

Although Madison stopped transcribing his rough notes, he appears to have continued sporadically to take them. Brief debates and comments are scattered amidst the lengthy extracts from the journal in the Notes after August 21. Unless he later invented or remembered such comments, he retained rough notes from the Convention. Although no rough notes have been found, the Notes offer some evidence as to what types of material Madison remained interested in recording.

Lengthy speeches disappeared. The absence may reflect the delegates' discussions. In McHenry's late August notes, he wrote comments such as "desultory debate" and "various debate." In reviewing the reports in late August and September, the delegates proceeded in sequential order. This disciplined approach likely made long speeches seem irrelevant. Madison's earlier Notes had focused on speeches as a strategic record but, by this point in the Convention, Madison may have known many delegates' preferences and seen little to be gained in recording others.[9]

The Notes suggest that the rough notes were very rough. Madison later faced difficulty in summarizing the topic. The first sentence often did not serve as a summary, and the subsequent sentences were disjointed. For example, Wilson tried again to add the negative on state laws to Congress's powers. Madison supported the issue and knew the arguments well. Nonetheless, despite some effort to connect the ideas, the paragraph was disconnected phrases.

> M[r]. Wilson considered this as the key-stone wanted to compleat the wide arch of Government we are raising. The power of self-defence had been urged as necessary for the State Governments—It was equally necessary for the General Government. The firmness of Judges is not of itself sufficient. Something further is requisite—It will be better to prevent the passage of an improper law, than to declare it void when passed.

There was no explanation of the reasons that judges were insufficient. There was no elaboration of the preference for preventing passage instead of voiding the law. Madison had recorded the various conclusions but apparently no reasons. Even greater incoherence appeared in a speech by Morris against a motion to require a two-thirds vote of each house on commerce regulations:

> M[r]. Gov[r]. Morris. opposed the object of the motion as injurious to Preferences to american ships will multiply them, till they can carry the Southern produce cheaper than it is now carried——A navy was essential to security, particularly of the S. States, and can only be had by a navigation act encouraging american bottoms & seamen—In those points of view then alone, it is the interest of the S. States that american navigation acts should be facilitated. Shipping he said was the worst & most precarious kind of property and stood in need of public patronage.

When Madison had transcribed his rough notes relatively contemporaneously, he had been comfortable inserting transitions and connections. He had felt confident about his ability to shape his rough notes into polished speeches. With the rough notes after August 21, he could expand his abbreviations into words. But he could only speculate as to the connections.[10]

This difficulty in reconstructing rationales several years later explains the repeated vague generalities. The delegate's position was clear—for or against the motion—but the reasoning had to be stated broadly. On the bankruptcy clause, Madison explained that "M[r]. Gov[r]. Morris said this was an extensive & delicate subject." Morris agreed "to it because he saw no danger of abuse by the power by the Legislature of the U- S." Similarly, Dickinson "was in favor of giving the eventual election [of the executive] to the Legislature, instead of the Senate—It was too much influence to be added to that body." These reasons—abuse of power and too much influence—were typical ideas that Madison could have easily inserted. On occasion, Madison appears to have not even bothered to reconstruct the reasons. He described a debate over ratification: "M^r. Ghorum urged the expedience of "Conventions" also M^r. Pinkney, for reasons, formerly urged on a discussion of this question." In these moments, Madison's rough notes proved no longer adequate.[11]

An odd aspect of the Notes after August 21 is Madison's assignment of motions. Madison managed to assign most motions to a particular delegate. When delegates speak, they often make, oppose, or amend a motion. Did the rough notes designate every motion maker, or did Madison guess on occasion? A comparison with McHenry's notes suggests the possibility of inaccuracy. For example, McHenry's notes include a lengthy speech by Morris favoring re-eligibility of the president. Madison appears to have described the same speech but linked it to the motion on electors and attributed the motion to Morris. Madison began to copy a phrase relating to ineligibility but crossed it out. Aligning the rough notes with the motions and votes in his Journal Copy must have posed problems. In this final section written much later, the reliability of the record becomes more speculative.[12]

The complexity of the final weeks of drafting, the sporadic nature of the rough notes, and a hiatus of several years contributed to the difficulties facing Madison in his eventual transcription. He may have omitted rough notes that he could not decipher. He may have abandoned comments that seemed out of place or irrelevant. He may have introduced errors in attempting to reconstruct his notes. The rough notes reflected a Convention that Madison could no longer completely recall.

Madison's speeches in this final period may be particularly unreliable. He recorded no lengthy speeches but did include shorter speeches and comments. These statements may have been based in his rough notes. Alternatively, Madison may have remembered making a comment and attempted to reconstruct his ideas from memory. Thus, they may reflect what he had said—but also, on certain occasions, what he believed or wished with hindsight that he might have said.

The most seemingly incoherent speeches may bear the closest resemblance to his rough notes. For example, Madison recorded his speech on the committee report relating to slavery. He wrote that he offered "a pretty full view of the subject." The details, however, remained obscure. Madison had difficulty. He crossed out words and moved them to new places as if attempting to create something comprehensible.

> He observed that the disadvantage to the S. States from a navigation act, ~~would~~ lay chiefly in ~~the~~ a temporary rise of freight, attended however with an increase of South[n] as well as Northern Shipping—with the emigration of Northern Seamen & merchants to the Southern States—& with a removal of the existing ~~& fetters~~ retaliations among the States ~~and with successful retalitaton on the injurious restrictions of foreign powers~~. . . .

The precise points are hard to decipher. His rough notes must have referenced retaliation—but he was no longer sure by precisely whom and to precisely whom. He copied the phrases but could not assemble them into a comprehensive argument.[13]

Madison may have omitted or reframed comments he made in his rough notes. Both Madison and McHenry described Madison's comments relating to treaties. McHenry described a distinction by Madison framed in the language of British precedent: "the Kings power over treaties final and original except in granting subsidies or dismembering the empire." Only these specific treaties "required parliamentary acts." Madison described having "hinted" at "a distinction" between "different sorts of Treaties." In Madison's version, the distinction was reversed and an apparently large group of "other Treaties" required the legislature's "concurrence." If Madison's rough notes included the British distinction, he either chose not to exclude it or reframed it.[14]

Two dramatic comments made by Madison against slavery raise concerns about accuracy. They represent the only two times that Madison spoke against slavery in the Notes. Both comments occurred in the Notes of August 25. The delegates debated the committee report stating that no prohibition on importation would be permitted prior to 1800. General Pinckney successfully moved to extend the date to 1808. Madison described himself stating:

Twenty years will produce all the mischief that can be apprehended from the liberty to import slaves. So long a term will be more dishonorable to the National character than to say nothing about it in the Constitution.

Later that day, he included a second comment:

M^r. Madison thought it wrong to admit in the Constitution the idea that there could be property in men. The reason of duties did not hold, as slaves are not like merchandise, consumed &c.

A similarity exists between Madison's first comment and Luther Martin's statement on August 21:

it was inconsistent with the principles of the revolution and dishonorable to the American character to have such a feature in the Constitution.

"Dishonorable," "character," and "constitution" occur in both sentences. Of course, Madison might have repeated Martin's comment four days later and written it down in his rough notes. But—and this interpretation is equally possible—Madison eventually may have decided to indicate some objection by himself to slavery in the Notes. In the lengthy debate over slavery on August 21 and 22, Madison recorded eighteen delegates with himself conspicuously absent. Madison's declaration that the Constitution should not admit there could be property in men was likely composed after August 25, 1787.[15]

A related concern about reliability occurs with Madison's comments which advance a specific constitutional interpretation. Earlier in the Notes, Madison tended to emphasize the complexity of interpretation. In this final section, Madison instead often argued for a particular interpretation.

At times, Madison placed the interpretation in his mouth. For example, he declared that "'arming' as explained did not extend to furnishing arms" and described the "primary object" of the militia clause as "to secure an effectual discipline of the Militia." Similarly, he explained that the insertion of "to offices," instead of "officers," would "obviate doubts that he might appoint officers without a previous creation of offices by the Legislature."[16]

In other places, Madison offered the interpretation as an omniscient narrator. For example, after "this Constitution" was added to the judiciary's jurisdiction, Madison gave the following explanation: "it being generally supposed that the jurisdiction given was constructively limited to cases of a Judiciary nature." He likewise followed an amendment relating to trial by jury with the explanation that "the object . . . was to provide for trial by jury of offences committed out of any State." These interpretive comments occur through to the end of the Convention. On September 15, "No person legally held to service or labour escaping into another" was altered by replacing "legally" with "under the Laws thereof." Madison provided a rationale: "in compliance with the wish of some who thought that term equivocal, and favoring the idea that slavery was legal in a moral view." In this final section—written later—Madison imposed a single interpretation for alterations. Some may have been in his rough notes but some likely reflect the distinct advantage of hindsight.[17]

Madison's record of himself was likely most accurate in comments that are least significant. On September 13, Madison included his motion to insert the words, "the day on which," in the procedures for presenting a bill. He explained, "in order to prevent doubts whether the day on which the bill be presented, ought to be counted or not as one of the ten days." Madison admitted that a "number of members" were "very impatient & calling for the question." His motion lost. In a moment like this one— with delegates frustrated by Madison—we glimpse the summer of 1787.[18]

The last view of Madison at the Convention comes from the letters he wrote in September 1787. On September 4, he wrote his father that the Convention would "probably continue but a short time longer." He promised to "forward the proceedings" as "soon as the tie of secrecy shall be dissolved." Two days later, Madison sent significant details to Jefferson in code. He felt "little scruple in disclosing what will be public here." He predicted that the Convention would end in a week or two. Although the final draft was not prepared, Madison was confident about the "outlines."[19]

Madison's perceptions reflected September 1787. He began with his significant success: the government would be "submitted to the people of the states." Ratification ensured that the government was not a government for the states but for the people. His description of congressional power focused on its breadth over large areas, rather than specific enumeration. It "will extend to taxation trade and sundry other general matters." With respect to limits on the states, Madison mentioned only one restriction, "from paper money," and added, "and in a few other instances." He referred to a "regular judiciary establishment" but offered no details. Madison did not distinguish between election and appointment. He used the phrase, "appointed biennially by the people," to refer to election. He used "chosen" to describe the state legislature's selection of senators and the people's election of representatives. The president was "cloathed with executive power," as if implying that executive power could have been placed elsewhere. The "mode of constituting the executive" remained "among the few points not yet finally settled." But Madison did not appear worried.[20]

The letter to Jefferson underscored Madison's disappointments. He still believed that the state governments were the problem. The plan did not "effectually answer its national object." It failed to restrict the states and would not "prevent the local mischiefs which every where excite disgust ag[ain]st the state governments." Madison was not sure it would be successful: "certain characters would "wage war against any reform whatever." Although he declared that the public would likely accept any government that "promises stability to the public Councils & security to private rights," he added a pessimistic aside, so long as "no regard" was given to "local prejudices or temporary considerations." Madison worried that if "the present moment be lost it is hard to say what may be our fate." The comment echoed a quotation he had written in his commonplace book as a young man: "There is a Critical Minute in every thing. . . . If it is miss'd, chiefly in revolutions of State, 'tis odds if it can be met with or perceived again." The Constitution was not what Madison wished, but failure presented a worse fate.[21]

By September 6, Madison knew he would sign the Constitution despite his reservations. After September 17, McHenry used his notes to explain his decision to sign despite concerns: "I distrust my own judgement . . . as I have had already frequent occasions to be convinced that I have not always judged right." In September 1787, if Madison had completed the Notes, a similar reflection on Madison's decision to sign might have appeared. The Notes might have ended with comments along the lines of the rather pessimistic letter to Jefferson. Instead, Madison makes no appearance in the September 17 Notes.[22]

The Notes for September 17 read as the conclusion to a drama. Morris and Hamilton—delegates whom Madison had recorded at length—made comments on the momentous occasion. Franklin, Gerry, and General Pinckney—delegates whom he had quarreled with—gave their thoughts. The other large state delegates commented—Gorham, King, and Wilson.

The two Virginia colleagues who had irked Madison appeared: Randolph explained his refusal to sign; Mason was not even given that privilege. Washington offered a rare comment. Even delegates who make almost no other appearance in the Notes were included: Williamson, Blount, and Ingersoll. But Madison wrote no lines for himself. Several years later, he may have been unable to reconcile his contemporary feelings of disappointment with his later knowledge of pragmatic success.[23]

Madison's letter a few days after the Convention's conclusion indicates that he was still wrestling with fundamental issues. His letter to Edmund Pendleton on September 20 described two "difficult" problems that characterized the Convention in Madison's mind. The first question was how to blend "stability & energy in the Government" with "the essential characters of the republican Form"? The second question was how to trace the "proper line of demarkation between the national and State authorities"? Madison remained fascinated with the "infinite diversity concerning the means" of solving the two problems even "among those who were unanimously agreed" on the ends.[24]

As evidence of this diversity of means at the Convention, Madison contemporaneously may have copied a detailed plan for government by Hamilton. The copy is on paper similar to that of the early Notes. A header in Madison's hand on the copy describes the plan being shared "about the close" of the Convention. The plan resembled an expansive version of the type of plan Hamilton had offered in June. In 1803, Hamilton argued that the plan copied by Madison at the end of the Convention did not include an executive on good behavior and that, by that point, he had abandoned that idea. The discrepancy between Hamilton's memory and Madison's copy would become controversial. Madison's copy describes an executive on good behavior. Whether Madison copied accurately the provision or altered it to demonstrate Hamilton's early June ideas to Jefferson is unknown. In important respects, it is irrelevant. If Hamilton willingly permitted Madison to copy a plan with an executive on good behavior, he presumably assumed that Madison was an understanding audience. In September 1787, Madison did not know that the Convention's work would prove successful nor that he would eventually need to distance himself from Hamilton.[25]

Madison could not view the Constitution and Convention as a detached observer. He explained to Pendleton that he would "forbear to make any observations" on the Constitution—"either on the side of its merits or its faults." Madison understood that the "best Judges" would have to be free from the "bias resulting from a participation in the work." Madison's participation—his failures and successes—and his reflection on that participation through the Notes left him with inevitable bias. If he had kept writing up his rough notes until the end of the Convention in September 1787, the Notes might have slowly petered out similar to his congressional diary in 1783.[26]

In September 1787, Madison had no time to waste transcribing rough notes. The fate of the Constitution remained uncertain. The final days of the Convention left Madison worried about the likelihood of success. He was concerned that the Constitution would be stopped or altered in Congress. On or around September 21, he left Philadelphia for New York to attend Congress. If the Constitution survived congressional scrutiny, was sent to the states, and successfully ratified, then Madison could return to finish the Notes. If the Constitution was not ratified, the Notes would serve as a narrative for Jefferson about the reasons for the failure.[27]

8

THE CONVENTION'S
CHANGING RELEVANCE

In the aftermath of the Convention, Madison left the Notes alone. He traveled immediately to New York, worrying about the Constitution's fate in Congress. If he brought his rough notes along, he was unlikely to have had the time or inclination to reconstruct them. Jefferson remained abroad. Not until the late summer of 1789 did Madison come to believe that Jefferson would return to the United States, and only then would he turn to the unfinished Notes.

Madison's understanding of the Convention altered over the two following years. Repeatedly, he explained parts of the Constitution for new audiences and new purposes. An October 1787 letter to Jefferson began the process of moving from engaged participant to one with omniscient hindsight. Madison's personal opinions were recast as those of the Convention; messy debates were presented as coherent choices among clear alternatives. Soon thereafter, for Alexander Hamilton's *Federalist* project, Madison constructed rationales and superimposed a single intent. At the Virginia ratification convention in the summer of 1788, he distanced himself from his apparent support for a consolidated government. By 1789, in the First Congress, he embraced interpretive questions arising from constitutional textual ambiguity. The congressional decision to add, rather than integrate, amendments left the Constitution's original text intact. Even as memories faded and the assumptions underlying the discussions grew remote, the proceedings of the Convention remained potentially politically relevant.

In the fall of 1787, Madison left Philadelphia with alacrity. He passed through Princeton on his way north, apparently refusing to remain long enough to acquire in person an honorary law doctorate from the college. By Monday, September 24, he was in New York. With two Virginia delegates having refused to sign the Constitution, support of Virginians in Congress seemed tenuous. Virginia delegate, Richard Henry Lee, wanted Congress to amend the document by including a "Bill of Rights." Lee also hoped to persuade the Confederation Congress to debate the Constitution paragraph by paragraph. Madison and others successfully argued that the Confederation Congress should not debate the Constitution. The two-day debate was then hidden from the public by removal from the congressional journal. Madison explained that the threat of "yeas & nays on the journals" had been "fortunately terminated" by an ambiguous resolution permitting a unanimous vote. A subsequent vote removed Lee's motions entirely from the journal. Washington approved of the "appearance of unanimity" and reassured Madison that most would not "peep behind the curtains." On September 28, the Constitution was transmitted to the states.[1]

Madison's memory of the Convention already was fading. After Mason published his objections to the Constitution, Madison wrote to Washington about his contrary recollections. With respect to Mason's complaint about the Senate treaty power, Madison commented: "If I do not forget too some of his other reasons were either not at all or very faintly urged at the time when alone they should have been urged." With respect to the senatorial term, Madison declared: "I recollect well that he more than once disclaimed opposition to it." And with respect to the foreign slave trade term, Madison noted: "My memory fails me also if he did not acquiesce in if not vote" in favor. The treaty and slave trade term involved debates after August 21, suggesting that any extant rough notes were of limited assistance. Madison thought Mason was advocating new reasons. It was not "candid to arraign the Convention for omissions which were never suggested to them" and not "prudent to vindicate the dissent by reasons which either were not previously thought of, or must have been wilfully concealed."[2]

As other recollections of the Convention appeared in print, Madison did not complain of any violations of confidentiality. Charles Pinckney privately printed a pamphlet, *Observations,* discussing his initial May plan. Washington rather snidely wrote that Pinckney is unwilling "to loose [sic] any fame that can be acquired by the publication of his sentiments." Madison believed Pinckney's printing of a congressional speech on Mississippi navigation was "too delicate" a subject "to have been properly confided to the press," but made no such comment about the Convention plan. In December, when versions of Franklin's September 17 speech appeared in print, Madison complained only about inaccuracy. He did not view with concern the publication itself.[3]

In letters written in October, Madison made little effort to defend the Constitution as perfect. Pendleton criticized the clause relating to interstate vessel traffic and duties as not "sufficiently explicit." Madison agreed that the "expression is certainly not accurate." The reason was that it had been "dictated by the jealousy of some particular States, and was inserted pretty late in the Session." Irritation at certain states similarly characterized his explanation to William Short about "the irregularities which may be discovered in its structure and form." Madison still saw the Constitution in terms of strategic politics.[4]

Nevertheless, Madison's desire to explain and justify began to revise his understanding. In a letter to Jefferson, Madison wrote as an omniscient narrator analyzing the proceedings. He ascribed his theory of the Constitution to the entire Convention. It was "embraced" that the government should "operate without" the intervention of the states but on the "individuals composing them." Although he summarized the "scale of opinions" on contested issues, he presented the differences far more systematically than the debate portrayed in his Notes. For example, on the discussion over slavery and exports, he described four alternatives. He explained there had been a need to adjust "the different interests of different parts of the Continent." Madison declared that "S. Carolina & Georgia were inflexible on the point of the slaves." He offered no reason for why their inflexibility controlled others. A narrative was becoming fixed in Madison's mind in which these two states would carry the blame.[5]

The letter's portrayal of the Convention did not match the Notes. Descriptions diverged. On the executive term, Madison wrote "the propositions descended from good-behavior to four years, through the intermediate terms of nine, seven, six, & five years." In the Notes, however, he had recorded others on the longer side—twenty, fifteen, eleven, and eight years. Madison winnowed the claims. Some statements were inconsistent with the Notes. He claimed, "No proposition was made, no suggestion was thrown out, in favor of a partition of the Empire into two more Confederacies." Although no such motion had been advanced, the Notes repeated various threats along those lines. Other descriptions were misleading. "The little States insisted on retaining their equality in both branches, unless a compleat abolition of the State Governments should take place." Altering geographic lines had been an argument of the Delaware deputies for equal state suffrage—but it had not been the smallest states alone who were interested in altering state governments, nor was complete abolition the only ground on which the small states had been willing to consider proportional representation.[6]

Madison hinted at his dissenting opinions but did not explicitly claim responsibility. He noted, "a few would have preferred a tenure during good behaviour—a considerable number would have done so, in case an easy & effectual removal by impeachment could be settled." Jefferson may have guessed that the approving tone indicated that Madison counted himself among the "considerable number." Madison similarly commented, "It was warmly urged that the judiciary department should be associated in the revision." Again, Jefferson may have concluded that "warmly urged" referred to Madison's position. Madison remained annoyed about losing proportional representation. Because the government "was to operate directly" on the people, it should be "drawn principally from the people immediately." The issue, however, "ended in the compromise which you will see, but very much to the dissatisfaction of several members from the large States." Madison again implicitly placed himself among the several members. He similarly did not agree with the executive in general, commenting that "tedious and reiterated discussions" occurred.[7]

One defeat above all others irked Madison. He devoted a significant portion of the letter to the failed negative over state laws. He depicted a narrow loss after "repeated discussions" and a final rejection by only "a bare majority." Madison portrayed the negative as a mechanism to regulate the proper scope of state authority. The "due partition of power" between local and general governments had been "the most nice and difficult" object of the Convention. The negative fell along a spectrum of solutions: "an entire abolition of the states"; an "indefinite power of Legislation" in Congress with a negative on state laws; an indefinite power and no negative; limited power and a negative. Madison drew on the explanatory section of the eleventh vice (apparently written by this point) from his Vices notes. He omitted unnecessary passages (the complaint about Rhode Island paper money and the lengthy discourse on religion). He reused the material to promote the negative.[8]

As Madison wrote, his image of the Convention changed. The choices were laid out in far clearer and starker terms than delegates perceived at the time. Blame was placed on voting coalitions winning by bare majorities or minority states refusing to budge. Personalities also explained results. Randolph had been unwilling "to commit himself." Mason was in "exceeding ill humour," and the "impatience which prevailed towards the close of the business, conspired to whet his acrimony." Madison added that Mason "considers the want of a Bill of Rights" to be a "fatal objection" and would consequently "muster every possible" complaint. Madison seemed to assume that Jefferson would share his opinion, not theirs.[9]

This letter and the other letters did not rely on the Notes. Madison was drawing on his memory. The incomplete Notes may have even seemed somewhat irrelevant. As he explained to Jefferson, Congress had approved a new three-year term in Paris for Jefferson. The Notes were unlikely to be read anytime soon.[10]

Between November 1787 and February 1788, Madison wrote essays that further revised his understanding of the Convention. He joined Alexander Hamilton's project to defend the Constitution in essays for New York newspapers. The project did not require the defense to be based on Convention discussions. In fact, Hamilton had been absent for an extended period of time. Hamilton's choices for co-authors were John Jay, who had never attended, and Gouverneur Morris, who had been repeatedly absent. Morris, however, declined, and Jay was able to contribute only a few essays because of illness. By mid-November, Hamilton invited Madison to help. Why Hamilton chose Madison for a replacement is unknown. Their service on the final committee may have indicated some overlap in understanding. Madison many years later described his suggestion of Rufus King, another member of the final committee, as a "proper auxiliary." Hamilton and Madison, however, wrote the essays alone.[11]

Prior to the invitation, Hamilton had formulated the essays' purposes. He would rebut the claim, "whispered in the private circles," that the states were "too great an extent for any general system." The essays would also reject the notion that regional interests required "resort to separate confederacies." The essays would show that the Constitution created a successful republican government over a large territory to control local interests. As Hamilton phrased it, the essays would establish the "utility" of the union, the "insufficiency" of the current confederation, the need for an "energetic" government, and the Constitution's conformity with the "true principles of republican government."[12]

Working with Hamilton altered Madison's perspective, liberating him from his disappointments with the Convention. His personal disappointments and grievances were irrelevant. The goal was to persuade objectors to ratify by offering counter-interpretations of the Constitution. Prior to the Federalist essays, Madison was drawn to focus on the annoying ways in which the Constitution had failed to fulfill his theory and analysis. Writing the essays marked a new beginning.

Madison's initial contributions drew heavily on his various notes to support Hamilton's arguments. Madison joined the project as Hamilton reached the problem of "faction." Scholars assign Federalist 9 to Hamilton and Federalist 10 to Madison, but both essays address faction and were complementary to each other. Federalist 10 used sections of the notes on the Vices of the confederation, in particular, the extended eleventh item on the injustice of state laws, and the October 24 analysis for Jefferson. Although Madison again described diverse interests in an extended republic, he abandoned the suggestion that the Constitution offered a specific political remedy. In the extended eleventh vice, after describing an abstract "modification of the Sovereignty," he ended by recommending as an "auxiliary" aspiration, a "process of elections" to extract the "purest and noblest characters." In the October letter, he argued explicitly for a negative on state laws. In Federalist 10, he simply asserted that the problem of factions would be solved by the extended republic. Interests would never become sufficiently powerful to dominate. Although modern scholars consider the essay profound, Madison may have been disappointed at the omission of a structural solution. But complaints about the failure to adopt his solutions or suggestions of future amendments had no place in the essay.[13]

In December, Madison contributed four essays drawing on his various notes on ancient and modern confederations. Federalist 14 employed convoluted, rather overwrought language and calculations of various distances to answer an objection "drawn from the great extent of country which the union embraces." Federalist 18, 19, and 20 addressed the lessons of historic confederacies to support three earlier Hamilton essays describing the Confederation's flawed theory of acting on states instead of individuals (a position that Madison asserted in the spring of 1787 and at the Convention). By 1816, Madison acknowledged that Hamilton might have originally started the essays and Madison finished them. He wrote in a copy of the *Federalist* in 1818, "What had been prepared by Mr. H. who had entered more briefly into the subject, was left with Mr. M, on its appearing that the latter was engaged in it, with larger materials, & with a view to a more precise delineation; and from the pen of the latter the several papers went to the Press." Hamilton then wrote sixteen essays enumerating the various "defects" in the existing confederation.[14]

Only in Federalist 37 did Madison's distinctive perspective on the Convention appear. The January 1788 essay was his finest contribution. It described a Constitution drafted in Convention as the outcome of delegates struggling with the inherent shortcomings of language, differing concerns, and unknown implications of restructuring political power. He insisted that the Constitution did not—could not—embody a single political theory. It was not written by "an ingenious theorist" and "planned in his closet or in his imagination." He cautioned those who looked for an "artificial structure and regular symmetry." Repeatedly Madison insisted that the Constitution necessarily had faults and was imperfect. Drawing on his earlier letter, he explained that the Convention could only "avoid the errors suggested by the past experience" and provide a mode of "rectifying their own errors, as future experience may unfold them." He insisted on the impossibility of a Constitution that solved all governmental and interpretive issues. No political science could "discriminate and define" the three powers or branches. Laws were necessarily "more or less obscure and equivocal, until their meaning be liquidated and ascertained" by interpretation. Indeed, because the Constitution required new concepts, the "unavoidable inaccuracy" was even greater. The "contending interests and local jealousies" of the states had increased difficulties. These "extraneous considerations" had required the sacrifice of "theoretical propriety." In words similar to Franklin's recently published September 17 speech, Madison argued that many delegates were "induced to accede to it" by the "deep conviction" of "sacrificing private opinions and partial interest to the public good." The essay implied the author had been among those delegates. Federalist 37 insisted that the Constitution could not be read as the product of a single intent.[15]

In the succeeding essays, Madison tried to mollify objectors. He argued that it was not necessary that the Constitution "should be perfect; it is sufficient" that the Articles of Confederation were "more imperfect." The argument of Federalist 38—anything was better than the Articles—was not by itself particularly persuasive. In Federalist 39, Madison insisted that fundamental allegations about the Constitution were inaccurate. It was "neither a national or a federal constitution; but a composition of both." Madison's bias was still apparent: the "national countenance of the Government" was "disfigured by a few federal features," but such a "blemish is perhaps unavoidable in any plan." In Federalist 40, he sought to legitimize the Convention's authority by describing the Constitution as "an expansion of principles" in the Articles instead of being "absolutely new." The "degree of enlargement" gave the "new system, the aspect of an entire transformation of the old." Madison did not seem persuaded himself. He argued alternatively that, if the Convention had exceeded its powers, "the means should be sacrificed to the end" to "accomplish the views and happiness of the people of America." Madison was trying to advance arguments that he did not embrace, but he remained reluctant to concede the points entirely.[16]

Slowly, Madison became comfortable with arguments designed to counter opposition interpretations. When Madison turned to discuss the general welfare clause in Federalist 41, he referred to the Convention. He sought to rebut the "very fierce attack" that the general welfare clause was "an unlimited commission to exercise every power which may be alledged to be necessary for the common defence or welfare." Madison pointed to the semicolon, instead of the "longer pause" of a period, as supporting the interpretation. As Madison knew, these arguments diverged from alternative interpretations of the Convention's records. The clause in the Constitution and the Articles used different language. The printed drafts seemed to indicate that the period became a semicolon after the September 12 draft; indeed, on Washington's amended copy, no change was reflected. In the essay, Madison ended by suggesting that the clause had been copied from the Articles and the opponents would not have been ones to argue that the Confederation Congress had such power. Madison, however, had at one time hoped the Confederation Congress did indeed have broader powers.[17]

For the subsequent two essays, Madison drew on the Notes but revised the material to create the impression of a uniform, consensus interpretation. In Federalist 42, Madison rewrote his speech in the Convention into the general intent of the delegates. The essay adopted the reasons and order of his August 17 speech on congressional power over felonies and crimes at sea: vagueness of felony at common law; problems of English statutes; issue of foreign law; problem of state laws; advantage in uniformity; and the power of definition. Madison's ideas became the collective understanding. In Federalist 43, Madison took the opposite approach with respect to the treason clause. He erased concerns at the Convention—including his own—about the language. At length, the delegates in the Notes argued over the language. Madison had initially complained that "the definition [was] too narrow" and worried about the possibility that the states held authority to punish treason. Certain states had voted against the addition of "confession in open court" because the words were "superfluous." The Notes left ambiguous whether anyone—never mind, everyone—was completely satisfied with the language. The Federalist essay, however, ignored the Notes and the disputes. The essay insisted that the Convention had inserted a "constitutional definition of the crime" and "proof."[18]

Madison was creating arguments. That is not to say that they may not have been stated by some delegates or imagined by others. But the Federalist essays were products of Madison's mind after the Convention. The Notes provided little help because they had not focused on the interpretive problems that were arising in the debates over ratification. In fact, where Madison knew the drafting history, he likely considered it advisable not to reveal it. For example, in Federalist 56, Madison defended in general terms the constitutional requirement of "a representative for every thirty thousand inhabitants" as guaranteeing "both a safe and competent guardian." He knew, however, how that precise number occurred in the Constitution. On the last day, possibly at the request of Washington, the delegates agreed to substitute thirty thousand for the forty thousand on the engrossed Constitution. To explain a change on September 17 in deference to the Convention's presiding officer hardly seemed appropriate.[19]

Despite Madison's insistence in Federalist 37 that the Constitution was not planned by a single mind or a single theory, the essays gradually began to reshape the Convention as proceeding logically through alternatives and choosing the least objectionable. In Federalist 44, while considering the clause giving the government power "To make all Laws which shall be necessary and proper for carrying into Execution the foregoing Powers," Madison surveyed alternatives to the clause's language. He assumed the power needed to exist: "Without the *substance* of this power, the whole Constitution would be a dead letter." First, the delegates could have followed the Articles' approach of expressly delegated powers. Madison rejected the idea as requiring constant recurrence to the "doctrine of *construction* or *implication*." The government would be forced to either betray the public interest and do nothing or violate the Constitution by using the powers. Second, the delegates could have attempted "a positive enumeration." That approach, however, would require a "complete digest of laws" and "all the possible changes which futurity may produce." Third, a "negative enumeration" could have been used but was equally "chimerical." Lastly, the Constitution could remain silent, "leaving these necessary and proper powers, to construction and inference." Madison thought silence was pointless because "[n]o axiom is more clearly established in law, or in reason, than that wherever the end is required, the means are authorised." In the end, the clause was the best choice, and "a better form" could "not have been substituted." In this moment, Madison's rationale seemed to reflect his personal analysis.[20]

Despite the effort to rationalize the Constitution, Madison had not altered some of his core beliefs. He criticized the government under the Articles as a compact with no "higher sanction than a mere legislative ratification." He emphasized the "examples of antient and modern confederacies" that showed the tendency of "the members to despoil the general Government." He remained convinced that the legislative department draws "all power into its impetuous vortex." He repeatedly emphasized that the "maxim"—the "legislative, executive and judiciary departments ought to be separate and distinct"—did "not mean that these departments ought to have no *partial agency* in, or no *controul* over the acts of each other." He alluded to the desire for "some qualified connection between this weaker department" (the executive) and "the weaker branch of the stronger department" (the Senate). He thought it possibly that "a people spread over an extensive region" would still be "subject to the infection of violent passions; or to the danger of combining in the pursuit of unjust measures." He remained worried about the small states. If the structure was "insufficient to subdue the unjust policy of the smaller states, or their predominant influence in the councils of the senate," the larger states could fall back on the fact that "they hold the purse." Scattered throughout the essays, Madison hinted at his discontent.[21]

Although Madison tended to write with the voice of an omniscient narrator, he became confessional in discussing the three-fifths clause in Federalist 54. At the end of the essay, Madison acknowledged that the reasoning behind the clause "may appear to be a little strained." He insisted, however, "on the whole, I must confess, that it fully reconciles me to the scale of representation, which the Convention have established." Writing in the voice of "our southern brethren," Madison explained that "our slaves" had "the mixt character of persons and of property." He acknowledged that if "the laws were to restore the rights which had been taken away, the negroes could no longer be refused an equal share of representation." But Madison devoted no space to those like Morris who had given speeches against slavery at the Convention. Instead, he approvingly described the "compromising expedient of the Constitution . . . which regards them as inhabitants, but as debased by servitude below the equal level of free inhabitants, which regards the *slave* as divested of two fifths of the *man.*" Madison then indulged in a long soliloquy about the importance of the representation of property—seemingly a euphemism for slavery—in government. The arguments were reminiscent of his attempt at the Convention to justify a bicameral legislature founded on the regional division over the legality of slavery. Madison again presented his opinions justifying the three-fifths clause as those of the entire group of delegates.[22]

Madison's last essays on the Senate returned to the theme of Federalist 37, his most significant essay, and his perpetual fascination with ancient confederacies and the problem of the extended republic. In Federalist 62, he emphasized that the Constitution was not based on a single theory. In describing equal state suffrage, he wrote, "it is superfluous to try by the standard of theory, a part of the constitution which is allowed on all hands to be the result not of theory." As evidence, Madison quoted the Convention's letter to Congress. The Constitution was the result " 'of a spirit of amity, and that mutual deference and concession which the peculiarity of our political situation rendered indispensable.' " Madison criticized the "fruitless anticipation of the possible mischiefs" instead of the contemplation of "advantageous consequences." In Federalist 63, Madison emphasized that the fact that an extensive republic would likely prevent interests from assembling "ought not to be considered as superseding the use of auxiliary precautions" such as a Senate. The end of the essay happily returned to survey ancient confederacies for insights on the Senate.[23]

Then Madison stopped writing. Hamilton wrote twenty-one additional essays about the judiciary and the executive—topics that had never particularly interested Madison at the Convention. The process of writing anonymously encouraged Madison to conflate his thoughts with those of the Convention and, conversely, to advance arguments that diverged from his descriptions in the Notes. Instead of the political struggles depicted in the Notes, Madison presented a rational process of analysis and resolution. He described multiple paths, explained which one had the fewest objections, and then argued the Convention had taken that one. Although he insisted that the Constitution could not be understood as the product of a single theorist or theory, the essays converted the complicated political process into the thoughts of a single mind.

Madison knew that the essays did not necessarily reflect his beliefs. He wrote to Jefferson, "Though carried in concert, the writers are not mutually answerable for all the ideas of each other there being seldom time for even a perusal of the pieces by any but the writer before they were wanted at the press and sometimes hardly by the writer himself." Jefferson reassured him that in "some parts it is discoverable that the author means only to say what may be best said in defence of opinions in which he does not concur." The essays were a political strategy, one that further distanced Madison from the Convention.[24]

At the Virginia ratification convention in June 1788, Madison faced attack for positions he had held at the Convention. Again, he advanced explanations that differed from the Notes. Even before the Virginia Convention, he planned to draw on his participation at the Philadelphia Convention. He would address objections that "proceed from a misconception of the plan, or of the causes which produced the objectionable parts of it," and "contribute some explanations and informations which may be of use." Madison did not expect to limit his justification to those from the Convention. King wrote Madison that the ratification debate should include "every reasonable explanation" as well as "arguments really new" in support of the Constitution.[25]

By the summer of 1788, references to the Convention had been made at other conventions and in essays. An American observer in London commented derisively on "the petty dialogues and paltry anecdotes" about "conventional committees and private conversations." Delegates disagreed over recollections. In the Massachusetts convention, Gerry described the vote on the right of suffrage in the Senate as 6 to 5, adding "if my memory serves me." He disagreed with a prior explanation for equal representation in the Senate as only a "partial narrative of facts." Similarly, Caleb Strong apologized because his "memory was not sufficiently retentive to enable him immediately" to recollect the reason for biennial elections instead of annual ones. In South Carolina, Pierce Butler "endeavor[ed] to recollect the reasons" that guided the committee that drafted the impeachment clause. Personal notes were cited as evidence. In Maryland, Luther Martin supported his account "not merely from my own recollection but from minutes which I believe to be very correct, in my possession." James McHenry offered an explanation to John Carroll, noting it was "copied in substance from my note book of the transactions of the convention, which I wrote down daily, and is besides fresh in my memory so there can be no mistake upon my part." In New York, Lansing and Hamilton debated the "intention of the framers of the Constitution" with respect to the Senate. In October 1788, Lansing transcribed and shared "Judge Yates's Information," apparently on Hamilton's opinions at the Convention. These references spread by word, letter, and printed debates of ratification conventions. Madison was sent "about sixty pages of the debates" of the Pennsylvania Convention and the "address of the minority" at the Maryland ratification convention. By the time the Virginia Convention assembled in June 1788, the Philadelphia Convention was disputed territory.[26]

Two accusations about the Convention caused particular consternation. The first allegation was that some delegates wanted to abolish the state governments. In the New York convention, Lansing claimed that Hamilton suggested "the state governments ought to be subverted." Hamilton interrupted him. The exchange "produced a warm personal altercation between those gentlemen, which engrossed the remainder of the day." The second allegation was that certain delegates had aspired to a monarchical style of government. In May 1788, Daniel Carroll wrote Madison about a rumor that "more than 20 Members of the Convention were in favor of a Kingly Government." Carroll's letter raises the possibility that Madison's name was involved. McHenry allegedly had a list of monarchists on his printed August draft. McHenry, in turn, said that "the names having *for* annexed to them, Mr. Mercer said, were for a king." John Mercer, however, insisted that the list had referred to "a National Gov[ernmen]t," not a monarchical one. Mercer, a Maryland delegate, had briefly attended, only from the committee of detail report to mid-August. The accusation raised concerns for political careers. Carroll believed that he not been elected to the Confederation Congress because of the list. Statements at the Convention were being seen as politically fatal.[27]

By the time the Virginia Convention began on June 2, 1788, the Constitution was close to ratification. Eight states had ratified (Delaware, Pennsylvania, New Jersey, Georgia, Connecticut, Massachusetts, Maryland, and South Carolina). On June 21, New Hampshire ratified, making it the decisive ninth state. As Pauline Maier notes, "Information traveled slowly in the eighteenth century." The Virginians were unlikely to have known the status of the New Hampshire ratification. Moreover, without two geographically critical states—New York and Virginia—even the ratification of the other states might be meaningless. The New York convention began on June 17, ratifying in late July. Virginia ratified on June 25 by a narrow vote of 89–79.[28]

At the Virginia Convention, for the first time Madison had to deal with the possibility that his words would be recorded in print. The ratification process had encouraged the popularity of printed debates. The Convention was open to the public. David Robertson was permitted to take shorthand notes and publish the debates. In the summer of 1788, however, only the first week (June 2–9) of Robertson's debates appeared in print. The remainder did not appear until 1789. Although Robertson knew shorthand, he had difficulty hearing certain speakers, including Madison. The printed speeches differed from members' recollections. Madison described "laughing" with William Grayson "over a paragraph in one of his speeches." The printed debates remained a product of partial memory and generous extrapolation.[29]

From the outset of the Virginia Convention, Madison faced allegations about his positions. Patrick Henry and George Mason accused the Philadelphia delegates of planning to destroy the states and form a national government tilted towards monarchy. Henry sarcastically referred to "those worthy characters" who felt "the necessity of forming a great consolidated Government." Mason declared that the Constitution would "annihilate totally the State Governments." The states needed to be made secure "by drawing the line between the general and State Governments." Henry alleged that the Constitution "squints towards monarchy." He predicted it would produce a "Consolidated Government" in which the "Government of Virginia" would no longer be a "State Government." These words—"consolidation," "annihilation," "monarchy"—became opponents' characterization of the Constitution's creation of a national government.[30]

The accusations infuriated Randolph and Madison. Although Randolph's early disappointments had led him to refrain from signing the Constitution, he was a strong advocate of ratification in the Virginia Convention. On June 9, after one remark by Henry, Randolph gave a lengthy speech disdaining the legendary orator's "aspersions, and his insinuations" and declaring them not "compatible with the least shadow of friendship." On June 19, when Mason insinuated that some intended the Constitution to produce a "national consolidated government" and "destroy the state governments," Madison "interrupted" and asked "who the gentlemen were to whom he alluded." Mason retreated, stating that neither Madison nor the other Virginia delegates advocated it. Shortly thereafter, Mason noted that "his memory had never been good, and was now much impaired from his age."[31]

In the volume of debates published by Robertson that summer, Madison made no overtly controversial comments. He initially demurred from speaking at any length. When Madison spoke, his voice was too "low" to record accurately. His rambling remarks adopted a moderate position, arguing that the government was "not completely consolidated,—nor is it entirely federal." He sought refuge in history, drawing on "a review of ancient and modern Confederacies," summarizing various confederacies and reading "sundry passages" on Holland. He focused on problems under the Confederation and avoided discussing the Convention. Then he became sick and was "laid up with a bilious attack." Until the summer of 1789, only these comments by Madison appeared in print.[32]

In the latter part of the Convention, however, Madison referred to the Philadelphia Convention and repeatedly implied a single universal intent of the delegates. On Article I, sixth section, clause eight, Madison explained "such considerations as led the convention to approve." On the third section, he gave the "reason of the exception." On the fourth and fifth sections, he discussed what "was thought." In places, he described his positions as if they had been those of the entire group. It would have been "dishonorable to have recourse" to the British law of felony and so a "technical term of the law of nations is therefore used." On another clause relating to congressional power, Madison commented that it was not "within the limits of human capacity" to "delineate on paper, all those particular cases and circumstances in which legislation by the general legislature would be necessary, and leave to the states all the other powers." Therefore, the "particular powers which are found necessary to be given, are therefore delegated generally, and particular and minute specification is left to the legislature." Although some explanations may have accorded with the delegates' general understandings, others were his beliefs or new rationales created for the Virginia audience. His goal was to obtain ratification. A comment by Henry Lee of Westmoreland reveals the strategy. Madison and Randolph, who were "in the Grand Convention have proved incontestably, that the fears arising from the powers of congress, are groundless."[33]

On occasion, Madison cagily distanced himself from the Convention. With Randolph now favoring ratification, Madison admitted a "peculiar difficulty in that of the Executive." He stated, "according to my view . . .

a more accurate attention" might have "exclude[d] some of the objections now made to it." Nevertheless, the section deserved "the indulgence of a fair and liberal interpretation" because "precision was not so easily obtained as may be imagined." Although he described the "reasoning of some gentlemen" in the debate over a two-thirds vote for commerce regulation, he also noted, "I wish I could recollect the history of this matter, but I cannot call it to mind with sufficient exactness." Madison's memory—or lack thereof—seemed on occasion to relate to his current political purposes.[34]

Slavery produced a lengthy description of the Convention. Madison referenced the debate over the foreign slave trade. He blamed Georgia and South Carolina. He asserted that the "southern states would not have entered" otherwise into the union. He spoke almost as if quoting particular comments at the Convention:

> The gentlemen from South-Carolina and Georgia argued in this manner:—"We have now liberty to import this species of property, and much of the property now possessed, has been purchased, or otherwise acquired, in contemplation of improving it by the assistance of imported slaves. What would be the consequence of hindering us from it? The slaves of Virginia would rise in value, and we would be obliged to go to your markets."

The Notes, however, most similar to these occur on August 22 and eventually described only the concern about the rise in value of Virginia's slaves. If the other comments appeared in Madison's rough notes from the Convention, he refrained from including them. Similarly, although the Notes indicated opposition to the foreign slave trade, at the Virginia Convention, Madison described no such controversy. He commented, "Great as the evil is, a dismemberment of the union would be worse." Madison offered no hint at his own role in instigating the focus on slavery but placed blame squarely on two states south of Virginia.[35]

Madison depicted proslavery protections of the Constitution. The Virginia convention, with nearly 300,000 people enslaved in the state (almost half the people held in slavery in the United States), was a different context from Philadelphia. Madison stated that the fugitive slave clause offered "a better security than any that now exists." According to Madison, a person escaping to a free state under the Articles of Confederation "becomes emancipated" by the laws of the free state. The fugitive slave clause therefore was "expressly inserted to enable owners of slaves to reclaim them." Madison similarly argued that there was "no power to warrant" ending slavery "in that paper" (the Constitution). Addressing possible power under the general welfare power, Madison pointed to southern political strength: "Can any one believe, that the American councils will come into a measure which will strip them of their property, discourage, and alienate the affections of five-thirteenths of the union." In essence, if two southern states had been able to force the foreign slave trade provision on the rest, political power would continue to protect southern slaveholders. To reassure the Virginians, Madison depicted a Constitution grounded in acceptance of slavery.[36]

Madison presented only some of Jefferson's likely influential views. Despite protesting that it is not "right for me to unfold what he has informed me," Madison described Jefferson as "captivated with the equality of suffrage in the senate." He omitted Jefferson's lengthy and thoughtful criticisms, in particular, relating to the absence of a bill of rights. Madison was sufficiently aware of the slant to confess to Jefferson that he had taken "the liberty to state some of your opinions on the favorable side."[37]

Despite Madison's apparent care with his comments, he found his views at the Virginia Convention made him politically vulnerable. Unlike many Virginians, Madison worried about adding a list of rights. Patrick Henry insisted that Madison was not "to be trusted with *amendments*" since he had argued that "not a [letter of the Constitution cou[l]d be spared." Madison lost the election to the Senate—although standard historical accounts argue that he did not really want the position.[38]

When Madison sought election to the House of Representatives, his comments remained an obstacle. Opponents described Madison's statements at the Virginia Convention that the Constitution was "the nearest to Perfection of any thing that Could be obtained." Rumors circulated that Madison was suppressing the second volume of the Virginia Convention debates to hide evidence of his opinions "until the Election should be over." Madison wrote letters declaring that the Constitution "ought to be revised" to include "all essential rights, particularly the rights of Conscience in the fullest latitude, the freedom of the press, trials by jury, security against general warrants &c." The new position proved successful. In mid-February 1789, he was elected to the House of Representatives.[39]

Amidst the effort to ensure election to Congress, Madison learned that Jefferson hoped to return briefly to the United States. In November 1788, Jefferson wrote that he hoped to return "for the summer only" and "pass as much time as possible with you." That December, Madison wrote Washington, Randolph, and Jefferson about a future "task" that he had planned to do during the congressional recess. He noted to Washington that it would be assisted by having access to the papers of Congress. If Madison contemplated copying the official journals of the Convention in order to complete the Notes, he might have believed the journals were stored with congressional papers. Madison, however, proceeded to Virginia to secure election. The Notes remained incomplete.[40]

In the spring of 1789, the new government slowly assembled in New York. By late June, Madison was awed by the challenge. He wrote to Jefferson: "We are in the wilderness without a single footstep to guide us. Our successors will have an easier task. And by degrees the way will become smooth short and certain." Madison liked his analogy and reused it in a letter to his father. Others understood the "great many perplexities in your progress of carrying the Constitution into effect." Transition from government under the Articles to government under the Constitution raised numerous questions.[41]

As a member of the new House of Representatives, Madison also confronted a shift toward greater public access to legislative proceedings. Although the Senate adopted the older closed-door approach, the House of Representatives permitted reporters and printed debates. Madison promptly sent the first printing of the *Congressional Register* to Jefferson so he would have "*some idea* of the discussions in the new Legislature." Madison complained about inaccuracy. He sniped, "You will see at once the strongest evidences of mutilation & perversion, and of the illiteracy of the Editor." After reading the printed debates, Henry Lee wrote Madison about the "contradictions which seem occasionally to be exhibited by the same speaker, the lameness of stile & crudeness of matter." In particular, Madison's speeches were difficult to record. "Mr. Madison spoke low," the *Gazette* commented, and its reporter was unable to follow a speech displaying "great theoretical knowledge of the general subjects of discussion." Inaccuracy was a problem, but it permitted speakers to disassociate themselves from comments after the fact.[42]

Sporadically during the first months, the members addressed the Constitution's meaning. In early May, Madison's Virginia colleague, Theodorick Bland, argued that a duty on coasting vessels was unconstitutional. Bland advanced an interpretation making duties largely impossible. Madison argued "the construction of the article [was] simple, and easy to comprehend." Bland lost. A newspaper described the argument over the "true meaning of the clause." Conversely, in a debate over regulation of the time and manner of oath administration for state officers, Elbridge Gerry argued that the Constitution did not give Congress the power unless resort was made to the necessary and proper clause. Bland and others asserted that Congress had the power under the supremacy clause and the oaths clause. In a debate over the duration of the revenue bill, Madison argued that the "spirit of the Constitution, and the structure of the government, rendered it improper to pass a perpetual revenue law." The Constitution was susceptible to multiple interpretations.[43]

The Constitution's relationship to slavery arose almost immediately. On May 13, 1789, Virginia representative Josiah Parker unsuccessfully moved for a duty on imported slaves of ten dollars. Parker wished the Constitution had prohibited "importation altogether." James Jackson of Georgia argued that, although "the fashion of the day" was to "favor the liberty of slaves," the slaves were "better off in their present situation, than they would be if they were manumitted." Madison occupied a middle ground. The government was prevented from a total prohibition on importation by the "terms of Constitution and principles of justice." The Constitution, however, had been "formed" to "give some testimony of the conscience of America, with respect to the nature of the African trade." Madison saw the Constitution as representing a compromise.[44]

One particular controversy over interpretation fascinated Madison. As the House began to draft legislation establishing the three executive departments (foreign affairs, treasury, and war), dispute arose over a provision that permitted the president to remove the heads of the departments. Fisher Ames from Massachusetts explained the difficulty: "It must be admitted, that the constitution is not explicit on the point in contest; yet the constitution strongly infers, that the power is in the president alone." The removal power was debated extensively in May and mid-June 1789.[45]

Madison was the principal spokesperson favoring executive removal power. In May, he argued from structural principles. The removal power was "absolutely necessary" so that the president would be "in a peculiar manner, responsible" for the conduct of subordinate officers. It would be a "fatal error" to have officers serving by "tenure of good behavior" and removable only by congressional impeachment. The principle that executive officers have the "highest possible degree of responsibility" was "one of the most prominent features of the constitution" and a principle that "pervades the whole system." To lessen the responsibility was contrary to the "spirit and intention" of the Constitution. Only if "saddled upon us expressly by the letter of that work," could executive responsibility be limited.[46]

By mid-June, Madison shifted toward a separation-of-powers analysis. He acknowledged that the Constitution "does not perfectly correspond with the ideas I entertained of it from the first glance." In speeches from June 16 to June 22, Madison emphasized separation of powers. He explained, "We ought always to consider the constitution with an eye to the principles upon which it was founded." The power to displace officers was an executive power and not a legislative power. As an executive power, it belonged to the president under Article II ("The executive power shall be vested in the President"). Madison argued that his interpretation "expresses the meaning of the constitution" as "by fair construction" and consistent with "liberty."[47]

Members were uncertain. Some disagreed with Madison as a privileged interpreter of the Constitution. South Carolina's William Smith acknowledged Madison as a gentleman "of great abilities" and a "member of the convention that formed the constitution." Nonetheless, Smith rejected the argument that "all powers incidental to the executive department, are vested in the president." Another member, Pennsylvania's Thomas Hartley, "owned he had some doubts" and thought others "might be in the same predicament." He believed that the president could exercise the "prerogative" despite being "not fully convinced that the power of removal vested by the constitution in the president." Interpreting the Constitution was turning out to be difficult.[48]

Madison loved the "very interesting discussion" over the removal power. He noted that, in the published debates, "the reasonings on both sides are mutilated, often misapprehended, and not unfrequently reversed." Madison emphasized the textual "silence." The Constitution "has omitted to declare expressly by what authority removals from office are to be made." Adopting his favorite form of analysis—describing possible, logical positions—Madison laid out four "constructive doctrines." The final interpretation favored executive removal power as "most consonant to the frame of the Constitution." It satisfied "the policy of mixing the Legislative & Executive powers as little as possible." It accorded with "the responsibility necessary in the head of the Executive Department." Madison assumed the removal debate was not unique in its interpretive challenges. In words reminiscent of Federalist 37, he declared that "the exposition of the Constitution is frequently a copious source, and must continue so until its meaning on all great points shall have been settled by precedents."[49]

Simultaneously, Madison sought to amend the Constitution. He had promised to favor amendments and, on May 4, announced that he would propose amendments. He wrote Jefferson that the amendments would include a "Bill of rights, incorporated perhaps into the Constitution." The addition of amendments was not at all inevitable. When the issue was raised on June 8, other members thought amendments should wait. Roger Sherman noted that the congressional agenda was rather full: the executive needed to be organized; the judiciary had not yet been created; and revenue issues remained incomplete. Nonetheless, Madison gave his famous, lengthy speech introducing and explaining his proposed amendments. Madison promptly sent the newspaper report to Jefferson on the "form and extent" of his amendments.[50]

Madison wanted a revised Constitution. He proposed incorporating the language into the Constitution's text in the same way that alterations to the printed drafts had been made at the Convention. He wanted to alter the apportionment clause to regulate the number of representatives. In that respect, he had "always thought" that "part of the constitution defective, though not dangerous." He added a provision that barred the legislature from varying sitting members' compensation. Compensation was not "likely to be abused," but nonetheless the Constitution permitted a "seeming impropriety." He offered a provision preventing appeals to the Supreme Court for small debt. The amendments were cast as mild improvements. Madison was most lukewarm about an amendment that followed those "proposed by the state conventions" and declared the existence of reserved powers in the states. The words would do "no harm," although they might "be considered as superfluous" and "deemed unnecessary." Likely influenced by the removal debate, he included an amendment describing a principle of separation of departments or powers. Much later in the summer, he commented that the amendment would "serve to explain many cases that may arise under the Constitution, and can do no harm."[51]

The proposed amendments also included rights. Some of Madison's rights were reminiscent of his description in the Notes of Pinckney's proposed rights. Language stated that the list did not include all rights, addressing Madison's concern that the enumeration of "particular exceptions" would "disparage those rights" not included. The "equal right of conscience, freedom of the press," as well as criminal trial by jury, were applied to the states to prevent "the abuse of certain powers in the state legislatures." Later in the summer, Madison argued this amendment ("No State shall violate the equal rights of conscience, or the freedom of the press, or the trial by jury in criminal cases") was "the most valuable amendment on the whole list." Madison was still hoping to restrain the power of the state legislatures.[52]

For Madison, the rights fit within his understanding of the Constitution. The government was given significant powers. As he explained, "even if government keeps within those limits, it has certain discretionary powers with respect to the means." Moreover, the necessary and proper clause "enables them to fulfil every purpose for which the government was established." Rights might "tend to prevent the exercise of undue power." The future judiciary would serve "in a peculiar manner the guardians of those rights." Although Madison acknowledged that rights might be thought "paper barriers," he argued that they "have a tendency to impress some degree of respect" and might be a means "to control the majority."[53]

Although Madison planned to integrate or interweave the amendments into the text of the Constitution, Roger Sherman insisted that they must be "supplemental" clauses. Those members favoring supplemental amendments argued that the original document had a special status. The "sacred constitution" was "lodged in the archives of Congress." The "long and animated debate" was "very ingenious and interesting." Eventually, Sherman's position proved successful. The amendments would be listed separately. As a consequence, the original Constitution and the Convention that wrote it remained significant.[54]

Madison was not comfortable with the implicit suggestion that the Convention had been engaged in a "sacred" endeavor. Sherman wanted members to change the alterations made on the last day of the Convention to the size of the House of Representatives. The size of a representative's district was dropped from 40,000 to 30,000 persons. Sherman described the change as if it had been illegitimate. He claimed that, throughout the Convention "a majority" had favored 40,000 and the change arose "after the constitution was agreed to" and at the wish of George Washington. Madison asked members to "not be influenced by what had been related to have passed in the convention." They should "determine upon their own sense of propriety." For Madison, the history of the Convention was not necessarily binding.[55]

Eventually, on August 24, 1789, the House sent seventeen amendments to the Senate. Madison's influence remained strong: a redesign of apportionment; a limit on altering compensation; a list of rights; an explicit bar on state infringement of speech, press, conscience, and juries in criminal cases; a statement preventing the enumeration from denying or disparaging other rights; a declaration regarding separation of powers; and an affirmation of the states' reservation of certain powers. Behind closed doors, the Senate significantly altered the amendments. A month later, on September 28, 1789, twelve amendments were finally approved by both houses and signed by the speaker. They were subsequently sent to the states for ratification. The first and second amendments addressed apportionment and compensation; amendments three through twelve were what would become known as the bill of rights.[56]

The debate over amendments once again reshaped Madison's understanding of the Convention. Over the preceding two years, Madison's explanations had varied considerably. He showed little inclination to interpret the Constitution solely from the stance of the Convention. He embraced a robust method of interpretation—spirit, principles, structure, text—with a pragmatic desire to make the government function. Yet the loss of his approach to amendments indicated that the Convention might retain relevance. With the amendments supplement, the text created by the Convention remained visually intact. The reference to the Constitution as "sacred" recast the Convention as involved in an endeavor greater than an operational government. By August 1789, Madison glimpsed a future in which the Convention was more than simply successful. For the first time in two years, the Notes taken for himself and Jefferson acquired a new, potentially significant purpose.

V

COMPLETING THE NOTES

9

CORRECTING AND
REVISING THE NOTES

Jefferson's return and Madison's growing awareness that the 1787 Constitution would remain untouched, despite amendments, made completion of the Notes a worthwhile endeavor. In the fall of 1789, Madison turned back to the Notes. Although Edmund Randolph warned of the inevitability of mingling events of the Convention with subsequent discussions, the advice was disregarded. For assistance, Madison made a personal copy of the official Convention journals. He then integrated material from this Journal Copy with his remaining rough notes. As he composed the Notes after August 21, he may have recast his comments and speeches. Madison also revised the Notes, adding and detailing procedural details. Three new sheets with his early June speeches also replaced less satisfactory original versions.

These changes and many small editorial revisions began to transform the Notes from a diary into a report of debates. The integration of the official journals gave new attention to procedural and textual details. Replacement of the June speeches cast a political coherence over Madison's opinions. For Madison, the project also had consequences. As the Convention retreated into the memory of many delegates, Madison became more committed to his revised version. Although the Convention was history, the work of revision made it seem deceptively present.

In the fall of 1789, Madison expected that Jefferson would return from France. Jefferson had asked permission to return, and, in late June, Madison had forwarded to him approval from John Jay. The delay in transatlantic correspondence, however, left uncertain the timing. In September, Madison heard that "Mr. Jefferson is expected to arrive soon." In early

October, Madison thought that "Mr. Jefferson may be daily expected." In November, Madison told Jefferson he could not wait any longer for him. Eventually, Madison received a letter that implied an arrival near the beginning of December.[1]

After returning to the United States, Jefferson was expected to join the new government. On September 26, the Senate confirmed Jefferson's appointment as secretary of state. If accepted, he would join an impressive array in the administration: John Adams as vice-president, Alexander Hamilton as secretary of treasury, Henry Knox as secretary of war, and Edmund Randolph as attorney general. Washington, Hamilton, and Randolph had been at the Convention. Adams was abroad but returned to participate in the Massachusetts ratification. Knox was secretary of war during the Confederation and an active advocate behind the scenes favoring the Convention and ratification. Jefferson was the only high-level officer who was absent during the entire period. The Notes of the Convention might be helpful in familiarizing him with decisions and issues.[2]

In late August 1789, Madison read over the first days of the Notes. He found them unsatisfactory. He explained to Edmund Randolph that he had been "looking over the notes" of Randolph's "introductory discourse" at the Convention. Madison was "anxious for particular reasons to be furnished with the means of preserving this as well as the other arguments in that body." His request was made "with an earnestness" permitting no "delay."[3]

Madison wanted Randolph to write the initial speech introducing the Virginia plan in May 1787. The Notes did not allow Madison to "do justice to the substance of it." The original entry merely stated:

> M^r. Randolph opened the main business in a long speech in which he pointed the various defects of the federal system, the necessity of transforming it into a national efficient Government, and the extreme danger of delaying this great work, concluding with sundry propositions as the outlines of a proper form.

The brief summary did not elaborate the underlying purposes. Moreover, by August 1789 the description was open to misinterpretation. After the ratification debates, a "federal" system was good rather than defective. In contrast, words such as "national" and "efficient" system might be read as a plan to abolish the states. The failure to include the speech in detail also implied a lack of precision about the Notes as a reliable record. As a solution, Madison wanted Randolph to "make out & forward me the scope of your reasoning." The two-year hiatus was of no concern to Madison.[4]

Randolph refused. He sent Madison his original notes for the speech. Randolph commented that he did not care "as to the form, in which they are submitted to the eye of a friend." "Friend" may have included Jefferson as well as Madison. Nevertheless, Randolph offered an apparent warning. He did not recreate—in his words, "dilate"—the speech. He "found it impossible to retrace the subject" from his notes. More importantly, he would "mingle inadvertently much of what I have heard since, without being able to separate it from what occurred then." For Randolph, it was impossible to recover his precise thoughts of May 1787.[5]

Although Madison would ignore Randolph's caution, he faced similar frustrations over the discrepancy between actual speeches and the versions published in contemporaneous printed debates of Congress. In late September, the House debated the lack of accuracy in printed reports of congressional debates. One representative, South Carolina's Aedanus Burke, was infuriated at the "glaring deviations from the truth" and the "thick veil of misrepresentation and error." Reporters wrote arguments that were contradictory and sometimes "never made." They mutilated and suppressed statements. They favored certain members and certain issues. Madison also had seen "very great misconceptions" of his speeches. If the House sanctioned printed debates, however, Madison believed members could not disregard the printed versions of speeches. Madison explained that he was "not responsible" for the reports of his speeches. He did not want to deal with the "inconvenience" and "the trouble of correcting and revising" them. The phrase—correcting and revising—was neatly ambiguous and implied ensuring accuracy and rewriting to counter misinterpretation.[6]

The failure to correct and revise a speech created problems for Madison that month. One of his political correspondents, Tench Coxe, had read "with considerable alarm a statement of one of your Speeches" in the printed debates. Madison had commented about "the deportment of Congress . . . and upon the qualities or characters of some of the members." Another friend, John Dawson, wrote that the comments had been "the subject of general conversation—that it had excited the apprehensions of many, and the displeasure of some." Madison blamed the printed report. It omitted "the occasion which produced" the comments. Moreover, it "interpolates personal reflections which I never meant, w[hi]ch could not properly be expressed, and which I am assured by a number of gentlemen attending at the time, was not countenanced by any thing that fell from me." Madison subsequently corrected the comment in the newspaper.[7]

The new congressional printed debates raised an additional problem for the Notes. The Notes contained comparatively little procedural information about motions and textual alterations. The rough notes for the end of the Convention were likely skeletal and difficult to decipher. The obvious guide to the Convention—the official Convention journals—had not been published. By unknown means, sometime likely in September and October 1789, Madison acquired temporary possession of the official Convention journals. He presumably borrowed them from Washington; however, no record of the transfer has been discovered. The consistency in composition suggests that he copied them relatively quickly. However Madison acquired access to the original journal, the Journal Copy suggests that he perceived his opportunity to be a relatively fleeting one.

Madison created a personal copy of the official Convention journals. He began with Monday, August 20—suggesting that his first purpose was to use the copy to complete his Notes. In the end, however, he copied the entire journal of the Convention as well as the journal of the Committee of the Whole House. The official journals may have disappointed Madison in one crucial respect. William Jackson, the Convention's secretary, had only a partial entry for September 15, no entry for September 17, and no details about alterations made on the final three days. By mid-October, Madison had likely completed the copying task. He explained that he had remained in New York to complete "some business which I can execute in this City only." This Journal Copy gave him a personal record as if the journal had been printed.[8]

The process of creating the Journal Copy altered Madison's memory of the Convention. He relived the Convention out of order. The Convention had begun with broad principles and ended with a document; however, in copying first August 20 to September, the text and textual alterations near the end of the Convention loomed in importance. The hours Madison spent copying motions about language and alterations of language while he was also participating in congressional debates about the meaning of the Constitution imbued the words with new significance. Returning then to the beginning of the Convention would have placed the larger political debates in a new context. Knowledge of the outcome highlighted certain strategies and emphasized the failure of others. The Journal Copy presented a different narrative from the incomplete Notes or Madison's memory. Perhaps most importantly, the Journal Copy provided security for Madison about the record that would appear with the eventual publication of the official records. Madison knew that his version of the final days could not be contradicted by an official source.

Even as Madison copied the journals, he expected Jefferson's imminent arrival. On October 4, he expected Jefferson's arrival "every day" and was in "anxiety" to see him. Jefferson did not arrive. On October 9, Madison left for Philadelphia, still hoping to make his journey to Virginia "coincide" with that of Jefferson. In Philadelphia, Madison again waited in vain. He was ill from about October 11 to 25. Finally, he journeyed to Virginia alone but remained ill. Writing to Hamilton on November 19, Madison apologized for having been "too much indisposed for some time" to write. Through mid-November, revising the Notes was likely far from his mind.[9]

Jefferson's delay altered the Notes. If Jefferson had returned from Paris and met Madison in New York in October 1789, he might have been shown the incomplete Notes and the Journal Copy. The two manuscripts resembled the materials Jefferson had relied on in the past for legislative intelligence: Madison's legislative diary and an official legislative journal. The Journal Copy contains a few clues that Madison may have expected it to be read with the Notes. In the Journal Copy on June 13, Madison wrote in small print at the end of the entry, "see debates of convention," and three dates. On June 15, he similarly noted in the margin with respect to Paterson's proposals: "see them in debates June 15 taken by JM." Conversely, in the Notes for August 22—the first day of the later composed Notes—Madison did not copy the committee report from his Journal Copy. Instead, he wrote: "See the Report in the Journal of the Convention of this date."[10]

Did Jefferson know of the existence of the Journal Copy? If he did, no reference has surfaced. Without knowledge of the Journal Copy, Jefferson might never have known or understood that the original Notes ended with August 21. He might have guessed—or Madison might have told him. But, perhaps, Madison later saw no reason to acknowledge the Notes' deficiencies and no reason to explain his temporary possession of the official records. Jefferson may have believed—Madison may have silently implied—that the Notes were finished in September 1787.

At Montpelier in November and December 1789, Madison likely turned to the incomplete Notes. The idea of integrating and adding the Journal Copy to the Notes came slowly to Madison. His initial plan may have been to create an appendix. Only remnants of the appendix—if one existed—remain. The beginning of the appendix may have included the list of delegates, the rules, two letters from Rhode Island to the Convention, and June 5 motions relating to inferior tribunals. The list of delegates and the rules—neither included in the original Notes—were information typical of printed legislative debates. The remaining materials reflected the political culture of the fall of 1789. Rhode Island had not ratified the Constitution. The letters to the Convention, however, showed that important Rhode Islanders supported its work. The letters became irrelevant after Rhode Island's ratification in late May 1790. In September 1789, the debates over the judiciary bill discussed the Convention's ideas about inferior courts. In the summer of 1787, however, Madison had little interest in the judiciary and on June 5 had skipped that material. Inclusion of the motions suggested Madison's desire to revise the Notes to bear on contemporary debates. Indeed, Madison was thinking about appendices in August 1789. He described his preference for the incorporation of amendments to the Constitution in these terms—as "the project of adding them by way of appendix to it." Nevertheless, the Notes' appendix approach was abandoned as Madison decided to integrate more extensive material from the Journal Copy into the Notes.[11]

Madison used the Journal Copy to create the post–August 21 section of the Notes. The section interspersed the journal material with comments by delegates and a few Madison speeches. The integration of the Journal Copy made it appear that Madison had recorded almost every textual alteration during the Convention. Instead of reflecting Madison's earlier casual and sporadic interest in textual changes, the Notes silently absorbed the secretary's record of the official textual alterations. An illusion of deep interest in the details of the text was cast over the Notes. Madison's record for August 22 demonstrates the integration. The style differed from the early Notes. He did not abbreviate his name, and he included the first initial for Martin and Pinckney. He rearranged the words and phrases from the Journal Copy. The overlap appears below.

Journal Copy entry:
> It was moved & 2[ded] to commit the 6 sect. of the 7 article
> which pass[d] in the affirmative
> and a Committee (of a Member from each State) was appointed by ballot of the honorable M[r]. Langdon, M[r]. King, M[r]. Johnson, M[r]. Livingston, M[r]. Clymer, M[r]. Dickinson, M[r]. L. Martin, M[r]. Madison, M[r]. Williamson, M[r]. C. C. Pinkney & M[r]. Baldwin, to whom the 2 remaining clauses of the 4th & 5th and 6th sections were referred.

Madison's Notes:
> On Question for committing 6 sect. as to navigation to a member from each State—N.H. ay—Mas. ay. C[t] no. N. J. no. P[a]. ay. Del. ay. M[d]. ay. V[a]. ay. N. C. ay. S. C. ay. Geo. ay.
> The Committee appointed were M[r]. Langdon, King, Johnson, Livingston, Clymer, Dickenson, L. Martin, Madison, Williamson, C. C. Pinkney, & Baldwin.
> To this committee were referred the two clauses above mentioned, of the 4 & 5. sect: of art. 7.

Madison's approach to copying appears in small idiosyncrasies. He dropped "honorable." He copied "Mr. Langdon" but then decided to exclude "Mr." from all the names. His paraphrases either consciously obscured the fact of copying or unconsciously reflected a preference for succinct summaries.[12]

Errors in the Journal Copy reappeared in the Notes. On August 22, a motion included the phrase, "nor any ex post facto laws." In the Journal Copy, Madison skipped the word "any": "The Legislature shall pass no bill of attainder nor ex post facto laws." The Notes therefore omitted "any": "The Legislature shall pass no bill of attainder, nor ex post facto laws." Similarly, Madison followed his stylistic decisions in the Journal Copy. Prior to August 22, Madison usually wrote the article number and the section number: "Art. VII. sect. 4." The secretary typically reversed the order, placing the section number first. Madison copied this style in the Journal Copy: "2d. sect. of 7 art." After August 21, when he wrote the Notes, he used this style, "2[d]. sect. art: 7." The process of copying from a copy left subtle traces.[13]

On occasion, the challenge of melding the Journal Copy and the rough notes showed. On August 30, the Journal Copy recorded, "'But no religious test shall ever be required as a qualification to any office or public trust under the authority of the U. States' which pass^d unan: in the affirmative." Madison copied the motion in the Notes. He added that Gouverneur Morris and General Pinckney "approved the motion"—names likely drawn from the rough notes or his memory. He then began to write "which"—planning to follow the Journal Copy: "which pass^d unan." He stopped, however, perhaps recalling that his usual practice was to write "nem con" to indicate a unanimous result. He scratched out "which" and concluded, "The motion was agreed to nem: con."[14]

In some places, the Notes so closely track the journal as to suggest that Madison's rough notes were unreliable or nonexistent. On August 23, the Notes followed a large section of the Journal Copy entry, sporadically inserting names and brief comments. Italics indicate words that do not appear in the journal.

M^r. Govr Morris moved to strike ~~out~~ the following words out of the 18 clause "enforce treaties" *as being superfluous, since treaties were to be "laws"* . . . which *was agreed to nem: contrad:*

M^r. Govr Morris moved to alter 1st. part. of 18. clause—sect. 1. art. VII *so as to read* "to provide for calling forth the militia to execute the laws of the Union, suppress insurrections and repel invasions". which *was agreed to nem: contrador*

On the question then to agree to the 18 clause of sect. 1. art: 7. as amended it passed in the affirmative *nem: contradicente.*

Mr C—Pinkney moved to add as an additional power to be vested in the Legislature of the U.S. "To negative all laws passed by the several States interfering in the opinion of the Legislature with the General interests and harmony of the Union;" provided that two thirds of the members of each House assent to the same" *This principle he observed had* ~~at~~ *formerly been agreed to. He considered the precaution as essentially necessary: The objection drawn from the predominance of the large <States> had been removed by the equality established in the Senate—Mr. Broome 2^ded. the proposition.*

M^r. Sherman thought it unnecessary; the laws of the General Government being Supreme & paramount to the State laws according to the plan, as it now stands.

M^r. Madison proposed that it should be committed—He had been from the beginning a friend to the principle; but thought the modification might be made better.

Madison may have known that Morris made the first motion based on rough notes, or he might have simply added it based as his best recollection. The comments by Pinckney and Sherman were broad and generic. They might have been recorded in the rough notes but also easily added. Madison included eight other speakers indicating that at least some of the entry came from rough notes. Nonetheless, without the rough notes, distinguishing later composition from original transcription is impossible.[15]

Beginning with September 6, Madison had particular difficulty integrating his rough notes with the Journal Copy. The committee reports had proposed language and, in turn, the language had been altered further by the delegates. Indeed, Madison seems to have had difficulty at the place where historian Max Farrand declared, with the advantage of examining all known records: "From this point on in this day's records it seems hopeless to determine the order of questions and votes." Madison switched from one type of paper to another, almost as if he had stopped out of frustration and returned later to the project. He followed his Journal Copy by including on September 6 an addition that may have been made on September 7. As the Notes continued, some motions seem likely to have been drawn from rough notes, and the reliance on the Journal Copy becomes less apparent. Elsewhere, the journal's language erratically appears, for example, in formal phrases such as "in order to take up the following." On occasion, Madison began to copy the Journal Copy and then decided to alter its record. The sources—his rough notes, his Journal Copy, and his memory—did not always align.[16]

The final days of the Convention posed the most significant problem. The secretary's vote tallies recorded sixty votes between September 12 and 17. Most of these votes, however, were not recorded in the journal. Moreover, the final text of the Constitution indicated additional alterations. The secretary's summary for September 12 stated that the draft was "read by paragraphs, compared, and in some places corrected and amended." Brief entries for September 14 and 15th were struck out in the journal. In the end, Madison tried to make sense of his rough notes, the changes recorded on his printed draft, and the changes that he knew must have occurred. On September 12, he focused on the shift from three-fourths to two-thirds on the veto. He included a few comments about juries in civil cases. He recorded a brief discussion over Mason's motion for a committee to frame a bill of rights—and the 10–0 vote in opposition. Although the journal made no reference to the appointment of a committee on sumptuary regulations, Madison included it. He could not sort out the proper place to include substitute sections for establishing the government and thus located them at the end of an entry. Although Madison was uncertain that the Notes were accurate, he also knew that the official record could not easily contradict them.[17]

Madison struggled with the divergence between what had mattered in September 1787 and what was relevant two years later. Although the delegates had agreed paragraph by paragraph to a letter to Congress transmitting and explaining the Constitution, Madison did not include a copy. Instead, he would eventually note, "here insert a transcript of both," referring to the letter and the printed report of the Constitution. The letter—significant at the time—focused attention on Congress rather than the larger ratification process. The final two days—September 15 and 17—reflected the advantage of hindsight. The inclusion of a motion about whether members could see the official records after the Convention was answered ambiguously—perhaps as protection for the Journal Copy. The last sheets of the Notes (possibly composed even later) incorporated two published Franklin comments about the final day. Their guarded optimism about the Constitution represented an alternative to Madison's original uncertainty and disappointment.[18]

The degree of hindsight is difficult to ascertain. One example discussed previously in Chapter 7, however, suggests that Madison included at least some significant comments in light of later concerns. On August 25, as the delegates debated the time limit before Congress could prohibit the foreign slave trade, Madison recorded his comment:

> Twenty years will produce all the mischief that can be apprehended from the liberty to import slaves. So long a term will be more dishonorable to the National character than to say nothing about it in the Constitution.

The statement was idiosyncratic. In the original Notes, Madison never spoke against slavery; indeed, he had been willing to constitutionalize slavery as the basis for a bicameral Congress. Moreover, the comment bears marked resemblance to Luther Martin's comment on August 21:

> it was inconsistent with the principles of the revolution and dishonorable to the American character to have such a feature in the Constitution.

The repetition of key terms—*dishonorable, character, Constitution*—is typical of Madison's paraphrasing. He might have made such a statement on August 25, 1787, and recorded it in his rough notes—but it could have also been contemplated and composed two years later.[19]

Over the preceding two years, Madison's views of slavery had shifted ever so slightly. In the fall of 1789, Madison wrote a memorandum on slavery that argued for African resettlement as an "encouragement to manumission" and "the best hope yet presented of putting an end to the slavery in which not less than 600,000 unhappy negroes are now involved." Like Jefferson's comments in the *Notes on the State of Virginia,* Madison believed that a multiracial free society was "rendered impossible" by the "prejudices of Whites" based "principally from the difference of colour" that "must be considered as permanent and insuperable." In the spring of 1790, Madison participated in the congressional debates over petitions against slavery. In March, a committee report addressed congressional powers "relating to the abolition of slavery." The committee denied congressional power to interfere with the emancipation of slaves or with the "internal regulation" of states relating to slavery. Madison's stance was cagey. On the one hand, he wanted the printed journals to show the proceedings with "the implication that Congress will exercise the power vested by the constitution whenever it should be requisite." On the other hand, Madison wanted to "quiet" southern state concerns by "recognizing that Congress had no power whatever to prohibit the importation of slaves prior to the year 1808, or to attempt to manumit them at any time." In a letter, Madison distanced himself from South Carolina and Georgia. He characterized the two states as "intemperate beyond all example and even all decorum" by pleading "for the lawfulness of the African trade itself." Madison was no supporter of abolition, but he recognized and hoped that the foreign slave trade would be banned in all states. As he copied the final section of the Notes, he may have been unable to resist recasting himself as an explicit supporter of the seemingly inevitable limitation.[20]

Madison used the Journal Copy to revise the earlier section of the Notes. Some additions are obvious; others considerably more subtle. During the early days of the Convention, Madison had placed each entry on a page and left large blank spaces. Material added in these spaces or to the end of the entry often blended almost seamlessly with the original entry. Elsewhere, Madison squished the new text making the addition obvious.

Where no space remained, Madison attached twenty-two slips of paper. Some slips are small; others cover nearly a page. Some were designed to cover crossed-out material. Others were intended to be flipped up, with the continuation of material on the other side. Madison may have attached the slips using sealing wax; Jefferson had attached similar slips to his *Notes on the State of Virginia*. Pins may also have been used; the Hamilton plan, for example, was apparently attached by a pin in the early 1790s. No slips were inserted for the new post–August 21 section. Two slips date from considerably later, likely after 1820.[21]

Even small revisions reflected the passage of the two years since the Convention. Madison had not originally listed the delegates' names. The official journal listed the delegates as they had arrived. When Madison had made the Journal Copy, he had followed the secretary's use of honorifics, referring to Washington and Randolph as "His Excellency," and others as "the Honorable" and "Esq[r]." Titles, however, were rapidly vanishing. In Congress in May 1789, Madison had opposed titles for officers, favoring "total neglect and disregard to things of this nature." In revising the Notes, Madison omitted the honorifics. He added the names at the beginning of early entries and placed the names in a boxed note in the bottom corner where he had no space on June 2. The rules were another aspect omitted originally from the Notes. Madison added them. The additions diminished the diary appearance of the Notes.[22]

Madison's original procedural terms were altered to conform to the official journal. Summaries of multiple clauses—the "other clauses giving power necessary to preserve harmony among the States and so forth"—were converted to a list of specific clauses. General sentences describing the "Clauses relating" were revised to precise explanations: "The remaining Clauses of Resolution 4th." "Proposition" became "resolution," and numbers were added. The revisions left the impression of technical accuracy. Madison even revised his original "adjourned" or "adj." to favor the formal journal. In some places, he may have shaved the original words. Combining the closing in the journal of the Committee of the Whole House and the journal of the Convention, he ended the early days with "The Committee then rose & the House adjourned." The revised consistency hid the spontaneity, inconsistency, and procedural imprecision of the original Notes.[23]

Motions that had been omitted were now inserted. Some additions are almost indiscernible. For example, on May 25 and June 20, Madison carefully added discussion of the Delaware deputies in blank spaces left on the page. Originally, Madison had paid little attention to the Delaware delegates and their instruction barring them from voting to alter state equal suffrage. He had likely assumed that one small state would not carry too much power. Two years later, emphasizing the role of the Delaware delegates cast an inevitable compromise over the proceedings and downplayed Madison's political miscalculations. Only the awkward spacing between the final sentences betrays the additions.[24]

The insertions of the journal language, particularly with the slips, transformed the selective recording. On May 30, a slip containing the detailed motions on suffrage and free inhabitants was substituted for the casual reference in the original Notes to "at length" proposals. Similar motions were inserted relating to suffrage, taxation, and apportionment throughout early July. Madison's lack of interest in the judiciary was replaced with motions on the judiciary (June 5), piracies and capture (June 12), and jurisdiction (June 13). A slip included the language of the supremacy clause motion (17 July). Another slip inserted the detailed description of the executive as it was finally approved on July 26. Where descriptions had ended with "&c"—for example, "to organize Militia &c"—the precise language was added. Madison even replaced his comment—"to substitute the words of the British Statute"—with the specific definition of treason. The revisions demonstrated textual precision lacking in the original Notes.[25]

Madison made revisions to acknowledge Pinckney's contributions. On May 29, language was inserted referring to Pinckney's draft. Madison may have assumed he could acquire a copy; he added, "insert the draught." He used a slip to enumerate the powers proposed by himself and Pinckney on August 18. Another slip included the detailed language in which Pinckney described his proposals for rights on August 20. Intriguingly, the slip covered Madison's original record. The similarity between Madison's original Notes and his proposed language in Congress in the 1789 debates was hidden.[26]

Some slips reflected repeated efforts at revision. The slip on May 25 with the delegates' names may have been written as part of the appendix and converted to a slip. A June 1 slip relating to executive powers demonstrates at least three moments of revision. The original Notes described, only in general terms, a motion on executive power, appointments, and additional congressional powers. Madison initially used the blank space to write in a "Note" to explain the division and debate. A slip was then added describing the precise division of his motion. Still later, probably after 1818, Madison may have added the state vote tally. Revision continued.[27]

The many small changes had a significant collective impact. Madison's revisions obscured the legislative diary foundations, replacing them with a veneer of legislative debates. Even the most subtle alterations changed the Notes. The consistency of certain revisions indicates that Madison had settled on a tone (measured, cautious, precise) and a voice (objective and detached). Of equal importance, the neatness of the alterations suggests that Madison initially assumed the revised manuscript would be read.

Revisions were not made at one time; indeed, they likely occurred over a long period. Some small editorial changes were made as Madison originally wrote the Notes. Some revisions were obviously made in later decades. Ascertaining the precise timing of any particular revision is difficult. This section discusses categories of revisions regardless of possible timing. Because nearly every sheet of the early sections of the Notes contains revisions, this section selects some significant patterns.

Recognizing the revisions is not always straightforward. Madison wrote over letters to alter words. He may have removed words by shaving the surface of the paper (the eighteenth-century equivalent of erasing). Additions made at the end of a paragraph or entry leave little evidence. In certain places, Madison crossed the original words out so darkly as to render them illegible. He deleted speeches by General Pinckney and Ellsworth. He obliterated lines in his own speeches. New technologies may eventually allow conservators at the Library of Congress to discover what bothered Madison. Nonetheless, many revisions can be easily seen in the transcript reproduced in the *Documentary History of the Constitution*.[28]

Madison altered characterizations by adding detachment. The very first entries were gossipy and epistolary. In fact, the original opening of the Convention read like a letter:

> The General was accordingly unanimously elected by ballot, and conducted to the chair by M[r]. R. Morris and M[r]. Rutlidge; from which he thanked in a very emphatical manner the Convention for the honor they had conferred on him, reminded them of the novelty of the scene of business in which he was to act, lamented his want of the requisites for it; and claimed the indulgence of the House towards the involuntary errors which his inexperience might occasion.

"The General" became "General Washington." Madison deleted the awkward "very emphatical" and wrote, "from which in a very emphatic manner." He replaced "the requisites" with the more politic, "better qualifications." In the following sentences, Madison rendered illegible a sentence comparing Franklin to Washington. He replaced a snide explanation for Franklin's inability to nominate Washington with a more factual comment on the weather and health. Opinions had become neutral description.[29]

Throughout the manuscript, Madison repeatedly deleted or altered characterizations. He described Butler's comment as "rather cautious." The sentence was revised to read, "After some general observations denoting a cautious temper," then altered again to state "of a guarded character"—and was finally struck completely. He had recorded his own speech using the words, "brought grave doubts"; he deleted "grave." He muted his critique of Ellsworth. Originally, he had stated that Ellsworth's reasoning "at different times did not well. . . ." He revised it to "did justice to the able and close reasoning of Mr. E but must observe that it did not always accord with itself." Madison deleted the strong comment in his July 5 speech: "These observations w^d. show that he was not only fixed in his opposition to the Report . . . but was prepared for any want that might follow a negative of it." He similarly removed his edgy commentary at the end of Martin's June 20 speech: "This was the substance of a very long speech." Madison's explicit personal comments vanished.[30]

The terms used for concepts were replaced. Some revisions related to a shift that occurred during the Convention; other revisions reflected a distinction that had arisen afterward. References to "civil Society" and "federal Society" became the more contemporary "civil government" and "federal government." Similarly, a reference to "Constitution"—not clearly meaning the document—was altered to "Government." The phrase, "no salary or emolument," became "no salary or compensation." The "equality of votes" was changed to the more theoretical "principle of representation." The "misdeeds" of the states became "unconstitutional proceedings." The "election" of judges was made more specifically "appointment." Similarly, "electing persons" became the more precise "electing representatives." And "freeholders" were revised to "qualified voters." The verb, "fixing," was made more specific to distinguish legislation alteration from constitutional enactment by adding, "fixing by y^e. Constitution." When a delegate referred to Congress—meaning the Congress of the Confederation—Madison added "existing" so the sentence would not be misread as a description of future congressional powers. Madison even repeatedly replaced "demagogue"—converting it to "pretended patriots" (May 31) and "leading partisans" (June 2). These distinctions—many of which arose during or after the Convention—appeared as if they had always existed.[31]

Madison paid attention to discussions of slavery. On May 30, he had originally written, "the words free inhabitants might occasion debates which would divert the Committee" from the representation issue. He revised the phrase to, "the number of free inhabitants," thus making the concern one of numbers rather than slavery itself. Originally, Madison had been imprecise in the words used to denote people held as slaves. Madison now fussed with descriptions. On July 9, Madison added "slaves" after "negroes" in Paterson's statement, "He could regard negroes in no light but as property." Although Madison had recorded "negroes" as if the word could mean slaves, the sentence now specified slaves. On July 11, Madison did the opposite, replacing "slaves" with "blacks" in Williamson's speech to make it consistent with the description of a motion for "considering blacks as equal to Whites."[32]

Madison's revisions reflected concern about sentences taken out of context or at risk of being misunderstood. General statements became more precise, making them more difficult to interpret broadly. Mason's comment—"Rebellion is the only case in which the public force can be exerted ag[ain]st its Citizens"—became "Rebellion is the only case in which the military force of the State can be properly exerted." Public force was narrowed to military force. Sherman's statement—"they were willing to trust Cong[res]s with more power"—became "trust Cong[res]s with more power to draw a revenue from Trade." Power was narrowed to trade revenue. Gerry's statement—"the inconveniency of excluding a few worthy individuals"—was limited with the addition of "who might be public debtors or have unsettled acc[oun]ts." Morris's desire that "the subject at large might undergo reconsideration" became clarified as the "whole constitution of the Executive might undergo reconsideration." Gorham's speech—"Public bodies feel no responsibility and give full play to intrigue & cabal"—was made more specific by the addition of "personal" before "responsibility." The theoretical "principle of democracy to starve the public servants" was converted to a cultural "maxim." With subtlety, general statements were narrowed.[33]

Even the smallest revisions shifted the meaning. In two comments by Morris, Madison revised one word and altered the interpretation. First, Morris stated, "The Rich will strive to establish their dominion & enslave the rest. . . . The only security ag[ain]st them is to form them into a separate interest." Madison changed "only security" to "proper security."

The original sentence had insisted on only one solution; the revised sentence suggested a mere opinion as to the most appropriate solution. Second, Morris dramatically declared, "We cannot annihilate the States; but we may perhaps take out the teeth of the serpents." Madison deleted "the States." The sentence was considerably more ambiguous: "We cannot annihilate but we may perhaps take out the teeth of the serpents." The states were no longer serpents.[34]

A few additional words similarly moderated strong statements. Madison originally recorded Morris's protestation that he was "reduced to the dilemma of doing injustice to the Southern States or to human nature, and he must therefore do it to the former." Madison's insertion of, "was compelled to declare himself reduced to" softened the sentence. With another bold Morris speech, Madison used the same technique: "Domestic slavery is the most prominent feature in the aristocratic countenance of the proposed Constitution." Madison added a prefatory phrase, "He would add that domestic slavery. . . ." The revision converted an apparent fact into mere opinion. Other strong sentences were excised. Madison cut Wilson's comment, "Here then a fundamental principle of free Gov[ernmen]t is violated." Wilson did not like equal state suffrage, but it no longer violated a fundamental principle.[35]

Madison fussed with his speeches, repeatedly temporizing. The government would "be stable and durable" if resting on the people. Madison changed the phrase to "more stable and durable." He had written that it "would rarely if ever happen that the Executive would, have firmness eno' to resist the Legislature." By adding "constituted as ours is proposed to be," his comment was limited to this particular executive. He had described "the two extremes before us are a perfect independence & a perfect incorporation, of the 13 States." Lest "perfect independence" sound overly positive, it was revised to "perfect separation." The comment that the Convention "was reduced to the delusion of either departing from justice" became less extravagant by replacing "delusion" with "alternative." The words "evil" and "interested" were deleted from the sentence: "evil mentioned by Col Mason of the zeal of interested men." The word "obnoxious" was similarly removed from "obnoxious partizans of the opposite faction." He cut "extremely" in "the word revenue was extremely ambiguous." Each change moderated his comments.[36]

At times, revision bordered on fussiness, particularly in his own speeches. In a June 19 speech, Madison had originally written, "He illustrated the position by the story of the Amphyctionic Confederates."

The casual word, "story," was replaced with the more technically correct "history." Similarly, an imprecise phrase, "during a certain period of the war" became "during a considerable period of the war." A succinct, informal sentence—"He thought not."—was deleted. The threat of the final sentence was diminished after Madison replaced "could" with "might": "Let them [the western states] have an equal vote, and a more objectionable minority than ever might give law to the whole." In a July 14 speech, Madison altered "no superstructure would be raised" under equality of state suffrage to the milder "no proper superstructure." He modulated a blunt argument ("the perpetuity it would give to the North[er]n ag[ain]st the South[er]n Scale") by converting it to the passive voice ("the perpetuity it would give to the predominance of the North[er]n ag[ains]t the South[er]n Scale was a serious consideration"). With each revision, Madison became ever more finicky, precise, and unemotional.[37]

Other alterations were made as if Madison were a copy editor intent on obscuring the informal nature of the Notes. For any "M" or blank space for his name, "Madison" was inserted. Various misspelled names were corrected: Gherry to Gerry; Franklyn to Franklin. Eventually, the Pinckneys acquired the "c" missing in "Pinkney" and, where "General" or the context did not sufficiently distinguish them, a first initial. Madison altered repetitions of a word. In the sentence, "certain rules by which the parties were to be bound, and certain rules by which their subjects were to be reciprocally governed," the first "rules" was altered to "duties." Where he had written "communicate" and "communication," he changed "communication" to "intercourse." He fixed missing parallels. Madison reworked for improved parallel structure an Ellsworth speech on the governmental structure as "partly national, partly federal." Initially the speech stated only that "equality of voices was conformable to the federal principle." Madison revised a prior sentence to make it "conformable to the national principle." To the outline summary of Wilson's speech, Madison added words. "Revision of the laws—no such check" became "Revision of the laws provided for in one: no such check in the other." New verb tenses erased the present tense and created an objective sensibility. Even small verbs were changed. In the middle of Gerry's speech, Madison had written: "He is for waiting till people feel more the necessity of it." The "is" made it ambiguous whether "he" referred to Gerry or Madison. Madison changed "is" to "was." The imperfections in writing were fixed.[38]

Cross-references were systematically added. Madison had often taken notes on a speech without including an aspect that a later speaker found of particular interest. In the original Notes, speakers referred to earlier comments, but the comment itself was missing. Madison inserted these earlier cross-references. George Read remarked on May 30 about the prior instruction of "the deputies from Delaware." Madison went back and wrote in the instruction in the May 25 entry. On June 4, members referred to Randolph's tripartite executive. Madison revised Randolph's June 2 speech to note that he was in "favor of three members" of the executive from "different portions of the Country." On June 7, Madison referred to Dickinson's desire for "family weight"; a previous Dickinson's speech was revised to include "family weight & other causes." On June 13, Madison similarly added a sentence about "money bills" in a Butler speech to explain a later Madison comment. On July 2, delegates described Bedford's previous "rash" language. To the initially mild version of Bedford's speech, Madison added, "we have been told with a dictatorial air." On August 7, Madison added "by ye Constitution" to his question about the reasons "for fixing the time of Meeting for the Legislature." The addition made coherent subsequent references to a distinction between time "fixed by the Constitution" and by ordinary legislation. The cross-references made the Notes appear to be comprehensive.[39]

The purpose of footnotes changed. Originally, Madison used an occasional footnote to expand the Notes beyond the Convention proceedings. For example, the July 5 footnote reported on committee proceedings and blamed Franklin and Sherman; the July 13 footnote similarly discussed committee discussions. As Madison revised, he added new explanatory footnotes. Intriguingly, in the post–August 21 section, the footnotes described compromises. Commenting on General Pinckney's comment on the importation of slaves on August 29, a footnote stated that an "understanding on the two subjects of navigation and slavery, had taken place between those parts of the Union, which explains the vote on the Motion." A September 5 footnote included, "This explains the compromise mentioned above." A September 9 footnote even referred to the prior footnote: "This was a conciliatory vote, the effect of the compromise formerly alluded. See Note Wednesday Sep[r]. 5." The explanation in footnotes created an air of detachment and objectivity about the debates.[40]

As Madison revised the original section of the Notes, new footnotes offered interpretation. A slip added to May 28 offered background on the pre-Convention discussion on the voting rules. Other footnotes similarly provided explanations: a June 7 footnote on the debate over election by state legislatures; a June 12 footnote on the vote on the Senate salary; a June 25 footnote on the vote on the second branch. Madison also decided that his integrated original "N.B." (nota bene) comments, which had been part of the entries, should be moved to footnotes. Some of these revisions may have come later as if Madison was writing for a future copyist. He wrote "transfer" on some textual comments as if instructing a copyist. For example, "this hint was probably meant in terrorem to the smaller States" was marked with the instruction, "the note to be transferred to the bottom margin." Regardless of timing, the footnotes demonstrated a new understanding of the manuscript. Madison divided the Notes into two voices: objective debates in the text; personal explanations in the footnotes. The legislative diary had vanished.[41]

The revisions demonstrate Madison's desire to convert the Notes to resemble printed debates. As Madison revised, his small changes, often seemingly innocuous, reduced the confusions, ambiguities, and uncertainties of the summer of 1787. In creating an illusion of consistency, the Notes composed in the summer of 1787 were gradually lost.

At some point, likely relatively early in Madison's project of revision, he inserted three replacement sheets into the Notes. The precise timing of this insertion is uncertain, but the late summer or fall of 1789 up through 1790 seems a plausible range. Madison may have composed the replaced sheets before completing the Notes, or he may have composed them afterwards. Three new sheets of paper permitted more significant revision to his speeches than was possible by altering words or adding slips. The substitution of a few sheets was unlikely to have been troubling to Madison. He had wanted Randolph to compose his introductory speech. Revising a few pages of his speeches—themselves composed after the fact—was unlikely to have given him even a moment's pause. Madison likely viewed the original versions as not doing justice to his arguments.

The replaced sheets seemed to include awareness of new concerns. As a collateral consequence of replacement, Madison's speech on inferior courts on June 5 was likely revised with evidence of later issues. Although the final sentence reflected Madison's earlier concerns ("A Government without a proper Executive & Judiciary would be the mere trunk of a body without arms or legs to act or move."), the revised speech described problems that would arise without inferior courts—issues raised during ratification and the debates over the new judiciary act. Appeals would be "multiplied" and even so were not always a "remedy." The parties would have "to bring up their witnesses, tho' ever so distant from the seat of the Court." Madison included his motion that the "National Legislature be empowered to institute inferior tribunals." With precision, Madison noted that he and Wilson had "observed" that there was "a distinction between establishing such tribunals absolutely, and giving a discretion to the Legislature to establish or not establish them." The Notes explicitly thus addressed the Constitution's relationship to inferior courts and seemed to indicate the relationship between the motion and the 1789 debates. Madison may have believed that he was clarifying a purpose that had not been evident in his original Notes, or the distinction may have become apparent only after June 1787.[42]

The significant reason for the replacements was Madison's lengthy June 6 speech. In the original Notes, the June 6 speech represented a significant revision because it likely included arguments from June 4. The replaced speech drew on sources that reflected subsequent and repeated revisions of the original ideas: the revised eleventh Vice, the October 1787 letter to Jefferson, and Federalist 10. The June 6 speech declared that the "only remedy" for factions was "to enlarge the sphere, & thereby divide the community into so great a number of interests & parties." The statement diverged from the approach favored by Madison in the summer of 1787. Then he preferred structural mechanisms to control interests and wanted the new governmental structure to control state legislatures. In replacing the sheet, Madison may have believed that he was clarifying that the insight of the enlarged sphere first occurred to him in early June 1787. But the belief represented a significant revision of the Convention. It made the specific solutions advanced by Madison over the course of the Convention–almost all of which lost—seem irrelevant. In shifting the focus away from his original losing structural solutions and toward an insight about size, Madison made himself a prophet of the future Constitution.[43]

One idiosyncratic sentence suggests that the speech may have been composed during the congressional debates over slavery in spring 1790. Madison stated: "We have seen the mere distinction of colour made in the most enlightened period of time, a ground of the most oppressive dominion ever exercised by man over man." The sentence only tenuously related to the speech. Moreover, in June 1787, no one recorded Madison offering such criticisms. In March 1790, however, these same phrases appeared in the congressional debates over slavery. The words, "distinction of color," appeared in the petition from the Pennsylvania Abolition

Society presented to Congress under Benjamin Franklin's signature in February 1790. In the debates, South Carolina's William Smith defended "the abominable practice ... of one man exercising dominion over another." Madison may have consciously or unconsciously absorbed the antislavery rhetoric from the debates in Congress.[44]

The extent of Madison's revisions to the original versions of his speeches is unknown. The final replaced speech by Madison on June 6 defended the revisionary power. By 1789–1790, Madison knew the speech reflected a dead end. Although the revisionary power was rejected, Madison may have still believed that some mergers of judiciary and executive did not violate the principle of separate and distinct powers. Madison's aspiration to a less rigid principle of separated powers may explain the retention of the basic argument. Were other aspects subtly altered? Did the odd expression, "co-ordinate Departments," reflect the new governmental structure? Did the reference to the judiciary as a protector of the "rights of the people at large" arise from his later arguments describing a role of the judiciary with a bill of rights? Unless his original sheets from the Notes are found, we are left with speculation.[45]

In replacing sheets, Madison equally may have been interested in deleting material. On the third sheet replaced apparently by Madison, his speeches are not unusual. One speech focused on the evils of the state legislatures; the other speech advocated a broad negative. Missing, however, is a Madison assertion recorded by multiple note takers on June 8: that a line could not be drawn between the state and national governments. In October 1787, Madison wrote Jefferson about the idea: "the impossibility of dividing powers of legislation, in such a manner, as to be free from different constructions by different interests, or even from ambiguity in the judgment of the impartial." At significant length, Madison explained the impossibility of drawing lines among powers. This insight formed the grounds for his commitment to the negative. Federalist 37 echoed the concern. But by 1789, this insistence on the impossibility of such line drawing may have been awkward. During the ratification debates, the argument had been linked to the abolition of the states. Recent debates in Congress had repeatedly sought to discern the boundaries of state and national powers. The recently passed Judiciary Act established the federal courts as arbiters of the line and bound the state courts to follow national law. Two years after the Convention, Madison may have wanted to minimize his initial conviction that it was impossible to partition state and national powers. In particular, he may have thought it advisable to soften the degree to which he had repeatedly tilted in favor of national power.[46]

Why did Madison bother to replace pages that addressed topics in Madison's October 1787 letter to Jefferson? Jefferson had the letter, and it was unlikely that he would have completely forgotten it. Perhaps Madison wanted to recast his earlier ideas as tentative rather than deep-seated convictions stated at the Convention. Perhaps Madison wanted to emerge in the Notes as the progenitor of a new political science. Perhaps Madison was already contemplating an audience beyond Jefferson. The motivations are unknowable.

The dating of the replacements, revisions, and writing of the post–August 21 section is similarly uncertain. Madison likely created the Journal Copy from the official journals by October 1789. His illness in November probably prevented him from beginning a sustained effort before the winter. Around December 26, Madison took "a ride to Monticello" to see Jefferson. Madison wanted to persuade Jefferson to accept the secretary of state position and remain in the United States. The meeting may have been rushed. Jefferson had written a letter for Madison, but he "forgot to give it." If Madison mentioned the Notes, Jefferson made no comment in subsequent letters. Into January 1790, Jefferson professed a desire to return to France. In a letter to Washington, Madison explained that Jefferson was not enthusiastic about "domestic service." In late January, Washington wrote that the position was "*very* important" but put the decision in Jefferson's hands. Even at the end of January 1790, Madison remained uncertain if Jefferson would "remain in America, or return to France." If Jefferson returned to France, the Notes would be significantly less useful to him.[47]

In the meantime, in January 1790, Madison traveled back to New York for Congress. His journey north took far longer than he expected. His letters complained of illness. To Washington, he described the "slight complaint in my bowels," which had become "a pretty severe dysentery." To his father and Jefferson, he similarly wrote of travels slowed by dysentery and hemorrhoids. Nevertheless, on January 20, 1790, Madison began to attend Congress. Almost a month later, Jefferson wrote accepting the position as secretary of state. On March 21, Jefferson arrived in New York. He likely had not yet read the Notes. Through the spring of 1790, Madison likely continued to work on revising the Notes.[48]

10

THE INFLUENCE OF MR. JEFFERSON

In late 1789, Thomas Jefferson returned to a different United States from the one he left in 1784. He had missed the Annapolis Convention, the Philadelphia Convention, the ratification debates, the election of George Washington, the slow commencement of the new government, the early disputes over interpreting the new Constitution, and the decision to amend the Constitution with twelve amendments. His perspective had been dominated by French political rhetoric contrasting republicanism and monarchy. He came to the Constitution as a reader. His information about American constitutional politics had been filtered by correspondents and visitors. On his return, Jefferson continued to rely on preexisting legal and political arguments. Only where the Constitution was explicit, did Jefferson accept that the new text altered matters. By diminishing the significance of the Convention, Jefferson promoted his constitutional interpretations as equally legitimate.[1]

The Notes helped form Jefferson's perception of the changes in American politics that had occurred in his absence. By early 1791, he read selections from the Notes, although he may not have read them carefully and in their entirety. Gradually, Jefferson became convinced that Hamilton and his allies were secretly devoted to a more monarchical government. Later that spring, Jefferson's nephew began to copy the Notes. Jefferson also decided to keep his own political notes, focusing in large part on Hamilton. By 1792, Hamilton's Convention plan became evidence of hidden monarchical tendencies that made necessary Jefferson's promotion of a political party devoted to republican government. In the Notes, five sheets were replaced, each containing a Madison speech or vote capable of being read as aligned with Hamilton. Incipient plans for publication of the Notes, if they were made during these years, never came to fruition. Jefferson retired, and Madison married. By 1799, when Jefferson urged publication, Madison demurred. In succeeding decades, the Notes remained unpublished.

Jefferson returned with views framed by the aspirations and anxieties of the French Revolution instead of firsthand experience with American political changes. He superimposed a French republican lens on American politics. For Jefferson, danger lay with would-be monarchists rather than state governments. Salvation lay with republican government rather than national or federal government. A letter for Madison brought back by Jefferson from France emphasized the French perspective. The most famous phrase discussed the "principle that the earth belongs to the living, and not to the dead" and criticized the idea of an enduring legal document. Jefferson calculated nineteen years as the longest period for which a political society could bind itself. The larger section, however, focused on France: the "principle that the earth belongs to the living, and not to the dead, is of very extensive application and consequences, in every country, and most especially in France." The five-year hiatus from American politics reframed Jefferson's political lens.[2]

Madison disagreed with the application of French revolutionary philosophy to the United States. He rejected Jefferson's philosophical starting point, the "law of nature," in favor of "conveniency." He cautioned, "However applicable in Theory the doctrine may be to a Constitution, in [sic] seems liable in practice to some very powerful objections." With a certain wry fondness, Madison noted that "our hemisphere must be still more enlightened before many of the sublime truths which are seen thro' the medium of Philosophy, become visible to the naked eye of the ordinary Politician." If Jefferson possessed the "eye of the philosophical Legislator," Madison perceived himself as an ordinary politician.[3]

Despite the different perspectives, the two men were collaborating on political matters within a week of Jefferson's arrival in New York in the spring of 1790. Correspondents perceived the close relationship. Randolph, for example, sent material to Madison with a "duplicate, that one may be put into mr. [sic] Jefferson's hands, if you approve." The two men may have held unvoiced political ambitions. A year earlier, Madison had mentioned to Jefferson, in a letter wishing him an "expeditious and safe passage across the Atlantic," that the "President has been *ill*." When Washington fell sick later that spring, Jefferson wrote of "very near

losing the President" and commented that two of three doctors pro-
nounced Washington "to be in the act of death." Washington nevertheless remained president for two terms and lived almost another decade
until December 1799.[4]

The first months were difficult for Jefferson as he struggled to adjust
to the new political world. An initial opinion by him as secretary of state
coincided with Madison's interpretation on whether the Senate could
alter the decision to send a minister to a foreign country. Madison argued that the power was "Executive and vested in the President by the
Constitution." Jefferson's letter made the same precise point. Jefferson initially had no apparent animosity towards Hamilton. He may have bro-
kered the famous compromise of 1790 between Madison and Hamilton
over dinner, although historians disagree on the details, relative involvement, and motives. The Potomac would become the seat of government;
a congressional plan permitting the assumption of state debts from the
war would move forward. The congressional politics were murky and
Madison wrote that "the votes printed furnish no clue, and which it is
impossible in a letter to explain to you." Jefferson later justified his assistance to Hamilton. During his absence, he "had lost a familiarity with
its [American] affairs" and "had not yet got into the train of them."[5]

Jefferson was uninterested in the Constitution. His advice on the study
of law recommended "Virginia laws" and "other American histories." His
report on weights and measures did not refer to the Constitution. His
opinion on arrearages in soldiers' pay in Virginia and North Carolina relied on common law and the laws of Virginia. When asked to address
the constitutionality of the residence bill on the capitol location, Jefferson
sidestepped the Constitution. His analysis began with natural rights. He
argued that Congress possessed a "natural right of governing itself" and
of fixing the time and place of meeting unless limited by the Constitution. Jefferson analyzed each constitutional provision as subsidiary to the
natural right. He concluded that Congress could alter its natural right of
adjournment by ordinary law without involving the Constitution. Jefferson did not interpret the Constitution as supplanting the pre-1787
constitutional structure with which he was familiar.[6]

During these first months in New York, Jefferson left no mention of
the Notes. Madison may have been working to complete them, or Jefferson may have been too busy to read them. In September 1790, Madison traveled with Jefferson to Virginia. The Notes are not on the packing
lists of two boxes of books sent to Philadelphia. The two men traveled

to Mount Vernon to see Washington and to Gunston Hall to see George Mason. But their correspondence provides little evidence of their intentions. If Madison brought the Notes with him to Virginia, he may have discussed them with Jefferson or even lent them.[7]

At Monticello, Jefferson began to contemplate acquiring a personal copy of the Notes. In October 1790, Jefferson wrote to see if his nephew, Jack Eppes, would be interested in coming to Philadelphia to do copying. The Eppes family was close to Jefferson. Francis Eppes had married Elizabeth Wayles, the sister of Jefferson's wife, Martha. After Martha died in 1782, the family had taken care of Jefferson's two daughters while he was in France. In 1784, Jefferson's daughter, Lucy, and the Eppes's daughter, Lucy, died of whooping cough. The Eppes eventually would send Jefferson's surviving daughter, Polly, to France with Sally Hemings, the fourteen-year-old enslaved girl, in May 1787. Jefferson maintained his correspondence with the Eppes family until his return to the United States. The choice of Jack Eppes carried an assumption about likely loyalty and discretion to Jefferson. Jack could "read law" and do "writing in my office." There would be "a great deal of drudgery in merely copying." In mid-October, Francis Eppes wrote that Jack would come. He preferred Jack "being in your Family to any other situation in the World." Jefferson had acquired a copyist.[8]

In early November 1790, Jefferson and Madison returned to Philadelphia to stay at the boarding house establishment run by Mrs. House and her daughter, Mrs. Trist. Jefferson had postponed his departure from Virginia because of "the desire of having Mr. Madison's company." Madison left behind instructions to the Montpelier overseers that included that the "Negroes" should be treated with "all the humanity & kindness consistent with their necessary subordination and work." He had changed little, if any, of his attitudes towards slavery.[9]

By February 1791, Jefferson had read at least one day of the Notes. In an opinion to Washington on the constitutionality of the national bank, Jefferson argued that the Convention had rejected a congressional power of incorporation. Jefferson drew on and accepted the Notes' description of the Convention proceedings for September 14.

The surrounding politics of the national bank were complicated. Hamilton had proposed the idea of a national bank in December 1790. Madison and certain Virginians disliked the idea. It supported an economic vision of the United States less dependent on southern agriculture. More-over, the proposed location in Philadelphia reinforced anxieties that the new capital would not be located on the edge of Virginia. Hamilton ini-tially seemed confident about the constitutionality. Indeed, opposition was late to form, arising on the third reading of the bill in February 1791. Even then Jefferson predicted that the "bank will pass." He preferred to increase "agricultural representation" in Congress and "put that interest above that of stock-jobbers." The bill passed by large margins, and Wash-ington signed it.[10]

In the congressional debates, Madison cited the Convention to argue that Congress had no authority to incorporate the bank. He "well rec-ollected" that "a power to grant charters of incorporation had been proposed in the general convention and rejected." For other members, however, the absence of an explicit power did not resolve the question. Roger Sherman viewed the bank as a necessary and proper means to ful-fill congressional power to regulate finances. Another member "proceeded to cite numerous instances" of powers "deduced under the constitution by necessary implication." The interpretive approach followed by Congress since 1789 seemed to support the bank. Fisher Ames explained,

> If Congress may not make laws conformably to the powers plainly implied, tho not expressed in the frame of government, it is rather late in the day to adopt it as a principle of conduct: A great part of our two year's labor is lost . . . for we have scarcely made a law in which we have not exercised our discretion with regard to the true intent of the constitution.

Indeed, Madison was accused of personal inconsistency. A member re-called his successful argument "that the power of removal from offices . . . was by construction and implication, vested, by the constitution, in the President—for there could be no pretence that it was expressly granted to him." To some observers, Madison's interpretive approach had changed.[11]

Unable to draw on a personal recollection of the Convention, Jefferson referred to knowledge of the proceedings—knowledge that came from the Notes. He minimized the relevance of the Constitution. Unless the Constitution had an explicit provision providing authority—which it did not—congressional power did not exist. He argued that the bank vio-lated traditional state common law doctrines against mortmain, alienage, and descents. He claimed that the Convention rejected an incorporation power based on fears of the bank:

It is known that the very power now proposed *as a means,* was rejected *as an end,* by the Convention which formed the constitution. A proposition was made to them to authorize Congress to open canals, and an amendatory one to empower them to incorporate. But the whole was rejected, and one of the reasons of rejection urged in debate was that then they would have a power to erect a bank, which would render the great cities, where there were prejudices and jealousies on that subject adverse to the reception of the constitution.

The description paraphrased the Notes. King's comments in the Notes on September 14 stated: "The States will be prejudiced and divided into parties by it—In Philadª. & New York, It will be referred to the establishment of a Bank, which has been a subject of contention in those Cities." The Notes gave Jefferson the ability to reinterpret the Convention.[12]

Other interpretations were possible based on the account in the Notes. Indeed, Jefferson even acknowledged that he described only "one of the reasons." The Notes cited Franklin's motion to add a power to cut canals and Madison's suggestion of "an enlargement of the motion into a power 'to grant charters of incorporation where the interest of the U.S. might require & the legislative provisions of individual States may be incompetent.'" Several short comments were made, including King's implication that the explicit power was unnecessary. The original canal motion was restored and failed (3–8). Madison explained in the Notes, "The other proposition fell of course, as including the power rejecting." The Convention had rejected a specific power to cut canals, but the reasons and relationship to general incorporation were unclear.[13]

The references to the Convention in Jefferson's opinion were sufficient to have led Washington to suspect Madison's Notes as the source. In possession of the official Convention journals and vote tallies, Washington knew the records provided little evidence supporting the September 14 interpretation. The official records contained no evidence of Madison's alleged motion. The journal provided no details for September 14. The secretary's voting tallies confirmed only the motion on canals. If Madison attempted to introduce an explicit power on September 14, the Notes were the only evidence. Hamilton may have also assumed that Madison had shared a portion of the Notes with Jefferson. Although the bank passed, the episode suggested that Jefferson was willing to engage in interpretation of what happened at the Convention. His use of the material drawn from Notes to limit the Constitution may have raised concerns.[14]

For Jefferson, the bank bill hinted at potential contemporary political usefulness of the Notes. Several days after writing his opinion on the bank bill, Jefferson wrote a comment about the advantage of copies of records. The "multiplication of copies" placed them "beyond the reach of accident." Madison later explained that Jefferson's copy of the Notes would "double the security agst. destructive casualties." In March, Jefferson wrote Francis Eppes: "the sooner Jack can now come the better."[15]

Jefferson nurtured a growing belief that members of Washington's administration aspired to a more monarchically styled government. In the spring, he described himself as "anti-monarchical, and anti-aristocratical." Others favored the "Halfway-house" of the English constitution. In May, he was the obvious, anonymous author of a blurb referring to "the political heresies which have sprung up among us" for an edition of Thomas Paine's *Rights of Man.* In a letter to Washington, Jefferson insisted that John Adams had "views of drawing the present government to the form of the English constitution."[16]

In late May, Madison and Jefferson traveled north to New York, Vermont, and Connecticut. Although some contemporaries suspected secret political motives, historians have been unable to find explicit evidence of a plan to develop northern support for a republican political effort. The two men's records are devoid of any political comments. The journey apparently improved their health. Jefferson had "great hopes it has rid me of my head-ach, having scarcely had any thing of it during my journey," and Madison's health was "very visibly mended." Even if the men advanced no explicit opposition strategy, the trip did not alter Jefferson's belief about monarchical leanings in the administration. It likely made the strength of Jefferson's conviction completely apparent to Madison. Indeed, by the end of the summer, they persuaded Philip Freneau to found the *National Gazette* to promote Jefferson's incipient republican political movement.[17]

The close political alliance was noticed. Richard Peters wrote Jefferson that Madison was seen as the "*Fox* of America"—and as "cunning." In return, Jefferson invited him for "a bad dinner, a good glass of wine" and suggested implicitly that Madison might join them. Charles Pinckney wrote Madison, "I have not the honour to know Mr: Jefferson" and insinuatingly added, "I am told you are very intimate with him."[18]

In the meantime, Jack Eppes had arrived in Philadelphia. By May, Jefferson encouraged him to "write an hour or two to learn the stile of business and acquire a habit of writing." Jefferson attempted to improve Eppes's handwriting. Eppes later noted, "I fear you will suppose from this letter I have forgot your injunctions." He apologized, "the badness of the hand will be excused when I inform you I had no knife that could make a pen."[19]

Eppes made a partial copy of the Notes for Jefferson. Eppes gave little effort to making a perfect copy and he did not proofread. He seems likely to have copied the Notes over a considerable period; indeed, they may not have been completed until his return to Virginia several years later. Apparently unlike the Notes, the copy bore a title, *Debates of the Grand Federal Convention, Taken by a member.* The title gave an integrity and coherence to the copy absent from the original Notes.[20]

The three sections of the copy reflected the structural division of the Notes in the early 1790s. The first part began in May and ended with the Report of the Committee of the Whole House on June 20. The second part began oddly and abruptly partway through the proceedings for July 18 and ended on August 21. The third part began on August 22 and extended through September 17. Blank pages in the Notes after June 20 and August 21 emphasized the divisions. In fact, the sections may have been grouped or sewn separately. Although the first section reflected the procedural stage of the Committee of the Whole House, the other two divisions reflected Madison's composition of the Notes. The August and September section was the product of the later-completed Notes. The July 18 section began after the controversial vote on executive tenure. A more coherent narrative division would have broken the Notes before the first draft of the Constitution. Eppes nonetheless followed the manuscript.[21]

Madison likely still had the Notes from June 21 to July 18. Eppes never copied this section. The missing section covered the debates over the committee report through the vote on executive tenure. Madison either was contemplating altering certain sheets or was in the process of doing so. The first and last sheets of the uncopied section are replaced sheets. Jefferson's copy was written reflecting Madison's revisions, not the original Notes.[22]

In mid-March 1791, Madison was working on his writing. He wrote, "I am just settled in my harness for compleating the little task I have allotted myself." Jefferson invited Madison to live with him—to "come & take a bed and plate with me." Madison declined, noting that his "papers and books are all assorted, around me." The task may have involved the Notes or notes for newspaper essays written later in the fall of 1791.

Although the essays did not draw on the Notes, the two projects may have become intertwined as components of the larger political strategy contemplated by the two men.[23]

Jefferson's copy was entwined with his conviction that Hamilton was opposed to republican government. Years later, Eppes recalled that the Notes established that Hamilton, "the idol of the Federal party was not a Monarchist in Theory merely, but the open zealous and unreserved advocate for the adoption of the monarchical system in this Country." In copying the Notes, Eppes copied Hamilton's speech and plan in June, as well as the copy made by Madison of Hamilton's alleged plan at the end of the Convention. The copy seemed to prove that the Convention had been tainted by monarchical elements.[24]

The copying project was conducted in secrecy. Eppes remembered that the copying was so "confidential" that for "years after the copy was taken" he never mentioned the existence of Jefferson's copy. In 1810, in writing Madison, Eppes with some irritation noted that he had learned several years earlier that others knew "the fact" of Jefferson's copy. Eppes concluded it was "unnecessary to impose on myself the same rigid silence." In 1791, however, Jefferson's copy was confidential and related to his larger political purposes.[25]

In mid-August 1791, Jefferson began to keep his own notes about political matters. These notes, known as the *Anas*, focused significantly on Hamilton's apparent monarchical tendencies. Perhaps with an eye to a future reader, Jefferson justified the accuracy of his notes. With respect to the record of one conversation, he explained that it was "nearly as much at length as it really was, the expressions preserved where I could recollect them, and their substance always faithfully stated." Jefferson eventually made what he described as a "calm revisal" of the *Anas*, and he may have toned down some comments against Hamilton.[26]

Throughout the *Anas*, Jefferson compiled evidence of monarchical tendencies in American political leaders. The first note recorded a private conversation about John Adams between Jefferson and Hamilton. Adams was described as having been sympathetic to hereditary rule, and Hamilton predicted that American government would likely eventually follow the "British form." Later, Jefferson referred to Gouverneur Morris as "a high flying Monarchy-man" who kept the "President's mind constantly poisoned with his forebodings." A repeated theme involved

Jefferson's efforts to persuade Washington of the danger. In February 1792, he told Washington that the "treasury possessed already such an influence as to swallow up the whole Executive powers." In March, he warned of "such legislative constructions of the constitution" to support an "unlimited government." In a small document written in difficult-to-read Sheltonian shorthand, Jefferson laid out his "Agenda to reduce the government to true principles."[27]

Hamilton's plan at the Convention was among Jefferson's concerns. In August 1792, Washington complained of the "internal dissentions" between Jefferson and Hamilton. Jefferson offered no apology in his explanatory letter. Hamilton planned to "undermine and demolish the republic." Referring obviously to the Convention, Jefferson alleged that Hamilton had hoped for "a king and house of lords" and a general government with "power to make laws binding the states in all cases whatsoever." Jefferson argued that Hamilton's subsequent actions aimed to achieve this goal. The insinuation about the June speech was designed to show that Hamilton's ideas "flowed from principles adverse to liberty." He was "a man whose history, from the moment at which history can stoop to notice him, is a tissue of machinations against the liberty of the country which has not only recieved [sic] and given him bread, but heaped it's honors on his head." Jefferson had been "duped" by Hamilton and "made a tool for forwarding his schemes, not then sufficiently understood by me."[28]

Additional evidence about the Convention appeared in the *Anas*. George Mason told Jefferson that the Constitution had been altered in the final weeks from one which he would have "set his hand and heart to." New England and most southern states formed a new coalition over the foreign slave trade, and the "great principles of the Constitution were changed in the last days of the Convention." Mason described several incidents of alleged manipulation. He claimed that Yates and Lansing never voted "in one single instance" with Hamilton, who "was so much mortified at it that he went home."[29]

As the *Anas* continued, Hamilton became Jefferson's nemesis. Jefferson insisted that Hamilton belonged to a "numerous sect who had monarchy in contemplation." The Convention loomed large as the foundation of Hamilton's plan:

> I had heard him [Hamilton] say that this constitution was a shilly shally thing of mere milk and water, which could not last, and was only good as a step to something better. That when we reflected that he had endeavored in

the Convention to make an English constitution of it, and when failing in that we saw all his measures tending to bring it to the same thing it was natural for us to be jealous.

Jefferson copied an account about a dinner where Hamilton allegedly defended monarchy. He described an inaccurate rumor that Hamilton had written a pamphlet in opposition to Thomas Paine's *Common Sense*. He recorded another "fact"—this one told to him thirdhand—about an alleged "plan for establishing a monarchical government" in the United States by Hamilton prior to 1787. By February 1793, Jefferson wrote a document—never found by historians—entitled "history of A. Hamilton."[30]

Jefferson charted Hamilton's influence in the administration. He compiled a list of "paper-men" holding investments. The list included important Convention members: Sherman, Ellsworth, King, Dickinson, Morris, and Johnson. Jefferson wanted Congress "cleansed of all persons interested in the bank or public stocks." At the end of December 1792, Jefferson learned of the "affair of Reynolds & his wife." The relevant facts of Hamilton's affair with Maria Reynolds are complicated, and the Virginians were principal investigators. Jefferson believed that Hamilton had given Washington tainted advice because of the affair. After a meeting on a treaty with France, Jefferson concluded that questions in Washington's handwriting "were not the President's" but that "the language was Hamilton's, and the doubts his alone." By December 1793, when the *Anas* ended, Hamilton, the Convention, and monarchical government were irrevocably intertwined in Jefferson's mind.[31]

For Jefferson, American politics had become a contest between republican government and a return to British-influenced monarchical politics. The word "republic" was a key term and political signal, meaning more than a type of political structure. Washington caught the word in a draft. He told Jefferson that "certainly ours was a republican government" but the government had "not used that stile in this way." Jefferson, however, employed "republic" as a political brand. Even in the omission of the word, Jefferson saw proof of antirepublican sympathies. He described secondhand information that Hamilton had not addressed "the Minister of the *republic of France,* but always as the minister of France." By August 1793, Jefferson was referring to the "Republican party." That fall, Jefferson was delighted when Randolph "by accident" had written the phrase, "our republic," into a Washington speech.[32]

Washington repeatedly rejected the insinuations about Hamilton that Jefferson directed his way. The *Anas* were filled with the record of the president's cautions, seemingly to imply that Washington was, at best, naïve and, at worst, deluded. In July 1792, Washington thought "there were suspicions against a particular party which had been carried a great deal too far." He acknowledged that there "might be *desires,* but he did not believe there were *designs* to change the form of government into a monarchy." In another carefully recorded conversation in October, Washington rejected Jefferson's claim. There were not "ten men in the U.S. whose opinions were worth attention" who hoped to transform "this government into a monarchy." Finally, Washington warned Jefferson about his republican party. Washington "believed the views of the Republican party were perfectly pure, but when men put a machine into motion, it is impossible for them to stop it exactly where they would chuse or to say where it will stop."[33]

Jefferson's allegations posed a significant threat to Hamilton. In 1792, an article appeared in Freneau's *National Gazette* referring to Hamilton's views at the Convention. The article alleged that Hamilton had opposed the Constitution because it was "too *republican*" and promoted "the *British Monarch* as the *perfect standard.*" In response, Hamilton wrote an essay stating that the "highest-toned" propositions had been voted for by some who now were considered "pre-eminent for republican character." Madison and the Virginians were the obvious target. Hamilton added that he could say no more because the "deliberations of the Convention which were carried on in private, were to remain undisturbed." The official records were not a problem for Hamilton. His plan had never been introduced; he had often been unable to vote; he had been absent much of the summer. The most damning vote was the one on executive tenure and that recorded the Virginians' favorable vote. His fear was more likely the publication of Madison's Notes or, perhaps more troubling, only Hamilton's speech and plan. Soon thereafter, Hamilton began to explain the context in which he had advanced his Convention proposals for terms of good behavior for the Senate and president. The Madison-Jefferson alliance seemed to betray the understanding under which Hamilton had lent to Madison his early Convention plan and joined in writing the Federalist essays.[34]

The role of the Notes in creating or confirming Jefferson's beliefs is difficult to judge. At a minimum, Jefferson learned of Hamilton's June speech and plan from the Notes. He accepted them as Hamilton's true convictions, rather than as strategic or possibly inaccurately recorded materials. If Jefferson had never read the Notes carefully—or had read only selectively—Hamilton's plan was evidence confirming Jefferson's biases.

Jefferson's interpretation reversed the significance of his absence in France during the Convention. France represented the embrace of republicanism; the Convention had become the secret betrayal of republicanism. By virtue of being in France, Jefferson gave himself an innocence that other American politicians lacked. His subsequent reconfiguration of American politics obscured and recast the Convention. Jefferson no longer was a political leader who had failed to participate in the founding; he was the only one untainted by it.

Madison became a willing ally to the narrative that a monarchist party had arisen at the Convention. In a remarkably short time, Madison shifted to support Jefferson's fears of a conspiracy to abandon republican policies and create a monarchical government. From the fall of 1791 through 1792, Madison wrote anonymous political newspapers essays. These essays gradually moved toward explicit support of a republican party. Madison's replacement of the five sheets containing speeches made in late June and July were plausibly made during this period. These replacements either promoted Republican Government or diminished evidence of Madison's support for what had become recast as monarchical positions.

Madison's understanding of the Notes had altered over the past decade. In 1790, Madison articulated what information should be included in legislative *debates*. That April, Madison asked Edmund Pendleton to write down the Virginia proceedings regarding the Stamp Act in 1765. Madison outlined the information that should be included. Pendleton was to "*briefly* note on paper—by whom & how the subject commenced in the assembly, where the resolutions proposed by Mr. Henry *really* originated, what was the sum of the arguments for and against them, and who were the principal speakers on each side; with any little anecdotes throwing light on the transaction, on the characters concerned in it, or on the temper of the Colony at the time." Pendleton sent information after noting that he had not actually been present at the debates. Madison reassured him, "knowing the accuracy & extent of your intelligence on all such interresting [*sic*] occurrences, I consider the particulars with which you have favor[e]d me as not the less authentic on that account." Authenticity for Madison remained surprisingly flexible.[35]

In November 1791, Madison began to write anonymous essays for Freneau's *National Gazette*. Madison favored large words and muted ideas. Although the essays did not yet advocate a republican brand, they linked consolidation to monarchical government. One essay described "consolidation" as worse than "schism" because it was "the high road to monarchy." The essays were less interesting than the underlying "Notes on Federal Governments" that he compiled in preparation. Madison surveyed the size of the nation, external dangers, public opinion, education, religion, domestic slavery, checks, reasons for keeping separate government departments, general government, and the best distribution of people in a republic. The notes for the "influence of the size of the nation" included the reference: "See Convention Notes—letter to Mr. Jefferson on federal negative on State laws Federalists No. X et alia." The essays formed a bridge between Madison's views at the Convention and the approach advocated by Jefferson.[36]

In the months that followed, these anonymous essays advanced what had become a seemingly shared agenda of Madison and Jefferson. An essay for the *National Gazette* alleged that some people were yet "openly or secretly attached to monarchy and aristocracy; and hoped to make the constitution a cradle for these hereditary establishments." Madison differentiated the "Republican party, as it may be termed" from those who were "more partial to the opulent than to the other classes of society." These latter people "debauched themselves into a persuasion that mankind are incapable of governing themselves." In another anonymous essay, Madison asked, "Who are the best keepers of the people's liberties?" The "Anti-republican" saw the people as "stupid, suspicious, licentious." The "Republican" saw "the people" as the solution. Key words— "opulent," "aristocratic," "the people"—were signals of underlying political commitments.[37]

The political shift did not pass unnoticed. Madison noted that an opposition pamphlet described him as having "sacrificed his principles & prostrated his understanding from an implied complaisance to the ambitious & malicious views of his friend." Indeed, Madison was arguing against positions he had advanced at the Convention: a willingness to reduce the states; a commitment to a small Senate and a lengthy executive; a desire for a national government with a negative on state laws; a defense of elites and an opulent minority. Aligned with Jefferson's republican politics were Madison's defense of proportional representation, his acceptance of slavery, and his defense of southern interests.[38]

The Notes presented difficulties. The five replaced sheets included speeches inconsistent with this republican rhetoric. A brief list highlights the potential concerns:

1. June 21: Madison's speech on encroachments, the states as corporations, and possible abolition of state governments (b.30)
2. June 23: Madison's speech against absolute disqualification for office and mode for acquiring the fittest candidates (b.33)
3. June 26: Madison's speech praising the Senate and the need to represent the more affluent minority (b.37)
4. June 29: Madison's speech on reducing the power of the states and the danger of states (b.42)
5. July 17: Madison's speech on the relative danger of executive, judiciary, and legislature (b.62)
6. July 17: Madison's speech on the executive and monarchy (b.62)
7. July 17: Vote on motion for an executive serving on good behavior (b.62)

Madison could not completely rewrite the speeches or even hope to claim he had not spoken. Too many members remained alive. Some members had notes. Many had powerful memories. But he could ensure that sentences—in his handwriting—would not be used as evidence against him.[39]

Other note takers' versions of these Madison speeches usually contain an idea or statement that had become controversial. As Madison replaced these sheets, sentences and ideas, evident in the notes of others, vanished. The revised pages included the speeches—but not the specific sentence. Moreover, Madison subtly recast his aspiration for the form of government to be established by the Constitution as "Republican Government"—the touchstone of Jefferson's agenda. Although "republic" and even "republican Government" appear occasionally in the Notes, the prominence of the term is striking in these speeches. In the June 26 speech, for example, Madison declared the purpose as "a plan which in its operation w[oul]d decide forever the fate of Republican Gov[ernmen]t. In the July 17 speech, Madison emphasized the "preservation of Republican Gov[ernmen]t." Madison's purpose at the Convention had been revised to align explicitly with Jefferson's contemporary political agenda.[40]

The vote favoring an executive tenure on good behavior—impossible to erase—was contextualized. The official records revealed the July 17 vote. The vote tallies—which Madison may or may not have seen—

recorded Virginia's favorable vote. Madison could not claim the vote had not been taken or that the Virginians had not voted favorably. The replaced pages added an explanation. The vote was "not to be considered as any certain index of opinion." Some affirmative votes were intended to "alarm" others and "facilitate final arrangement of a contrary tendency." In his October 1787 letter to Jefferson, Madison had distinguished between the few who favored the tenure and a larger number who would have supported it "in case an easy & effectual removal by impeachment could be settled." He had written as if he had been in the latter group. In replacing the paper, Madison reworked the explanation, altering the distinction to provide evidence of a large group who quietly favored monarchy.[41]

Madison may have wanted to replace one additional speech: his August 7 speech on suffrage. The speech began with an acceptable proposition that the right of suffrage had been a fundamental article of "republican Government." But Madison continued by arguing that "freeholders"—property owners—would be safe "depositories of Republican liberty." He added that in the future the "majority" would not have property and the majority would therefore render insecure the "rights of property & public good." By the early 1790s, this speech was overly favorable toward property holders and too adamant that the majority would endanger liberty and property. Two revised versions of this speech exist. A lengthy version appeared in an appendix prepared by John C. Payne before Madison's death. An introductory comment stated that the August 7 speech did "not convey the speaker's more full and matured view of the subject, which is subjoined." An earlier revision may also exist: another speech appeared in the appendix bearing only the vaguest resemblance but approximately the same length. It would have fit into the space if the sheet had been replaced. Similar to Madison's National Gazette essay on property in 1792, it described the "fundamental principle" that "men cannot be justly bound by laws in making which they have no part." It discussed that persons and property were "both essential objects of government." It attempted to revise Madison's meaning in the new republican political environment. Madison, however, never replaced the speech.[42]

Were the five sheets replaced with an eye towards publication? If Jefferson read the Notes in their entirety, the replacements suggest contemplation of the Notes as part of his political agenda. If Jefferson never read the Notes carefully—or at least had not read the mid-June to mid-July section—then Madison's replacements suggest an effort to retroactively align Madison's positions with those of Jefferson. Did Jefferson know of the replacements? The friendship between Madison and Jefferson favors

Jefferson's knowledge, but even between great friends, there are often secrets. In fact, a friendship may depend on a secret. If Jefferson had long
misunderstood Madison's stance in the Convention, it was far too late
to have remediated it.

In late 1792, Madison and Jefferson believed that Washington would
retire. Jefferson thought the announcement might occur "even after the
meeting of Congress." Madison drafted a farewell address, but Washington served a second term. Jefferson retired to Monticello. He was sick
and suffering from rheumatism. He wrote Madison that he did not plan to
return to public life. As he later explained to his daughter, "from 1793. to
1797. I remained closely at home, saw none but those who came there, and
at length became very sensible of the ill effect it had upon my own mind,
and of it's direct & irresistible tendency to render me unfit for society, &
uneasy when necessarily engaged in it." Eppes returned to Virginia—and
may have continued to copy the Notes for Jefferson at Monticello.[43]

In 1793, Madison's life once again changed. His stay at the boarding
house in Philadelphia came to an end. Mrs. House died, and Eliza Trist
planned to sell the establishment. By June 1794, Madison had formed
an attachment to Dolley Payne, a Philadelphia widow. In September 1794,
they married. The correspondence between Madison and Jefferson declined, and the dynamic of their friendship seemed to subtly change. When
Madison traveled to Virginia in the late summer of 1794, he barely found
time to visit Jefferson.[44]

Madison likely replaced other sheets between 1792 and 1796. First, Madison inserted a replacement sheet for September 7–8. In the process, he
mistakenly left a gap in the proceedings on September 8. Another sheet—
likely the final one added to the Notes—compensated for this missing
material. Second, far more speculatively, Madison may have replaced in
part the sheets describing the final two days of the Convention. Resolution of these matters will depend on future scholarship.[45]

The September 7–8 proceedings were recorded with difficulty. In the
official journal of the Convention, Washington had inserted certain words
in pencil, apparently disagreeing with the journal's record. The order and
substance of the motions may have been confused. In the Notes, the sheet
for September 7 (b.121) is different from other surrounding sheets. Eppes
noticed that material was missing between this sheet and the subsequent
one. Madison must have replaced the original sheet but left the remaining
material unfinished. Madison eventually added a new sheet (b.122) for

September 7–8 but made no effort to fill it. His writing scrawls across the pages. It ended abruptly halfway down the last page: "M^r. Madison objected to a trial of the President by the" and then with plenty of space to write, Madison added the carry word: "Senate." There was no effort to disguise the addition. Madison added this last sheet when he had no interest in obscuring the addition.[46]

The matter under debate involved the treaty power, in particular, the relationship among the president and the Senate and treaties of peace. The treaty power had been the subject of repeated controversy among Jefferson, Madison, and Hamilton. Jefferson had disagreed with others in Washington's administration with respect to the Neutrality Proclamation and the Jay Treaty. In July 1793, Hamilton published essays related to the treaty power under the pen name, Pacificus. Jefferson wanted Madison to disagree: "For god's sake, my dear Sir, take up your pen, select the most striking heresies, and cut him to peices [sic] in the face of the public." Madison somewhat grudgingly complied, writing a series of essays under the pen name Helvidius. In September 1795, Hamilton again wrote essays discussing the treaty power, this time under the pen name Camillus. In nearly identical words, Jefferson again asked Madison to "for god's sake take up your pen, and give a fundamental reply to Curtius & Camillus." Instead of writing essays, in October 1795 Madison visited Jefferson at Monticello to discuss objections to the Jay Treaty.[47]

By early 1796, the Convention proceedings became a focus in the treaty power debate. In January in the final and thirty-eighth Camillus essay, Hamilton dared Madison to disagree with his depiction of the Convention: "To suppose them capable of such a denial were to suppose them utterly regardless of truth." Hamilton argued that the "intent of the provision" was to provide "the most ample latitude . . . which the exigencies of National Affairs might require" for any type of treaty and competent "to controul & bind the legislative power of Congress." On March 19, Washington deposited the official journals with the state department. The Convention proceedings were now a matter of public record. Washington then wrote an official message in support of the treaty and in agreement with Hamilton. The message relied in part on the official records and a Convention vote on August 23, 1787 apparently rejecting the requirement that treaties had to be separately ratified as laws.[48]

The appearance of the official records, including the official journal, worried Madison. On April 4, he wrote Jefferson, suggesting that the last sheets of the Notes would demonstrate that Washington should not have deposited the official records. Then in Congress on April 6, Madison gave a lengthy speech denying Hamilton's and Washington's interpretation. Of equal importance, the speech sought to draw attention away from the official records of the Convention. After disagreeing with the Hamilton-Washington interpretation of the Convention, Madison attempted to diminish the authority of the Convention. He argued that the more legitimate meaning of the Constitution was to be drawn from the records of the ratification conventions. Madison knew the paltry extent of these records. The replacement of these two sheets may relate to this controversy or the similar one in 1793.[49]

A final mystery lies with the last four sheets of the Notes. Did Madison compose the detailed description of the September 15 proceedings after Eppes copied the manuscript? The Eppes copy of September 15 is missing, but the page numbers imply it was considerably shorter than the current material in the Notes. The evidence is ambiguous. Although these sheets are on a different paper from all but the replaced sheet for September 7, Eppes appears to have copied the September 17 sheets. Replacing the sheets would have allowed Madison to describe in detail the alterations made toward the end of the day on September 15. Further study may elucidate the mystery or, equally plausibly, leave it unresolved.[50]

Regardless of precise chronology, the final sheets were likely in place by the end of 1796. Jefferson had possession of the end, if not the entire, Notes manuscript at Monticello that spring. If Eppes was still copying, the enterprise was likely completed during the year. On September 25, 1796, Eppes wrote Jefferson that he hoped to marry Jefferson's daughter, Maria. If Jefferson and Eppes discussed the copy, the evidence may lie in the six letters exchanged between September 1795 and June 1796, which have never been located.[51]

In late June 1796, Madison returned to Virginia and remained for the summer. Madison may have reacquired the Notes—or some portion—from Jefferson. At some point, Madison learned of the missing material on September 7–8. The last sheet composed by Madison was likely the one that filled the gap. In November 1796, Madison returned to Philadelphia and, in December, announced his retirement from politics.[52]

The end of Washington's second term brought a change in Jefferson's fate. In December 1796, Jefferson was elected vice president. Adams was elected President. As Jefferson returned to politics in March 1797, Madison returned to Virginia.[53]

Others suspected that Madison might have notes about the Convention. In January 1795, Madison's friend, Samuel Stanhope Smith, inquired about notes. Stanhope wanted to offer a course at the College of New Jersey (subsequently Princeton). He asked, "whether you have preserved any notes of your discourses on the federal constitution, or the constitution of Virginia—or of any reflections you have made on these subjects." Smith noted, "no man understands better than you."[54]

Jefferson continued to view the Notes in terms of his political agenda. The knowledge that the Notes were in publishable form was not a secret. In early 1799, Jefferson wrote Madison, "in a society of members between whom & yourself is great mutual esteem & respect, a most anxious desire is expressed that you would publish your debates of the Constitution." The "society" is thought to have been the American Philosophical Society, of which Jefferson had become president in 1797. Indicating an earlier discussion of the Notes' publication, Jefferson referred to Madison's likely concern as "personal." More important reasons, however, favored publication. Jefferson added, "something is required from you as a set-off against the sin of your retirement." He ended, "I beg of you to turn this subject in your mind." Jefferson predicted "a revulsion of public sentiment" against the Adams administration. He believed the "constitution will then recieve [sic] a different explanation." The Notes were evidence. Jefferson concluded, "Could those debates be ready to appear critically, their effect would be decisive."[55]

On February 8, 1799, Madison wrote back with considerably less enthusiasm about publication. He did not absolutely refuse. He put off the decision until they could discuss it: "I shall be better able to form & explain my opinion by the time, which now approaches when I shall have the pleasure of seeing you." The Notes had become a "whole volume"—a defined manuscript. And, like Jefferson, Madison described the Notes using a formal title: the "Debates of the Convention."[56]

But Madison worried that Jefferson had not read the entire Notes. He noted, "And you will have the advantage of looking into the Sheets attentively before you finally make up your own." The emphasis on "attentively" hints that Jefferson read the Notes selectively and not perhaps carefully. Madison worried that the Notes would not support Jefferson's interpretation. He explained that "the whole volume ought to be examined with an eye to the use of which every part is susceptible." He was conscious that other note takers had notes. He warned of other "reports of the proceedings that would perhaps be made out & mustered for the occasion." These reports would not necessarily confirm the Notes or Jefferson's position. Madison was not at all certain that the Notes would ultimately support Jefferson's desire for a different explanation of the Constitution. Madison cautioned, it "is a problem what turn might be given to the impression on the public mind."[57]

Madison worried about the "intimate connection" between the "personal view" and the "public" view. Nothing in the Notes would harm Jefferson's reputation. For Madison, however, the "expediency" of publication weighed rather differently. Over the past decade, the surviving group of Convention's delegates had already begun to shrink. Benjamin Franklin, James Wilson, George Mason, Roger Sherman, George Read, Nathaniel Gorham, David Brearley, Daniel Carroll, Daniel Jenifer of St. Thomas, William Houston, and William Livingston, had died. Nonetheless, many allies and foes remained alive, and Madison's version of his positions were precarious. Despite Jefferson's visit in March 1799, Madison's personal concerns trumped Jefferson's political expediency. Jefferson was unable to persuade Madison of the advantages of publication. Jefferson also may have decided that the Notes would not be as helpful as he had hoped. The Notes were not published.[58]

Jefferson was already moving on to a different interpretation of the Constitution. In the fall of 1798, Jefferson had drafted resolutions for the Kentucky legislature in opposition to the Adams administration; Madison had drafted similar ones for the Virginia legislature. These resolutions abandoned the language of "constitution" for the term, "compact." Jefferson's draft of the Kentucky Resolutions declared, "a compact under the style and title of a Constitution for the US." In August 1799, Jefferson described the "palpable violations of the constitutional compact by the Federal government" and the "true principles of our federal compact." The Notes—as diary or debates—did not support the constitutional compact interpretation. Indeed, Madison's speeches and his theory of the Constitution since the spring of 1787 held that the Constitution must not be a compact. Avoiding a compact had been Madison's overarching goal and one, despite his disappointments, that he believed had succeeded. Ironically, Madison's deepest anxiety at the Convention was turned to a new political use. Jefferson knew Madison would not publish the Notes. Perhaps, with a sense of relief, Madison put the Notes aside.[59]

CONCLUSION

In the years after 1787, Madison's Notes had shifted from a legislative diary to a volume of conventional debates. In August 1815, Thomas Jefferson wrote John Adams, "Do you know that there exists in MS. the ablest work of this kind ever yet executed, of the debates of the Constitutional convention of Philadelphia in 1788?" Perhaps assuming 1788 was when Madison wrote the manuscript, Adams wrote: "Mr. Madison's Notes of the Convention of 1787 or 1788 are consistent with his indefatigable Character." Jefferson emphasized the almost implausible detail of the account. The "whole of everything said and done" was "taken down by Mr. Madison, with a labor and exactness beyond comprehension."[1]

Adams correctly predicted, "I shall never see them; but I hope Posterity will." In retirement, Madison continued to revise the Notes. These revisions sought to bring the material into conformity with other printed materials about the Convention. Madison acknowledged only some of the printed sources for his revisions. He enlisted his brother-in-law, John C. Payne, in the creation of a transcript of the Notes designed to be published with other correspondence and documents of Madison. But when Jefferson and Adams died on July 4, 1826, the Notes remained unpublished.[2]

As the years passed, Madison grew increasingly wary about contemporary uses of the Convention proceedings and predicted a posthumous publication. By 1829, he was the last living member of the Convention. In the spring and early summer of 1836, his health failed. Dolley Madison's grandniece noted that the physicians were "anxious to prolong" Madison's life until July Fourth—precisely a decade after Adams' and Jefferson's deaths. Madison did not participate in a death for posterity. He "refused to take the necessary stimulants" and died on

June 28, 1836. He was eighty-five years old. After nearly fifty years, the Notes would be published.[3]

After 1799, Madison appears to have put the Notes aside for almost two decades. Beginning in 1801, Madison served as secretary of state during Jefferson's presidency. Jefferson even wrote that Madison "had no leisure to write" after he joined the administration. Subsequently, in 1809, Madison was sworn into office as president, serving two terms. Only with his retirement in 1817 did he turn to focus on the Notes.[4]

In the intervening years, the controversy over Hamilton's and Madison's positions at the Convention continued to trouble Madison. Before Hamilton's untimely death in 1804, he had attempted to explain the context of his Convention plan. In an 1803 letter, Hamilton implicated Madison. He wrote, "if I sinned against Republicanism, Mr. Madison was not less guilty." Hamilton declared that he had "never contemplated the abolition of the State Governments." He attempted to explain the shifting meanings of republican government and the context in which his and other "experimental propositions" had been advanced. Hamilton defended his June 1787 approach as compatible with republican government because the officials would have been elected by the people and held office on "temporary or *defeasible* tenure." He described the July vote on the executive on good behavior. He emphasized that Virginia had voted in favor and therefore Madison must have "concurred" in the vote. Hamilton also detailed the circumstances under which Madison had acquired a copy of his plan. In language similar to that on the heading of Madison's copy of the plan, Hamilton stated that Madison had been given his plan "about the close" of the Convention, "perhaps a day or two after." Hamilton insisted that the president's tenure was for three years. Hamilton's letter may have come to Madison's attention during his presidency; in 1812, it was reprinted in the *Weekly Register*.[5]

In the summer of 1810, Madison searched for the Hamilton plan in Hamilton's handwriting. Eppes wrote that he himself did not remember the plan existing in Hamilton's handwriting. Jefferson similarly replied that he did not have a plan in Hamilton's hand. He supposed it to have been copied in "your Original manuscript" on the "date of June 18." If Madison did not have his "MS. of the debates with you," Jefferson would "copy it from my copy." In subsequent years, Hamilton's son insisted that Madison had misrepresented his father's speech and merged the two different plans. Madison's search suggests uncertainty over the copy in the Notes or the attempt to create a record.[6]

After Madison's retirement from the presidency in 1817, his assistance was repeatedly requested with new publications relating to the founding period. The publishers Gales and Seaton wanted to produce a "Legislative History of our Country," and Madison agreed to lend necessary records to their effort. He helped Jacob Gideon with a new edition of the *Federalist Papers* (1818) by attributing authorship of each essay to himself or Hamilton. Madison's list differed from the one left by Hamilton before his death. The divergences created nearly two centuries of controversy.[7]

Most important among these publications was the printing of the official records of the Convention in 1819. When the new secretary of state, John Quincy Adams, had inquired about publication, Madison had been less than enthusiastic. Nevertheless, once Congress had authorized publication, he aided Adams by filling in the omissions in the official journal for the last two days. Based on his Notes, Madison created motions for these days. He confirmed the date on which Hamilton's plan had been presented. He also tried to help Adams sort out the vote tallies without motions. The introduction to the *Journal, Acts, and Proceedings of the Convention* explained that Madison had assisted, using his "own minutes." The *Journal* made public the existence of Madison's Notes.[8]

Although Madison had copied the journals, the *Journal* compiled significant material about the Convention that was not in Madison's possession. Adams printed the delegates' credentials, the amended Virginia resolutions, the Paterson and Hamilton plans, and the various drafts of the Constitution. He assigned votes to motions and inserted vote tallies throughout. One document eventually caused Madison considerable consternation. Adams included a plan "furnished by Mr. Pinckney." Madison had never recorded the Pinckney plan. The secretary had not kept a copy of either the Virginia or Pinckney plan in the records. Madison also explained that he did "not find the plan of Mr. Charles Pinkney" among his papers. Adams acquired a plan from Pinckney. It was eventually discovered that Pinckney had sent a document written in or after 1797—around the time that Jefferson was urging publication of the Notes. Controversy has followed the Pinckney plan. Historians currently believe that the 1797 version contained elements of Pinckney's original plan with conflations or revisions. In later years, Madison became obsessed with apparent inaccuracies in the plan.[9]

Initially, one apparent discrepancy about the *Journal* bothered Madison. In June 1820, Madison wrote Adams that he had been "turning over a few pages of the Journal." A "casual glance" had noticed a "passage which erroneously prefixed my name" to the proposition relating the motion for a constitutional executive council on September 7. Madison stated Mason—not Madison—had made the motion. He offered as support his "recollection" and notes, which "contain the observations" of the speakers. Madison admitted to having a copy of the official journal, which he referred to as "the original Journal according to my extract." "Extract," of course, understated the extent of Madison's copy. Madison wondered if the "degree of symphony in the two names"—Madison and Mason—might have led to a copying error. Madison was perhaps writing from an experience with that confusion. Madison's concern about September 7 is curious. He had considerable trouble in the Notes with the events of September 7 and apparently eventually replaced an original sheet or two. Moreover, support for the council may have seemed to suggest veracity to claims that Madison favored a certain approach to the executive branch.[10]

The *Journal* led Madison to revise the Notes again. He inserted footnotes and described discrepancies in motions and votes between his Notes and the *Journal*. He referred to the *Journal* as the "printed Journal." The footnotes did not explain the divergences. Madison left ambiguous whether he or the *Journal* was incorrect. He may not have known.[11]

Within several years, a more controversial record of the Convention appeared—one in which Madison's role was depicted as he had feared. In 1821, *The Secret Proceedings and Debates of the Convention* compiled new and old material, including an extensive selection of Robert Yates's notes of the Convention. A smaller portion had been printed in 1808 in a New York newspaper and in 1813 in *The American Law Journal*. Yates's notes ended on July 5, when he had left the Convention. The Convention proceedings were interpreted through the lens established by the first document in the collection: Luther Martin's lengthy speech to the Maryland Convention in late 1787. He described a covert group that wished "to abolish and annihilate all state governments, and to bring forward one general government, over this extensive continent, of a monarchical nature." Madison figured prominently in the *Secret Proceedings* as a member of the group opposed to state governments.

The edition included speeches that Madison had worried about since the early 1790s.[12]

Publicly, Madison criticized the *Secret Proceedings*. He pointed to the comments about the states as corporations as examples of "the extreme incorrectness." He suggested Yates and Lansing had represented "strong prejudices." These views had "warped" the notes "to an unfavorable understanding of what was said." Madison implied that any troubling comments that appeared were the product of political bias.[13]

The accuracy of Yates's notes has been controversial. Yates's original notes were not extant in the 1820s. The notes were composed from a manuscript by John Lansing copied from Yates's "original manuscript" and "certified" as a "true copy." Lansing's copy unfortunately has never been found in entirety. The printed versions were prepared by Edmond Charles Genet. Genet's editorial intervention has been assumed to have been significant and biased. He was briefly the French minister to the United States in 1793 until Washington requested his recall. Genet stayed in the United States after marrying the daughter of New York governor, George Clinton. The inevitable creativity required to transcribe rough notes, however, may explain the notes as much as political manipulation. Two pages found from Lansing's copy indicate the approach taken to convert fragments and ambiguous statements to speeches. For example, "A Leap in the dark" became "I do not chuse to take a leap in the dark." Genet increased the emotional charge of certain words, omitted duplicative ideas, and fixed cross-references. He tried to insert coherence where there appeared to be none. Did he also add material without support? Did he also deliberately alter meanings? Until the rough notes are discovered, the extent of his editorial intervention remains uncertain.[14]

Privately, Madison showed less concern about accuracy. He revised the Notes to include material drawn from the Yates notes. Max Farrand discovered over fifty insertions. A few changes related to procedural matters, for example, relating to the Delaware instruction barring the delegates from agreeing to vary equal state suffrage. But Madison also made a number of substantive additions. Rather than add the verbatim text, he paraphrased sentences, thereby disguising the origin. Madison shortened passages and reordered phrases. He kept key words and inserted synonyms for others. For example, Gerry's speech on June 11 was added:

Secret Proceedings (Gerry): The idea of property ought not to be the rule of representation. Blacks are property, and are used to the southward as horses and cattle to the northward; and why should their representation be increased to the southward on account of the number of slaves, than horses and oxen to the north?

Notes: M^r. Gerry thought property not the rule of representation. Why then sh^d. the blacks, who were property in ~~of~~ the South, be in the rule of representation more than the cattle & horses of the North.

Madison retained Gerry's question and terms (*rule of representation, blacks, property, south, north, cattle, horses*). The paraphrases and reversed order, however, made the copy appear to be merely a record of the same speech.[15]

The insertions mostly occurred in the section of the Notes that Eppes did not copy for Jefferson. Elsewhere, Madison inserted procedural matters and names for motions. But between June 22 and July 5 (when the Yates's notes ended), Madison revised the Notes by adding speeches in whole or part:

June 22: Madison, Hamilton, Gorham, Butler, Mason
June 23: General Pinckney, Sherman, Butler, Jennifer, Mason, Gerry, Hamilton, Rutledge
June 25: Johnson, Madison, Randolph, Read
June 26: Hamilton.
June 29: Ellsworth, Madison, Pierce
June 30: Ellsworth, Madison, Ellsworth, Franklin, Martin, Madison, Ellsworth, King.
July 2: Pinckney, Lansing
July 5: Wilson, Martin, Wilson.

He added sentences to speeches or even inserted an entire speech. Madison's additions were made where the Jefferson Copy would not reveal that the insertions had not been in the original Notes. At some point, he inserted in the margin—"From June 21 to July 18 inclusive not copied by M^r. Eppes"—as if forestalling any future questions.[16]

Madison even included a short speech given by him copied from the *Secret Proceedings.* On June 22, Wilson had moved that legislators' salary be set by the legislature. Madison apparently gave a speech unrecorded in the Notes. Yates, however, described Madison's opposition because members were "too much interested." It was "indecent that the legislature should put their hands in the public purse to convey it into their own." Madison lightly paraphrased: "M^r. Madison, thought the members . . . too much interested to ascertain their own compensation." He continued: "It w^d be indecent to put their hands into the public purse for the sake of their own pockets." Madison did not want to overlook such a compelling sentiment.[17]

According to the *Secret Proceedings,* Madison "intends to publish" his "memorandums of the controversies." The printed volume implicitly dared Madison to disagree at his peril. He presumably had evidence that would prove his version of the Convention. The public knew that Madison's Notes existed but whether they would confirm or deny the implications about his role remained a mystery.[18]

By the 1820s, Madison was once again considering publication. In the fall of 1821, Madison was urged to publish. A relative, John Jackson, argued that publication of what Madison was "known to possess in manuscript" was required for "justice & expediency." Jackson alluded to Madison's concern about his original positions. "If indeed you did propose to infuse more vigor, & strength into the national Government than it possesses," Jackson assured Madison that the recent war proved Madison correct. In return, Madison admitted that opinions in the Notes might have been "set out on negociating grounds more remote . . . than the real opinions" or in ways that omitted the "conditional reference"—in essence, the larger context.[19]

Nonetheless, Madison was still reluctant to publish. In a detailed letter to Thomas Ritchie, Madison sought to explain his position. He acknowledged that, "as the public has been led to understand," he possessed "materials for a pretty ample view of what happened" at the Philadelphia Convention. He did not intend that they "for ever remain under the veil of secrecy." Madison offered an array of reasons for delay. He wondered about posthumous publication or a publication "delayed till the Constitution should be well settled by practice, & till a knowledge of the controversial part of the proceedings of its framers could be turned to no improper account." The "controversial part" that worried him was left ambiguous. He referred to a Convention's rule that "'prohibited a promulgation without leave of what was spoken in it.'" Madison implied that "policy" might be considered to be "unexpired." Nevertheless, he stopped short of claiming a prohibitory rule. Madison left open future publication.[20]

In the meantime, Madison and his brother-in-law, John C. Payne, created a fair copy of the Notes. The revisions from the *Journal* and the *Secret Proceedings* had already been made. Payne followed instructions written by Madison to insert various drafts printed in the *Journal*. He included the Pinckney plan of May 29 and the June 19 Committee of the Whole resolutions from the *Journal*. Payne even copied John Quincy Adams' reconstructed list of resolutions used to write the first draft—a document not created by the Convention. No indication was made that the *Journal* was the source for these additions. In the fair copy, the Notes as taken by Madison appeared comprehensive and accurate.[21]

Payne was a careful copyist. Like Eppes, he offered the advantage of the confidentiality of a family member. The occasional insertion of a sentence in his handwriting suggests that the copy was read against the Notes and corrected. Eventually, Madison may have read it over. For example, Payne copied Article I, section 8 following the typographical arrangement in the *Journal:*

> Sect. 8. The Congress shall have power—
>   To lay and collect taxes, duties, imposts and excises:
>   To pay the debts and provide for the common defence and
>   general welfare of the United States; but all duties, imposts, and
>   excises, shall be uniform throughout the United States:
>   To borrow money on the credit of the United States: . . .

Subsequently, Payne altered the lines. He converted the colon to a semicolon and wrote in *To pay the debts,* crossing it out below. A footnote was added to explain that the two lines were not to be separate clauses; Madison may have been the author or instigator.[22]

In the fair copy, explanatory comments were located in the footnotes. Payne followed the instructions in the Notes to transfer explanatory comments from the entries into the footnotes. Other footnotes identified divergences in vote counts between the Notes and the *Journal*. Madison added new footnotes. For example, the September 12 report was copied from Madison's printed report. A footnote cast doubt on the *Journal,* which allegedly included "alterations subsequently made in the House." By the time the fair copy was complete, it had absorbed and responded to the other printed records of the Convention.[23]

In the fair copy, the Convention ended with success. In the Notes, Franklin's declaration that the carved sun on Washington's chair must be rising was followed by the disappointment of nonsigners. Payne reversed the order. The Constitution with signatories was followed by the names of the nonsigners. The last paragraph related Franklin's rising sun anecdote. The nonsigners were rendered insignificant, and the Convention given an optimistic conclusion.[24]

The controversial Hamilton materials received new explanations. On June 18, a footnote insisted that Hamilton had "seen" and "approved" the speech. The Hamilton plan was copied in the appendix under a heading that Hamilton "delineated the Constitution which he would have wished to be proposed by the Convention." Although clarifying that Hamilton had not proposed the plan, the explanation implied it reflected his agenda. The fair copy insisted on its substantive accuracy.[25]

The fair copy also sought to place Madison's speeches in a larger context. Although he could not alter his speeches through further revision, he could place the speeches in a broader narrative. The Convention Notes were intended to appear in the middle of other material from the 1780s. Payne copied Madison's legislative diaries in the Confederation Congress and selected correspondence. The concepts and concerns were to read as part of anxieties about the states and the absence of a national government with power. Madison also attempted to define—perhaps redefine—key controversial terms in contemporaneous correspondence. For example, in an 1824 letter, Madison argued that "consolidate" had shifted meanings. At the time of the Convention, it meant "to give strength and solidity to the Union of the States" but later meant "a destruction of the States, by transfusing their powers into the government of the Union." Madison implied that the subsequent meaning was "unknown to its founders." As writers suggested interpretations of available Convention sources, Madison repeatedly disagreed. By revising terms, Madison attempted to shape the context in which his Convention Notes would be read.[26]

Madison seemed to be keeping track of the living members. In late 1826, Jonathan Elliot asked if he could publish the Notes. Elliot was planning to publish volumes on the ratification debates and hoped for a supplementary publication on the Convention. He believed Madison and King were the only survivors of the Convention. Madison wrote back, noting

that Elliot had "overlooked" William Few. John Lansing and the secretary, William Jackson, also remained alive. Madison lent some of his
copies of ratification materials, but not the Notes. In February 1827,
Elliot made another effort to persuade Madison but was again apparently rebuffed.[27]

Madison had grown cautious about revision. In a draft letter—possibly
never sent—he declined Elliot's request to correct his speeches from the
Virginia ratifying convention. He paraphrased Randolph's words forty
years earlier: "If I did not confound subsequent ideas, and varied expressions, with the real ones, I might be supposed to do so." Madison acknowledged that some speeches were "defective, others obscure, if not
unintelligible, others again which must be more or less erroneous." Regardless, it was not "safe" or "fair" to alter them. He had not "in the
meantime ever revised them." At this point, he could not now "under-
take to make them what it may be believed they ought to be."[28]

In the implication that more contemporaneous revision was acceptable,
Madison reflected the practice of revision in legislative reporting. The
publication of congressional debates had expanded over the decades since
1789, but complaints of inaccuracy and political bias abounded. In 1834,
editors Joseph Gales and William Seaton "invited members of Congress
to revise their speeches before" publication. The *Congressional Globe* had
a similar revisal policy. The inherent limits of reporting—inaudible voices,
rapid speakers, misheard comments, mumbling—continued. Not until the
late 1840s, did the introduction of phonetic (Pitman) shorthand permit
significantly more accurate reports and allowed a stenographer to come
close to the speed of a speaker. Nevertheless, in 1873, when the new *Congressional Record* appeared with government reporters, it was described
as "substantially a verbatim report of the proceedings." A verbatim report was not considered attainable.[29]

By early 1827, Madison was leaning towards posthumous publication
as "most delicate and most useful." In April 1827, King died with his notes
unpublished. Late in his life, King had emphasized the context of the
Convention. He advocated greater appreciation for those delegates who
favored a "stronger organization than was adopted." King cautioned that
some propositions "ought not to be quoted against their authors, being
offered for consideration, and to bring out opinions, and which, though
behind the opinions of this day, were in advance of those of that day." The
following year William Few, John Lansing, and William Jackson died. By
1829, Madison had become the only living member of the Convention.[30]

Madison was concerned about other versions of the Convention. He wanted as a mere "matter of curiosity" to "compare the notes taken on the same subjects by different members." He requested a copy of Pierce's notes in the *Savannah Georgian*. He had reason to worry about Pierce. In 1788, in the *Georgia Gazette,* Pierce had described the object of the Convention as being to "consolidate the Union." Although the framework "must eventually draw" from the states "all their remaining sovereignty," Pierce declared it was "better [to] be consolidated than to remain any longer a confederated republic." Pierce also had defended the "high mounted" executive. The 1828 printing of Pierce's notes from May to June 6 included descriptions of Madison's speeches.[31]

Other accounts were disputed by Madison. A description of Franklin's "proposition for a religious service" had "every semblance of authenticity," but was "so erroniously [*sic*] given." In 1830, Jared Sparks asked if the Pinckney plan evidenced "later composition." Madison explained that he had meant to write Pinckney after it appeared in the *Journal,* but Pinckney had died. In 1831, Madison pored over the plan to establish its inauthenticity. Comparisons were prepared to demonstrate that the printed plan could not have been the one introduced by Pinckney in May 1787. By late November 1831, Madison concluded that the evidence was "irresistible" that the printed plan had not been introduced.[32]

Madison wrote letters explicating his memory of the Convention on constitutional topics (for example, the general welfare clause, congressional power over internal improvements and manufacturing). The publication of the Madison Papers' retirement series will undoubtedly cast further light on Madison's efforts at explanation during these years. He cited printed materials and did not include extracts from his Notes. Madison began to regret that his various earlier statements were being used to support nullification and other states' rights doctrines. With respect to debates over slavery, Madison stayed relatively aloof. He maintained his approach, outwardly stating that slavery was wrong and yet continuing to participate in it. He supported the American Colonization Society; indeed; his will gave a legacy of $2000 to the Society from the money raised by the publication of the report of the Convention. Yet his will did not free any person held as a slave.[33]

By the end of 1831, Madison knew that he was "the only living signer" of the Constitution. In the mid-1830s, Madison once again revised his depiction of the Convention, now arguing for complexity, a renewed appreciation for former opponents, and the possibility that his prior descriptions had been politically biased. Madison explained, "A proposition may be voted for, with a view to an expected qualification of it; or voted ag[ain]st as wrong in time or place, or as blended with other matter of objectionable import." He noted that a vote in the Convention record "may often have a meaning quite uncertain, and sometimes contrary to the apparent one." He found frustrating simplistic interpretations of the record. He explained that it was "quite possible that J.M. might have remarked that certain powers attributes of sovereignty had been vested" in Congress. He even implied that he might have offered statements advocating the states having little power. He acknowledged that he and Hamilton had "agreed to a certain extent . . . in the expediency of an energetic Gov[ernmen]t adequate to the exigencies of the Union." Madison emphasized that Hamilton had never proposed the plan to the delegates. Madison gave Gouverneur Morris full credit for the final draft of the Constitution:

> The finish given to the style and arrangement of the Constitution, fairly belongs to the pen of Mr. Morris; the task having, probably, been handed over to him by the Chairman of the Committee, himself a highly respectable member, and with the ready concurrence of the others.

Madison declared: "A better choice could not have been made, as the performance of the task proved." The comments suggested that Madison, Hamilton, and Morris had been in considerable agreement. He even cast doubt on his writings during the 1790s, concluding that they had been "too often tinged with the party spirit of the times."[34]

Most importantly, Madison slowly grasped the impossibility of reclaiming the original Convention. In an editorial note that he apparently intended to add to the Notes, Madison speculated on the discrepancies between the published Pinckney plan and the one he recollected. He defended Pinckney. Pinckney might have lost the original document and used a rough draft with "erasures and interlineations." The revisions might have been "confounded" with the "original text." Later, "after a lapse of more than thirty years," the revisions might have been "confounded also in the memory of the author." Madison suggested that having originally revised the document, Pinckney could no longer remember precisely what occurred and the order. The description of Pinckney's dilemma was Madison's own. Randolph had warned Madison of the inevitability of confounding the events of the summer of

1787 with subsequent beliefs. Nearly fifty years later, Madison finally agreed.[35]

When Madison died on June 28, 1836, his will ambiguously referred to the Notes. After describing his "careful and extended report of the proceedings and discussions" of the Convention, the will provided that "the report as made by me" should be published under Dolley Madison's "authority and direction." Madison's intention regarding the Notes was not explicit. The will left "all" of his "manuscript papers" to his wife, "having entire confidence in her discreet and proper use of them." Her original plan for the Notes remains a mystery. Dolley left her own papers to her niece, Annie Payne, with instructions that they were to be burned.[36]

Dolley Madison and John C. Payne further revised the fair copy of the manuscript. Before Madison's death, as his eyesight and handwriting diminished, the two had aided him in preparing his manuscripts. In the years since Payne had created the fair copy; small revisions had been made to the Notes and the fair copy. A few footnotes had been added and another effort made to explain the July 17 executive tenure vote. The appendix was rearranged and notes added. At some point, concern arose that Payne's additions could be misinterpreted. On the final page, Madison wrote: "The few alterations and corrections made in these debates which are not in my hand writing were directed by me and made in my presence by John C. Payne." As if attesting to the statement, he signed his name, "James Madison." After his death, other hands—Payne, Dolley Madison, and possibly even her niece Anna Payne—further revised the fair copy by adding editorial notes, often marked "Editor." Materials were added to the appendix; one of the added suffrage speeches bears a header describing it having been "found among his papers."[37]

By Madison's death, the Jefferson Copy had come into Madison's possession. The copy was transformed into a complete copy of the fair copy to be sent abroad for foreign publication or translation. A team of female relatives and clerks compared the fair copy to the Jefferson Copy and added missing material—words, lines, lengthy sections of multiple pages—to make it identical.[38]

After private publishers failed to offer a satisfactory price for the three proposed volumes, Congress purchased them for $30,000. Dolley

Madison was disappointed by the amount. In April 1837, she sent the fair copy to a box at the Bank of the United States in Washington.[39]

The transmission of the fair copy instead of the Notes was unacceptable to Senator William C. Rives. "The original manuscript of the Debates is that which Congress will expect to receive," Rives wrote Dolley Madison. In the congressional debates on the purchase, Rives had argued that "grave constitutional questions have turned upon the punctuation of some of the articles" of the Constitution. He emphasized that the "object is that we may have these manuscripts to appeal to as a genuine and authentic record." Rives had studied law with Jefferson and served in the House of Representatives in the 1820s and in the Senate in the 1830s. Dolley Madison and Payne consulted closely with Rives about publication plans, and he helped them write editorial footnotes to explain certain discrepancies. His wife, Judith Page Walker Rives, had assisted in the copying after Madison's death. Rives would go on to write the first major biography of James Madison, *History of the Life and Times of James Madison*. For these works, the state department loaned Madison's papers, many of which were not returned to the government until the 1940s with Rives's own papers. In the biography, Rives described the Notes as "an accurate memorial" and "an exact account." The fair copy— intended to be published by Madison—did not serve Rives' purposes.[40]

Regardless of Dolley Madison's initial intentions, she complied. She reassured Rives that her son, John Payne Todd, would bring the "original Debates." Rives, however, was warned that Todd's "intimates are the Blacklegs and Gamblers of Washington." They might "succeed in plundering Todd." Indeed, Todd would later sell Madison manuscripts to raise funds. With the Notes undelivered in March 1837, Dolley Madison sent a desperate letter to Todd: "the money will not be paid without these being first delivered." In April, the secretary of state, John Forsyth, acquired the box containing the Payne fair copy described as a "copy of the original manuscripts, prepared for publication with corrections." Only later did Todd deliver the original Notes. The Notes may have been stored in a small trunk. If so, the trunk may be the red morocco trunk with brass tack and handles, believed to have belonged to Dolley Madison, on display at the National Museum of American History.[41]

In 1840, the government used the fair copy to print a three-volume edition of Madison's papers. Under Attorney General Henry Gilpin's editorial eye, the revisions were acknowledged but minimized. The edition was published as the account prepared by Madison at his death. Although the edition included a facsimile image of the final page of the Notes, it was doctored to bring it into alignment with the printed version. This edition became the widely read version of the Notes when it was re-printed in Jonathan Elliot's *Debates on the Adoption of the Federal Constitution*.[42]

For almost ninety years, the Notes were largely forgotten. The manu-script remained at the state department in the Bureau of Rolls and Li-brary, but access was difficult. In the wake of the Constitution's 1887 centennial, criticism mounted about the division's apparent policy "to seclude from use the immensely valuable manuscript purchases and official records." A new chief of the Bureau of Rolls and Library, Andrew H. Allen, promised greater access. Madison's papers were repaired and bound into seventy-five large red leather volumes. Linen hinges were placed on the papers to permit attachment to heavy ledger paper. The Notes were apparently similarly treated.[43]

A literal transcription of the Notes showing Madison's revisions was published. Beginning in the summer of 1897, a young staff member, John P. Weissenhagen, detached the small slips of paper in the Notes. On paper in red ink, he noted the precise location of the slips. Each page of the Notes was transcribed, the type face set, and then the final page apparently proof-read twice. The editors used various fonts to demonstrate the revisions. The edition appeared in 1900 as part of *The Documentary History of the Constitution*. It remains the most accurate transcription of the Notes.[44]

Unfortunately, within a decade, this remarkable edition was consigned to obscurity. Reviewers minimized the significance of the revisions. The *American Historical Review* mockingly stated the edition was a "great boon to scholars, especially to those who are occupied with minute re-searches into constitutional history." The revisions made "very hard reading" and were "most commonly . . . not instructive." The reviewer concluded, "It is obvious that while this edition will be the ultimate au-thority, Elliot or Gilpin will be that ordinarily used." In 1914, the gov-ernment recommended against reprinting the edition.[45]

Other publications of Madison's record minimized the revisions. In 1902–1903, Gaillard Hunt, the leading Madison scholar of the day and future chief of the Division of Manuscripts for the Library of Congress, claimed to follow the "original manuscript . . . with rigid accuracy," but the text favored the fair copy. A 1920 edition by Hunt added footnotes describing revisions in the fair copy. An insightful reviewer, Francis Coker, criticized the edition for not making "constantly clear . . . what parts constitute a strictly contemporaneous record" and "what parts were added at a considerably later period." Although Max Farrand expressed greater interest in the revisions in his *Records of the Federal Convention of 1787* (1911), he showed only revisions with "significance." Farrand struggled with the revisions. It was "sometimes difficult and sometimes impossible" to know whether a revision was later. He suggested the "more radical" revisions arose when Madison had "accustomed himself to the idea of changes being necessary, or when he had forgotten the criteria of his earlier revision." In 1937, after the discovery of the Journal Copy, Farrand claimed that the "distinction" between the sources for the revisions "is not of so much importance." The Farrand edition and the Hunt edition (reprinted by Tansill, Koch, and others) remained the dominant texts throughout the twentieth century.[46]

Over the past century, the Notes remained difficult to study. In 1922, the manuscript was transferred to the Library of Congress. The Notes appear to have been hinged in large volumes when they were microfilmed in 1964. Subsequently, the Library removed them and disassembled the manuscript. Today, the Notes rest in two archival storage boxes in the Library's secured refrigerated vault.[47]

Since 1840, a single description of Madison's writing of the Notes— apparently from his own hand—has reassured readers. Repeated in most accounts of the Convention, Madison explained:

> In pursuance of the task I had assumed, I chose a seat in front of the presiding member, with the other members on my right and left hands. In this favorable position for hearing all that passed, I noted down, in terms legible, and in abbreviations and marks intelligible to myself, what was read to the chair or spoken by the members; and not losing a moment unnecessarily between the adjournment and re-assembling of the convention, I was enabled to write out my daily notes during the session, or within a few finishing days after its close, in the extent and form preserved in my own hand on my files.
>
> In the labor and correctness of this, I was not a little aided by practice, and by a familiarity with the style and train of observation and reasoning which characterized the principal speakers. It happened also that I was not absent a single day, nor more than the casual fraction of an hour in any day, so that I could not have lost a single speech, unless a very short one.

In fact, Madison never made this claim in print in his lifetime. In offering the Debates for publication, Dolley Madison and Rives used a description drawn from a "paper written by him." They claimed that it "guarantees their [the Debates] fullness and accuracy."[48]

The description, however, was not written completely by Madison. The words came from a document entitled, "A sketch never finished nor applied." Madison's handwriting trails off as he explains *when* he rewrote the rough notes taken during the Convention. He explained, "I was enabled to write out ~~during the intervals~~ my daily notes ~~in the extent &~~ ~~form~~." Dolley Madison completed the sentence and wrote the additional paragraph. Gaillard Hunt asserted that Madison had dictated these words before his death. Perhaps he did; perhaps not. Madison likely read them for his extremely shaky handwriting seems to appear on the page. But Madison did not write the explanation himself.[49]

Madison never asserted *in his own hand* that the Notes were contemporaneous. In the fifty years that he had possessed the Notes, he never settled on a precise explanation of their relationship to the Convention. Madison may have consented to the addition to his draft—and then again, who knows, perhaps on his deathbed he paused, unable to bring himself to swear to posterity that the Notes had been written in the summer of 1787. What was the original *extent & form* of the Notes? No one will likely ever know.

If original understandings of the Convention existed, we cannot retrieve them. Indeed, hours after the Convention ended for the day, Madison could no longer recover it precisely himself. From the initial day in May 1787, when Madison gathered and sorted his memory to write his first entry in his legislative diary, he was revising his understanding. In transcribing the rough notes, tracking strategic coalitions, recording the positions of Virginia colleagues, he imposed his personality and preferences. As his commitment for proportional representation in both houses lost, as the possibility of the negative on state laws faded, as the executive changed shape, as the southern states became convinced of their need to protect slavery, Madison intertwined the proceedings with his desires and disappointments. When he finished the Notes for Jefferson two years later, he brought a new interest in constitutional text and contemporary controversies. When he replaced speeches to share Jefferson's vision of republican politics, he subtly created an alternative interpretation of the Convention. When he shared the Notes with Jefferson, he inadvertently supported, if not set in motion, a new constitutional politics and approach to interpretation. He shifted the context of comments. Each revision—small and large—increased the distance from the summer of 1787. Over the years and decades, words, concepts, compromises shifted focus and took on new political meanings. Motivations were disputed; context lost.

The Convention could not see the Constitution until the final days. And from the moment the Constitution became visible, it was contested. The respect owed the framing generation demands appreciation for the political world in which they struggled to stabilize the country. The understandings of the Constitution shifted over the summer of 1787 and continued to transform through that fall into 1788, 1789, 1791, 1796, and 1799. Over the first decade, the Constitution survived and indeed began to become *the* Constitution.

Madison's narrative in the Notes was that of *James Madison, a member.* Beginning in 1787 and continuing for a half century afterwards, he struggled to understand what had happened that summer. Along the way, he and others made decisions and advanced accusations that he likely later regretted. Only near the end of Madison's life did he grasp the inescapable inevitability of confounding later ideas and expressions with "the real ones." Looking back, he suggested understanding for the others. So too, undoubtedly, he forgave himself.

THE EVIDENCE

ABBREVIATIONS

NOTES

ACKNOWLEDGMENTS

INDEX

THE EVIDENCE

The Manuscripts

Vices of the Political System of the United States

The Vices manuscript appears to have been constructed at two different times. The available evidence is suggestive of revision but does not permit certainty. Of the twelve vices, ten include a paragraph of observations. The last two vices are markedly different. The eleventh vice is the only one with a lengthy analysis; the twelfth vice is only a header. Moreover, the ink color—admittedly an unreliable marker—appears to change at the beginning of the extended discussion of the eleventh vice. The extended discussion begins with Madison's question: "To what causes is this evil to be ascribed?"[1]

Two different types of paper occur in the manuscript. The manuscript is composed of large sheets, each folded in half to form four pages. There are two full sheets followed by three half-sheets. The first two full sheets bear the watermark of a Bruges printer, Joseph De Busscher. Madison used this type of paper in his correspondence in the spring of 1787. The following half-sheet matches these two. The eleventh vice, the initial paragraph observation, and the beginning of the extended discussion appear on the last page of this half-sheet. If there had been a full sheet in place, the missing half would have provided space for the twelfth vice with a paragraph observation. The two half-sheets that complete the existing manuscript, however, are on paper by the English papermaker James Whatman. It may match the paper used by Madison at the Annapolis Convention and the Philadelphia Convention. Although the extended discussion begins on the De Busscher half sheet, most of it is written on the two Whatman half-sheets.[2]

This forensic evidence is consistent with two scenarios. First, the paper change could be coincidental with the manuscript written in the spring of 1787. Alternatively, the paper change could be significant. After originally writing the manuscript on three sheets of De Busscher paper, Madison returned later and ripped

243

off the final half sheet with the twelfth vice. He wrote new material in the space following the eleventh vice and then added two new half-sheets to complete his thoughts. He copied the twelfth vice heading but omitted the observation.

The alternative scenario of revision explains other curiosities. Other observations in the manuscript can be found in letters from March or April 1787. The extensive republic as *a solution* does not. The absence is unusual because Madison tended to send his good ideas to his correspondents. The *Madison Papers* editors were similarly puzzled over the relationship of the idea to contemporary political controversy. The discussion does not completely align with Madison's thoughts in the spring of 1787.[3]

Madison had reasons to revise the Observations on the Vices manuscript. He never used it for a possible opening address. Instead, as the Convention proceeded, the manuscript served as a useful compilation of concerns about the confederation and his theory for a new national governmental structure. Madison rearranged the topics for use in his June 19 speech. After the Convention, Madison used the manuscript for Hamilton's *Federalist* project, in particular, essays 10 and 51, and, at some point, for material with which to replace his original June 6 speech.

If Madison did revise the manuscript, he likely made the alteration during the latter part of the Convention or relatively soon after its close. The eleventh vice's extended republic is linked to the Convention but plausibly in this different chronological order.

Three Replaced Sheets (June)

Three sheets in the first section of the Notes do not match the surrounding notes or letters contemporaneously written by Madison. The first two sheets (b.11–12) contain Madison's significant June 6 speeches as well as a comment on June 5 on the inferior courts. The third sheet (b.14) contains Madison's speeches on June 7 and 8. Textual and paper evidence suggests these sheets were replaced.

The most persuasive textual evidence is the presence of material on the sheets copied from the official Convention journals. Madison copied these journals in the early fall of 1789. Elsewhere in the Notes for early June, his additions from his Journal Copy are visible. On these three replaced sheets, such additions appear integrated into the text; that is, they were included as the entries were written. On b.12, Madison recorded that Wilson moved "to add after 'National Executive' the words 'with a convenient number of the national Judiciary.'" The Journal Copy stated: "by adding after the words 'National Executive' the words 'with a convenient number of the National Judiciary.'" On b.14, Madison's language closely tracked the official journal:

> Notes: M^r. Gerry gave notice that he w^d. tomorrow move for a reconsideration of the mode of appointing the Nat^l. Executive in order to substitute an appointm^t. by the State Executives.

Journal Copy: Mr Gerry gave notice that he w^d. tomorrow move for the reconsideration of the Resolution which respects the appointm^r. of the National Executive when he sh^d offer to substitute the following mode of appointing the National Executive namely by the Executives of the several States.

Madison appears to have been using the Journal Copy as he wrote.[4]

In addition, stylistic differences are evident. In the original Notes, Madison referred to himself as "M." Only later did he return to the manuscript and add "adison." He followed this same practice in his congressional diary. On the three replaced sheets, however, Madison seems to have written "Madison." Madison originally wrote a casual "adj" for "adjourned." Later he revised this to adapt the formal ending used in the journal. On the replaced sheets, he adopted the formal ending.[5]

The three sheets do not match the surrounding sheets. The Notes from May through mid-June have the countermark, "J. Whatman," or a corresponding watermark. The six extant Madison letters written between May 27 and June 13 are on this paper. As the Catalogue describes, all three sheets instead have a GR watermark.

Most intriguingly, Madison made pseudo-revisions to the three sheets. The words crossed out and written above are the same. On b.11, he wrote, struck, and rewrote "state tribunals," "opposed," "M^r. Sherman," "indigence," "expected," and "Treaties." On b.12, he rewrote "insecure," "unavoidable," "reduced," and "means." On b.14, he crossed out and wrote "destroy," and "disobey." He may have simply wanted to make these words more legible. But the pattern is odd. Madison may have wanted the sheets to blend in with the surrounding sheets— going so far as to make them appear to be revised. The pseudo-revisions, if intentional, may also suggest that the replacements were made after Madison had begun to revise the Notes.[6]

The likely timing of the replacements is speculative. The three sheets appear in the Jefferson Copy. Based on current evidence, they appear to have been written between fall 1789 and 1791, perhaps between the fall of 1789 and the summer of 1790. This timing suggests that these Madison speeches should be interpreted with care. Madison's idea of the extensive republic as a solution may have been developed in a different chronological order. In conventional analyses, components of the idea appear in the extended discussion of the eleventh vice, the June 4 speech as recorded by others, the June 6 speech, the October 24, 1787 letter to Jefferson, and Federalist 10 (November 22, 1787). No other delegate definitively associated Madison on June 4 or June 6 with the idea. Madison's oft-quoted speech may not date in its entirety to June 6, 1787.[7]

Five Replaced Sheets (June–July)

Five sheets in the June–July section of the Notes do not match the surrounding sheets or letters contemporaneously written by Madison. Textual and paper evidence again suggests these sheets were replaced. The first four sheets include significant speeches by Madison: b.30 (June 21); b.33 (June 23); b.37 (June 26); b.42 (June 29). The last sheet, b.62, covers the vote on July 17 relating to executive tenure on good behavior. As with the earlier three sheets, the evidence has to be considered circumstantial in the absence of a discovery of any original sheets. Replacement provides an explanation for the discrepancies.

Because these sheets focus on speeches, the textual evidence is weaker than with the earlier replaced sheets. Madison, however, wrote "Madison" out in full. There are unfortunately few procedural motions with which to compare the Journal Copy. On b.30, for example, Madison wrote that Dayton "took his seat" using words similar to the official journal. He also oddly seemed to have recorded General Pinckney's motion in two different ways. Less significant evidence can be found but is only suggestive.[8]

More significantly, the first paragraph of Charles Pinckney's speech on June 25 (b.33) is a later creation by Madison. Madison had a copy of the speech in Pinckney's handwriting. That version began: "The people of the U.S. are perhaps the most singular. . . ." In the Notes, these words are written on the top of b.34 (an original sheet). On the prior replaced sheet (b.33), Madison created a new opening paragraph for the speech by rearranging and paraphrasing Pinckney's sentences. For example, "distinctions of fortune . . . and rank" (original) became "hereditary distinction of ranks" (replaced sheet). Madison made the actual first sentence appear as if it was the last half of a sentence from the previous page: "This equality of property & rank is likely to be continued for / The people of the U. States are perhaps the most singular. . . ." Eventually—and perhaps tellingly—Madison crossed out most of the invented paragraph. In modern editions, after two brief introductory sentences, the speech begins where Pinckney intended it to begin, on the original sheet.[9]

The five sheets are on different paper. Four sheets bear the countermark, T. French (b.33, b.37, b.42, and b.62). The fifth sheet (b.30) has a watermark with a "T" in the crown. No example of T. French paper is known in letters written by Madison in the summer of 1787.

The five replaced sheets also correlate to the uncopied section of the Jefferson Copy. Madison acknowledged in the margin that John Wayles Eppes never copied the Notes from June 21 to July 18. Eppes stopped copying after an original sheet (b.29) and began copying again with another original sheet (b.63). He did not copy from the first to the last replaced sheets (b.30 and b.62). This section appears to have been separated from the Notes. The timing of these replacements was likely later than the first set. They may have been composed between 1791 and 1796. Madison may have removed the section to revise it.[10]

August 22–September 17

The Notes from August 22 to September 17 involve an unconformity, a word that geologists use for a missing section of time. No evidence proves that these sheets were written in August–September 1787. Instead, available evidence suggests that the sheets were written at a later point in time, with the bulk likely composed in the year or so following the fall of 1789. This section involves the sheets from b.99 (August 22) to b.132 (September 17).

The most compelling evidence is the integration of material from the official journal of the Convention. Earlier in the Notes, Madison added slips or explicitly added material from the Journal Copy. In this section, however, there are no slips and no extensive visible additions. Instead, beginning with August 22, verbatim sections drawn from the journal alternate with brief descriptions of speeches. The appearance of superfluous words from the journal—such as "instant," "at the instance," "entered on," "to whom were referred"—indicate that the material was copied. The Convention rules barred Madison from copying the journal during the Convention, and Madison's copy likely dates from the late summer or fall of 1789. The Journal Copy is the source for much of the procedural material in the post–August 21 Notes. In at least one instance—and there may be more—Madison copied a textual error over into the Notes that he had made in the Journal Copy. He also reversed the order of the proceedings of September 13 because he reversed them in his Journal Copy. The majority of sheets include some integrated verbatim journal material, and the sheets without integrated journal material are similar in paper and style.[11]

The style of the Notes in the post–August 21 section differs from the earlier Notes. Madison wrote his name out in full, "Madison," instead of his usual practice of "M" or leaving a blank. The ubiquitous "Elseworth" of the early notes became "Elsworth." Madison also made relatively few corrections to the text.

Madison used new papers for this section. The twenty sheets from August 22 to September 6 are a different Whatman paper. The marks differ too significantly from the earlier Whatman paper to have been the result of the papermaking process. The eight sheets for September 6/7 and September 8–15 are on another paper. This paper has a distinctive variation of a GR watermark and appears in Madison's correspondence, but not during the summer of 1787. The sheet used for September 7/8 is on paper with the countermark "Taylor." This sheet was added relatively late, likely in response to Eppes, who noticed missing material. Five sheets (September 7 and September 15–17) are on paper with the countermark "Budgen." Similar paper was used for a slip containing the additional rules in May. None of these papers appear in the Notes prior to August 22. A final forensic curiosity is that this section may have been sewn together separately. At least on cursory comparison of b.98 and b.99, the holes in the margin of the later section do not align with the earlier Notes.

The papers used for this section cannot be definitively shown to match Madison's correspondence from the summer of 1787. The evidence is tentative. Madison is known to have written only five pieces of correspondence during these weeks. Two letters to McClurg (August 25 and September 1) have never been located. The small receipt to Blair (September 15) could not be located for this book by the Library of Virginia. Two letters are in the Library of Congress: the September 4 letter to Madison, Sr., and the September 6 letter to Jefferson. In May 2014, the Library placed the letters on a light table. Both letters are only half sheets. Only the top of the countermark appears. For September 4, the top of J and W are visible. For September 6, with less clarity, the top of J and W are also visible. None of the markers appear that easily distinguish the two Whatman countermarks. To my eye, the top of the J is located closer to the position of the early Whatman paper—but this evidence is rather slight. The two letters, however, establish that watermarks cannot prove the section to be original. The textual evidence of the Journal Copy's integration further supports that both entries were composed using the Journal Copy.[12]

The absence of the early Whatman paper from the later Notes is significant. Madison seems to have used his early Whatman paper in September 1787 to copy the Hamilton plan. The heading describes the copy made "about the close of the Convention in Philad 1787." If so, they may have been among his last sheets. The letter sent from Philadelphia to Edmund Pendleton on September 20 was on paper that was probably by Christian Bauman in Pennsylvania. Madison's letters from New York during the fall of 1787 use other papers.[13]

The Franklin speech and anecdote framing the opening and close of the September 17 entry offer additional evidence for later composition. In the Notes, Madison placed Franklin's speech at the beginning of September 17. Franklin explained that he did not "at present approve" of all sections, but he doubted "whether any other Convention we can obtain, may be able to make a better Constitution." He declared it astonishing "to find this system approaching so near to perfection as it does." The penultimate event that day was another Franklin observation. Looking at the president's chair with its rising sun motif, Franklin quipped that he had not known "whether it was rising or setting" during the Convention. He then said, "I have the happiness to know that it is a rising and not a setting Sun." This speech and anecdote, however, appeared in print after the Convention.[14]

In December 1787, Franklin's speech was published in the *American Museum*. At the Convention, Franklin had Wilson read the speech. Although Madison could have copied it before he left Philadelphia, the Notes' version is very similar to the printed version. Madison may have relocated the speech. McHenry reported that the Constitution was read, the representation clause altered, and then Franklin spoke. Madison, however, placed the speech immediately after the reading. From a procedural perspective, the placement was odd, as the speech made more sense once the business was complete. From a literary perspective particularly after ratification, however, the order made perfect sense. Franklin's speech foreshadowed the inevitable success of the Constitution.[15]

Similarly, the Franklin anecdote provided a perfect ending. In 1789, the Franklin anecdote was published in the *American Jest Book*. In the Notes, Madison introduced the anecdote using an awkward construction: "I have said he, often and often in the course of the Session." He curiously interjected an explanation for his knowledge of the comment: "observed to a few members near him." In the *American Jest Book* anecdote, Franklin talks to a "gentleman who sat next to him." Madison might have written down the anecdote, but he also easily could have copied it from the printed version.[16]

During the Convention, Franklin had been a source of some annoyance to Madison. Particularly after his death in April 1790, Franklin's imprimatur on the Constitution and the Convention provided a sense of closure to the Notes. This careful composition of the final day may indicate Madison's shift towards the larger public as a potential audience. As discussed in "Jefferson's Copy" below, it is possible that these Budgen sheets were composed after many other sheets in this section.

Madison's Journal Copy

In the fall of 1789, Madison made a copy of the official journals of the Convention. Madison's apparent title for the manuscript appears on the August 20 entry: "Copy of Journal of the Federal Convention." The Journal Copy was unknown to early scholars and remained in private hands until given to Yale University's Library. In 1930, Charles Keller and George Pierson argued that the Journal Copy was composed in September and early October 1789. Madison left New York on October 9, 1789, and the Journal Copy was presumably completed. In addition, they demonstrated that Madison used the Journal Copy to revise the Notes of the Convention prior to the Jefferson Copy. They established that the visible revisions of procedural matters were drawn from the Journal Copy and the slips in this process. Because Keller and Pierson's article postdated Farrand's *Records of the Federal Convention* (1911), these significant conclusions were never integrated into a documentary edition of the Notes.[17]

Evidence supports the 1789 creation of the Journal Copy. The Journal Copy includes a heading in Madison's hand referring to the manuscript as created in New York in September and October. Where a year might have originally been written, the page corner has been torn off. Nonetheless, the Journal Copy is on paper manufactured by Joshua Gilpin at the Brandywine Pennsylvania paper mill. Keller and Pierson established that Madison used this Brandywine paper for letters in June to September of 1789. Moreover, on several letters written in September and early October 1789, Madison erroneously wrote "1787." Keller and Pierson suggested that the error was the unconscious result of writing "1787" so often in the Journal Copy. In the research for this book, no evidence surfaced to contradict these conclusions. The dating of the Journal copy and the belief that Madison was not permitted access to the official journal during the

Convention are foundational assumptions on which the conclusions of this book are based.[18]

The official journals of the Convention were composed by the secretary, William Jackson. Jackson kept two journals: one covered the Convention proceedings; the other covered the early Committee of the Whole House proceedings. He also kept sheets with vote tallies, a small book of vote tallies, drafts of the Constitution, and other papers. On the evening of September 17, 1787, Jackson burned certain "loose scraps of paper." He gave the "Journals and other papers" to George Washington. No instruction regarding the journals appeared in the official records. Madison eventually wrote in the post–August 21 section of the Notes that Washington was to "retain the Journal and other papers, subject to the order of Congress, if ever formed under the Constitution." No one else at the Convention, however, recorded such an order. The journals were in a form that could have been printed; that is, they were journals as opposed to rough minutes. In the months after the Convention, they were not printed. In the spring of 1788, Luther Martin wrote "those very journals . . . ought to have been published" and described them as "in the possession of our late Honourable President." Between September 1787 and April 1796, Washington apparently retained the journals. In 1796, amidst controversy over the Jay Treaty, Washington deposited them with the secretary of state. Not until 1819, however, were they published.[19]

The manner in which Madison obtained the official journals remains a mystery. In the fall of 1789, Madison was serving as confidential advisor to Washington. Washington wrote him, "I am very troublesome, but you must excuse me. Ascribe it to friendship and confidence, and you will do justice to my motives." Although Washington kept careful diaries, no diary is extant from February 1789 to October 1789, the likely span in which Madison borrowed or returned the journals. In fact, Washington's extant 1789 diary begins with the record of the October 1 dinner attended by Madison before leaving New York. Madison seems likely to have borrowed the journals with Washington's permission, but there is no proof of that fact. Furthermore, it is unknown whether Washington was aware of Madison's Journal Copy.[20]

In copying the journals, Madison appears to have begun with August 20. In the Journal Copy, the page resembling a first page is Monday, August 20, 1787. That day—not May 14—has a prominent header: "Copy of Journal of the Federal Convention held in Philadelphia May 14 1787 from & after." On subsequent days, Madison included a header for each page: "Journal of the Federal Convention" followed by the day, date, and year. In the section for May to August 20, no such header appears. Madison originally started each day on a new page. With the exception of the brief entries for September 11 and 14, he maintained this approach. When he returned to the beginning of the journals, however, he began to copy entries sequentially on the same page. Madison likely began with Au-

gust 20, copied to the end of the Convention, and then returned to copy the proceedings from May to August 19, 1787.[21]

Time pressure or tedium underlay Madison's approach to the early proceedings. He combined the Journal of the Convention and the Journal of the Committee of the Whole House into single entries. The secretary used the same formal
sentences to describe the transition each day from Convention to Committee of
the Whole House and back to the Convention. Madison copied the formal proceeding for May 30; however, the following day, at the end of the proceeding, he
left a blank with instructions: "[see the form of yesterday & enter it here]." On
June 1, he simply left a blank after writing, "Mr Gorham reported." His interest
instead was with the substantive Committee of the Whole House proceedings.
He also copied the secretary's instructions to himself. On May 25 and June 1,
the secretary wrote: "(here insert the credentials)." Madison copied the words
but did not insert the credentials (indeed, he was likely not in possession of them).
Madison may have copied the additional rules of May 28 earlier on another
paper and so left a space, later returning to recopy the rules into his Journal Copy.
He was copying what he could not later reconstruct.[22]

Copying was not easy, and he made mistakes. On August 23, he lost his place.
On August 31, he wrote that a vote "pasd in the affirmative" three times, and
mistakenly wrote "affirmative" again, only to cross it out to correctly state "negative." On September 7, the secretary inserted a question and vote in the margin.
Madison realized after copying that he had missed the margin insertion. He then
squished it in. He miscopied August 8 and, in starting the day over, turned two
pages resulting in blank pages. Similarly, because the journal page had been apparently reversed for September 13, Madison copied it incorrectly. As Madison
wrote, he corrected small errors, inserting an occasional word and crossing out
others.[23]

Madison used brackets to indicate errors in the journal. On August 29, the
secretary did not report the vote on a motion. Madison wrote, "[no decision
here noted]. On June 2, the secretary did not finish a motion. Madison wrote,
"[here a blank left in ye original]." On June 9, the secretary used a printer's
hand—literally a little hand—to indicate an insertion. Madison copied it. He
made certain that anomalies would not later confuse him.[24]

In copying, Madison recognized that Washington had inserted several words
into the journal's rendering of the September 4 Report. Madison placed these
words in brackets. He added a note in the margin: "the words in [ ] interlined
with pencil by the President from the hand-writing." When Washington made
the insertions is unknown because he was president of the Convention and later
president of the country by the time of Madison's copy. On the following page,
Madison interlined the words: "[except treaties of peace]." Again he noted that
it was interlined in pencil in "Presidents hand." Madison kept a record of Washington's alterations.[25]

The secretary did not keep detailed records of September 14, 15, and 17. On September 14, the secretary recorded two initial motions and then summarized the proceedings, noting only that the Constitution was amended to the first article, first clause. He subsequently drew a line through the motions. Although the motions were legible, Madison did not copy them. Madison copied the summary paragraph (although altering "first" to "10th") and then wrote, "The Journal is not continued farther." The Journal Copy underscored the absence of official information about the final days.[26]

Madison's Journal Copy does not include the secretary's vote tallies. Jackson recorded the votes on loose sheets and in a small book. Copying the tallies would have been laborious but not impossible. If Madison obtained the vote tallies and made a copy, that copy has not been found. If Madison did not copy the tallies, he may have been unaware of their existence. Future research may establish whether Madison composed the final section with a copy of the vote tallies.[27]

Jefferson's Copy

Jefferson's copy of the Notes was created by John Wayles Eppes. Eppes later described the "particular and confidential manner" in which he had been instructed to copy the Notes. The Notes were stored in a "Trunk." Each day, "they were replaced and each original as copied was returned with the copy to Mr. Jefferson." Eppes likely began the copy in Philadelphia between the summer of 1791 and April 1793. He may have continued to work on the copy in Virginia. After Jefferson retired to Monticello in 1794, Eppes was a frequent visitor. In the spring of 1796, Jefferson possessed the last pages of the Notes at Monticello. Eppes may not have copied the Notes in chronological order. His handwriting changes throughout the manuscript, and a few pages might even be in the hand of a different person, although a handwriting expert would need to investigate that possibility. A tantalizing suspect is Jefferson's daughter, Maria (often called Polly) who had returned to Philadelphia with Jefferson in the fall of 1791. She married Eppes in October 1797.[28]

A partial duplicate of the Jefferson Copy was made with a letter press. For duplicates, Jefferson employed a letter press until he acquired his polygraph (a machine with two pens) around 1804. A letter press utilized moistened tissue-like paper placed on top of the original sheet, followed by another sheet. Under pressure in the press, the ink from the original bled through creating a blurred, but usually legible, copy. Even using ordinary iron gall ink, a copy could be made approximately within the first twenty-four hours. Press copies exist of other papers copied by Eppes for Jefferson. Presumably Eppes or Jefferson made the Press Copy. The Press Copy is incomplete. It includes the Committee of the Whole House proceedings and the debates over the Virginia resolutions (including Hamilton's June speech), Madison's speeches, and Hamilton's plan. Either only selected portions were made, or many pages have been lost over the years. The Press Copy shows the Jefferson Copy prior to later revisions to the Notes.[29]

The Jefferson Copy is titled, *Debates of the Grand Federal Convention*. The manuscript states: "Taken by a member." The inclusion of anonymous authorship suggests that the Jefferson Copy was made when Madison (or Jefferson) began to contemplate publication. Alternatively, it may reflect the conventional preference for a title page. Eppes included an appendix with Hamilton's plan and Randolph's plan.[30]

Eppes was not a perfect copyist. He read the manuscript phrase by phrase and copied it from memory. This approach—which is the way people ordinarily copy—meant that he imposed his stylistic tendencies on the manuscript. He skipped words. He adopted a unique style for the beginning of each delegate's comments. He placed a comma after the name and then capitalized the introductory verb. Eppes changed verb tenses. He replaced small phrases with others (e.g.,"for" in place of "in favor of"). He substituted synonyms: "part" for "article"; "powerful" for "violent." When the Eppes copy was proofread against the Notes in the 1830s, almost every page had to be fixed. Although some editorial corrections reflect Madison's later revisions, others were the result of Eppes's imperfect copying. Eppes did not manage to create a perfect duplicate.[31]

The revisions made the Notes difficult to copy. Madison had inserted new material, added the slips, and left instructions to move material. Eppes likely started to copy the Notes from the beginning of the manuscript because the early pages contain significant errors. Eppes tried to follow Madison's instructions; however, the first sheet of the Notes contained slips and was sufficiently revised as to be confusing. He copied the front of one slip but skipped the reverse side and the material covered by the slip. The error suggests that neither Madison nor Jefferson explained the manuscript to Eppes—and no one was proofreading Eppes's work. By the end of the Notes, Eppes had become a careful reader. He noticed that the debate on September 7 made no sense. He inserted a footnote: "There appears to be wanting in this place part of a days debate. . . ." Eppes was correct. Madison later added a sheet.[32]

The Jefferson Copy has three parts, each with a separate title page. The first part spanned May through the Committee of the Whole House Report on June 20. This first part appears to have been written in three sections. A section ended abruptly after the replaced sheets in the early June Notes (b.12), suggesting that Eppes perceived a division in the Notes. The second Part began in the middle of the proceedings for July 18 and ended after August 21. This division suggests that, at the time of the Eppes copying project, the post–August 21 section was distinct. The final part was originally labeled "part 3[d]." Only later, presumably in the 1830s with the addition of the June 21 to July 18 material, were the words altered to "part last."[33]

The Jefferson Copy is incomplete. In the 1830s, copyists worked with John C. Payne to bring the Jefferson Copy into conformity with the Payne transcript of the Notes. New pages were inserted and numerous words altered and sentences added. These pages are easily distinguished from the original sheets by Eppes. Because Eppes never copied the Notes between June 21 and the end of July 18, this section was written in the 1830s. In addition, a significant section of the Jefferson Copy from July 25 through August 13 is not extant. The page numbers suggest that Eppes copied these pages, but no Press Copy exists to confirm the existence of an initial copy. Third, beginning with September 6, three groups of pages are missing. Eppes presumably copied the pages, but when and why they disappeared is unknown. Among these are pages for September 15. According to the page numbers on the Jefferson Copy, only three pages (one sheet) are missing. In the Notes, however, two closely written sheets cover the proceedings. If the page numbers are accurate, the September 15 proceedings copied by Eppes must have been considerably shorter. If so—and this conclusion is highly speculative—the lengthy proceedings currently in the Notes were themselves a replacement and may represent Madison's effort to more comprehensively catalog the alterations made on September 15. It may be, however, that the page numbers are in error and the Notes were complete for these final days when Eppes made the copy or that Eppes simply accidently skipped the September 15 proceeding.[34]

Catalogue of the Notes

This catalogue lists the sheets (bifolia) and slips. Letters from Madison between May and September 1787 are placed after the sheet bearing that date. The sheets are numbered with the first sheet (May 14, 1787) given the number 1 and "b." (bifolium). Where relevant, the pages follow the dash. Slips are numbered to show the page on which the slip was attached, as well as the ordinal arrangement. Thus, slip 2, b.96-2 is the second slip attached to the second page of the ninety-sixth sheet. Although the arguments in this book are based primarily on textual evidence, I include watermark information. For my research, I also tracked whether material was added from the official journal or was integrated when originally written; whether the sheet was copied in the Jefferson Copy and Press Copy; and whether material from the Yates notes was added. For sheets likely replaced, I provide the introductory and concluding words of the sheet and the speaker to locate the material in other editions.

This book takes watermark information into account but has not relied on watermark evidence. Watermarks are imprecise, circumstantial evidence. Scholars continue to disagree on the degree of variation present in paper created from the same mold at approximately the same time. Further complexity results from the Whatman paper mill's use of a double mold. The mill created two sheets (each with watermark and countermark) at the same time. Uncertainty exists about the manner in which these sheets were cut and arranged for sale. A search of images in watermark catalogues in print and online shows similar watermarks in correspondence in the late 1780s and 1790s. Last, and perhaps most important, an individual may use a variety of papers and may return to use older papers. Watermark evidence may suggest that papers with the same watermark were written at approximately the same time but other explanations always need to be considered.[35]

The technologies and access available permitted classification of eleven marks: three Whatman watermarks; two Whatman countermarks; three watermarks with a crowned posthorn shield and a GR; and countermarks for T. French, Budgen, and Taylor. This classifications is more detailed than prior studies but further variations may be identified in the future. I accept that many other variations are the result of ordinary paper production. The sheets may have been shaved, resulting in the loss of a chain line. On certain sheets the mark is distorted by adhesion in the center margin, a consequence of earlier storage. Some sheets have been treated for conservation and repair. In 2008, the Library of Congress provided images for eleven images missing in the 2003 digital copy. On these new images, the mark is usually visible. On some digital images of the microfilm, the center of the mark can be seen. For this research, the Library graciously agreed to take a limited number of watermark digital images in August 2009. In May 2010, I examined the sheets on a light table with Library staff. In 2014, the Library helped me examine the September letters on a light table. Without the extraordinary Library staff, this research would have been impossible. Identification of the marks in Madison's letters has been particularly challenging. When this research was conducted, the Library's letters were bound in large volumes. More definitive study would require examination on a light table of correspondence from the mid-1780s to the 1790s.

I have written the descriptions without specialized terms so that the reader can understand the more obvious differences.

Whatman Paper

Five marks bear a mark associated with Whatman paper. A large sheet contained a countermark and a watermark, usually cut apart. The Whatman short-M is the likely countermark for PHW1 and PHW2. The Whatman long-M is the likely countermark for PHW3. By the nineteenth century, the marks of James Whatman the Younger were imitated by other papermakers. The marks in the first two-thirds of the Notes seem most plausibly to have been Whatman paper from the Turkey Mill paper mill. Whether the "Whatman" marks in the last third are from that paper mill or an imitator may be open to question. Other Whatman marks exist throughout Madison's correspondence.[36]

1. Whatman short-M. The diagonal strokes in the center of the "M" do not reach the baseline. The top left arm of the "T" crosses the chain line. Centered on 10 chain lines: J |W |HA |TM |AN. There may be two variations as a result of a double mold, paralleling the two Whatman watermark variations (PHW1 and PHW2). Appears May through August 21, Hamilton Plan, Randolph July 10 plan. Letters: June 10 and 13; probably September 4 and 6 (half sheets with only the tops of J and W visible).

2. PHW1. Posthorn crowned shield with appended W below. This variation is characterized by an elegant elongated ribbon attached to the posthorn at approximately the same laid line. Chain lines cut through the body of the horn on the opening side and through the mouthpiece on the opposing side. The opening of the horn neatly attaches to the horn on the left; slightly in on the right. The scrolls merge to a closed double line in the center of S. The W attaches to chain lines through outer curlicue. One tear drop at base of W tilts slightly. Appears from May through August 15. Letters: May 27 (two), June 6 (two), July 18, July 28.

3. PHW2. Similar to PHW1 with a nearly identical W cypher, but horn and shield differ. Characterized by a thicker, misaligned ribbon on the posthorn. The top of the mouthpiece is several laid lines below the top of the horn opening. The ribbon attaches to the horn unevenly. The chain line running through the horn's mouth only barely crosses into the body of the horn. The other chain line runs through the mouthpiece. The scrolls do not merge tightly in the center of the S. The W is attached with the chain lines through only the outer curlicue. The mark appears in James Hutson's article in the *Texas Law Review*. Appears May through August 13; twelve sheets. Letters: July 18, possibly July 28 (only corner of mark visible), possibly August 12 (bottom half visible and hinged in volume so difficult to distinguish from PHW1).

4. Whatman long-M. The "M" has a long downstroke in center. The "T" does not cross the chain line. Centered on ten chain lines: J|W|HA|TM|AN. Ten sheets; August 23 to September 6. No definitive correspondence from summer 1787 (see discussion of September letters above).

5. PHW3. Posthorn crowned shield with appended W. Distinguished from PHW1 and PHW2 because W attaches to chain lines such that the chain line runs through the center of the small inner circles on either side of the cypher. W is more spread; ribbon is less elongated. The top of the horn mouthpiece is approximately the same laid line as the top of opening. The ribbon attachment to the side of opening is above ribbon attachment on mouthpiece. Ten sheets; August 22–30. No summer 1787 correspondence.

Posthorn GR Watermarks

1. PHGR1 (centered). Posthorn crowned shield with appended GR. No T in crown. Centered on nine chain lines; G on chain line 5; R on chain line 6. Protuberances at top are more comma-shaped. Three sheets; June 5–6, 7–8. No summer 1787 correspondence.

2. PHGR2 (crown has T). Posthorn crowned shield with an appended GR, small T in the top of the crown. Ten chain lines. G and R attached to chain lines in middle of letters. Protuberances at top of shield are circle shapes. One sheet; June 21. No summer 1787 correspondence.

3. PHGR3 (spread ribbon). Posthorn crowned shield with appended GR. Watermark is off-center with G on fifth chain and R on sixth chain. Nine to ten

chain lines (tenth chain line may be shaved). Ribbon and posthorn stretched out. Protuberances resemble top of question mark. Eight sheets; September 6–7, 8–15. No summer 1787 correspondence.

Other Countermarks

1. T. French. Centered on ten chain lines: T | FR| EN| CH. Four sheets; June 23, 25, 26, 29; July 17–18. No summer 1787 correspondence.

2. Budgen. Centered on nine chain lines: |B U (on next chain line) | DG | EN. Five sheets; September 7, 15, 17; also slip 1, b.1-2. No summer 1787 correspondence.

3. Taylor. Centered on ten chain lines: T | AY | LO |R. 1 sheet; September 7 and 8. No summer 1787 correspondence.

Letter. Tuesday, May 15, 1787 (to Jefferson). J. DeB[usscher] paper.

Letter. May 5, 1787 (to Irvine). H. Van Delden (HSP).

Letter. Wednesday, May 16, 1787 (to Short). Crown watermark; partially visible and obscured by seal (Short Papers, DLC).

b1. Monday, May 14; Friday, May 25; Monday, May 28; Tuesday, May 29. PHW1.

> *Slip 1, b.1-1.* Friday, May 25 (list of delegates).

> *Slip 1, b.1-2.* Monday, May 28 (additional rules and footnote). Budgen (partially visible).

Letter. Sunday, May 27, 1787 (to James Madison, Sr.). Appears to be PHW1 (top of mark on folio).

Letter. Sunday, May 27, 1787 (to Edmund Pendleton). PHW1.

Letter. Sunday, May 27, 1787 (to Jones). Not extant.

b.2. Tuesday, May 29 (Randolph's resolutions). PHW1.

Inserted manuscript (Randolph's May 29 notes of speech; sent after August 21, 1789).

b.3. Wednesday, May 30. PHW2.

> *Slip 1, b.3-2.* Wednesday, May 30 (Read's motion to postpone).

> *Slip 1, b.3-3* (resolution on suffrage and free inhabitants).

> *Slip 2, b.3-3* (Madison's motions on suffrage).

b.4. Thursday, May 31. PHW1.

b.5. Thursday, May 31; Friday, June 1. PHW1.

> *Slip 1, b.5-4.* Friday, June 1 (division of Madison's motion and vote).

b.6. Friday, June 1; Saturday, June 2. PHW1.

b.7. Saturday, June 2. PHW1.

b.8. Saturday, June 2; Monday, June 4. PHW2.

b.9. Monday, June 4. PHW1.

b.10. Monday, June 4; Tuesday, June 5. PHW2.

> *Slip 1, b.10-3.* Tuesday, June 5 (motions on inferior tribunals, appointment, good behavior (admission of states added later)).

b.11. Tuesday, June 5; Wednesday, June 6. PHGR1 ["final jurisdiction in many cases" (Madison) . . . "diminished in proportion to the number among" (Madison)].

b.12. Wednesday, June 6. PHGR1. ["whom the blame or praise" (Madison) . . . "revisionary as to the Executive power." (King)].

b.13. Wednesday, June 6; Thursday, June 7. PHW2.

Letter. Wednesday, June 6, 1787 (to Jefferson). PHW1.

Letter. Wednesday, June 6, 1787 (to Short). PHW1 (folio; top half of mark). (Short Papers).

b.14. Thursday, June 7; Friday, June 8. PHGR1. ["[subordi]nate purposes" (Wilson) . . . Federal liberty" (Wilson)].

b.15. Friday, June 8; Saturday, June 9. PHW1.

b.16. Saturday, June 9; Monday, June 11. Whatman–short M.

Letter. Sunday, June 10, 1787 (to Monroe). Whatman–short M.

b.17. Monday, June 11. Whatman–short M.

b.18. Monday, June 11; Tuesday, June 12. Whatman–short M.

b.19. Tuesday, June 12; Wednesday, June 13. Whatman–short M.
Slip 1, b.19-3. Tuesday, June 12 (motions relating to ineligibility, piracies, captures, etc.).
Slip 2, b.19-3. Wednesday, June 13 (Randolph and Madison motion on jurisdiction of national judiciary; Pinckney and Sherman motion on judicial appointment).

b.20. Wednesday, June 13 (report of Committee of Whole House) (b-20-4 blank). Whatman-short M.

Letter. Wednesday, June 13, 1787 (to Ambrose Madison). WM: Whatman-short M. (Harvard University Library, Houghton Library).

b.21. Thursday, June 14; Friday, June 15. PHW1.
Slip 1, b.21-4. Friday, June 15. Wove paper (continuation of note on discrepancies between Patterson's propositions and copy "printed in the Journal").

b.22. Saturday, June 16. Whatman–short M.

b.23. Saturday, June 16; Monday, June 18. Whatman–short M.

b.24. Monday, June 18. Whatman–short M.

b.25. Monday, June 18. PHW1.

b.26. Tuesday, June 19. Whatman–short M.

b.27. Tuesday, June 19. Whatman–short M.

b.28. Tuesday, June 19; Wednesday, June 20. Whatman–short M.

b.29. Wednesday, June 20. Whatman–short M.

b.30. Thursday, June 21. PHGR2. ["Mr Jonathan Dayton from N. Jersey took" . . . "best, but is content with" (Sherman)].

b.31. Thursday, June 21; Friday, June 22. Whatman–short M.

b.32. Friday, June 22. Whatman–short M.

b.33. Saturday, June 23; Monday, June 25. T. French. ["Mr. Rutlidge, was for preserving" . . . "property & rank is likely to be continued for" (Pinckney).]

b.34. Monday, June 25. PHW1.

b.35. Monday, June 25. PHW1. [Out of order at DLC but placed here in order that corresponds to text and older numbers on mss.]

b.36. Monday, June 25. Whatman–short M. [Out of order at DLC but placed here in order that corresponds to text and older numbers on mss.]

b.37. Tuesday, June 26. T. French. ["The duration of the 2d. branch under consideration" . . . "concurred also in the general observations of [Mr. Madison] on the" (Hamilton).]

b.38. Tuesday, June 26. PHW1.

b.39. Tuesday, June 26; Wednesday, June 27; Thursday, June 28. PHW1.

Letter. Tuesday, June 26, 1787 (to Jones): Not extant.

b.40. Thursday, June 28. PHW1.

b.41. Thursday, June 28. PHW1.

b.42. Friday, June 29. T. French. ["Doctr. Johnson. The controversy must be endless" . . . "nor by themselves" (Madison).]

b.43. Friday, June 29; Saturday, June 30. PHW1.

b.44. Saturday, June 30. PHW1.

b.45. Saturday, June 30. PHW1.

b.46. Saturday, June 30; Monday, July 2. PHW2.

b.47. Monday, July 2; Thursday, July 5. PHW1.

b.48. Thursday, July 5. Whatman–short M.

b.49. Thursday, July 5; Friday, July 6. Whatman–short M.

Slip 1, b.49-1. Thursday, July 5 (motion on suffrage proportioned on general revenue payments).

b.50. Friday, July 6; Saturday, July 7. Whatman–short M.

b.51. Saturday, July 7; Monday, July 9. Whatman–short M.

b.52. Monday, July 9; Tuesday, July 10. Whatman–short M.

b.53. Tuesday, July 10; Wednesday, July 11. Whatman–short M.

b.54. Wednesday, July 11. Whatman–short M.

b.55. Wednesday, July 11; Thursday, July 12. Whatman–short M.

b.56. Thursday, July 12; Friday, July 13. Whatman–short M.

Slip 1, b.56-2. Thursday, July 12 (motion on representation proportioned to direct taxation).

b.57. Friday, July 13; Saturday, July 14. Whatman–short M.

Slip 1, b.57-1. Friday, July 13 (motion on representation based on apportionment).

b.58. Saturday, July 14. WM: PHW1.

b.59. Saturday, July 14; Monday, July 16. PHW1.

Slip 1, b.59-4. Monday, July 16 (motion apportioning representation and allocating representatives).

b.60. Monday, July 16; Tuesday, July 17. PHW2.

b.61. Tuesday, July 17. PHW1.

   Slip 1, b.61-2. Tuesday, July 17 (motion of supremacy clause).

b.62. Tuesday, July 17; Wednesday, July 18. T French. ["On the question on the words" . . . "making a fit choice." (Martin).]

b.63. Wednesday, July 18. PHW2.

b.64. Wednesday, July 18; Thursday, July 19. PHW1.

Letter. Wednesday, July 18, 1787 (to Jefferson). PHW2. (Folio; lower half of mark).

Letter. Wednesday, July 18, 1787 (to Ambrose Madison). PHW1. (NYPL).

Letter. Wednesday, July 18, 1787 (to Carrington). Not extant.

b.65. Thursday, July 19. PHW1.

b.66. Friday, July 20. PHW1.

b.67. Friday, July 20; Saturday, July 21. PHW1.

b.68. Saturday, July 21. PHW1.

b.69. Saturday, July 21; Monday, July 23. PHW1.

b.70. Monday, July 23. PHW1.

b.71. Monday, July 23; Tuesday, July 24. PHW2.

b.72. Tuesday, July 24; Wednesday, July 25. PHW1.

b.73. Wednesday, July 25. PHW2.

   Slip 1, b.73-4. Wednesday, July 25. Wove paper (motions on copies of proceedings for committee of detail and refusal of copy permission to members).

b.74. Thursday, July 26. PHW1.

   Slip 1, b.74-2. Thursday, July 26 (resolution on national executive).

b.75. Thursday, July 26; Monday, August 6 (Committee of Detail report on 75-3). PHW1.

Letter. Saturday, July 28, 1787. To Madison Sr. PHW1 (folio, top half).

Letter. Saturday, July 28, 1787. To McClurg. Not extant.

Letter. Saturday, July 28 [July 30,] 1787. To Ambler. No visible mark (Library of Virginia, less than folio).

Letter. Saturday, [July 28], 1787. To E. Pendleton. Possibly PHW2 (Library of Virginia, less than folio).

b.76. Monday, August 6. (Committee of Detail report). Whatman–short M.

b.77. Monday, August 6. (Committee of Detail report). Whatman–short M.

b.78. Monday, August 6. (Committee of Detail report). Whatman–short M.

b.79. Tuesday, August 7. PHW2.

b.80. Tuesday, August 7; Wednesday, August 8. PHW1.

b.81. Wednesday, August 8. PHW1.

b.82. Wednesday, August 8; Thursday August 9. PHW1.

b.83. Thursday, August 9. PHW2.

b.84. Thursday, August 9; Friday, August 10. PHW1.

b.85. Friday, August 10; Saturday, August 11. PHW1.

b.86. Saturday, August 11; Monday, August 13. PHW1.

Letter. Sunday, August 12, 1787. To Madison Sr. PHW1 or 2 (folio, bottom half).

Letter. Sunday, August 12, 1787. To E. Pendleton. Not extant.

b.87. Monday, August 13. PHW2.

b.88. Monday, August 13; Tuesday, August 14. PHW1.

b.89. Tuesday, August 14. PHW1.

b.90. Tuesday, August 14; Wednesday, August 15. PHW1.

b.91. Wednesday, August 15; Thursday, August 16. Whatman–short M.

Letter. Wednesday, August 15, 1787. To Grayson. Not extant.

b.92. Thursday, August 16; Friday, August 17. Whatman–short M.

b.93. Friday, August 17; Saturday, August 18. Whatman–short M.

    Slip 1, b.93-4. Saturday, August 18 (Madison & Pinckney propositions for powers).

b.94. Saturday, August 18. Whatman–short M.

Letter. Sunday, August 19, 1787. To Jefferson. Not extant.

b.95. Saturday, August 18; Monday, August 20. Whatman–short M.

    Slip 1, b.95-2. Monday, August 20 (Pinckney propositions on rights).

    Slip 2, b.95-3. Monday, August 20 (Morris propositions on council of state).

b.96. Monday, August 20; Tuesday, August 21. Whatman–short M.

    Slip 1, b.96-2. Monday, August 20 (motion on treason).

    Slip 2, b.96-4. Tuesday, August 21 (report on assumption of state debts and militia).

b.97. Tuesday, August 21. Whatman–short M.

    Slip 1, b.97-3. Tuesday, August 21 (Martin motion on requisitions).

b.98. Tuesday, August 21. Whatman–short M (98-3 and 98-4 blank).

b.99. Wednesday, August 22. PHW3. Page holes appear in different location from prior section.

b.100. Wednesday, August 22; Thursday, August 23. PHW3.

b.101. Thursday, August 23. PHW3.

b.102. Thursday, August 23. Whatman–long M.

b.103. Friday, August 24. Whatman–long M.

b.104. Friday, August 24; Saturday, August 25. PHW3.

Letter. Saturday, August 25, 1787. To McClurg. Not extant.

b.105. Saturday, August 25. Whatman–long M.

b.106. Saturday, August 25; Monday, August 27. PHW3.

b.107. Monday, August 27; Tuesday, August 28. PHW3.

b.108. Tuesday, August 28; Wednesday, August 29. PHW3.

b.109. Wednesday, August 29. PHW3.

b.110. Wednesday, August 29; Thursday, August 30. PHW3.

b.111. Thursday, August 30. PHW3.

b.112. Thursday, August 30; Friday, August 31. Whatman–long M.

b.113. Friday, August 31; Saturday, September 1. Whatman–long M.

Letter. Saturday, September 1, 1787. To McClurg. Not extant.

b.114. Monday, September 3, 1787. Whatman–long M.

Letter. Tuesday, September 4, 1787. To Madison, Sr. Only top of J and W visible (folio, top half).

b.115. Tuesday, September 4. Whatman–long M.

b.116. Tuesday, September 4; Wednesday, September 5. Whatman–long M.

b.117. Wednesday, September 5. Whatman–long M.

b.118. Wednesday, September 5; Thursday, September 6. Whatman–long M.

Letter. Thursday, September 6, 1787. To Jefferson. Only top of J and W visible (folio, top half).

b.119. Thursday, September 6. PHGR3.

b.120. Thursday, September 6; Friday, September 7. PHGR3.

b.121. Friday, September 7. Budgen.

b.122. Friday, September 7, Saturday, September 8. Taylor. (Eppes wrote, "there appears to be wanting in this place part of a days debate which. . . .")

b.123. Saturday, September 8; Monday, September 10. PHGR3.

b.124. Monday, September 10. PHGR3.

b.125. Monday, September 10; Tuesday, September 11; Wednesday, September 12. PHGR3.

b.126. Wednesday, September 12; Thursday, September 13. PHGR3.

b.127. Thursday, September 13; Friday, September 14. PHGR3.

b.128. Friday, September 14; Saturday, September 15. PHGR3.

Letter. Saturday, September 15. To Blair. Library of Virginia (not located by Library).

b.129. Saturday, September 15. Budgen.

b.130. Saturday, September 15. Budgen.

b.131. Monday, September 17. Budgen.

b.132. Monday, September 17. Budgen.

b.133. Copy of Hamilton Plan. Whatman–short M.

b.134. Copy of Hamilton Plan. Whatman–short M.

b.135. Copy of Hamilton Plan. Whatman–short M.

b.136. Copy of Hamilton Plan. Whatman–short M.

b.137. Randolph Plan, July 10 (folio). Whatman [appears that the T crosses the chain line as in Whatman short–M].

[Letter. September 18, 1787 [1789] (to Tench Coxe). This letter was misdated by Madison and was written in 1789. PJM, 12:409–10 n.1.]

Letter. Thursday, September 20, 1787 (to Pendleton). CB inside a heart.

Letter. c. September 28, 1787 (to Randolph). Not extant.

Letter. September 30, 1787 (to Madison, Sr. from New York). GR.

Letter. September 30, 1787 (to Washington from New York). R. Williams.

ABBREVIATIONS

Manuscript Sources

EJC   [Eppes's Jefferson Copy], James Madison Papers, 1780–1836, volume 1, Edward Everett Papers, Ms. N-1201, Vols. 229–231, Massachusetts Historical Society.

JMP   James Madison Papers, Library of Congress.

MJC   [Madison's Journal Copy], "'Journal' of the Federal Convention of 1787," United States Presidents Collection, General Collection, Beinecke Rare Book and Manuscript Library, Gen. Mss. 271, Box 1, f.49.

Notes   Madison's Original Notes on Debates in the Federal Convention, 1787, James Madison Papers, series 5e, Library of Congress.

Payne Copy John C. Payne's Copy of Madison's Original Notes on Debates in the Federal Convention, 1787, James Madison Papers, series 5f, Library of Congress.

PC   [Press Copy], Notes of the Federal Convention, James Madison Papers, 1781–1847, Ser. VI (NYPL).

Other

CWH   Committee of Whole House.

DHC   *The Documentary History of the Constitution, 1786–1870* (Washington, DC: Department of State, 1894–1905), 5 volumes.

DHFFC   *Documentary History of the First Federal Congress of the United States of America,* eds. Linda Grant De Pauw, Charlene Bangs Bickford, Kenneth R Bowling, Helen E Veit (Baltimore: John Hopkins University Press, 1972–2012), 20 volumes.

DHRC   *The Documentary History of the Ratification of the Constitution,* eds. John P. Kaminski, Gaspare J. Saladino, Richard Leffler, Charles H. Schoenleber, and Margaret A. Hogan (Madison: State Historical Society of Wisconsin, 1976–2013), 26 volumes.

DLC   Library of Congress.

DMDE   *Dolley Madison Digital Edition,* ed. Holly C. Shulman (Charlottesville: University of Virginia Press, Rotunda, 2004).

JCC   *Journals of the Continental Congress,* eds. Worthington C. Ford, Gaillard Hunt, John C. Fitzpatrick, and Roscoe R. Hill (Washington: Government Printing Office, 1904–1937), 34 volumes.

LDC   *Letters of Delegates to Congress, 1774–1789,* eds. Paul H. Smith, Gerald W. Gawalt, Rosemary Fry Plakas, and Eugene R. Sheridan (Washington: Government Printing Office, 1976–2000), 26 volumes.

LMCC   *Letters of Members of the Continental Congress,* ed. Edmund C. Burnett (Washington, DC: Carnegie Institution, 1921–1936), 8 volumes.

MHS   Massachusetts Historical Society.

NYPL   New York Public Library.

PAH   *The Papers of Alexander Hamilton,* eds. Harold C. Syrett and Jacob E. Cooke (New York, Columbia University Press 1961–1979), 26 volumes.

PGW (CS)   *The Papers of George Washington: Confederation Series,* eds. W. W. Abbott and Dorothy Twohig (Charlottesville : University Press of Virginia 1992–), 6 volumes.

PGW (PS)   *The Papers of George Washington: Presidential Series,* ed. Dorothy Twohig and W. W. Abbot (Charlottesville: University Press of Virginia 1987–2013), 17 volumes.

PJM   *The Papers of James Madison,* eds. William T. Hutchinson, William M. E. Rachal, and Robert Allen Rutland (Chicago:

University of Chicago Press, 1962–1977; Charlottesville: University of Virginia Press, 1977–1991), 17 volumes.

PJM (Gilpin)   *The Papers of James Madison,* ed. Henry D. Gilpin (Washington, DC: Langtree & O'Sullivan, 1840), 3 volumes.

PJM (PS)   *The Papers of James Madison, Presidential Series,* ed. Robert Rutland (Charlottesville: University of Virginia Press, 1984–2012), 7 volumes.

PJM (RS)   *The Papers of James Madison, Retirement Series,* ed. David B. Mattern (Charlottesville: University of Virginia Press, 2009–2013), 2 volumes.

PJM (SS)   *The Papers of James Madison, Secretary of State Series,* ed. Robert J. Brugger (Charlottesville: University of Virginia Press, 1986–2014), 10 volumes.

PTJ   *The Papers of Thomas Jefferson,* eds. Julian P. Boyd, L. H. Butterfield, and Charles T. Cullen (Princeton: Princeton University Press, 1950–), 22 volumes.

PTJ (RS)   *The Papers of Thomas Jefferson, Retirement Series,* ed. J. Looney (Princeton: Princeton University Press, 2004–), 10 volumes.

RFC   *The Records of the Federal Convention,* ed. Max Farrand (New Haven: Yale University Press, 1911; volume 4, 1937), 4 volumes.

SRFC   *Supplement to Max Farrand's The Records of the Federal Convention of 1787,* ed. James H. Hutson (New Haven: Yale University Press, 1987).

WJM   *The Writings of James Madison,* ed. Gaillard Hunt (New York: G.P. Putnam's Sons, 1900–1910), 9 volumes.

NOTES

Introduction

1. James Madison, Notes, JMP (DLC); PJM (Gilpin). For label, see digital images of Notes from Library of Congress provided to author with images labeled James Madison, *Debate Notes*, 1787, GR no. 142 (May 2003). On Treasures, see "American Treasures of the Library of Congress: Top Treasures Gallery," DLC, www.loc.gov/exhibits/treasures/tr00.html#caselist. I am indebted to Jack Rakove who suggested that this book was a "biography" of the Notes.

2. Notes survive in original or revised form by Robert Yates, John Lansing, Rufus King, William Pierce, Alexander Hamilton, James Wilson, James McHenry, George Mason, Pierce Butler, Gunning Bedford, and William Paterson. For discussion of other note takers, see RFC, 1:xiv–xxii; SRFC, xviii. On official record, see Mary Sarah Bilder, "How Bad Were the Official Records of the Federal Convention?" *George Washington Law Review* 80, no.6 (2012): 1620–1682. For modern editions, see [James Madison], *The Debates in The Federal Convention of 1787 which Framed the Constitution of the United States of America*, eds. Gaillard Hunt and James Brown Scott (New York: Oxford University Press, 1920); Edward J. Larson and Michael P. Winship, *The Constitutional Convention: A Narrative History from the Notes of James Madison* (New York: Random House, Modern Library, 2005).

3. *Outranks in, The Writings of James Madison,* ed. Gaillard Hunt (New York: G. P. Putnam's Sons, 1902), 3:ix. *at once,* Max Farrand, "The Records of the Federal Convention," *American Historical Review* 13 (1907): 44–65, quotation at 51–52; John P. Kaminski, "Madison's Gift," *Common Place,* 2, no. 4 (July 2002), http://common-place.org. For reprints, see James Madison, *The Debates in the Federal Convention of 1787* (Amherst, NY: Prometheus Books, 2007); Larson and Winship, *Constitutional Convention.*

4. *Them transcribed,* see Dolley P. Madison to the President (A. Jackson), 15 November 1836, in PJM (Gilpin), 1:xvi. For facsimile, see "Fac-simile of the

last page of Mr. Madison's Manuscript Debates of the Convention" in "Fac-similes of the Manuscripts of Mr. Madison carefully copied from the originals . . . ," PJM (Gilpin), 3:[backmatter after ccxlvi]; Eric Slauter, *The State as a Work of Art: The Cultural Origins of the Constitution* (Chicago: University of Chicago Press, 2009), 1–8. For publications, see DHC, 3; RFC. *the Debates,* Charles R. Keller and George W. Pierson, "A New Madison Manuscript Relating to the Federal Convention of 1787," *American Historical Review* 36 (October 1930): 17–30.

5. *There has,* SRFC, xx; see also James H. Hutson, "The Creation of the Constitution: The Integrity of the Documentary Record," *Texas Law Review* 65 (1986): 1–39; James H. Hutson, "Riddles of the Federal Constitutional Convention," *William and Mary Quarterly* 44 (1987): 411–423. On Hamilton charge, see John C. Hamilton, *The Life of Alexander Hamilton,* 2nd ed. (New York, D. Appleton & Co., 1841), 2:490–492 n.† & n. 492 n.*; John C. Hamilton, *History of the Republic of the United States as traced in the writings of Alexander Hamilton* (New York: D. Appleton, 1859), 3:301–302, 340, 344–348. For Crosskey claims, see William W. Crosskey, *Politics and the Constitution in the History of the United States* (Chicago: University of Chicago Press, 1953), 1:313 (addressing August 21 Notes), 2:1021 (addressing August 15 Notes); William W. Crosskey, "The Ex-Post-Facto Clause and the Contracts Clauses in the Federal Convention: A Note on the Editorial Ingenuity of James Madison," *University of Chicago Law Review* 35 (1968) (posthumously published from repeatedly revised draft): 248–254 (addressing August 28 Notes). On claim rejection, see Irving Brant, *James Madison: Commander in Chief, 1812–1836* (New York: Bobbs-Merrill Company, 1961), 435, 571 n. 18; SRFC, xxi–xxiii; Hutson, "Riddles," 411–423.

6. *Inspired by,* Larson and Winship, *Constitutional Convention,* 10. *impresses,* Bernard Bailyn, *The Ordeal of Thomas Hutchinson* (Cambridge: Harvard University Press, 1974), ix.

7. *Great collaboration,* Adrienne Koch, *Jefferson and Madison: The Great Collaboration* (New York: Knopf, 1950). Andrew Burstein and Nancy Isenberg give more attention to the 1780s in their chapter, "Partners Apart," in *Madison and Jefferson* (New York: Random House, 2010).

8. *They are far,* Hutson, "The Creation of the Constitution: The Integrity," 1, 35. *no more,* Frederic Irland, "The Reporter Who Became President," *McClure's Magazine* 24 (1905): 258–265; see also Hutson, "The Creation of the Constitution: The Integrity," 1, 33–34 (estimating 7–10% of proceedings at best). *Madison could not,* Hutson, "The Creation of the Constitution: The Integrity," 35. *Madison's diligence,* Richard Beeman, *Plain, Honest Men: The Making of the American Constitution* (New York: Random House, 2009), 85.

9. Lance Banning, *The Sacred Fire of Liberty: James Madison and the Founding of the Federal Republic* (Ithaca, NY: Cornell University Press, 1995), 8.

10. For an overview of the scholarship, see Alan Gibson, "Inventing the Extended Republic: The Debate over the Role of Madison's Theory in the Creation of the Constitution," in *James Madison: Philosopher, Founder, and Statesman*, eds. John R. Vile, William D. Pederson, and Frank J. Williams (Athens: Ohio University Press, 2008), 63–87. Excellent discussions of the conventional reading of the Vices and Federalist 10 are Larry D. Kramer, "Madison's Audience," *Harvard Law Review*, 112 (1999), 611–679, and Jack Rakove's writing, in particular, *James Madison and the Creation of the American Republic* (Glenview, IL: HarperCollins, 1990); Rakove, "James Madison and the Extended Republic: Theory and Practice in American Politics," in *This Constitution: A Bicentennial Chronicle* (Fall 1985), published by Project '87 of the American Political Science Association and American Historical Association. Over the past decade, political scientists such as Colleen Sheehan, Alan Gibson, Robert Martin, Jenna Bednar, and many others have written abundantly on the extensive republic and federalism. Recent historians and legal scholars who have focused on the relationship to the Constitution include Charles Hobson, Larry Kramer, Jack Rakove, Garry Wills, Gordon Wood, and Stuart Leibiger.

11. The relationship between "population and constitution-making" was emphasized in a note to the apportionment numbers in the first volume of *The Documentary History of the Ratification of the Constitution*, edited by Merrill Jensen in 1976 with associate editors John Kaminski and Gaspare Saladino. DHRC, 1:297–301. Recent scholarship emphasizing the relationship between slavery and political power includes works by David Waldstreicher, George William Van Cleve, John Kaminski, Paul Finkelman, Robin Einhorn, Matthew Mason, Don Fehrenbacher, Mark Graber, Gary Nash, and authors represented in *Contesting Slavery: The Politics of Bondage and Freedom in the New American Nation* (Charlottesville: University of Virginia Press, 2011).

12. For scholarship on the documentary record, see John Franklin Jameson, "Studies in the History of the Federal Convention of 1787," *Annual Report of the American Historical Association* (1902), 1:87–167 and works by Paul L. Ford, Worthington Ford, Gaillard Hunt, Max Farrand, William Crosskey, Irving Brant, James Hutson, Leonard Rapport, John Kaminski, and the editors of the Madison and Jefferson Papers. A helpful bibliographic aid is Carol D. Billings, "Sources for the Study of the Constitutional Era: A Bibliographic and Historiographical Essay," *Law Library Journal*, 81 (1989): 47–67. The paper collections of particular assistance to this book have been those of Madison, Jefferson, Dolley Madison, Alexander Hamilton, and George Washington, as well as the various collections related to the old Congress and the first Federal Congress. Historians and political scientists include Douglass Adair, Joyce Appleby, Bernard Bailyn, Charles Beard, Richard Bernstein, Max Edling, Alan Gibson, David Hendrickson, Charles Hobson, David Konig, Forrest McDonald, Pauline Maier, R. Kent Newmyer, Jack Rakove, Michael Kammen, John Vile, Gordon Wood, and

Peter Onuf. Legal scholars and legal historians include, among numerous others, Akhil Amar, Bruce Ackerman, Fabio Arcila, Hans Baade, Jack Balkin, Raoul Berger, Boris Bittker, Steven Calabresi, Thomas Colby, Saul Cornell, William Ewald, Daniel Farber, James Fleming, Barry Friedman, Jamal Greene, John Harrison, Richard Kay, Vasan Kesavan, Leonard Levy, Charles Lofgren, Gregory Maggs, John Manning, Maeva Marcus, William Meigs, Edwin Meese, Bernie Meyler, John Mikail, Robert Natelson, Caleb Nelson, Michael Stokes Paulsen, H. Jefferson Powell, Saikrishna Prakash, Michael Rappaport, Stephen Sachs, Suzanne Sherry, Louis Sirico, Peter Smith, Steven Smith, Lawrence Solum, Jacobus tenBroek, William Michael Treanor, Keith Whittington, and John Wofford. Narrative accounts have been written by Richard Beeman, Carol Berkin, Catherine Drinker Bowen, Frank Donovan, Max Farrand, Clinton Rossiter, David Stewart, as well as helpful compilations on the Convention by John Vile. On Madison and his circle, see Robert Alley, Lance Banning, Irving Brant, James Scott Brown, Edward Burns, Charles Cerami, Lynne Cheney, Francis Cogliano, Donald Dewey, Susan Dunn, Joseph Ellis, Joanne Freeman, Robert Goldwin, John Kaminski, Ralph Ketcham, Adrienne Koch, Richard Labunski, Stuart Leibiger, David Mattern, Richard Matthews, Drew McCoy, Marvin Meyers, Michael Meyerson, William Lee Miller, Gary Padula, Jack Rakove, Neal Riemer, Gary Rosen, Robert Rutland, Colleen Sheehan, Garrett Ward Sheldon, Sheila Simon, J. C. A. Stagg, Garry Wills, and the authors of essays in collected volumes (*James Madison and the Future of Limited Government,* ed. John Samples (Washington: Cato Institute, 2002); *James Madison: The Theory and Practice of Republican Government,* ed. Samuel Kernell (Stanford: Stanford University Press, 2003); *James Madison: Philosopher, Founder, and Statesman,* eds. John R. Vile, William D. Pederson, Frank J. Williams (Athens: Ohio University Press, 2008)). Scholars in the history of the book as it relates to legal texts include M. T. Clanchy, Walter Ong, David Hall, Ann Blair, Anthony Grafton, Robert Darnton, Eric Slauter, Alfred Brophy, Morris Cohen, John Gordan, Michael Hoeflich, Richard Ross, Stephen Wilf, and authors represented in two recent collections, *The History of the Book in America* (Chapel Hill: University of North Carolina Press, 2014–2015), 5 volumes, and *The Cambridge History of the Book in Britain* (Cambridge: Cambridge University Press, 2006–[2016]), 7 volumes. Several new and important books on the Convention, the Constitution, and Madison were published as or after this book was completed: Eric Nelson's *The Royalist Revolution: Monarch and the American Founding* (Cambridge: Harvard University Press, 2014); Colleen Sheehan's *James Madison, the Classics, and the Foundations of Republican Government* (Cambridge: Cambridge University Press, forthcoming); and Jonathan Gienapp's *The Transformation of the American Constitution: Politics and Justification in Revolutionary America* (tentative title). They will undoubtedly enrich this book's argument.

13. In August 2009, the Library of Congress graciously agreed to take a limited number of watermark images to establish certain variations. The Library provided supervised access to the manuscript in May 2009 and May 2010. In May 2010, the Library conservators and I studied each sheet on a light table. In addition, the digital microfilm images available through the Madison Papers have been helpful because the microfilm unintentionally captured parts of the watermark in the center margin on certain images. The Library also provided access to Madison's contemporary correspondence and in May 2014 permitted several letters to be placed on a light table.

14. Brant suggested that the W watermark designated "George Washington" instead of the more conventional Whatman watermark. He believed that the Taylor mark appeared in a February 15 letter to Jefferson. Although the letter remains hinged, it may resemble I TAYLOR as in a Madison letter of September 18, 1789. Madison to Jefferson, 15 February 1787; Madison to T. Coxe, 8 September 1787 [1789], JMP, series 1, 7. Brant referred to a letter *to* Madison on T. French paper, which does not establish Madison's use in summer 1787. Brant, *James Madison: Commander in Chief*, 435, 571 n. 18. Hutson and Rapport significantly improved on Brant's study but were constrained by technological limitations. SRFC, xx–xxv (noting assistance of Leonard Rapport on title page). The Hutson-Rapport studies did not include the Taylor watermark and did not realize there were significant variations among the Whatman marks. Rapport spent a "year in the Library of Congress examining James Madison's papers" but prior to significant developments in watermark scholarship. Rapport noted, "if Tom Gravell, his light box, and his books had come on the scene ten years earlier I would have been able to accomplish a lot more." Leonard Rapport, [Talk], 21 August 1997, 2 (courtesy of Jody Rapport) (paper may have been delivered under the title "Watermark Evidence for the Dating of Madison's Notes of the 1787 Constitutional Convention" given at the First International Conference on the History, Function, and Study of Watermarks, The Center for Textual & Editorial Studies, Virginia Tech, October 1996). I am grateful to Jody Rapport for searching her father's papers. For Jefferson Copy description, see the Evidence, the Manuscripts.

15. Pauline Maier, *Ratification: The People Debate the Constitution, 1787–1788* (New York: Simon & Schuster, 2010), 36.

16. Drew R. McCoy, *The Last of the Fathers: James Madison and the Republican Legacy* (Cambridge: Cambridge University Press, 1989). *his own,* Jack N. Rakove, *Original Meanings: Politics and Ideas in the Making of the Constitution* (New York: Vintage, 1997), 5.

17. DHC, 3:7–9.

18. RFC, 1:3.

1. The Genre of Legislative Diaries

1. *Proceedings,* William Bradford to Madison, 17 October 1774, PJM, 1:125–126.

2. Madison to William Bradford, 23 August 1774, PJM, 1:120–121.

3. JCC, 1:13 (Sept. 5), 25–26 (Sept. 6); *Journal of the proceedings of the Congress, held at Philadelphia, September 5, 1774* (Philadelphia: Printed by William and Thomas Bradford, at the London Coffee House, MDCCLXXIV. [1774]), 23. On procedures, see Edmund Cody Burnett, *The Continental Congress* (New York: MacMillan Co., 1941), 33–43; Calvin Jillson and Rick K. Wilson, *Congressional Dynamics: Structure, Coordination, and Choice in the First American Congress, 1774–1789* (Stanford: Stanford University Press, 1994), 43–67.

4. Herbert Friedenwald, "The Journals and Papers of the Continental Congress," *Pennsylvania Magazine of History and Biography* 21 (1897): 161–184, 361–375, 445–465; John C. Fitzpatrick, "A Rough Secret Journal of the Continental Congress," *American Historical Review* 27 (1922): 489–491; *Catalogue of the Papers of the Continental Congress: Miscellaneous Index* (Washington: U.S. Department of State, 1893), 7–8 (Bureau of Rolls and Library Bulletin No. 1).

5. See Friedenwald, "Journals," 361–362, 453; JCC, 11:535 (26 May 1778); Mary Sarah Bilder, "How Bad Were the Official Records of the Federal Convention?" *George Washington Law Review* 80, no.6 (2012): 1636–1637.

6. On English practices, see Benjamin Beard Hoover, *Samuel Johnson's Parliamentary Reporting: Debates in the Senate of Lilliput* (Berkeley: California University Press, 1953); Andrew Sparrow, *Obscure Scribblers: A History of Parliamentary Journalism* (London: Politico's Publishing, 2003); Nikki Hessell, *Literary Authors, Parliamentary Reporters: Johnson, Coleridge, Hazlitt, Dickens* (Cambridge: Cambridge University Press, 2012), ix–59; Arthur Aspinall, "The Reporting and Publishing of the House of Commons' Debates, 1771–1834," in *Essays presented to Sir Lewis Namier,* eds. Richard Pares and A. J. P. Taylor (London: Macmillan, 1956), 227–257; John Ferris, "Before Hansard: Records of Debate in the Seventeenth-Century House of Commons," *Archives* 20, no. 88 (1992): 198–207. On 1774 debates, see Peter D. G. Thomas, "The Beginning of Parliamentary Reporting in Newspapers, 1768–1774," *English History Review* 74 (1959): 623–636. On early American practice, see Mary Patterson Clarke, *Parliamentary Privilege in the American Colonies* (1943; New York: Da Capo Press, 1971), 232–233; Alison G. Olson, "Eighteenth-Century Colonial Legislatures and Their Constituents," *Journal of American History* 79 (1992): 543–567.

7. *Is it discoverable,* Madison to Bradford 28 July 1775, PJM, 1:159. On publications, see Bradford to Madison, 10 July 1775, PJM, 1:154–156.

8. *The Intelligence,* Elias Boudinot to George Washington, 17 March 1783, LDC, 20:30. *well authenticated,* Edmund Pendleton to Madison, 30 October

1780, PJM, 2:154–155. *Should you,* David Howell to Thomas G. Hazard, 26 August 1783, LDC, 20:596.

9. *Handed,* Pendleton to Madison, 27 August 1780, PJM, 2:66–67. *I shall,* Madison to Pendleton, 12 September 1780, PJM, 2:81. *such information,* Jones to Madison, 19 September 1780, PJM, 2:91. *other,* Madison to Jefferson, 18 March 1782, PJM, 4:101–102. For coded example to Randolph, see Madison to Randolph, 20 August 1782, PJM, 5:69–71. On ciphers, see Edmund C. Burnett, "Ciphers of the Revolutionary Period," *American Historical Review* 22 (1917): 329, 331–332; Ralph E. Weber, *United States Diplomatic Codes and Ciphers, 1775–1938* (Chicago: Precedent Publishing, 1979), 22–117.

10. *Few delegates, Letters of Members of the Continental Congress,* ed. Edmund C. Burnett (Washington: Carnegie Institute, 1921), 1:viii. *insensible,* Arthur St. Clair to Thomas FitzSimons, 10 March 1787, LMCC, 8:553.

11. *Illegal, products,* Hoover, *Samuel Johnson,* 32, 129. On English debates, see P. D. G. Thomas, "The Beginning of Parliamentary Reporting in Newspapers, 1768–1774," *English Historical Review* 74 (1959): 623–636; Aspinall, "Reporting," 227–257; Dror Wahrman, "Virtual Representation: Parliamentary Reporting and Languages of Class in the 1790s," *Past and Present* 136 (1992): 83–113; Mary Ransome, "The Reliability of Contemporary Reporting of the Debates of the House of Commons, 1727–1741," *Bulletin of the Institute of Historical Research* 19 (1942–43): 67–79; H. Hale Bellot, "Bibliographical Aids to Research: . . . Reports of Parliamentary Debates for the Period since 1660," *Bulletin of the Institute of Historical Research* 10 (1932–1933): 171–177. On American reprinting, see *The Parliamentary Register* (London: Printed for J. Almon, 1775), 1:76–79 (complaint of Governor Colden to the Earl of Dartmouth). For congressional library, see PJM, 6:81. On Jefferson's library, see E. Millicent Sowerby, *Catalogue of the Library of Thomas Jefferson* (Charlottesville: University of Virginia Press, 1983), 3:190–197. *printed debates,* Patrick Bullard, "Parliamentary Rhetoric, Enlightenment and the Politics of Secrecy: The Printers' Crisis of March 1771," *History of European Ideas,* 31 (2005): 313, 324.

12. On rise of American debates, see Charlene Bangs Bickford, "Throwing Open the Doors: The First Federal Congress and the Eighteenth-Century Media," in *Inventing Congress: Origins and Establishment of the First Federal Congress,* eds. Kenneth R. Bowling and Donald R. Kennon (Athens: Ohio University Press, 1999), 166, 170–171; Bilder, "How Bad," 1638–1639. *here quite,* Mathew Carey, *Mathew Carey: Editor, Author, and Publisher Autobiography* (1833; Brooklyn: Research Classics, 1942), 12; *Debates and Proceedings of the General Assembly of Pennsylvania on the Memorials praying a repeal or suspension of the law annulling the charter of the bank,* ed. Mathew Carey (Philadelphia: Carey and Co, Seddon and Pritchard, 1786). On Carey, see Earl L. Bradsher, *Mathew Carey, editor, author and publisher: a study in American*

literary development (New York: Columbia University Press, 1912), 4; Edward C. Carter II, "Mathew Carey in Ireland, 1760–1784," *Catholic Historical Review* 51 (1966): 503–527. On Thomas Lloyd, see Marion Tinling, "Thomas Lloyd's Reports of the First Federal Congress," *William and Mary Quarterly* 18 (1961): 519–545; *Proceedings and Debates of the General Assembly of Pennsylvania* (Philadelphia, 1787), 2 vols.; *Debates of the Convention, of the State of Pennsylvania, on the Constitution . . .* (Philadelphia, 1788), 2 vols.

13. For Carey's comments, see *Debates and Proceedings of the General Assembly of Pennsylvania,* preface. For shorthand, see Editorial Method, DHFFC, 10:xlvi–xlviii. On Lloyd's difficulties, see Tinling, "Thomas Lloyd," 530–531; DHFFC, 10:xxix–xxxiii.

14. *Personal Aide, Tory and Whig: The Parliamentary Papers of Edward Harley, 3d Earl of Oxford,* eds. Stephen Taylor and Clyve Jones (Rochester, N.Y.: The Boydell Press, 1998), xviii. *personal vanity,* John Ferris, "Before Hansard, Records of Debate in the Seventeenth Century House of Commons," *Archives* 20 (1992): 198–207, 207. *marks, erratic, Two Diaries of the Long Parliament,* ed. Maija Jansson (New York: St. Martin's Press, 1984), xv. *grammatical, The Parliamentary Diary of Sir Edward Knatchbull, 1722–1730,* ed. A. N. Newman (London: Royal Historical Society, 1963), 131. *leading role, The Parliamentary Diary of Sir Richard Cocks, 1698–1702,* ed. D. W. Hayton (Oxford: Clarendon Press, 1996), xiii. *Speeches,* Geoffrey Elton, *The Parliament of England 1559–1581* (Cambridge: Cambridge University Press, 1986), 10–11. On parliamentary diaries, see also *The Parliamentary Diary of Narcissus Lutrell, 1691–1693,* ed. Henry Horwitz (Oxford: Clarendon Press, 1972), vii–xiii; *The Parliamentary Diary of Robert Bowyer, 1606–1607,* ed. David Harris Willson (Minneapolis: University of Minnesota Press, 1931); A. P. W. Malcomson and D. J. Jackson, "Sir Henry Cavendish and the Proceedings of the Irish House of Commons, 1776–1800," in *The Irish Parliament in the Eighteenth Century: The Long Apprenticeship,* ed. David Hayton (Edinburgh: Edinburgh University Press, 2001), 128–146; Anthony R. Black, *An Edition of the Cavendish Irish Parliamentary Diary, 1776–1778* (Delavan, WI: Hallberg Publishing Corp., 1984), 1:ix–x.

15. Anchitell Grey, *Debates of the House of Commons, from the year 1667 to the year 1694* (London: D. Henry & R. Cave, 1763); [James Caldwell], *Debates Relative to the Affairs of Ireland in the Years 1763 and 1764* (London, 1766). *Re-establishment,* Grey, *Debates,* 10:v. *only,* ibid., vii. *confined,* [Caldwell], *Debates,* i–ii, viii. On Jefferson's copies, see Sowerby, *Catalogue,* 3:196–197. There are also examples of colonial legislative diaries indicating that no formal model was required.

16. *Scattered,* LMCC, 1:vi. On Middleton, see LDC, 18:xxiv. Congressional diarists included John Adams, James Duane, Richard Smith, Samuel Ward,

Thomas Jefferson, Thomas Burke, Benjamin Rush, Charles Thomson, Henry Laurens, John Fell, Samuel Holten, Thomas Rodney. LMCC, vi–vii.

17. [Adams, Notes of Debates in the Continental Congress], page 29 (7 October 1775), in John Adams diary 23, 22 [i.e., 23] September–25 October 1775, *Adams Family Papers: An Electronic Archive* (MHS), http://www.masshist.org /digitaladams/ (transcription from L. H. Butterfield, ed. *Diary and Autobiography of John* Adams, vol. 2 (Cambridge: Harvard University Press, 1961)).

18. Jefferson to Madison, 1 June 1783, PJM, 7:103–105. For notes, see PTJ, 1:299–329. The controversy over the notes lies outside this book, but for summary see Garry Wills, *Inventing America: Jefferson's Declaration of Independence* (1978; New York: Houghton Mifflin, 2002), 307–309.

19. *A prisoner,* Madison to Randolph, 29 October 1782, PJM, 5:225. *want,* Madison to Randolph, 26 November 1782, PJM, 5:329–30. On voting, see Note on Procedure in the Confederation Congress, *A Documentary History of the First Federal Elections,* eds. Merrill Jensen and Gordon DenBoer (Madison: University of Wisconsin Press, 1976), 1:18–19. For notes, see Madison's Original Notes on Debates in the Confederation Congress, 1782–1783, James Madison's and Thomas Jefferson's Notes of Debates, 1776–1788, series 5 (DLC); printed in PJM, vols. 5–8, JCC, vols. 23, 25, and LDC, vols. 19–21. Two other delegates, Arthur Lee and Theodorick Bland, Jr., were absent. LDC, 19:xxv. For example of similarity, compare Madison's letter to Randolph on Tuesday, November 5, with notes for November 4 and 5. PJM, 5:234–237, 242–245.

20. *Some days,* Jefferson to Madison, 26 November 1782, PJM, 5:326. For Jefferson's notes from congressional documents, see PTJ, 6:210–211, 212–213. *the communication,* Randolph to Madison, 29 November 1782, PJM, 5:338. *absence,* Madison to Jefferson, 6 May 1783, PJM, 7:18, 19. *perusal,* Jefferson to Madison, 31 August 1783, PJM, 7:298, 299.

21. For entries, see JCC, 23:857–859 (on Jefferson), 845–846 (Asgill). For struck comment, see PJM, 5:476–477. For entry on revenue plan, see PJM, 6:289–292; for memorandum, see PJM, 6:309–311. For background, see Andrew Burstein and Nancy Isenberg, *Madison and Jefferson* (New York: Random House, 2010), 89–104.

22. *Call any,* JCC, 814–816 (18 December 1782). *keeping,* ibid., 828–829 (23 December 1782). *very indistinct,* JCC, 25:849–850 (January 1783).

23. *The printed journal,* PJM, 5:293–294 n.1 (20 November). *standing,* PJM, 6:186, 187 (4 February 1783). For Madison's focus, see, e.g., PJM, 5:273–275 (14 November, discussion of a committee report on Vermont focused on Madison's motion to call a member to order for maligning Virginia); PJM, 6:116 (23 January 1783) (Madison's committee for a library of Congress); PJM, 5:268–269 (12 November, Madison's objections to phrase, "to take order").

24. *The most,* PJM, 5:442 (24 December); see ibid., 544, nn.16–17. For Rhode Island account, see Samuel Osgood to John Lowell, 6 January 1783, LDC, 19:540.

On impost, see PJM, 6:152–153 nn. 29–33; Burnett, *Continental Congress, 530–533*; Jack N. Rakove, *The Beginnings of National Politics: An Interpretive History of the Continental Congress* (Baltimore: Johns Hopkins Press, 1979), 308–329; Ralph Ketcham, *James Madison: A Biography* (Charlottesville: University of Virginia Press, 1990), 116–120; Keith Dougherty, *Collective Action under the Confederation* (Cambridge: Cambridge University Press, 2001), 60–62.

25. *Constituents,* Madison to Randolph, 28 January 1783, PJM, 6:155, 156. *still more,* PJM, 6:141, 143 (28 January). *would leave,* PJM, 6:158, 161 (29 January). *Va.,* PJM, 6:198 (7 February); JCC, 24:110 (6 February) (Mercer's appearance). Lee disliked Madison, years later calling him "a supporter of public knaves" with the "vanity to suppose himself superior to all other persons, conducting measures without consulting them and intolerant of all advice or contradiction." See Irving Brant, *James Madison: The Nationalist, 1780–1787* (Indianapolis: Bobbs-Merrill Company, 1948), 199 (quoting letter from 1790).

26. *True,* PJM, 6:270 (21 February). *owed,* PJM, 6:141, 147 (28 January). *that the,* Elton, *The Parliament,* 10–11.

27. *For rating,* PJM, 6:407–408 (28 March). *only material,* PJM, 6:487–498. On three-fifths ratio, see Donald L. Robinson, *Slavery in the Structure of American Politics, 1765–1820* (New York: Harcourt Brace Jovanovich, 1971), 155–167. On different earlier ratio, see Burnett, *Continental Congress,* 225–226.

28. *Mutual,* PJM, 6:492. For discussion of Billey, see Madison to Madison, Sr., 8 September 1783, PJM, 7:304–305. On Madison and slavery, see "James Madison's Attitude towards the Negro," *Journal of Negro History* 6 (1921): 74–102; Elizabeth Dowling Taylor, *A Slave in the White House: Paul Jenning and the Madisons* (New York: Palgrave Macmillan, 2012); Lawrence Goldstone, *Dark Bargain: Slavery, Profits, and the Struggle for the Constitution* (New York: Walker & Company, 2005), 189–190; *A Necessary Evil,* 245, 268–275; Lance Banning, *Sacred Fire of Liberty: James Madison and the Founding of the Federal Republic* (Ithaca, NY: Cornell University, 1995), 83.

29. *Been much,* Madison to Jefferson, 20 September 1783, PJM, 7:352–353. For April and May entries, see JCC, 25:960–967. *danger,* PJM, 7:176–177 (21 June). *incommodious,* Madison to Randolph, 13 September 1783, PJM, 7:314, 315. *scarcely,* Madison to Jefferson, 20 September 1783, PJM, 7, 352, 354. On attendance, see PJM, 7:xvii.

30. On Floyd, see Ketcham, *James Madison,* 108–111, Brant, *James Madison, The Nationalist,* 283–287; Lynne Cheney, *James Madison: A Life Reconsidered* (New York: Penguin, 2014), 99–100. For letter, see Madison to Randolph, 13 October 1783, PJM, 7:373–375. *perusal,* Jefferson to Madison, 31 August 1783, PJM, 7:298, 299. *obey,* Madison to Jefferson, 20 September 1783, PJM, 7:352. For summary, see Notes on Congress' Place of Residence, [c. 14 October 1783], PJM, 7:378–382. *better,* Jefferson to Madison, 31 August 1783, PJM, 7:299.

31. For 1787 Notes in the Confederation Congress, see Editorial Note, Notes on Debates, PJM, 9:275–276; Original Notes on Debates in the Congress of Confederation, 1787, Madison Papers, series 5 (DLC) [images 697–724]. *Nothing,* PJM, 9:284 (20 February 1787), 309 (13 March). *little,* William Irvine to James Wilson, 6 March 1787, LMCC, 8:551.

32. For entries, see February 20, February 21, March 13, March 20, March 21, March 28, April 2, April 11, April 12, April 18, April 25 in JCC, 33:719–739. On report and letters, see PJM, 9:291 (21 February); Madison to Pendleton, 24 February 1787, PJM, 9:294–295; Madison to Monroe, 25 February 1787, PJM, 9:298; Madison to Randolph, 25 February 1787, PJM, 9:299. For April notes and letter, see PJM, 9:372 (11 [10] April), Madison to Randolph, 15 April 1787, PJM, 9:378–380.

33. On Gardoqui, see JCC, 8:725 (13 March), 730 (29 March). For speech, see PJM, 9:404–406. On secrecy, see Rhode Island delegate James Mitchell Varnum's comment that "every thing essentially relating" to the "western territory and navigation of the Mississippi" is "upon the Secret Journals." James Mitchell Varnum to the Governor of Rhode Island, 4 April 1787, LMCC, 8:571.

34. PJM, 9:331 (23 March); JCC, 32:129.

35. For speech, see PJM, 9:326–327 (21 March 1787). For April entries, see JCC, 33:734–738 (18 April–25 April). For description of enlistment, see PJM, 9:275–279 (19 February 1787). On Madison's role, see JCC, 32:62–64.

36. *The opinion,* PJM, 9:372 (11 [10] April 1787); see 9:375 (12 April 1787). For Madison's views, see Madison to Randolph, 15 April 1787, PJM, 9:378, 379–380. For King's efforts, see King to Gerry, 11 April 1787, LMCC, 8:573–574. On Madison's motion, see Motion on Congressional Rule of Order, [10 April 1787], PJM, 9:371–372 n.1.

37. *Nothing,* Notes on Debates, 26 April 1787, PJM, 9:407; Original Notes on Debates, 1787, PJM [image 724].

2. The Practice of Working Notes

1. DHRC, 1:187 (21 February 1787).

2. For discussion, see Mary Sarah Bilder, "James Madison, Law Student and Demi-Lawyer," *Law & History Review* 28 (2010): 389–449.

3. *Many,* Madison to Madison, Sr., 3 December 1784, PJM, 8:172. *other,* Madison to Jefferson, 22 January 1786, PJM, 8:472, 473–474, 477.

4. For letters from Jefferson, see, e.g., Jefferson to Madison, 25 April 1784, PJM, 8:23–26; Jefferson to Madison, 7 May 1784, PJM, 8:28; Jefferson to Madison, 8 May 1784, PJM, 8:29–32. For Monroe, see Monroe to Madison, 7 November 1784, PJM, 8:125–126; Monroe to Madison, 15 November 1784, PJM, 8:140–142. For Grayson, see Grayson to Madison, 1 May 1785, PJM,

8:274–276; Grayson to Madison, 27 June 1785, PJM, 8:309–311. *way of,* Lee to Madison, 16 February [1786], PJM, 8:493.

5. On "constitution," see Mary Sarah Bilder, "Colonial Constitutionalism and Constitutional Law," in *Transformations in American Legal History: Essays in Honor of Morton J. Horwitz,* eds. Alfred Brophy and Daniel W. Hamilton (Cambridge: Harvard University Press, 2009), 28–57. *any person,* Articles, IV, DHRC, 1:87. *difficult point,* Madison to Randolph, 10 March 1784, PJM, 8:3–4; see Randolph to Madison, 27 January 1784, PJM, 7:415–418 n.2.

6. *The debates,* Jefferson to Madison, 1 June 1783, PJM, 7:103. *notes,* Jefferson to Madison, 7 May 1783, PJM, 7:23, 24, 27 n.14. Madison later claimed that he had planned to write an account of the Revolution and early Confederation. PJM, 7:344 n.30.

7. *A few,* Madison to Jefferson, 3 October 1785, PJM, 8:373, 374–375. *We are either,* Washington to Madison, 30 November 1785, PJM, 8:428, 429. On Madison, see Jack N. Rakove, *The Beginnings of National Politics: An Interpretive History of the Continental Congress* (Baltimore: Johns Hopkins Press, 1979), 361–372. On the Mount Vernon conference, see Stuart Leibiger, *Founding Friendship: George Washington, James Madison, and the Creation of the American Republic* (Charlottesville: University of Virginia Press, 1999), 49–50.

8. Notes on Ancient and Modern Confederacies, PJM, 9:3–24, JMP, General Correspondence (DLC). The James Madison Papers editors date the notes April–June? 1786. For Montesquieu, see *The Spirit of the Laws,* trans. Anne M. Cohler, Carolyn M. Basia, and Harold S. Stone (Cambridge: Cambridge University Press, 1989), Book 9, 131–137. On contest, see *The Monthly Review* 71 (December 1784), Article 12, 531–539; J. De Meerman, *Discours . . .* (Hague, 1784) (winning essay). Jefferson sent *Felice's Code de l'humanite* and the *Encyclopedie methodique.* See Madison to Jefferson, 16 March 1784, PJM, 8:6, 11 (requesting books on confederacies); Jefferson to Madison, 25 May 1784, PJM, 8:42; Madison to Jefferson, 18 March 1785, PJM, 8:247, 249; Madison to Jefferson, 18 March 1786, PJM, 8:500, 501–503. For comparison, see *Spirit of Laws,* 133 (end of sentences omitted silently); PJM, 9:4.

9. "An Abstract of the General Principles of Ancient and Modern Confederacies," *The Writings of George Washington,* ed. Jared Sparks (Boston: Russell, Odiorne . . . , 1835), 9:521–528; George Washington Papers (DLC), Series 8d (titled by DLC, "Notes on James Madison Jr. Forms of Government") (beginning at image 344); Leibiger, *Founding Friendship,* 73. Washington's copy lacks the final heading for the "Gryson Confederacy." George Washington Papers, image 366. *Jealousy,* PJM, 9:22. *Continental,* Madison to Monroe, 14 March 1786, PJM, 8:497–498; Madison to Monroe, 19 March 1786, PJM, 8:504, 505.

10. *Originated,* Stephen Higginson to John Adams, quoted in Irving Brant, *James Madison: The Nationalist, 1780–1787* (Indianapolis: Bobbs-Merrill Com-

pany, 1948), 384. *brainchild,* PJM, 9:115–119 (discussing responsibility). *reme-dial,* Madison to Monroe, 14 March 1786, PJM, 8:497–498.

11. See Madison to John Francis Mercer, 16 July 1783, PJM, 7:228 (containing closing: "Done in bed in my Chamber in the Hotel at the Corner of Market & 5 Streets in the City of Philada. at ½ after 6 oClock, on the 16 of July annoque Dom: 1783"); Madison to Jones, 19 September 1780, PJM, 2:91, 92 n.8; PJM, 7:xvii. On Trist, see Introduction, "The Travel Diary of Elizabeth House Trist: Philadelphia to Natchez, 1783–1784," ed. Annette Kolodny, in *Journeys in New Worlds: Early American Women's Narratives,* eds. William L. Andrews, et al. (Madison: University of Wisconsin Press, 1991), 183–199; for correspondence, see letters regarding Trist in PJM, vols. 8 and 9.

12. For letters, see Madison to Ambrose Madison, 8 September 1786, James Madison Papers (NYPL); Madison to James Monroe, 11 September 1786, JMP, Series 1, General Correspondence (DLC). I am grateful to Thomas Lannon (NYPL) for generous assistance with digital watermark images. It appears to match the Whatman paper of the early Notes. A watermark catalogue of Madison's correspondence would be required to know for certain whether Madison used this Whatman paper prior to the fall of 1786 and during the time between Annapolis and the Philadelphia Convention. For purchases, see Madison to Ambrose Madison, 8 September 1786, PJM, 9:120, 121. Newspaper advertisements can be electronically searched for 1785 and 1786 in Philadelphia and Baltimore showing the sale of fine writing paper and post-sized paper.

13. On the Annapolis Convention, see DHRC, 1:176–185; Rakove, *The Beginnings,* 369–375; Lance Banning, *Sacred Fire of Liberty: James Madison and the Founding of the Federal Republic* (Ithaca, NY: Cornell University, 1995), 73–75; Keith Dougherty, *Collective Action under the Confederation* (Cambridge: Cambridge University Press, 2001), 141–143; Louis Ottenberg, "A Fortunate Fiasco: The Annapolis Convention of 1786," *American Bar Association Journal* 45 (1959): 834–837, 877–882.

14. *Subservient,* Madison to Jefferson, 12 August 1786; PJM, 9:93, 96. *necessarily,* Rufus King to Jonathan Jackson, 3 September 1786, LMCC, 8:458, 460. *prolonged,* Madison to Ambrose Madison, 8 September 1786, PJM, 9:120.

15. For documents and overview, see DHRC, 1:176–185. *a uniform system,* DHRC, 183. *the sudden,* Madison to Monroe, 11 September 1786, PJM, 9:121. On the Annapolis Convention records, see Mary Sarah Bilder, "How Bad Were the Official Records of the Federal Convention?" *George Washington Law Review* 80, no. 6 (2012): 1627–1628; Howard H. Wehmann, "The 'Lost' Records of the Annapolis Convention, 1786–1986," *Manuscripts,* 38:101–104 (1986).

16. *The expediency of extending,* Madison to Monroe, 11 September 1786, PJM, 9:121–122. *important,* DHRC, 1:184.

17. For attendance, see DHRC, 1:185, 230. New Jersey's William Houston also attended both conventions. *which declares,* Act electing and empowering

delegates, 3 February 1786, DHRC, 1:203; see David Brian Robertson, *The Constitution and America's Destiny* (Cambridge: Cambridge University Press, 2005), 122.

18. *Long time,* Henry Lee Jr. to Madison, 19 October 1786, PJM, 9:143, 144. For discussion, see Gaillard Hunt, *The Life of James Madison* (New York: Doubleday, 1902), 137; Brant, *Nationalist,* 341. *best,* Monroe to Madison, 25 September 1786, PJM, 9:134. On trip, see Monroe to Madison, 7 October 1786, PJM, 9:142–143.

19. *Dissolution,* see PJM, 9:152 (ante 31 October 1786); Notes for Debate on Trade and Paper Money, PJM, Series 1, General Correspondence [DLC]. For bill, see Bill Providing for Delegates to the Convention of 1787, PJM, 9:163–164. *purpose,* An Act for appointing deputies . . . , 23 November 1786, DHRC, 1:196–198. For appointment, see ibid., 1:198.

20. On journey, see Madison to Trist, 10 February 1787, PJM, 9:259. On delegation, PJM, 9:266, 269–672. On illness, see Grayson to Madison, 22 November 1786, 9:173–175. On Carrington and Lee, LDC, 24:xxvii. *revive,* Madison to Pendleton, 9 January 1787, PJM, 9:243, 245. *just,* Jefferson to Madison, 30 January 1787, PJM, 9:247, 249–251.

21. For delegations, see DHRC, 1:230; LDC, xviii–xxvii, 672. *the season,* William Pierce to St. George Tucker, 14 April 1787, LDC, 24:221. *great,* William Grayson to William Short, 16 April 1787, ibid., 24:226.

22. *State boat,* Randolph to Madison, 7 March 1787, PJM, 9:303–304. On resignation and replacement, see DHRC, 1:198 n.3. On Washington, see Madison to Jefferson, 19 March 1787, PJM, 9:317–318; Washington to Randolph, 9 April 1787, PGW (CS), 5:135–136. *take,* Madison to Jefferson, 23 April 1787, PJM, 9:398, 401.

23. *Partial,* Madison to Randolph, 11 March 1787, PJM, 9:307; *propensity,* Madison to Pendleton, 24 February 1787, PJM, 9:294, 295. *an end,* John Dawson to Madison, 15 April 1787, PJM, 9:381. *shall we,* William Pierce to George Turner, 19 May 1787; LDC, 24:282. *I hope,* Madison to Pendleton, 24 February 1787, PJM, 9:295. *partition,* Madison to Randolph, 8 April 1787, PJM, 9:371.

24. *Some general,* Randolph to Madison, 27 March 1787, PJM, 9:335. *adopt,* Washington to Madison, 31 March 1787, PJM, 9:342, 344. *thorough,* Madison to Washington, 21 February 1787, PJM, 9:285, 286. *leading ideas,* Madison to Jefferson, 19 March, 1787, 9:317, 318–319.

25. *Some outlines,* Madison to Washington, 16 April 1787, PJM, 9:382, 383. *individual,* Madison to Randolph, 8 April 1787, PJM, 9:368, 369–370; Madison to Washington, 16 April 1787, PJM, 9:383–385 (quotes come from both the letters to Randolph and Washington). Madison to Randolph, 8 April 1787, PJM, 9:367. The Randolph letter is reproduced from a contemporaneous file copy made by Madison—a somewhat unusual practice for him. PJM, 9:371. Wash-

ington abstracted Madison's plan. Notes on the Sentiments of John Jay, Henry Know, and James Madison, [c. April 1787], PGW (CS), 5:163, 164–166.

26. *The aggressions,* Madison to Washington, 16 April 1787, PJM, 9:384. *Figure,* William Grayson to William Short, 16 April 1787, LDC, 24:226, 227.

27. *An address,* Randolph to Madison, 27 March 1787, PJM, 9:335. James Madison, Vices of the Political System of the U. States, JMP, Series 1, General Correspondence; PJM, 9:345–358 (dating mss. to April–June). Madison later noted that Daniel Carroll made a copy for Charles Carrollton. That copy has never been located. Carroll did not attend the Convention until July 9. The manuscript has visible revisions not reflected in PJM, 9:345–358.

28. Vices, PJM, 9:354–357 ("To what causes is this evil to be ascribed? These causes lie. . . ."). For summary of conventional relationship between manuscript and Federalist 10, see, e.g., Lynne Cheney, *James Madison: A Life Reconsidered* (New York: Penguin, 2014), 123–124; Ralph Ketcham, *James Madison: A Biography* (Charlottesville: University of Virginia Press, 1990), 186–187; Adam Tate, "James Madison, 1780–1787: Nationalism and Political Reform," in *A Companion to James Madison and James Monroe,* ed. Stuart Leibiger (Malden, Mass.: Wiley-Blackwell, 2013), 39, 53–55; Ralph L. Ketcham, "Notes on James Madison's Sources for the Tenth Federalist Paper," *Midwest Journal of Political Science* 1 (1957): 20–25; Mark G. Spencer "Hume and Madison on Faction," *William and Mary Quarterly,* 3d series, 59 (2002), 869–896; William Lee Miller, *The Business of May Next: James Madison and the Founding* (Charlottesville: University Press of Virginia, 1992), 22–33. On the Vices, see Jack Rakove, "James Madison and the Constitution," *History Now,* September 2007 (Gilder Lehrman Institute for American History), at www.gilderlehrman.org/historynow /09_2007/historian2.php; Jack N. Rakove, "James Madison and the Extended Republic: Theory and Practice in American Politics," This Constitution: A Bicentennial Chronicle, APSA and AHA (Fall 1985); Randall Strahan, "Personal Motives, Constitutional Forms, and the Public Good: Madison on Political Leadership," in *James Madison: The Theory and Practice of Republican Government,* ed. Saul Kernell (Stanford: Stanford University Press, 2003), 63, 67–72.

29. For cautionary note by editors, see PJM, 9:358 n.10; see also Jack N. Rakove, *Original Meanings: Politics and Ideas in the Making of the Constitution* (New York: Vintage, 1997), 220–221 and 401 n.39. For discussion of the eleventh vice, see Banning, *Sacred Fire of Liberty,* 115, 207–208; Rakove, *Original Meanings,* 48–56. For discussion of manuscript, see the Evidence, the Manuscripts: Vices of the Political System of the United States.

30. *Internal,* Madison to Washington, 16 April 1787, PJM, 384. On impotence, see Eric Slauter, *The State as a Work of Art: The Cultural Origins of the Constitution* (Chicago: University of Chicago Press, 2009), 73–74.

31. *Existing,* Madison to Madison Sr., 1 April 1787, PJM, 9:358, 359.

3. The Success of the Opening Days

1. *An alarm,* Edward Carrington to Jefferson, 24 April 1787, LDC, 24:253, 254. *effect,* Grayson to Monroe, 30 April 1787, LDC, 24:262.

2. For a particularly well done account of the gathering at the outset of the Convention, see Richard Beeman, *Plain, Honest Men: The Making of the American Constitution* (New York: Random House, 2009), 22–85.

3. For numbers, see Washington's diary [May 14–May 19], RFC, 3:20–21; William Shippen to Thomas Shippen, 14 May 1787, SRFC, 1–21. *sour,* George Washington to Arthur Lee, 20 May 1787, RFC, 3:22. For list, see *Pennsylvania Journal and Weekly Advertiser,* 19 May 1787, RFC, 3:21. On guests, see Eliza House Trist to Jefferson, 6 June 1787, PTJ, 11:403–405.

4. George Mason to George Mason Jr., 20 May 1787, RFC, 3:22–24; George Mason to Arthur Lee, 21 May 1787, ibid., 3:24.

5. Madison to Randolph, 8 April 1787, PJM, 9:368, 371.

6. For Virginia population, see Population and Constitution-Making, 1774–1792, DHRC, 1:297–301. The 1790 census enumerated the nonslave population at 454,983 and the slave population at 292,627. Another 61,247 nonslave and 12,430 enslaved persons lived in Kentucky. The enslaved Virginia population represented nearly half of the entire enslaved population in the 1790 census. The Convention is thought to have used a number of 420,000 for the total Virginia population with 280,000 non-white persons. Ibid., 300. *ultimately,* Madison to Randolph, 8 April 1787, PJM 9:368, 371.

7. *Lesser States,* Madison to Washington, 16 April 1787, PJM, 9:382, 383. *copied draft,* Read to Dickinson, 21 May 1787, RFC, 3:24–26. *proposed,* Jacob Broom to Thomas Collins, 23 May 1787, SRFC, 16–17. On Pinckney plan, see Beeman, *Plain, Honest Men,* 93–98.

8. *Mortified,* Rufus King to Jeremiah Wadsworth, 24 May 1787, RFC, 3:26.

9. Notes, b.1-1; DHC, 3:7–8.

10. For charge, see Confederation Congress calls the Constitutional Convention, 21 February 1787, DHRC, 1:185, 187.

11. Madison to Pendleton, 27 May 1787, PJM, 10:11. For other letters, see Madison to Madison, Sr., 27 May 1787; Madison to Jones, 27 May 1787, PJM, 10:10–12. For "free," see Madison to Pendleton, 27 May 1787, JMP, series 1. On franking, see Resolution of Congress, 23 April 1787, RFC, 3:17.

12. My appreciation to the conservation staff for noticing the scored margin.

13. Notes, b.1-1; DHC, 3:8–9. The entry was heavily revised. The quoted passage is my interpretation of Madison's original record. "of of" is the DHC editors reading of the original. The Delaware credentials were added later. On the secretary, see Mary Sarah Bilder, "How Bad Were the Official Records of the Federal Convention?" *George Washington Law Review* 80, no.6 (2012): 1621–1631.

14. On Pinckney, see Marty Matthews, *Forgotten Founder: The Life and Times of Charles Pinckney* (Columbia: University of South Carolina Press, 2004), 40. On Jefferson's similar spelling of Franklin as "Franklyn," see Bill Bryson, *Made in America: An Informal History of the English Language in the United States* (New York: W. Morrow, 1994), 44. A curiosity about the Notes is that speeches by General Pinckney often, although not entirely, appear on replaced sheets (e.g., June 6, June 21, June 26, August 22).

15. Madison to Madison, Sr., 27 May 1787, PJM, 10:10.

16. *To gain,* John Dawson to Madison, 15 April 1787, PJM, 9:381. *Convention,* Edward Carrington to Jefferson, 24 April 1787, LDC, 24:253, 255.

17. *Any entry, nothing,* Journal (Convention), 29 May 1787, DHC, 1:54. *licentious,* ibid., 28 May 1787, ibid., 53. For initial rules, see ibid., 28 May 1787, ibid., 1:50–53. Madison's description of the reason for the rules was added to the original entry likely after the fall of 1789 and used the language of the official journal, Notes, DHC, 3:13. The description does not appear in the Jefferson Copy; however, Eppes may have overlooked the material as it was covered by a large note. EJC, 28 May 1787 (section copied by nineteenth-century transcribers). On rules, see Bilder, "How Bad Were the Official Records of the Federal Convention?," 1641–1643.

18. *Confidential,* Hawkins to Jefferson, 9 June 1787, PTJ, 11:414. *at Liberty,* R. D. Spaight to Governor Caswell, 12 June 1787, RFC, 3:46. *I have,* Washington to George A. Washington, 10 June 1787, PGW, 5:224, 226. *rules,* Madison to Jefferson, 6 June 1787, PJM, 10:28–29.

19. *All,* George Mason to George Mason, Jr., 1 June 1787, RFC, 3:32–33. *propriety,* Nathan Dane to Rufus King, 19 June 1787, ibid., 3:48. *to forget,* Manasseh Cutler, Journal, 13 July 1787, ibid., 3:58, 59. On Beckley, see James Monroe to Jefferson, 27 July 1787, ibid., 3:65 (discussing the negative).

20. *Profound,* Edward Carrington to Jefferson, 9 June 1787, PTJ, 11:407, 409–411. Carrington's letter may reflect information from Madison prior to June 10. Madison's 10 June letter to Carrington, as well as any prior letters, are not extant. Edward Carrington to Madison, 13 June 1787, PJM, 10:52, 53 n.1. Carrington's letters seem to have a Madisonian sensibility. For the Otto letter, see Louis-Guillaume Otto to Comte de Montmorin, 10 June 1787, RFC, 3:39–45; in *Documents of the Emerging Nation: U.S. Foreign Relations, 1775–1789,* eds. Mary A. Giunta and J. Dane Hartgrove (Wilmington, DE: Scholarly Resources, 1998), 254–259 (English translation). For letters, see Madison to Jones, 27 May 1787, PJM, 10:12, and 26 June 1787, PJM, 10:79; Madison to McClurg, ca. 25 August 1787, PJM, 10:157 and ca. 1 September 1787, PJM, 10:161. In addition, Madison wrote to Carrington on June 10.

21. *At liberty,* Nathaniel Gorham to Nathan Dane, 3 June 1787, SRFC, 46–47. *independent,* Washington to David Stuart, 1 July 1787, RFC, 3:51.

22. *Secrecy,* Nicholas Gilman to Joseph Gilman, 31 July 1787, RFC, 3:66. For Gorham letter, see Nathaniel Gorham to Caleb Strong, 29 August 1787, ibid., 3:75 (referring to the seventeenth article by the typo in the draft). For Madison letter, see Madison to Jefferson, 6 September 1787, PJM, 10:163–165 (partially in code).

23. *Long,* Washington to Lafayette, 6 June 1787, RFC, 3:34. *As the,* Washington to George A. Washington, 3 June 1787, PGW, 5:217, 219 (p.s.). *for the,* William Samuel Johnson to son, 27 June 1787, RFC, 3:49. *during, whole,* George Mason to Beverley Randolph, 30 June 1787, RFC, 3:50.

24. Madison to Jefferson, 6 June 1787, PJM, 10:28. On newspaper coverage, see *Commentaries on the Constitution: Public and Private,* vol. 1 (1981), DHRC, 13:120–123; John K. Alexander, *The Selling of the Constitutional Convention: A History of News Coverage* (Madison, WI: Madison House, 1990), 62–63; John P. Kaminski, *Secrecy and the Constitutional Convention* (Madison: University of Wisconsin-Madison, 2005).

25. Notes, b.1-3 (May 29); DHC, 3:13. On journal and possible publication, see Bilder, "How Bad," 1639–40, 1644–1645.

26. Notes, b.1-2 (May 28); DHC, 3:10.

27. Notes, b.1-1 (May 25), b.1-2 (May 28), b.1-3 (May 29).

28. Notes, b.1-3; DHC, 3:13–14. For McHenry, see RFC, 1:24–26. For Paterson, see ibid., 1:27–28. For Bedford, see SRFC, 4:27.

29. Notes, b.1-3; DHC, 3:14. For blank page, see b.1-4. Madison added and then later struck: "See the propositions at a subsequent page of this debate." For Resolutions, see b.2-1-4; DHC, 3:16–20. Madison was copying. On the eighth resolution, Madison began to write "Judiciary" but only got as far as "Ju" before he realized that the words were "National Judiciary." Similarly, with the twelfth resolution, he mistakenly began to copy the thirteenth, and had to line out those words and finish with the correct words of the thirteenth resolution. Because the resolutions were not a final report, the secretary did not retain the original proposed copy. Multiple copies of Randolph's resolutions are extant. Two Virginia copies exist, those of Madison and Washington. In addition, James McHenry, David Brearley, William Paterson, and John Dickinson left copies. See RFC, 1:27 n.20; Appendix C, RFC, 3:593–594; SRFC, 28. Jameson and Farrand discuss divergences between Madison's copy and others involving the sixth resolution on the negative and the ninth resolution on supreme and inferior tribunals. John Franklin Jameson suspected that Madison's copy reflected the plan as it had been revised slightly in the first two weeks of the Convention. John Franklin Jameson, *Studies in the History of the Federal Convention of 1787* (Washington, DC: Government Printing Office, 1903; reprinted from Annual Report of the American Historical Association for 1902, 1:87–167), 103–111. Max Farrand concluded that Madison's plan was the plan as originally introduced. Appendix C, RFC, 3:593–594.

30. *The national,* Journal (CWH) (May 31), DHC, 1:202. *Legislative,* Notes (May 31), DHC, 3:32. *the other,* Notes (May 31); DHC, 3:33. For vote, see Journal (CWH), DHC, 1:203.

31. For official mention of plan, see Journal (Convention) (May 29), DHC, 1:55. *confessed,* Lansing, Notes (May 29), SRFC, 4:26. For plan, see Charles Pinckney's Plan (by James Wilson), DHRC, 1:245–247. For summary of plan and debate, see Richard Beeman, *Plain, Honest Men: The Making of the American Constitution* (New York: Random House, 2009), 93–98. Beeman suggests that Pinckney may not have given the speech that he later published as given on May 29. Beeman rejects the idea that Pinckney borrowed from Madison.

32. See Charles Pinckney's Plan (by James Wilson), DHRC, 1:245–247; Virginia Resolutions, ibid., 243–45. I have not independently investigated the Wilson notes. Because the plan was reported to the Committee of Detail, which Wilson was on, it would be useful to know whether the notes can be definitively dated to May 1787 or to the more general period of the Convention. For discussion of plan, see sources listed in note to DHRC, 1:245–246.

33. Notes, b.3-1 to b.3-4.

34. *Verbal,* DHC, 3:21 (May 30); *by several,* ibid., 3:25. For paragraph, Notes, b.3-4; DHC, ibid., 3:24–26;. Madison later added two paragraph symbols.

35. DHC 3:23 (May 30). For speeches, see ibid., 3:21–22. For an outstanding account of the underlying political strategies of the Convention, see David Brian Robertson, *The Constitution and America's Destiny* (Cambridge: Cambridge University Press, 2005).

36. For pattern, see letters in the Evidence, Catalogue; J. Franklin Jameson, "Review of *Writings of James Madison* by Gaillard Hunt," *American Historical Review* 7 (1902), 573–575, 575 (commenting that of 137 letters from Madison while in Philadelphia attending Congress, only 26 were not written on Tuesday). For example, on Monday, June 11, Madison wrote: "The Alterations made in clause, (compare its original State with the Report of Comt^e of whole)." The Report was submitted on Wednesday, June 13. DHC, 3:108. The pattern was not absolute. For discussion of example of Notes written after Thursday, June 29, see Chapter 5, note 25.

37. Note on 9 July 1787 committee report, GR no. 142, 148a (LC 2003 image, GR-142-0565) (also containing list of states and numbers). For other similar numbers, see RFC, 1:572–574; SRFC, 160–161. The Notes follow this language. DHC, 3:295. For report, see Journal (Convention), DHC, 1:83–84. For partial copy of 24 October 1787 letter, see JMP (DLC), series 1; for letter, see PJM, 10:205–220.

38. As an example, compare Rufus King's version and Madison's version of speeches by George Mason and John Dickinson on the council of revision on June 6. DHC, 3:79, b.13-1 (not a replaced sheet); RFC, 1:144–145.

39. *We cannot,* RFC, 1:90 (2 June). *A limited,* DHC, 3:50 (2 June). *A vig[orou]s,* RFC, 1:90 (2 June). *such an,* DHC, 3:49 (2 June).

40. *Repub[lic]s*, RFC, 1:90 (2 June). *If antient,* DHC 3:50. For example of concepts, compare King's version of Mason's speech favoring a restraining power without distinction between an executive veto or council of revision, and Madison's version suggesting that Mason favored a council of revision (Madison's preference). RFC, 1:144; DHC, 3:79 (6 June). For example of vocabulary, compare King's version of Dickinson's description that the council "mingles separate Orders" to Madison's version that it "involved an improper mixture of powers." Ibid.

41. *Wandering,* RFC, 1:60 (31 May). *necessary, premature,* ibid., 1:58. *constantly,* DHC, 3:26. *dupes,* ibid., 3:27–28. *grand,* DHC, 3:27. *confidence, necessary,* ibid., 3:28.

42. For seventh resolution, see DHRC, 1:243, 244 ("Resd. that a National Executive be instituted . . . ; it ought to enjoy the Executive rights vested in Congress by the Confederation"). For Notes quotations on June 1, see DHC, 3:35–37 (June 1). For Notes quotations on June 2, see ibid., 3:51–52. Madison later revised Randolph's speeches on both days to refer to the three being drawn from different regions. Ibid., 3:37; 52.

43. DHC, 3:66–67 (5 June). For original location of "hint" at conclusion of Wilson speech and later instruction to move sentence to "bottom margin," see b.10-4.

44. *Discourse,* DHC, 3:49. For visual appearance, see Notes, b.8-1–b.8-2.

45. DHC, 3:50–51.

46. For copied speech, see DHC, 3:43–48. The speech was copied on b.7-1–b.7-4. *The motion,* DHC, 3:48. *Doctr Franklyn,* ibid., 3:43. On spelling, see Bryson, *Made in America,* 44. Madison, Notes (2 June), DHC, 3:48. Franklin was the president of the Pennsylvania Society for the Abolition of Slavery. The Society had written an address that it hoped Franklin would present to the Convention. SRFC, 44–45. Franklin never presented it. For second reference to Franklyn, see DHC, 3:113 (12 June). Franklin successfully deleted "liberal" after Madison had successfully had "fixt" added to the provision on compensation for members.

47. *I was, it appeared,* RFC, 1:59 (31 May). *What his,* DHC, 3:33 (31 May).

48. *At present,* RFC, 1:60 (31 May). *some,* DHC, 3:33 (31 May). *Mr. Madison,* RFC, 1:128 (5 June). *hinted, rather,* DHC, 3:63–64 (5 June).

49. *The best,* RFC, 1:70 (1 June). *an Executive,* RFC, 1:74 (1 June). For absence of Madison comment, see DHC, 3:36–37 (Madison's comment missing between Wilson and Gerry). For vote on June 4, see Journal (CWH), DHC, 1:208 (7–3). For state tally, see DHC, 1:227. For Madison's description of vote, see DHC, 3:54 ("Wythe ay but gone home").

50. For second resolution, see DHRC, 1:243. *in Proportion,* SRFC, 31 (30 May).

51. Journal (CWH), DHC, 1:199, 200–201 (30 May). Madison seconded Randolph's resolution.

52. DHC, 3:23, 24, 26; Notes, b.3-3–b.3-4.

53. Notes, b.3-4; DHC, 3:24–26. The type is rendered as in the Notes, b.3-3. For final page, see DHC, 3:25–26; b.3-4.

4. Struggling with Speeches

1. *Very,* RFC, 1:110 (4 June). For similar description by King, see RFC, 1:108 (4 June). For Madison's Notes, see DHC, 3:52–62. The only speech by Madison in the original Notes for June 4 discussed problems with an executive negative. Ibid., 57. The section beginning "It was moved by M^r. Wilson . . ." was likely added later. The original entry likely ended after "that a national judiciary be established." Ibid., 61 (compare to Journal (CWH), DHC, 1:209).

2. On council of revision, see Resolution 8, DHRC, 1:244 (composed of "the Executive and a convenient number of the National Judiciary"). For procedural history on June 4, see Journal (CWH), DHC, 1:209–210.

3. For Pierce, see RFC, 1:110. For King, see RFC, 1:108. The notes of Pierce and King undoubtedly suffer from similar problems to Madison's Notes. See RFC, 1: xix–xxi. They are offered as an alternative description of events, not as verifiable fact.

4. *Safety, check,* RFC, 1:108 (King). *Judges, strictly,* RFC, 1:110 (Pierce).

5. *Objection,* Journal (CWH), DHC, 1:209–210 (4 June); RFC, 1:95 (Journal). For rule, see Journal (Convention) DHC, 1:54 (29 May). The secretary recorded initially that Thursday, June 7, was assigned for reconsideration but struck Thursday and wrote "Wednesday." Journal (CWH), DHC, 1:210. For June 6 vote, see Journal (CWH), DHC, 1:214 (6 June). For tally, see DHC, 1:227 (3–8).

6. *Constitutionality,* DHC, 3:54–55 (Gerry) (4 June).

7. For existing speech, see DHC, 3:72–74, RFC, 1:134–136 (6 June). For replaced sheets, see b.11–b.12. For discussion of speech's importance, see James H. Hutson, "The Creation of the Constitution: The Integrity of the Documentary Record," *Texas Law Review* 65 (1986): 1, 35 ("some political scientists" regard the speech as "among the most important delivered"); Ralph Ketcham, *James Madison: A Biography* (Charlottesville: University of Virginia Press, 1990), 200 (declaring it "his most important speech of the Convention"). The speech is reprinted as "Speech in the Federal Convention on Factions," *James Madison, Writings,* ed. Jack N. Rakove (New York: Library of America, 1999), 92–93; "Election of Representatives," *Selected Writings of James Madison,* ed. Ralph Ketcham (Indianapolis: Hackett Publishing, 2006), 49–50. Hutson points out the speech "as delivered must have been far briefer" than the one in the Notes. Hutson, "Creation," 35. For suggestions that this speech includes remarks from June 4, see RFC, 1:110 n.25 (disputing Jameson's belief that the speech was given on June 6 and stating that it "is possible" that Madison "inserted in his record of his

remarks on June 6 a portion of his speech on June 4); PJM, 10:25–26 n.1 (mis-interpreting Farrand to claim that Pierce recorded a second Madison speech on June 4). John Franklin Jameson suggested that Pierce may have "fused two speeches" made on June 6; however, he began with a caveat: "If Madison's re-port is right." At the time, Jameson did not know that King's notes assigned the speech to June 4. John Franklin Jameson, "Notes of Major William Pierce on the Federal Convention of 1787," *American Historical Review* 3 (1898): 310, 323. Farrand concluded that Madison's notes for the end of June 4 "were quite defective," and he may have "inserted in his record of his remarks of June 6 a portion of his speech on June 4." RFC, 1:110 n.25. I believe Farrand reached the more plausible conclusion. Pierce's notes were printed in 1828; King was pre-paring to print his notes sometime after 1818. Both men may have made errors in assigning speeches to various dates. Moreover, both men might have written their notes up several days later like Madison and in so doing confused various speeches, and later revisions may have been made. Nonetheless, the correspon-dence between the two favors their dating over that of Madison. For compo-sition, see Chapter 10 and the Evidence, the Manuscripts, Three Replaced Sheets.

8. The two motions considered on June 6 were (1) to elect the first house by the state legislatures instead of "the people"; (2) to add "a convenient number" of the judiciary to the executive negative. Madison seconded the motion to add the judiciary. Journal (CWH), DHC, 1:213–214. For various accounts, see RFC, 1:141 (Yates: Madison arguing for extensive basis to national government); 143–144 (King: Madison arguing for elections in enlarged sphere); 144 (King: Madi-son advocating for check of executive and judiciary); 147 (Pierce: Madison dis-cussing apparently the first branch); Lansing (Madison speaking against election by state legislatures). King's notes are marked June 5; however, they contain the speakers and motions of June 6. Only one extant note offers any evidence sup-porting Madison's link between elections, interests, and the extensive territory on or around June 6: Hamilton's undated note marked "Principles." RFC, 1:146–147 (describing Madison's ideas as "extent to render combinations on the ground of interest difficult" and elections to refine representation). Hamilton's note hints that Madison developed the idea of extensive territory making difficult interest combination. Unfortunately, whether Hamilton's note reflects the June 6 pro-ceeding is not clear. The note has no date. On uncertainty in dating, see ibid., 146 n.13; PAH, 4:161 n.1; Worthington C. Ford in "Alexander Hamilton's Notes in the Federal Convention of 1787," *American Historical Review* 10 (October 1904): 97. There are two numbers likely added at an unknown time on the docu-ment. One (106) places it before 107, apparently notes for 8 June, 1787. The other (75) places it before 76, apparently notes for 16 June, 1787. Constitutional Convention: Notes Taken in the Federal Convention [1787, June 1–26], Speeches & Writings, Hamilton Papers (DLC) (microfilm). Prior to Ford's investigation, it

was not apparent that the notes even related to the Convention; indeed, whether the note was always part of the set of Convention notes is also unknown. Ford, "Alexander Hamilton's Notes," 97. Hamilton intermingled comments made by others with his own thoughts. As the editors of the *Hamilton Papers* remark, it is not "always possible to determine whether an opinion recorded in his notes was made by one of the delegates or represented his own thoughts, for he sometimes inserted his own ideas into the record he made of remarks by others." Notes Taken in the Federal Convention, PAH, 4:161, n.1. Hamilton may have understood Madison better than other note takers—or the note could reflect a discussion outside of the Convention. For discussion of an additional alternative possibility that the note relates to the two men's discussions in writing Federalist essays 9–10, see Chapter 8, note 13. Quotes from King notes.

9. The original speech on the first branch may have resembled the current version. Pierce's description and the original introduction to the eleventh vice resemble the comment on the objects of a national government: "the necessity of providing more effectually for the security of private rights, and the steady dispensation of Justice." Other elements are likely later additions, including the comment on slavery. The sixth vice had included "3. Where slavery exists the republican Theory becomes still more fallacious." But for whom the existence of slavery makes representative government fallacious was not apparent. The original speech on the Council may have been even stronger. The "two objections" to the Council are worded similarly to his June 4 record of Gerry's and King's criticisms. See DHC, 3:77–78 (6 June); DHC, 3:54–55.

10. On July 21, Madison and Wilson again sought to amend the executive negative by adding the judiciary. Journal (Convention), DHC, 1:105; DHC, 3:390. Madison recorded two speeches that he gave in defense. DHC, 3:391–392, 395–396. *no hope,* Madison to William Short, 6 June 1787, PJM, 10:31. *result,* Madison to Jefferson, 6 June 1787, PJM, 10:28, 29.

11. For replaced sheet, see Notes, b.14. For Thursday vote, see Journal (CWH), DHC, 1:215 (7 June). For Friday vote, see ibid., 1:216 (8 June) (altering "to negative all laws passed by the several States contravening in the opinion of the national legislature, the articles of union; or any treaties subsisting under the authority or the union" to "all laws which to them shall appear improper").

12. For Dickinson's speech, see DHC, 3:80–81. *more coolness,* DHC, 3:82–83; Notes b.13-2. *If each,* SRFC, 57. *Ideas,* RFC, 1:158.

13. *Let our,* RFC, 1:158–159 (King). For similar versions, see ibid., 1:157 (Yates); SRFC, 57 (Lansing). *abolish, attempt,* RFC, 1:158–159 (King). *If the,* DHC, 3:83–84. Madison included Dickinson's comment that the "attempt to abolish the States altogether . . . would be impracticable, would be ruinous." Ibid., 84. Later Madison seemed to worry that Dickinson's speech suggested Madison was contemplating consolidation and added a confusing footnote insisting that the issue involved the "principle" of proportional representation and alluding to

concerns about the size of the second branch to "throw light on this discussion." Notes, b.13-4.

14. For large district proposals, see DHRC, 1:245, 246 (Pinckney's plan proposing "four Districts"); RFC, 1:58 (Pierce) ("to divide the union into districts from which the Senators should be chosen"); Journal (CWH), DHC, 1:215 (June 7) (proposing "elected by the people in Districts to be formed for that purpose"). King described the June 7 proposal as "convenient Districts." RFC, 1:159. *election,* DHC, 3:85. *same Opinion,* SRFC, 58. *Mr. Madison,* RFC, 1:190. For replaced Madison speech, see b.14-1; DHC, 3:85–86. For Sherman and Pinckney comments on districts, see DHC, 3:86–87. *unfair,* RFC, 1:159 (King). On a procedural motion to postpone Dickinson's motion to enable the large district motion to be voted, only Pennsylvania voted aye. If Madison voted with Wilson and Morris, he was outvoted within the Virginia delegation. Journal (CWH), DHC, 1:215; DHC, 1:244. Because only the state votes are known, dissenting individual votes—likely known by the delegates—remain invisible. On the subsequent vote that the members be chosen by state legislatures, Madison was likely outvoted within the delegation. The vote was unanimous, 11–0. DHC, 1:215, 227, 244. On May 31, Madison voiced concern about large districts related to the possibility that less competent men from a larger state would be elected over those from a smaller state. DHC, 3:31 (31 May). The concern related to the "influence of the smaller States" rather than the states' identity. At the time, Madison may have been attempting to persuade the small states to favor the original approach of the Virginia plan, which involved the first branch choosing among persons nominated by the state legislatures. DHRC, 1:243–244 (fifth resolution). The Virginia plan's approach was rejected and, as Madison noted, "a chasm [was] left in this part of the plan." DHC, 3:32.

15. *All laws,* Journal (CWH), DHC, 1:216. King described the difference as between "in certain instances" to a "general Negative." RFC, 1:171. For speech, see RFC, 1:171 (King); SRFC, 61 (Butler); SRFC, 60 (Lansing); RFC, 1:169 (Yates).

16. Notes, b.14-3; DHC, 3:88–89.

17. DHC, 3:93; b.15-2. Madison eventually may have worried that the line "dissolution of the States" could be taken out of context to suggest he had proposed abolition of the states and replaced it with "dissolution of the Union." Ibid.

18. Journal (CWH), DHC, 1:216, 227; DHC, 3:93–94.

19. For Franklin speech, see DHC, 3:102–106; b.16-4–b.17-4 (June 11). For Wilson and Mason speeches, see DHC, 3:52–53, b.8-3–b.8-4 (Wilson, June 4) and DHC, 3:58–60, b.9-3–b.9-4 (Mason, June 4).

20. For Paterson speech, see b.14-4–b.16-2; DHC, 3:97–99.

21. On length, see Journal, DHC, 1:217 ("After some time passed in debate"). For Brearley speech, see DHC, 3:95–96 (*Virg[ini]a, weight*). For other version of Brearley speech, see RFC, 1:184 (King), 1:191 (Paterson), 1:181–182 (Yates);

SRFC, 62 (Lansing), 64 (Bedford). In Madison's version, Brearley refers to the "disparity" under the "quota" of Congress—suggesting that he used the three-fifths clause. DHC, 3:96. According to Lansing, Brearley based his figures on numbers of "free inhabitants." SRFC, 62. For similar figures, see RFC, 1:190 (Paterson), 190 n.24 (noting similar documents in Wilson and Brearley papers). The Paterson numbers are based on "quota of tax" and Bedford refers to the last congressional requisition, suggesting that the numbers assumed a three-fifths clause.

22. *I shall,* RFC, 1:184 (punctuation *sic*). *One [remedy],* DHC, 3:96.

23. *Striking,* DHC, 3:97; Notes, b.15-4–b.16-2.

24. *New partition,* Wilson speech, see DHC, 3:99–100. *admitted,* DHC, 3:100. *so much,* DHC, 3:100. The postponement was not formal, see Journal (CWH), DHC, 1:217.

25. For omitted motions relating to the Virginia Plan, resolution 9, see Journal (CWH), DHC, 1:222–223 (12 June); DHC, 3:117. For Randolph's replacement motion, seconded by Madison, see DHC, 1:223 (13 June). *relating,* DHC, 3:117 (also showing later slip additions). *several members,* DHC, 3:108 (discussing resolution 13 on amending the "national Constitution" on 11 June). For list of nine questions on 12 June, see DHC, 3:113–114. Similarly, see omission on motions relating to republican government clause. DHC, 3:108 (11 June).

26. *Fix the equitable,* DHC, 3:107, b.18-1. The actual language did not refer to the congressional act and was more technical: "in proportion to the whole number of white and other free Citizens and inhabitants of every age, sex and condition, including those bound to servitude for a term of years, and three fifths of all other persons not comprehended in the foregoing description, except Indians, not paying taxes in each State." Journal (CWH), DHC, 1:218. For vote, see DHC, 3:107; DHC, 1:227 (9–2). The additional discussion written at the end of the prior sheet containing Franklin's speech (from "On the question for agreeing to Mr Kings" to "N.J. & Del: in the negative") was added later, likely at two different times. See b.17-4; DHC, 3:106–107. The paraphrase of Butler's speech was added from Yates. RFC, 1:196

27. For Paterson, see RFC, 1:207, 208. For Butler, see SRFC, 70. For Lansing, see SRFC, 69. For Yates, see RFC, 1:205–206.

28. For discussions of slavery and the Constitution, see Donald L. Robinson, *Slavery in the Structure of American Politics, 1765–1820* (New York: Harcourt Brace Jovanovich, 1971), 168–247; David O. Stewart, *The Summer of 1787: The Men Who Invented the Constitution* (New York: Simon & Schuster, 2007), 75–85; Richard Beeman, *Plain, Honest Men: The Making of the American Constitution* (New York: Random House, 2009), 67–68; 152–155; 200–225; Lawrence Goldstone, *Dark Bargain: Slavery, Profits, and the Struggle for the Constitution* (New York: Walker & Co., 2005), 100–195; Paul Finkelman, *Slavery and the Founders: Race and Liberty in the Age of Jefferson,* 2nd ed. (Armonk, NY: M.E. Sharpe, 2001), 3–36; George Van Cleve, *A Slaveholders' Union:*

Slavery, Politics, and the Constitution in the Early Republic (Chicago: University of Chicago Press, 2010), 103–183; David Brion Davis, *The Problem of Slavery in the Age of Revolution, 1770–1823* (Ithaca, NY: Cornell University Press, 1975); Steven Lubet, *Fugitive Justice: Runaways, Rescuers, and Slavery on Trial* (Cambridge: Harvard University Press, 2010), 11–22; Margot Minardi, *Making Slavery History: Abolitionism and the Politics of Memory in Massachusetts* (New York: Oxford University Press, 2010), 13–28.

29. *The particular,* RFC, 1:208. *detail be,* RFC, 1:206.

30. For votes, see Journal (CWH), DHC, 1:218 (describing the second branch right of suffrage according to the rule "established for the first"), 227 (vote tallies).

31. For report, see DHC, 3:120–123, b.20-1–b.20-3. For squished comments, see DHC, 3:120; b.19-4. The editors of the *Documentary History* assumed the squished words were added. The heavy use of abbreviations and style is more indicative of June 1787 composition. On omission by Eppes, see EJC, June 13 (later slip added with Williamson's speech).

32. *Instability,* DHC, 3:111 (the "s" to vices is a revision to b.18-3). *consider,* DHC, 3:111. On argument with Franklin over salary, see DHC, 3:112–113. *stability,* DHC, 3:115–116. *too much,* DHC, 3:118. *generally,* DHC, 3:119.

33. DHC, 3:120–123.

34. The blank page is b.20-4.

35. *Give an opportunity,* b.19-4; DHC, 3:120. *I think,* Madison to Ambrose Madison, 13 June 1787, PJM, 10:51.

5. An Account of Failed Strategies

1. *Taken,* Madison to Jefferson, 18 July 1787, PJM, 10:105 .

2. *Contradistinguished,* DHC, 3:123; b.21-1. *N.B.,* DHC, 3:124, b.21-1–b.21-2.

3. DHC, 3:124.

4. DHC, 3:124 (introducing comment with "M^r. Dickenson said to M^r. M"); b.21-2.

5. DHC, 3:124. Madison emphasized that members had been permitted to take copies. For discussion of various versions, see RFC, 3:611–615. After the Journal was published in 18 19, Madison added a footnote explaining that his version differed from the Brearley reprinted copy but a "confidence is felt . . . in its accuracy." DHC, 3:128.

6. DHC, 3:128; b.22-1–b.23-2 (16 June).

7. For Paterson's speech, see DHC, 3:130. For Randolph's speech, see DHC, 3:136. *Why,* DHC, 3:131–132. *2. Representation,* DHC, 3:132–133.

8. *A total,* SRFC, 77. *will absorb,* RFC, 1:270 (Paterson). *will absorb,* RFC, 1:263. *proposes,* RFC, 1:267. *which latter,* RFC, 1:257. For Madison, see DHC, 3:129.

9. DHC, 3:138–151; b.23-3–b.25-2.

10. *A compleat,* DHC, 3:142. *the States,* DHC, 3:138. *subordinate,* DHC, 3:144. *had not been, Corporations,* DHC, 3:163 (19 June).

11. *Extent,* DHC, 3:144. *separate,* DHC, 3:145 (Madison inserted "debtors & Creditors). *firmness,* DHC, 3:146. Madison records Hamilton using "for life" in the speech and "good behavior" in the plan. DHC, 3:150. Impeachment was covered. DHC, 3:151. *monarch,* DHC, 3:148. For discussion of executive, see DHC, 3:147–148. *In his private,* DHC, 3:145. For various interpretations of Hamilton's plan, see Louise Burnham Dunbar, *A Study of "Monarchical" Tendencies in the United States from 1776 to 1801* (1922; New York: Johnson Reprint, 1970), 77, 82–98; Clinton Rossiter, *1787: The Grand Convention* (New York: Macmillan Company, 1966), 177–178; Richard Beeman, *Plain, Honest Men: The Making of the American Constitution* (New York: Random House, 2009), 166–170.

12. *Sketch,* DHC, 3:149; b.24-4–b.25-1. *All laws,* DHC, 3:151 (X). *The Senate,* DHC, 3:150 (VI). For discussion of versions of Hamilton's plan, see RFC, 3:617–618. Farrand favored the accuracy of the Madison plan based largely on his belief in Madison's accuracy. Jameson was more neutral. The sketch may not have been written at the same time as the account of the speech. The final two pages of the sheet were left blank suggesting that he had already written Tuesday, June 19, on a new sheet. Notes, b.25-3–b.25-4. "On these articles . . . reasoning" appears to have been added. Notes, b.25-2.

13. *Did not mean,* DHC, 3:149. On interpretation in the 1790s, see Chapter 10.

14. For other versions of Madison's speech, see RFC, 1:329–330 (King's version largely a summary of ancient confederacies); RFC, 1:325–326 (Yates's version discussing state violations and ancient confederacies); SRFC, 95 (Lansing's version similar to Yates). For Madison's version, see DHC, 3:151–162; b.26-1–b27-3. *reviewed,* DHC, 3:156; b.26-3. On appendix possibility, see Charles R. Keller and George W. Pierson, "A New Madison Manuscript Relating to the Federal Convention of 1787," *American Historical Review* 36 (October 1930): 25. For earlier notes, see Notes on Ancient and Modern Confederacies, 9:3–24. If the Confederacies were paper B, then presumably Madison had in mind a paper A. There appears to be no reference to paper A in the Notes on June 19 unless it was removed. The obvious suspect for paper A would seem to have been the Vices notes.

15. Compare DHC, 3:154–160 with Vices of the Political System, PJM, 9:345, 348–358. I have structured the speech using brackets to indicate my organizational headers and numbers to indicate Madison's original numbers. The absence of material from the extended discussion of the eleventh vice also supports the idea that Madison had not yet formulated those ideas. Although Hamilton had focused on the extensive country—the issue addressed by the extended eleventh vice—Madison's speech included no similar discussion.

16. *Mr Randolph's, was in fact,* DHC, 3:162. For vote, see Journal, DHC, 1:225 (19 July). The secretary also recorded that the Committee officially reported that "they do not agree to the propositions" by Paterson. Ibid. Madison skipped a postponement motion. The proceedings of July 19 ended the Journal of the Committee of the Whole House.

17. DHC, 3:162; b.27-3 (illegible word in heading). The heading probably more closely resembled a heading before Madison added an "Of." *by a,* DHC, 3:162. *much of,* 164 (King). For Hamilton, see DHC, 3:163. *government,* DHC, 3:166. Randolph noted that he accepted the language but "did not admit it for the reasons assigned." Ibid. The motion passed unanimously. DHC, 3:167.

18. For June 21 speech, see b.30; DHC, 3:179–181. For June 29 speech, see b.42; DHC, 3:237–239. For June 28 speech, see b.49-5–b.50-3; DHC, 3:228–233.

19. *Not because,* DHC, 3:190 (22 June) (later moved to a footnote). *friends,* DHC, 3:190.

20. DHC, 3:234, b.40-4. For Franklin's speech as originally recorded, see DHC, 3:234. At a later time that summer, Madison crossed out this summary and copied Franklin's speech onto a separate sheet. DHC, 3:235–237; b.41-1–b.41-2 (last two pages left blank; a section of the blank page missing and repaired). Farrand did not reproduce the summary. RFC, 1:450 n.12. For objections, see DHC, 3:234–235. For absence of record of motion, see Journal (Convention), DHC, 1:76–77.

21. RFC, 3:366 (21 June) (King). Madison's version used far more complicated language. DHC, 3:178.

22. *Subordinate,* DHC, 3:163 (19 June). *States, rights,* RFC, 1:331, 332 (19 June) (described by Farrand as King's notes for his speech). Madison's version did not contain the word, "corporation(s)." DHC, 3:163–164.

23. *That there,* RFC, 1:367 (King). *Legislatures,* SRFC, 106 (Lansing). *any state,* RFC, 1:363–364.

24. For existing replaced speech, see DHC, 3:179–181; b.30-2–b.30-3. Madison raised this theme of concern over encroachment and demarcation between state and general government in a letter to Jefferson in October 24, 1787, and in Federalist essays 45 and 46 in late January 1788. PJM, 10:208, 428–432, 438–444.

25. *Fallacy,* DHC, 3: 228. *the conditions, mere counties,* DHC, 3:232. *perfect,* DHC, 3:232. *equalization,* 232–233. For Yates version, see RFC, 1:455–456. June 28 may be an example of writing the Notes on a day other than Wednesday. On Wednesday, June 27, and Thursday, June 28, Madison recorded the same motion relating to Lansing's striking "not." The motion occurred on Thursday. The confusion seems likely to have been the result of writing up the Notes of Wednesday and Thursday (largely the long speech of Luther Martin) after Thursday. DHC, 3:224, 227; Journal (Convention), DHC, 1:76.

26. *Compromise,* RFC, 1:476 (describing dispute over conception of a state on 475). *the lowest,* RFC, 1:477. *have the States,* RFC, 1:479. Yates had a similar version. RFC, 1:471–472 ("The states . . . are only great corporations, having the power of making by-laws.").

27. For existing replaced speech, see DHC, 3:240; b.42-3–b.43-4. Madison used the following speeches (on an original sheet) to suggest sympathetic understandings. Hamilton emphasized that the states were "a collection of individual men." The people, not "the artificial beings resulting from the composition," ought to be respected. DHC, 3:242. Gerry described the "advocates" for the states as "intoxicated with the idea of their sovereignty." DHC, 3:244.

28. See Journal (Convention), DHC, 1:77–78 (29 June), 78 (30 June); DHC, 3:247–248. On New Hampshire abolition, see David Menschel, "Abolition without Deliverance: The Law of Connecticut Slavery, 1784–1848," *Yale Law Journal* 111 (2001):183, 184 n.3; Arthur Zilversmit, *The First Emancipation: The Abolition of Slavery in the North* (Chicago: University of Chicago Press, 1967), 117 (describing history of interpretation that the state bill of rights abolished slavery).

29. For June 23 speech, see DHC, 3:196–197, b.33-2–b.33-3. For June 26 speech, see DHC, 3:214–216, b.37-1–37-3. For June 30 speech (original), see DHC, 3:252–255, b.44-3–b.44-4.

30. For cynical, see Sherman, DHC, 3:195. For suspicious, see King, DHC, 3:195. For laudatory, see Wilson, DHC, 3:195. *other offices,* DHC, 3:194, b.32-4 (original sheet). For motion and vote, see Journal (Convention), DHC, 1:71, 247.

31. *Necessary,* SRFC, 109. *patriotism,* RFC, 1:392. *most capable,* DHC, 3:196–197. The replaced speech includes a center section on the problems with appointments. It discussed the "appointment of strangers on these recommendations" and candidates who "would hover round the seat of Govt or be found among the residents there" and court the members. It was not recorded by Yates or Lansing and seemed somewhat unrelated to Madison's purpose in the motion. The final sentence suggesting that no one would have served in the Virginia legislature if rendered incapable of serving in Congress seems likely to have been in the original. It reflected Madison's experience.

32. *Five Classes,* SRFC, 112. *see it Monday,* DHC, 3:264, b.56-2 (2 July). For Madison's copy in the Notes, see DHC, 3:199–207, b.34-1–b.35-2 (last two pages blank). The thirty-fifth sheet is misnumbered as 46 in the Library of Congress's 2008 digital images. The thirty-sixth sheet is misnumbered similarly as 45. At the end of Madison's copy, he wrote: "The residue of this speech was not obtained." The replaced sheet is b.33. For discussion of Madison's later revision, see Chapter 9. The loss of context for the speech resulted in Farrand adding an explanatory footnote: "Relating to the composition of the upper house." RFC; 1:397. For another version of Pinckney's speech and plan, see RFC, 1:410–412 (Yates). For the speech in the Madison papers, DHC, 3:789–795; SRFC, 113–118

(printed in different order). Yates records Madison suggesting that there were "great differences of opinion" over the clause and it should be postponed until the "mode of representation" was determined. Seven states disagreed. Madison omitted his motion in his original notes. He later would revise the Notes to insert the comment from Yates's notes. DHC, 3:210. Madison eventually also revised "see it" on July 2 to "form the States into classes, with an apportionment of Senators." DHC, 3:264.

33. DHC, 3:199–207. For draft, see SRFC, 113. Subsequent speakers responded to the point about the extensive country. Wilson argued that the "extent of country" suggested that the second branch be elected by electors chosen by the people. DHC, 3:208–209. Ellsworth argued that the states were necessary to "support a Republican Govt." over distances. Madison revised the sentence to add "over so great an extent of Country." DHC, 3:210.

34. *Distinctions, landed, Balance,* SRFC, 119 (Lansing). *Property,* SRFC, 120 (Butler). *The Senate,* SRFC, 119 (Lansing). Yates's notes resemble Lansing's in greater detail and length.

35. For replaced version, see DHC, 214–216, b.37-1–b.37-3. *He [Madison],* DHC, 3:217 (original sheet) (eventually revised by Madison to omit the "He was right"). *the position,* DHC, 3:219 (original sheet). *important,* DHC, 3:222 (original sheet).

36. DHC, 3:221 (original sheet, 26 June). For description, see DHC, 212 (original sheet, 25 June). For vote on term, see Journal (Convention), DHC, 1:73 (25 June), 247 (7–3–1, Pennsylvania and Delaware voting with Virginia). For vote on election, see Journal (Convention), DHC, 1:72 (25 June), 247 (9–2, Virginia and Pennsylvania opposed).

37. *Compromise,* DHC, 3:245–247. Johnson made a similar suggestion at the outset of June 29. DHC, 3:237 (29 June). *we are,* RFC, 1:478. *reasoning,* DHC, 3:252. *Mr. E.,* DHC, 3:252–253.

38. *An equal,* Journal (Convention), DHC, 1:78 (30 June). For Bedford speech, see DHC, 3:259–261. *intemperance,* DHC, 3:262. *warm & rash,* DHC, 3:268 (2 July). For Yates's version, see DHC, 1:501 ("Sooner than be ruined, there are *foreign powers who will take us by the hand*").

39. For failed vote on equal vote in second branch, see Journal (Convention), DHC, 1:78 (2 July), 248 (5–5–1). For committee, see Journal (Committee), DHC, 1:79, 238 (9–2) (New Jersey and Delaware opposed). *hit on,* DHC, 3:264. *peculiar,* DHC, 3:263–264 (stating the three states by name). General Pinckney technically proposed the committee. DHC, 3:264. *delay,* DHC, 3:269.

40. Journal (Committee), DHC, 1:79; DHC, 3:269.

41. For Morris's speech, see DHC, 3:264–268. For attendance, see Charles Warren, *The Making of the Constitution* (1928; reprinted, Boston: Little, Brown and Co., 1937), 810–811 (Hamilton leaving on June 29; Morris arriving on July 2); see also Gordon Lloyd, The Constitutional Convention Attendance Record

(http://teachingamericanhistory.org/convention/attendance/). Morris also suggested somewhat similar to Madison's inducement idea that a "Senate for life will be a noble bait." DHC, 3:267.

42. For July 5 report, see Journal, DHC, 1:79–80. For Madison's version, see DHC, 3:270. Footnote appears on b.47-3. *merely,* DHC, 3:271.

43. DHC, 3:271–273.

44. *Manner,* DHC, 3:278. *We cannot,* DHC, 3:275. *he would,* DHC, 3:278. In Lansing's notes, Bedford commented that "Gentlemen have threatened in Terms very indelicate, tho' they have generally moderated their Voices when they did so." SRFC, 150. *What if,* DHC, 3:293.

45. On vote, see Journal (Convention), DHC, 1:82 (7 July) (whether equal state suffrage would "stand part of the report"); 249. Massachusetts and Georgia were divided. *several votes,* DHC, 3:291 (7 July). For July 9 committee report, see Journal (Convention), DHC, 1:83. The committee was comprised of Morris, Gorham, Randolph, Rutledge, and King. Journal (Convention), DHC, 1:81 (6 July). *Report is,* DHC, 3:296. *the Combined,* DHC, 3:297. For Brearley's numbers, see DHC, 1:331 (based on tax quotas, 27 Sept. 1785). Brearley organized in terms of size, and that is followed here.

46. For Randolph plan, see b.137 (GR_142_0559), 147e–f (2003); DHC, 5:437–438; 3:345 n.‡; RFC, 3:55–56. For location in the original 1840 edition, see PJM (Gilpin), 3:Appendix, vii–viii.

47. DHC, 3:254–255; b.44-4. For other versions of Madison's speech, see RFC, 1:504 (Paterson); RFC, 1:496–497 (Yates); SRFC, 131 (Lansing).

48. DHC, 3:298.

49. *Warmly,* DHC, 3:298. *some,* DHC, 3:298. For committee, see Journal (Convention), DHC, 1:84 (9 July); DHC, 3:299. The eleven-person committee included King, Sherman, Yates, Brearley, Morris, Reed, Carroll, Madison, Williamson, Rutledge, and Houston. For report, see Journal (Convention), 1:84–85; DHC, 3:299. Madison gave only the numbers in the Notes. States are arranged in order of original Brearley arrangement.

50. DHC, 3:299–300 (10 July).

51. *Considered,* DHC, 3:300 (10 July). *dividing,* DHC, 3:300 (10 July). *property,* DHC, 3:320 (12 July). *lamented,* DHC, 3:322 (12 July). *it was,* DHC, 3:320 (12 July). *allotted,* DHC, 3:326–327 (13 July). For the reader, Madison included a likely original footnote explaining Read's suspicion that in the committee Madison and Morris had recommended fewer representatives for their states in order to lessen the share of taxation. The footnote did not entirely deny Read's suspicion. DHC, 326 n.; b.56-4. Madison eventually struck the footnote.

52. For Gorham, see DHC, 3:309, 317 (11 July). *He had,* DHC, 3:316 (11 July); see also DHC, 3:311 (agreeing with Morris but going along). *the Southern,* DHC, 3:323 (12 July); b.56-4. *difficulties,* DHC, 3:317 (11 July). For vote, see Journal (Convention), DHC, 1:91–92, 251 (6–2–2) (the motion related

to the census and linked representation to direct taxation and based it on the 1783 ratio) (New Jersey and Delaware voted no; Massachusetts and South Carolina divided).

53. *The dilemma,* DHC, 3:318 (11 July). *high time,* DHC, 3:321 (12 July) (echoing Davie's comment in favor of slavery). *A distinction,* DHC, 3:329 (13 July).

54. DHC, 3:329–330 (13 July). Madison took the only extant notes of the debates between 10 July and 14 July.

55. *M^r.,* DHC, 3:336. For Pinckney's scheme, see Journal (Convention), DHC, 1:93–94; DHC, 3:335 (14 July) (recommending 36 representatives for second branch, apparently by dividing the July 10 figures in half and rounding up). For speech, see DHC, 3:338–341. Madison tallied the votes under equal state suffrage: five states to the South and eight to the North. Although under proportional representation, the Northern side would "still outnumber the other," Madison predicted "not in the same degree . . . and every day would tend towards an equilibrium."

56. For vote refusing to postpone equal state suffrage and substitute Pinckney's proportional representation proposal, see Journal, DHC, 1:94; 251 (14 July) (4–6). *M^r.,* DHC, 3:343. For King memorandum, see RFC, 2:12 (15 July). Only Pennsylvania, Maryland, Virginia, and South Carolina voted in favor of postponement. With Gorham's attendance, assuming neither Gerry nor Strong voted differently, the vote would have been 4–5–1.

57. *Including,* DHC, 3:343–344. For vote, see Journal (Convention), DHC, 1:94; 251 (16 July) (5–4–1).

58. *The large,* DHC, 3:345–346 (16 July). For Paterson comment, see DHC, 3:346. *so readily,* DHC, 3:346. For adjournment votes, see Journal (Convention), 251 (first vote, 5–5; second vote, 7–2–1). For debate, see DHC, 3:346–347.

59. For blank space, see b.60-2; DHC, 3:347. For commentary, see DHC, 3:347–348.

60. DHC, 3:348.

61. *Probably approved,* DHC, 3:349. On enumeration debate, see DHC, 3:329–351. For Morris's comment, see DHC, 3:350. For vote, see Journal (Convention), DHC, 1:96–97; 251 (2–8).

62. For Madison speech on negative, see DHC, 3:351–351. For vote, see Journal, DHC, 1:97; 251 (3–7) (Massachusetts, Virginia, and North Carolina in favor).

63. *Judiciary,* DHC, 3:353. *valid,* DHC, 3:353. For supremacy clause motion, see DHC, 3:353; b.61-2 (original sheet). Madison interestingly described it with the language "shall be observed by their Courts" instead of the more technical language binding the state courts regardless of state law. Journal (Convention), DHC, 1:97. The DHC editors showed the language approving of the motion nem. com. as a revision. Although it looks like the words were inserted after the

motion and the next line were written (they seem to be written into the space), it may be that they represent a relatively contemporary revision by Madison as he was writing originally. They predate his decision to insert a slip with the language of the motion. DHC, 3:353, Slip 1, b.61-2.

64. For Morris's speeches on popular election, see DHC, 3:353–354, 355–356. For vote, see DHC, 3:357; Journal (Convention), DHC, 1:97, 252. For Martin's on electors, see DHC, 3:357. For vote, see Convention (Journal), DHC, 1:98 (margin). Williamson stated that popular election would favor the "largest State" (likely Pennsylvania) because in Virginia, "[h]er slaves will have no suffrage." DHC, 3:357. For vote to strike "ineligible a second time," see Journal (Convention), DHC, 1:98, 252 (6–4) (Virginia opposed). For good behavior vote, see Journal (Convention), DHC, 1:98; 252 (4–6).

65. For replaced sheet, see b.62; DHC, 3:358–363. Yates and Lansing had left the Convention around July 5. King and Paterson had no regular notes. Madison included two speeches of his own. If he followed his pattern in replacing speeches, he retained the analysis but deleted troubling conclusions. Both speeches contain sentences similar to later speeches given by Madison suggesting that he may have borrowed the lines in revising. The first speech suggested that the reasons supporting judicial tenure on good behavior also applied to the executive. The beginning of the replaced speech resembles Madison's speech on July 19. In the second speech on July 17, Madison opposed monarchy. This speech is similar to his July 21 speech on legislative vortex. It is even conceivable that he did not originally give one or both speeches. For first speech, see DHC, 3:359–360. For second speech, see DHC, 3:361. For July 19 speech, see DHC, 3:378 (first two sentences similar to first July 17 speech). For July 21 speech, see DHC, 3:392 (similar vortex argument). According to Madison, Dr. McClurg made the motion. McClurg made little other appearance in the Notes except for being noted as having agreed with Madison in two votes in June and a comment about the executive's means to enforce laws. Madison later added and then deleted that he had "actively promoted" McClurg's appointment to the Convention. *actively,* DHC, 3:359 n.*. In late July, McClurg left the Convention and continued to correspond with Madison. Madison's two letters to him have never been found. If the letters contained further discussion of the executive tenure, Madison or McClurg may have eventually destroyed them. For attribution to McClurg, see DHC, 3:358. For mention of McClurg in divisions, see June 4 vote on the single executive and June 8 vote on extending the negative. DHC, 3:54 (4 June); 94 (8 June). On August correspondence, see PJM, 10:120 (ca. 28 July, not found), 134–136 (5 August) (McClurg describing his presence as producing a vote division), 161 (ca. 1 September, not found), 165–166 (10 September). *held by,* DHC, 3:378 (19 July). For votes, see DHC, 3:362. On the replaced sheet, Madison later added footnotes to the motion and his speech suggesting that the tenure represented something other than Madison's preferred outcome. For

footnote on motion, see b.62-1 (describing it as intended to promote ineligibility for a second term; the theory being that a tenure on good behavior was the only alternative mechanism for executive independence). The footnote repeats the substance of the McClurg speech. DHC, 3:362. For footnote on speech, see b.62-2. The absence of spacing suggests that the footnotes were added to the pages. The DHC editors erred in placing the two comments as footnotes. The * note ended at "tendency"; "The avowed . . . office" was added later. Madison scratched out and revised that addition. The insertion shown vertically in the margin in the DHC appears to have been in the handwriting of John C. Payne. The † note was only slightly revised. Notes, b.62-4.

6. Acquiring a New Role

1. Madison to Jefferson, 18 July 1787, PJM, 10:105–106. Jefferson did not receive the letter until December 19, 1787. PTJ, 11:601.

2. DHC, 3:372–376. For Federalist 10, see PJM, 10:263–270 (22 November 1787).

3. *National,* DHC, 3:363; Journal (Convention), DHC, 1: (18 July). For omissions, see DHC, 3:367. On inferior tribunals, see DHC, 3:368–369 (18 July). *criticisms, the jurisdiction,* DHC, 3:369. *entirely,* DHC, 3:399–400 (21 July).

4. For July 23, see DHC, 3:403. *articles,* DHC, 3:404. On voting, see DHC, 3:412–413. For "N.H.," see DHC, 3:411 (writing "N.H." over his initial habit of "Mas.").

5. *Given day,* DHRC, 1:250 (res. 15). *interregnum,* DHC, 3:369 (18 July). *the Constitutional,* DHC, 3:370–372. *better,* DHC, 372 (18 July).

6. *Incompetent,* DHC, 3:410–411 (23 July). *Southern,* DHC, 3:379 (19 July). *best,* DHC, 3:426 (25 July).

7. *Defending,* DHC, 3:391–391. *Theory,* DHC, 3:395. For debate, see DHC, 3:390–399 (21 July).

8. *Reminded,* DHC, 3:414. For votes, see DHC, 3:414.

9. *Took,* DHC, 3:422 (24 July). *object,* DHC, 3:422–423. Morris agreed, explaining that "the bridge may be removed."

10. DHC, 3:423; Journal, DHC, 1:109 (24 July).

11. On executive debates, see DHC, 3:423–435 (25–26 July). For vote, see DHC, 3:435. For clause, see Journal (Convention), DHC, 1:110–111 (26 July).

12. *Election,* DHC, 3:432–434. For landed property qualification, see DHC, 3:435. For Madison's opposition, see DHC, 3:436, 438–439. For seat, see DHC, 3:442.

13. *Adjourned,* DHC, 3:443. For referral, see Journal (Convention), DHC, 1:109 (24 July).

14. For votes, see vote tallies, DHC, 1:255 (not recorded in Journal).

15. For Madison's copy of report, see DHC, 3:444–458; b.75-3–b.78.4. Madison began the copy at the bottom of the third page of the sheet containing the notes for July 26 as if he wrote both at the same time (explaining the initial incorrect date of July 27 for 26). For Madison's printed Report, see Committee of Detail Report (Madison) (COD), no. 143 (DLC). Madison never wrote changes on this draft. If he tracked changes on a draft, he used another copy.

16. For words corrected, see DHC, 3:452. On printer error, see DHRC, 1:269 n.1; RFC, 2:177 n.3. On the printed draft, a lengthy enacting style was given ("by the House of Representatives, and by the Senate of the United States, in Congress assembled"), but the committee apparently changed it before August 6. Madison copied the intended version: "the Senate and Representatives in Congress assembled." DHC, 3:448 (article VI, section 11); see RFC, 2:180 n.4. Madison made both changes on his printed copy. COD Report (Madison).

17. DHC, 3:503; b.85-2.

18. *M^r. Sherman,* DHC, 3:461–462; b.79-3. *He had,* DHC, 3:465–466, b.80-1. July had been originally written across the top of the page; Madison wrote August over it. DHC, 3:458, b.79-1.

19. *Children,* DHC, 3:466 (7 August). *If not,* DHC, 3:466 (7 August). For run-on, see DHC, 3:461–462 (Sherman), 468 (Franklin), 477 (Morris). For "And," see DHC, 3:463 (Randolph), 477 (Morris). *was strongly,* DHC, 3:458 (7 August). *Treaties,* DHC, 3:359 (7 August).

20. Compare Madison's version, DHC, 3:497 with Journal (Convention), DHC, 1:122 (11 August). *sect.,* DHC, 3:480; Convention (Journal), DHC, 1:119 (9 August). For August 9, see DHC, 3:490; Journal (Convention), DHC, 1:118; RFC, 2:240 n.16.

21. *M^r. Williamson, M^r. Carrol,* DHC, 3:505 (11 August). *after,* DHC, 3:505–506. For example of skipped motions and votes, see DHC, 3:513, 523, 535. For example of nontechnical language, see DHC, 3:531, 535, 536, 541. For override, see DHC, 3:540. For missed proceedings at end, see DHC, 3:523 (13 August), 535 (14 August). *&c.,* DHC, 3:548 (16 August).

22. DHC, 3:532.

23. *Executive,* DHC, 3:536; Journal (Convention), DHC, 1:126. *a short,* DHC, 3:541; Journal (Convention), DHC, 1:127. For August 16 speech, see DHC, 3:543. *felony,* DHC, 3:550. For examples from 18 August–21 August, see DHC, 3:568, 569–570, 573, 577, 580–581.

24. *Saw no,* DHC, 3:539 (15 August). *We grow,* DHC, 3:540. *complained,* DHC, 3:540. *not possible,* Madison to Madison, Sr., 12 August 1787, PJM, 10:146.

25. DHC, 3:474–475 (8 August).

26. DHC, 3:476–478.

27. *never,* DHC, 3:510 (10 August). *reasons,* DHC, 3:511.

28. For motion to strike, see DHC, 3:479 (8 August). *no advantage,* DHC, 3:480. For Randolph's notice for reconsideration, see DHC, 3:480, 482, 484–485 (9 August). *compromise,* 506 (11 August); 513 (13 August). On past votes, see DHC, 3:519 (13 August). For vote, see DHC, 3:522 (13 August). At some later point before the Jefferson Copy, Madison wrote a note in the margin to explain Washington's vote. b.88-3.

29. *Of plunder,* DHC, 3:524 (Mercer), 525 (Gerry's description of Mercer). *It is,* DHC, 3:529 (14 August). For technicalities, see DHC, 3:523 (later revised).

30. For speeches, see DHC, 3:467–468 (7 August), 485–486 (9 August), 508–509, 510–511 (13 August), 491–492 (9 August), 495–496 (10 August), 517–519 (13 August), 504–505 (11 August), 563 (18 August), 543 (16 August), 580–581 (21 August), 568 (20 August).

31. DHC, 3:467–468. *supported,* RFC, 1:210. *in fav[o]r,* RFC, 2:208. For Madison's likely plan to replace this speech, see Chapter 10.

32. For discussion, see Mary Sarah Bilder, "James Madison, Law Student and Demi-Lawyer," *Law & History Review* 28 (2010): 389–449.

33. DHC, 3:458–460 (Article 3) (7 August); Journal (Convention), DHC, 1:113.

34. *Legislature,* DHRC, 1:261 (Article 3). *fixing,* DHC, 3:461 (7 August). For debate, see DHC, 3:462–463. On vote, see DHC, 3:463; Journal (Convention), DHC, 1:113.

35. For motion, see DHC, 3:485 (9 August). *in the,* DHC, 3:485–486. *very,* DHC, 3:486. For Randolph, see DHC, 3:487, 490. On vote, see DHC, 3:490; Journal (Convention), DHC, 1:117.

36. For language, see DHRC, 1:261 (Article 4, section 2). For motion, see DHC, 3:471 (8 August). *vague,* DHC, 3:471.

37. For language, see DHRC, 1:261 (Article 5, section 1). *A Senator,* DHC, 3:482 (9 August). *to prevent,* DHC, 3:482. *words of,* DHC, 3:491 (9 August). *not only,* DHC, 3:493.

38. For Report's language, see DHRC, 1:264 (Article VII, section 1). *commerce,* DHC, 3:545. *foreign,* DHC, 3:545. *constitute inferior,* DHC, 3:549.

39. *To make,* DHC, 3:552 (17 August). For their motion, see DHC, 3:553. For McHenry, see RFC, 2:320. For Madison's record, see DHC, 3:553–554; b.93-2–b.93-3. For votes, see Journal (Convention), DHC, 1:129, 230 (tally stating "last question repeated"); RFC, 2:319 n.10. Madison later added a footnote to attempt to bring his record into conformity with the Journal.

40. *And emit,* DHRC, 1:264 (16 August). For comments, see DHC, 3:546–548. *became,* DHC, 3:548. For vote to strike, see DHC, 3:548; Journal (Convention), DHC, 1:128, 230 (9–2).

41. On Madison's law study, see Bilder, "James Madison, Law Student." For Report language, see DHRC, 1:264 (Article VII, section 1). For discussion, see

DHC, 3:549–551 (17 August). For motions, see Journal (Convention), DHC, 1:129.

42. For list, see Journal (Convention), DHC, 1:130–131 (18 August). From "That Funds" through "post-roads" match motions proposed according to the Notes. See RFC, 2:325 n.4. The Notes, however, are the only evidence. For Madison's list, see DHC, 3:554–555.

43. *Sev[e]ral*, DHC, 3:554. For language, see DHC, 1:130–131. The Notes also omitted the names of a committee appointed to consider the state debts. DHC, 3:558–559; Journal (Convention), DHC, 1:132.

44. DHC, 3:565 (20 August).

45. Compare DHC, 3:565 with Journal (Convention), DHC, 1:133–135.

46. *Organizing*, DHC, 3:565 (20 August). For proposal, see Journal (Convention), DHC, 1:135–136.

47. *And support, more, To make*, DHC, 3:560 (19 August). For motions, see Journal (Convention), DHC, 1:132.

48. *To enact*, DHC, 3:567 (20 August); Journal (Convention), 1:137. For discussion, see DHC, 3:567–568.

49. For Report's language, see DHRC, 1:264. *liable*, DHC, 3:568 (20 August). For motion, see Journal (Convention), DHC, 1:137, 230.

50. *Concerning*, DHC, 3:568 (20 August). For general references to statute, see DHC, 3:568, 569, 571. The statute dating to 1351 was Treason Act, 25 Edw. 3, stat. 5, c. 2; see Note, "Historical Concept of Treason: English, American," *Indiana Law Journal* (1959), 35:70–80; R. Kent Newmyer, *The Treason Trial of Aaron Burr: Law, Politics, and the Character Wars of the Early Republic* (Cambridge: Cambridge University Press, 2012), 60; Carlton F. W. Larson, "The Forgotten Constitutional Law of Treason and the Enemy Combatants Problem," *University of Pennsylvania Law Review* 154 (2006): 863, 870–873.

51. For discussion, see DHC, 3:568–573, b.95-4–b.96-3. For thirteen votes, see Journal (Convention), DHC, 1:138–139. The vote tally included a failed motion to commit the section. DHC, 1:231. The fourteen appear in RFC, 2:337–339.

52. For Report, see DHRC, 1:264–265 (Article VII, Section 3). For discussion, see DHC, 3:573 (20 August).

53. *Friday*, DHC, 3:574; b.96-4. *to organize*, DHC, 3:574. y^e, DHC, 3:580. *&*, DHC, 3:581. w^d, DHC, 3:581.

54. *May not*, DHC, 3:580 (21 August). For vote, see DHC, 3:583; Journal (Convention), DHC, 1:143, 231. *for reducing*, DHC, 3:582. *national*, DHC, 3:580.

55. For Report, see DHRC, 1:265 (Article VII, section 4). For motion, see Journal (Convention), DHC, 1:143 (21 August). *to strike*, DHC, 3:583.

56. For discussion, see DHC, 3:584.

57. b.98-3 (21 August)–b.98-4 (blank). For division, see EJC, [201] (21 August). Madison may not have written the notes of Tuesday, August 21 immediately following the proceedings. Nonetheless, on the evidence currently available, the Notes written in the summer of 1787 end with b.98 on Tuesday, August 21.

7. The Complexity of Drafting

1. *Indisposition,* Madison to Jefferson, 18 July 1787, PJM, 10:105. For missing letter, see Madison to McClurg, [ca. 25 August 1787], PJM, 10:157. *Not surprized,* McClurg to Madison, 5 September 1787, PJM, 10:162.

2. *First day,* Madison to Jefferson, 6 September 1787, PJM, 10:163. Only between August 27 and August 30 was Madison not likely to have been actively engaged in committee work.

3. For time, see Journal (Convention), DHC, 1:132 (18 August) (describing time as 10:00 to 4:00 with no adjournment motion allowed).

4. The August 22 committee addressed Article VII, sections 4 (no duty on exports or migration of people or prohibiting importation), 5 (no tax unless in proportion to census), and 6 (no navigation act without a two-thirds legislative vote). The committee suggested that the fourth section include a provision that the migration and importation shall not be prohibited prior to 1800 by a tax or duty. It left the fifth section as it was, and struck out the sixth section that said navigation acts required a two-thirds vote of both houses. The committee was similar to that appointed the previous week on August 18; however, Madison replaced Mason, and Martin replaced McHenry. The committee on postponed matters was so busy that McHenry noted after it and the Rutledge committee reported on Saturday September 1, the Convention adjourned "to let the committee *sit.*"

5. For debts and militia committee (Livingston chair), see Journal (Convention), DHC, 1:131–133 (18 August), 140–141 (21 August), 146 (22 August), 147–148 (23 August). For August 6 holdover committee (Rutledge chair), see DHC, 1:130, 133 (18 August), 133–137 (20 August), 144–146 (20 August), 150 (23 August) (Senate treaty and judicial appointments clause). For Article VII slavery committee (Livingston chair), see DHC, 1:143–144 (22 August) (Langdon, King, Johnson, Livingston, Clymer, Dickinson, Martin, Madison, Williamson, C. C. Pinckney, Baldwin), 151 (24 August), 155–156 (25 August), 166 (29 August), 170 (30 August), 171 (31 August). For duties committee (Sherman chair), see DHC, 1:157 (25 August), 162 (28 August), 173 (31 August). For bankruptcy committee, see DHC, 1:165 (29 August) (not elected), 174 (1 September), 173 (3 September). For postponed matters committee, see DHC, 1:173 (31 August) (Gilman, King, Sherman, Brearley, G. Morris, Dickinson, Carroll, Madison, Williamson, Butler, Baldwin) (Brearley chair), 174 (1 September), 175–176 (3 September), 176–180 (4 September), 180–183 (5 September), 183–186 (6 Sep-

tember), 186–188 (7 September), 188–191 (8 September). For final draft committee, see DHC, 1:191 (8 September) (Johnson, Hamilton, G. Morris, Madison, King) (Johnson chair), 193 (10 September), 194 (12 September), 195–196 (13 September), 196–197 (14–15 September). The report in the Madison Papers of the postponed matters committee is not in his handwriting. He wrote, "Query if this report be not in the handwriting of Mr Sherman? More probably in that of Mr Brearly." It appears that "except treaties of peace" was added. The copy in the Notes was likely made from the journal because it included a word ("immediately") that was added to the journal entry but had not been present in the report on September 4. U.S. Constitutional Collection, MMC 2323 (DLC), Box 1, folder 3; DHC, 3:669; RFC, 2:498 n.12.

6. For Johnson's committee service, see DHC, 1:165.

7. Journal (Convention), DHC, 1:145. On discussion, see Jane Butzner, *Constitutional Chaff: Rejected Suggestions of the Constitutional Convention of 1787* (New York: Columbia University Press, 1941), 103–104. For copy permission, see DHC, 1:146. The Notes' reference was "See the Report in the Journal of the Convention of this date." DHC, 3:592. In contrast, Madison included a committee that does not appear in the Journal. On Thursday, September 13, Madison recorded Mason's suggestion for a committee to address "sumptuary regulation." DHC, 3:737–738. Given the absence of an official record, Madison drew on rough notes. The committee was described in revolutionary-era terms: to "report articles of Association for encouraging by the advice the influence and the example of the members of the Convention, œconomy frugality and american manufactures." The members were older delegates: Mason, Franklin, Dickinson, Johnson, and Livingston. The committee—if it existed—never gave a report. Its appearance reflected Madison's tendency to use the Notes to convey Mason's seemingly antiquated ideas to Jefferson. For official absence, see Journal (Committee), DHC, 1:195–196, 241. By September, Madison and Mason were opposed. Joseph Jones wrote Madison, "it is *whispered* here" that there was "great disagree[en]t" among the delegation. On "a very important question," Madison and the "the General" were "together." Mr Mason was "alone and singulir [*sic*] in his opinion." Jones believed it may have involved ratification and came from "the fountainhead," implying Madison or Washington as the source. The debate on ratification occurred on August 31, and Madison wrote McClurg sometime that weekend. Jones to Madison (ca. 13 September 1787), PJM, 10:166–167.

8. For reconstructed amended draft on September 10, see DHRC, 1:270–284. For September 12 report, see DHRC, 1:284–296. Madison's printed copy has only a few of the changes made on the final two days. For Madison's printed copy, see Committee of Style, GR 144; DHC, 3:720. He did not copy the draft into the Notes. DHC, 3:719–720.

9. For McHenry's notes, see RFC, 2:378 (22 August), 406 (24 August).

10. For Wilson, see DHC, 3:602 (23 August). For Morris, see DHC, 3:638 (29 August).

11. M^r. Govr., DHC, 3:664 (3 September). *was in,* DHC, 3:682 (5 September). M^r. *Ghorum,* DHC, 3:656 (31 August).

12. For McHenry, see RFC, 2:407 (24 August) (relating to electors). For Madison's version, see DHC, 3:610–611 (24 August) (striking "being disqualified to be reappointed"). For motions, see Journal (Convention), DHC, 1:152, 233. If Madison later copied the vote tallies, some identification may have been made based on that record's attribution of certain motions, for example, "To agree to M^r. Morris's amendment of the 1st clause of the report of the Committee of eleven." DHC, 1:232.

13. DHC, 3:649–640 (29 August) (later insertions omitted), b.109-3.

14. *The Kings power,* RFC, 1:395 (23 August). *hinted,* DHC, 3:606 (23 August).

15. *Twenty,* DHC, 3:616 (25 August), b.105-1. M^r. *Madison,* DHC, 3:618, b.105-3. "Consumed" was underscored and the underscore later marked for deletion. b.105-3. For Martin, see DHC, 3:583 (21 August). For slavery debate, see DHC, 3:583–584 (recording Martin, Rutledge, Ellsworth, Pinckney on 21 August), 585–591 (recording Sherman (thrice), Mason, Ellsworth, Pinckney, General Pinckney (twice), Baldwin, Wilson, Gerry, Dickinson, Williamson, King, Langdon, Rutledge, Morris, Butler, Read, Randolph on 22 August).

16. *Arming,* DHC, 3:596. *primary,* DHC, 3:597 (23 August). *to offices,* DHC, 3:612 (24 August).

17. *This Constitution,* DHC, 3:626 (27 August). *the object,* DHC, 3:628 (28 August). *No person,* DHRC, 1:295 (Article IV, section 3). *in compliance,* DHC, 3:755 (15 September).

18. DHC, 3:739 (13 September).

19. *Probably,* Madison to Madison, Sr., 4 September 1787, PJM, 10:161. *little,* Madison to Jefferson, 6 Sept. 1787, PJM, 10:163–164.

20. Madison to Jefferson, 6 September 1787, PJM, 10:163 (removed italics indicating originally coded words).

21. Madison to Jefferson, 6 September 1787, PJM, 10:163–164. *There,* PJM, 1:9 (commonplacing the Memoirs of the Cardinal de Retz) (copied by Madison c. 1759).

22. *I distrust,* RFC, 1:649 (17 September). For September 17, DHC, 3:761–771.

23. DHC, 3:761–771.

24. Madison to Pendleton, 20 September 1787, PJM, 10:171.

25. For plan, see DHC, 3:771–778, b.133-136 (Article IV, section 9 on President on "good behavior"). For Hamilton's later position, see Hamilton to Timothy Pickering, 16 September 1803, RFC, 3:397–398. The header reproduced in the *Records* emphasizing the "personal opinion of Hamilton," does not appear in the Notes manuscript. RFC, 3:619, DHC, 3:771. It is not in the Jefferson Copy. EJC, Appendix. The Gilpin edition does not include it. PJM (Gilpin),

3:Appendix, xvi. The Jefferson Copy contains the "Editor" note regarding Hamilton's belief that the term was three years. PJM (Gilpin), 3:Appendix, xvi. The 1803 letter curiously uses similar language to Madison's header that the plan was "communicated to Mr. Madison about the close of it, perhaps a day or two after."

26. Madison to Pendleton, 20 September 1787, PJM, 10:171.

27. On date, see PJM, 10:xxv. On Madison's concerns, see Pauline Maier, *Ratification: The People Debate the Constitution, 1787–1788* (New York: Simon & Schuster, 2010), 36.

8. The Convention's Changing Relevance

1. On Lee, see Pauline Maier, *Ratification: The People Debate the Constitution, 1787–1788* (New York: Simon & Schuster, 2010), 53, 56–58; DHRC, 1:322–340. On removal from journal, see DHRC, 58–59. *yeas & nays,* Madison to Washington, 30 September 1787, PJM, 10, 179, 180. *appearance,* Washington to Madison, 10 October 1787, PJM, 10:189. For transmittal, see DHRC, 1:340.

2. Madison to Washington, 18 October 1787, PJM, 10:196–197.

3. For pamphlet, see Charles Pinckney, *Observations on the Plan of Government submitted to the Federal Convention, In Philadelphia, on the 28th of May 1787* (New York: Francis Child, 1787); RFC, 3:106 (discussing printing history before 14 October 1787 and reprinting in late October and November *State Gazette* (South Carolina)). *to loose,* Washington to Madison, 22 October 1787, PJM, 10:203, 204. *too delicate,* see Madison to Washington, 14 October 1787, PJM, 10:194. On Franklin speech, see Madison to Washington, 20 December 1787, PJM, 10:333–335. For various printings of speech, see PJM, 10:335 (discussing excerpted commentary on speech in early December papers); "Doctor Franklin's final speech in the late federal convention," *American Museum, or Repository* (Philadelphia, Mathew Carey), December 1787, vol. 2, no. 6, 558–559 (2d edition subscription list including Madison and Washington).

4. *Sufficiently,* Pendleton to Madison, 8 October 1787, PJM, 17:519, 523. *expression,* Madison to Pendleton, 28 October 1787, PJM, 10:223 (relating to Article 1, section 9, clause 6). *the irregularities,* Madison to William Short, 24 October 1787, PJM, 10:220–221.

5. Madison to Jefferson, 24 October 1787, PJM, 10:205–220; PTJ, 12:270–286. Other readers were assumed. Madison wrote Short about it and made a rare partial file copy. See Madison to William Short, 24 October 1787, PJM, 10:220; editorial note, PJM, 10:205–206. In August 1834, Nicholas Trist made an extract. See Editorial Note, PJM, 10:205. A number of revisions appear in the letter; the editors suggest without explanation that some were done contemporaneously. For example, the words "private rights" were originally "private

and public faith." The sentence, "a majority when united by a common interest or passion can not be restrained from oppressing the minority," originally referred to "the predominant party" instead of the majority, and "suppressing" instead of "oppressing." PTJ, 12:285–286, nn. 22, 31–33.

6. Compare Madison to Jefferson, 24 October 1787, PJM, 10:205, 207–209; DHC, 3:417 (24 July) (specific suggestions on terms).

7. Madison to Jefferson, 24 October 1787, PJM, 10:207–209, 215.

8. Madison to Jefferson, 24 October 1787, PJM, 10:209–214. On the eleventh vice, see PJM, 9:354. As the *Madison Papers* editors explain, Madison was concerned with rebutting Brutus I (18 October 1787), DHRC, 13:411, 417. Brutus argued that the "idea of an extensive republic" was not borne out in history, nor in theory (citing Montesquieu). If government officers were given "honor and emolument," they would become the "proper objects for ambitious and designing men" who would use their power for "gratifying their own interest and ambition." Ibid., 420. Some of Madison's word revisions may be responses to this essay.

9. Madison to Jefferson, 24 October 1787, PJM, 10:215–216.

10. For appointment, see Madison to Washington, 14 October 1787, PJM, 10:194–195.

11. On *Federalist* project, see DHRC, 13:486–494; PJM, 10:259–263; *The Federalist,* ed. Robert Scigliano (New York: Modern Library, 2000); Douglass Adair, "The Authorship of the Disputed Federalist Papers," *William and Mary Quarterly,* 3rd series, 1 (1944), 97–122. On King, see DHRC, 13:487.

12. Federalist 1 (Hamilton), DHRC, 13:494–497 (27 October 1787).

13. Federalist 9 (Hamilton), DHRC, 14:158–163 (21 November); Federalist 10 (Madison), DHRC 14:175–181 (22 November). *process,* Vices, PJM, 9:345, 357; Madison to Jefferson, 24 October 1787; PJM, 10:205, 209–214. It may be that the two essays reflected prior conversations between Hamilton and Madison. In the undated page of Hamilton's notes, the "two principles" resemble Federalist 10's two "great points of difference" between democracy and a republic. One difference related to the system of election: "public views" are "refine[d] and enlarge[d]" by "passing them through the medium of a chosen body of citizens" (Federalist 10); "a process of election calculated to refine representation of the people" (Hamilton's notes). The other difference involved consequences of the size of the country: "renders factious combinations less to be dreaded" (Federalist 10); "render combinations on the grounds of interest difficult" (Hamilton's notes). Hamilton worried in the notes that an "influential demagogue" could still arise. Federalist 10 acknowledged that "men of factious temper, of local prejudices, or of sinister designs" could betray the people. He noted it was less likely to happen in large districts. As Douglass Adair pointed out, Federalist 10 also incorporated David Hume's thought. Douglass Adair, "The Tenth Federalist Revisited" and "'That Politics may be reduced to a Science': David Hume, James

Madison, and the Tenth Federalist," *Fame and the Founding Fathers,* ed. Trevor Colburn (New York: W. W. Norton, 1974), 75–106. Madison and Hamilton were committed to responding to the dominant critique of a large republic from Montesquieu, discussed at the Convention, and raised early in the ratification debates by Brutus. The conventional chronology for Madison's intellectual development of the insistence that the problem would not arise has been the extended eleventh Vice, the June 6 Convention speech, the October 22 letter to Jefferson, and, finally, Federalist 10. It may be, however, that the extended eleventh Vice was written after May 1787 and the June 6 speech written as late as the fall or winter of 1789. An alternative chronology may prove to be the extended eleventh Vice (written most likely during the Convention or at its immediate conclusion), the October 24 letter, Federalist 10, and the rewritten June 6 speech.

14. Federalist 14, DHRC, 14:313–317 (30 November); Federalist 18, DHRC, 14:381–386 (7 December), Federalist 19, DHRC, 14:390–395 (8 December), Federalist 20, DHRC, 14:410–413 (11 December). On explanation and *What,* see DHRC, 14:381 (quoting 1818 notation in *Federalist* copy). Madison had taken additional notes on confederacies. See PJM, 10:273–283 (dating to before 30 November 1787). *defects,* Federalist 21, DHRC, 14:414 (12 December).

15. Federalist 37, DHRC, 15:343–348 (11 January). The essay drew on earlier letters. See Madison to Archibald Stuart, 30 October 1787, PJM, 10:233–234 (comparison should be made to prior system, not the "theory, which each individual may frame in his own mind"); Madison to Stuart, 14 December 1787, PJM, 10:325–326. The essay also seemed to allude to the Franklin publication. Franklin noted, it "astonishes me, Sir, to find this system approaching so near to perfection." Federalist 37 commented, "It is impossible for any man of candor to reflect on this circumstance, without partaking of the astonishment."

16. *Should,* Federalist 38, DHRC, 15:353–360 (12 January). *neither,* Federalist 39, 15:380–386 (16 January). *an expansion,* Federalist 40, DHRC, 15:403–410. Federalist 40 stated that, to address the powers of the Convention, one "ought in strictness" to inspect the commissions. Madison, however, did not have copies of the delegates' credentials in the Notes. Although the secretary of the Convention apparently retained them, they were not copied into the official journal. See Mary Sarah Bilder, "How Bad Were the Official Records of the Federal Convention?" *George Washington Law Review* 80, no.6 (2012): 1666–1667.

17. Federalist 41, DHRC, 15:418–425 (19 January). Madison ignored the verb change between the Articles and the Constitution. The Articles provided, "All charges of war, and all other expenses that shall be incurred for the common defense or general welfare," to be permitted from the general treasury. DHRC, 1:86, 89. The Constitution used the phrase, "to pay the Debts and provide for the common Defence and general Welfare. . . ." DHRC, 306, 309. On the engrossed Constitution, section 8 appears to be one sentence:

> Section 8. The Congress shall have Power To lay and collect Taxes, Duties, Imposts and Excises, to pay the Debts and Provide for the common Defence and general Welfare of the United States; but all Duties, Imposts and Excises shall be uniform throughout the United States;
>
> To borrow Money on the credit of the United States; . . .

DHRC, 1:309. Madison seemed to be arguing that the semicolon had meaning; *general welfare* referred to the remaining aspects of the "sentence"; i.e., the subsequent enumerated powers ("To . . ."). The significance, if any, of the punctuation is uncertain. The August 6 report used semicolons to separate various powers, but section 1 stated only, "The Legislature of the United States shall have the power to lay and collect taxes, duties, imposts, and excises;." DHRC, 1:264; DHC, 1:293. The clause first appeared in the committee report on September 4 (which included Madison): "The Legislature shall have power to lay and collect taxes, duties, imposts, and excises, to pay the debts and provide for the common defence and general welfare of the United States." Convention (Journal), DHC, 1:177 (4 September 1787). The September 12 report made two punctuation changes: the addition of a semicolon added after "excises"; periods at the end of the phrases describing powers. The report provided:

> Sect. 8. The Congress may by joint ballot appoint a treasurer. They shall have power
>
> To lay and collect taxes, duties, imposts and excises; to pay the debts and provide for the common defence and general welfare of the United States.
>
> To borrow money on the credit of the United States.

DHRC, 1:289. On the printed copy used by Washington and Jackson, the apparent punctuation change is the addition of a colon after the "general welfare of the United States" to add the phrase, "but all Duties, Imposts and Excises shall be uniform throughout the United States." PGW (CS), 5:324; George Washington Papers, 1741–1799, series 4, General Correspondence, 1697–1799 (microfilm image 232–234). Madison's printed copy shows no alteration. DHC, 3:724. When the punctuation altered, who altered it to the series of semicolons, the issue of whether the change carried the meaning suggested by Madison, and the merits of arguments surrounding the various punctuation issues lie outside this book.

18. Federalist 42, DHRC, 15:427, 428 (22 January). For Madison's speech, see DHC, 3:550 (17 August). Federalist 43, DHRC, 15:439, 440 (23 January). For Convention discussion over treason, see DHC, 3:568–573 (20 August).

19. Federalist 56, DHRC, 16:129, 132 (16 February) (attributing essay to Madison). For September 17 change, see DHRC, 1; Denys P. Myers, "The History of the Printed Archetype of the Constitution of the United States," S. Doc. No. 49, at 49, reprinted in *The Green Bag: An Entertaining Journal of Law, 2d series,* 11:217 (2008). According to Madison, the motion for the change was made by Gorham, and the President (Washington) spoke in support.

20. *To make,* Constitution, art. 1, section 8, clause 18. *Without,* Federalist 44 (43), DHRC, 15:469–473 (25 January).

21. *Higher sanction,* Federalist 43, DHRC, 15:445. *examples,* Federalist 45, DHRC, 15:477. *all power,* Federalist 48, DHRC, 16:3, 4. *maxim,* Federalist 47, DHRC, 15:499. *some qualified,* Federalist 51, DHRC, 16:43, 45 (attributing essay to Madison). *a people,* Federalist 63, DHRC, 16:292, 294 (1 March) (attributing essay to Madison). *insufficient,* Federalist 58, DHRC, 16:154, 156 (20 February) (attributing essay to Madison).

22. Federalist 54, DHRC, 16:107–111 (attributing essay to Madison).

23. *it is superfluous,* Federalist 62, DHRC, 16:232, 233 (17 February). For discussion of attribution, see *The Federalist,* ed. Robert Scigliano (New York: The Modern Library, 2000), xvi–xli. *ought,* Federalist 63, DHRC, 16:292, 294 (1 March).

24. *Though,* Madison to Jefferson, 10 August 1788, PJM, 11:225–227 (partially in code). *some,* Jefferson to Madison, 18 November 1788, PJM, 11:353.

25. *Proceed,* Madison to Ambrose Madison, 8 November 1787, PJM, 10:243, 244. *every,* Rufus King to Madison, 16 January 1788, PJM, 10:376.

26. *The petty,* John Brown Cutting to Jefferson, 11 July 1788, DHC, 4:770, 773. *if my,* Elbridge Gerry to the Vice President of the Convention of Massachusetts, 21 January 1788, RFC, 3:263–264. *memory,* Caleb Strong in the Massachusetts Convention, 15 January 1788, RFC, 3:247. *endeavor,* Debate in the South Carolina Legislature, 16 January 1788, RFC, 3:248, 250. *not merely,* Luther Martin, Reply to the Maryland Landholder No. X, 7 March 1788, DHRC, 16:342. *copied,* McHenry to Rev. John Carroll, 16 June 1788, "Papers of Dr. James McHenry on the Federal Convention of 1787," *American Historical Review* 11 (1906): 595, 622–623. *intention,* RFC, 3:337 (June 1788). *Judge Yates,* John Lansing to Abraham Yates and Melancton Smith, 3 October 1788, RFC, 3:352, 353. *about sixty,* Tench Coxe to Madison, 16 January 1788, PJM, 10:375 (to be forwarded to Rufus King). *address,* Daniel Carroll to Madison, 28 May 1788, PJM, 11:66–67.

27. For Lansing-Hamilton exchange, see *The Debates and Proceedings of the Constitutional Convention of the State of New York* (New York: Francis Childs, 1788), 28 June 1788, 122–123; PAH, 5:135–136 (newspaper account). *more than,* Daniel Carroll to Madison, 28 May 1788, PJM, 11:62, 64. *the names,* McHenry to Rev. John Carroll, 16 June 1788, "Papers of Dr. James McHenry on the Federal Convention of 1787," *American Historical Review* 11 (1906):595, 622–623; see document III–IX, ibid., 619–624 (letters describing controversy). *a National,* John Mercer to Madison, 28 May 1788, PJM, 11:62, 64. The other names on the list have not been discovered; neither McHenry nor Mercer's draft of the Committee of Detail has been found.

28. Maier, *Ratification,* 252–253; see ibid., 255–314.

29. Maier, *Ratification*, 258–259; DHRC, 9:897–900; PJM, 11:72–76. For Robertson's debates, see *Debates and other proceedings of the Convention of Virginia, convened at Richmond, on Monday the 2d day of June, 1788, for the purpose of deliberating on the Constitution recommended by the Grand Federal Convention. To which is prefixed, the Federal Constitution* (Petersburg: Hunter & Prentis, 1788), vol. 1. Volumes 2 and 3 were printed in 1789. Charles Evans, *American Bibliography* (Chicago: Columbia Press, 1912), 7:278; DHRC, 8:xlv. Robertson printed a revised version in 1805. See *Debates and other proceedings of the Convention of Virginia . . .* 2nd ed. (Richmond: for Ritchie & Worsley and Augustine Davis, 1805). *laughing,* Madison to Eliza House Trist, 21 May 1789, PJM, 12:175–176.

30. *Those worthy, Debates,* 1:36 (4 June 1788). *annihilate,* ibid., 1:43 (4 June). *by drawing,* ibid., 1:46 (4 June). *squints,* ibid., 1:69 (5 June 1788). *Consolidated,* ibid., 1:172–173 (9 June).

31. *Aspersions, Debates,* 1:187 (9 June). *national, Debates* (1805), 371–372. *his memory,* RFC, 3:331 (retreating from another interpretation).

32. *Low, Debates,* 1:95. *not completely,* ibid., 1:102. *a review,* ibid., 1:134–136. *laid up,* Madison to Rufus King, 9 June 1788, 11:102.

33. *Such considerations, Debates* (1805), 263. *reason of,* ibid., 261. *was thought,* ibid. *dishonorable,* ibid., 378. *within,* ibid., 311. *in the grand,* ibid., 139.

34. *Peculiar,* ibid., 377. *reasoning,* ibid., 443–444.

35. *Southern states,* ibid., 322. For August 22 speeches, see DHC, 3:587–588 (Pinckney, General Pinckney, and Baldwin).

36. *A better, Debates* (1805), 322. *no power,* ibid., 444. For 1790 census, see DHRC, 1:300.

37. *Captivated, Debates* (1805), 235; see Jefferson to Madison, 20 December 1787, PJM, 10:336–339 ("captivated by the compromise of the opposite claims of the great & little states"). *the liberty,* Madison to Jefferson, 24 July 1788, PJM, 11:196, 197 (in code).

38. On concerns about a bill of rights, see Madison to Jefferson, 17 October 1788, PJM, 11:295, 297–300. *to be trusted,* George Lee Turberville to Madison, 16 November 1788, PJM, 11:346–347. On Senate election, see Madison to Randolph, 17 October 1788, PJM, 11:304–305; Carrington to Madison, 19 October 1788, PJM, 11:305–306. On November 9, Carrington wrote that Madison had lost the Senate. Carrington to Madison, 9 November 1788, PJM, 11:336.

39. On election, see Madison to Randolph, 2 November 1788, PJM, 11:328, 329. *the nearest,* Benjamin Johnson to Madison, 19 January 1789, PJM, 11:423, 424. *ought to be,* Madison to George Eve, 2 January 1789, PJM, 11:404, 405. On election, see Ketcham, *James Madison,* 275–277; Richard Labunski, *James Madison and the Struggle for the Bill of Rights* (New York: Oxford University Press, 2006), 140–177.

40. *For the summer,* Jefferson to Madison, 18 November 1788, PJM, 11:353, 355. *task,* Madison to Washington, 2 December 1788, PJM, 11:376, 377; Madison to Randolph, 23 November 1788, PJM, 11:362; Madison to Jefferson, 8 December 1788, PJM, 11:381, 384. For speculation on task, see PJM, 11:363, n.1.

41. *We are,* Madison to Jefferson, 30 June 1789, PJM, 12:267, 268; see Madison to Madison, Sr., 5 July 1789, PJM, 12:278. *great many,* Samuel Johnston to Madison, 8 July 1789, PJM, 12:284, 285. For similar sentiment, see Washington to Madison, 5 May 1789, 12:131, 132 ("the first of every thing *in our situation* will serve to establish a Precedent").

42. On access, see Jones to Madison, 28 May 1789, PJM, 12:188; DHFFC, 10:xi–xx. *some idea,* Madison to Jefferson, 9 May 1789, PJM, 12:142–143; see also Madison to Monroe, 13 May 1790, PJM, 12:159–160. *contradictions,* Lee to Madison, 10 June 1789, PJM, 12:212. *Mr. Madison,* 9 April 1789, 10 DHFFC 27 (published 15 April 1789).

43. For Bland, see *Debates,* 4 May 1789, DHFFC, 10:394, 410. *the construction,* ibid., 410. *true,* 408 (*Daily Advertiser*). On oaths, see *Debates,* 6 May 1789, ibid., 481–487. *spirit, Debates,* 15 May 1789, DHFFC 10:691.

44. *Importation, Debates,* 13 May 1789, DHFFC, 10:644. On motion, see ibid., 642. *the fashion,* ibid., 646. *terms,* ibid., 647–649. On debate, see John P. Kaminski, *A Necessary Evil?: Slavery and the Debate over the Constitution* (Madison, WI: Madison House, 1995), 201 (stating that Parker acted "obviously under instructions from James Madison").

45. *It must, Debates,* 18 June 1789, DHFFC, 11:978, 979. On May 19, the House first debated the issue and decided "by a large majority" that the president should have the power. Ibid., 10:718–719. From June 16 to June 24, the power of removal was further debated. DHFFC 10:lxii. Discussions of the 1789 debates for modern interpretations of executive power lie outside the scope of this book.

46. *Absolutely, Debates,* 19 May 1789, DHFFC, 10:727. *highest,* ibid., 10:735.

47. *Does not, Debates,* 16 June 1789, DHFFC, 11:867. *We ought, Debates,* 22 June 1789, DHFFC, 11:1032. *expresses, Debates,* 17 June 1789, DHFFC, 11:927.

48. *All powers, Debates,* 18 June 1789, DHFFC, 11:985. *owned, Debates,* 22 June 179, DHFFC, 11:1035.

49. *Very interesting,* Madison to Edmund Pendleton, 21 June 1789, PJM, 12:251, 252. *the reasonings,* 24 June 1789, PJM, 12:258. For other letters on removal debate, see Madison to Samuel Johnston, 21 June 1789, PJM, 12:249, 250; Madison to Tench Coxe, 24 June 1789, PJM, 12:257. *silence,* Madison to Pendleton, PJM, 12:252. *most,* Madison to Johnston, PJM, 12:250.

50. On introduction, see Labunski, *James Madison,* 191–192. *Bill of rights,* Madison to Jefferson, 27 May 1789, PJM, 12:185, 186. For Sherman, see *Debates,* 8 June 1789, DHFFC, 11:815. For June 8 speech, see *Debates,* 8 June 1789,

804 (*Daily Advertiser* version), 805 (*Daily Gazette* version), 806 (*Gazette of the United States* version), 818–827 (*Congressional Register* version). *form and extent,* Madison to Jefferson, 13 June 1789, PJM, 12:217, 218. For relevant records, see *Creating the Bill of Rights: The Documentary Record from the First Federal Congress,* eds. Helen E. Veit, Kenneth R. Bowling, and Charlene Bangs Bickford (Baltimore: Johns Hopkins Press, 1991). For amendments, see *Creating,* 11–14.

51. For June 8 speech, see *Debates,* 8 June 1789, DHFFC, 11:818–827. *serve to, Debates,* 18 August 1789, DHFFC, 11:1296 (*Gazette of the United States*).

52. For June 8 speech, see *Debates,* 8 June 1789, DHFFC, 11:818–827. *the most valuable, Debates,* 17 August 1789, DHFFC, 11:1292.

53. *Debates,* 8 June 1789, DHFFC, 11:818–827.

54. *Supplemental, Debates,* 13 August 1789, DHFFC, 11:1208. *sacred,* ibid., 11:1209. *long,* ibid., 11:1209–1210.

55. For discussion, see *Debates,* 14 August 1789, 11:1249–1250.

56. See *Creating,* 37–41, 47–50, 3–5, 11; Labunski, *James Madison,* 235–240.

9. Correcting and Revising the Notes

1. For approval, see Madison to Jefferson, 30 June 1789, PJM, 12:267. *Mr. Jefferson,* Madison to Tench Coxe, 17 September 1789, PJM, 12:404. *Mr. Jefferson,* Memorandum for George Washington, [ca. 8 October 1789], PJM, 12:433, 434. For November letter, see Madison to Jefferson, 1 November [1789], PJM, 12:439. For likely arrival, see William Irvine to Madison, 23 November 1789, PJM, 12:454.

2. For appointment, see PTJ, 15:2; Madison to Jefferson, 8 October 1787 [1789], PTJ, 12:433.

3. Madison to Randolph, 21 August 1789, PJM, 12:348, 349.

4. *Do justice,* Madison to Randolph, 12 August 1789, PJM, 12:348, 349. For Notes, see DHC, 3:13–14 (29 May); b.1-3. *make out,* PJM, 12:349. Madison may have planned to copy Randolph's expanded speech into the remaining space on the page and the blank fourth page. b.1-3–b.1-4.

5. Randolph to Madison, 26 September 1789, PJM, 12:421.

6. For debate, see DHFFC, 11:1502–1506 (26 September 1789).

7. *With considerable,* Tench Coxe to Madison, 9 September 1789, PJM, 12:394, 395–397. *the subject,* John Dawson to Madison, 13 September 1789, PJM, 12:399, 400. For Madison's explanation, see Madison to Coxe, 18 September [1789], PJM, 12:409, 410. The comments related to 3 September 1789 in the N.Y. *Daily Advertiser,* 7 September 1789, and were subsequently corrected on 10 September. See PJM 12:396–397 n.1.

8. *Some business,* Madison to Henry Lee, 4 October [1789], PJM, 12:425, 427. For August 20, see MJC, August 20. On Madison's copying process, see

the Evidence, the Manuscripts, Madison's Journal Copy. For official record, see Journal (Convention), DHC, 1:196–197.

9. *Every day,* Madison to Henry Lee, 4 September [1789], PJM, 12:425, 427. *coincide,* Madison to Jefferson, 8 October [1789], PJM, 12:433. On Philadelphia, see Madison to Jefferson, 1 November [1789], PJM, 12:439. On illness, see PJM, 12:xxiv. *too much,* Madison to Alexander Hamilton, 19 November 1789, PJM, 12:449.

10. See MJC, 13 June, 15 June. For August 22, see DHC, 3:592. Madison later revised "See" to "Here insert."

11. For Madison's copy of Rhode Island letters, see Notes, GR142, 147g–j (labeled Note C and Note F). For official copies, see DHC, 1:275–276, 277–279. For delegates list and rules, see Slip 1, b.1-1, Slip 1, b.1-2, b.1-4. The page with a Rhode Island letter contains words ("until the president pass him") indicating that the prior, now missing, page contained the May 28 rules. GR 142, 147g; DHC, 1:53. On Rhode Island ratification, see Pauline Maier, *Ratification: The People Debate the Constitution, 1787–1788* (New York: Simon & Schuster, 2010), 458–459 (29 May 1790). For June 5 motions, see GR 142, 147i (tracking Journal (CWH), DHC, 1:211); MJC, 5 June (tracking Journal (CWH)); Notes, Slip 1, b.10-3 (rephrased). For Madison's views on courts, see, e.g., Madison to Pendleton, 23 September 1789, PJM, 12:418–419; DHFFC, 1353. Madison eventually rewrote the passage when he added it as a slip; however, the appendix is drawn from the journal with a few idiosyncrasies (e.g., the substitution of "namely" for "to wit" and the omission of "C."). His interest in the issue of inferior tribunals may explain the "&c, &c" for language relating to the admission of states. 147i. The Notes contain apparently early references to "Note A" (b.1-1), "Note B" (b.1-2), "Note E" (b.3-3). For argument favoring initial appendix, see Keller and Pierson, *A New Madison,* 25. *the project,* Madison to Alexander White, 24 August 1789, PJM, 12:352–353.

12. MJC, 22 August; Notes, DHC, 3:591; Journal (Convention), DHC, 1:143–144.

13. For motion, see Journal (Convention), DHC, 1:145–146; MJC, 22 August; Notes, DHC, 3:592. Madison later revised by adding "any." *Art. VII,* DHC, 3:578 (21 August). Compare Journal (Convention), DHC, 1:145 ("2nd section of the 7 article") with MJC, 22 August ("2d sect. of 7 art.") with Notes, DHC, 3:592 ("2d sect. art: 7").

14. MJC, 30 August; Notes, DHC, 3:652–653.

15. Notes, DHC, 3:601–603 (23 August); MJC, 23 August; Journal (Convention), DHC, 1:149. Careful examination of the votes may yield evidence on whether Madison likely copied the vote tallies.

16. *From this,* RFC, 2:517 n.3. The paper changes partway through September 6. Notes, b.118, b.119; DHC, 3:687. For particular difficulties, see DHC, 3:689. Madison followed the journal in including in the amended report on September

6: "and the concurrence of a majority of all the States shall be necessary to such choice." DHC, 3:693 (later adding explanatory footnote); MJC, 6 September; Journal (Convention); DHC, 1:186 (showing words added in), 187 (showing words added 7 September). *in order,* DHC, 3:712 (10 September); MJC (10 September); Journal (Convention); DHC, 1:192. For example of alteration relating to 1808 unamendable provision, see DHC, 3:712–713; Journal (Convention); DHC, 1:192 (10 September); MJC (10 September) (following Journal Copy through "provid" until realizing that he wanted to attribute responsibility, although not clearly the language itself, to Rutledge for the 1808 provision).

17. For votes, see DHC, 1:241–242, 227–229. For unrecorded votes and alterations, see RFC, 2:582–583, 604–606, 610–611, 621–622, 641. For Journal, see DHC, 1:196–197. Madison copied only part of the entry for September 14 and added: "The Journal is not continued farther." MJC, 14 September. On September 12, the Journal reflected only the veto change, the bill of rights committee, and duties. DHC, 1:194. For sumptuary committee, see DHC, 3:737–738 (13 September). For substitute sections, see DHC, 3:739–740; DHC, 1:195–196, 241.

18. For letter, see Journal (Convention), DHC, 1:273–274 (draft); DHC, 3:719 (12 September). For records motion, see DHC, 3:770 (17 September); Mary Sarah Bilder, "How Bad Were the Official Records of the Federal Convention?" *George Washington Law Review* 80, no.6 (2012): 1663–1665.

19. *Twenty,* DHC, 3:616. *it was,* DHC, 3:583.

20. *Encouragement.* Memorandum on an African Colony for Freed Slaves, [ca. 20 October 1789], PJM, 12:437–38. For Jefferson's comments, see Thomas Jefferson, *Notes on the State of Virginia* (London: John Stockdale, 1787), 229–233. On petition and debates, see DHFFC, 8:314–338; see also George Van Cleve, *A Slaveholder's Union: Slavery, Politics, and the Constitution in the American Republic* (Chicago: University of Chicago Press, 2010), 187–203; John P. Kaminski, *James Madison: Champion of Liberty and Justice* (Madison, WI: Parallel Press, 2006), 37–39; John P. Kaminski. *A Necessary Evil? Slavery and the Debate over the Constitution* (Madison, WI: Madison House, 1995), 201–230. *relating,* House Committee Report, 5 March 1790, DHFFC, 8:335–337. The delegates disagreed over the relevance, if any, of alleged understandings at the Convention. Thomas Scott of Pennsylvania argued, "[N]or can I think it satisfactory to be told that there was an understanding between the northern and southern members, in the national convention, on this subject." He added, "When we are considering our constitutional powers, we must judge of them by the fact of the instrument . . . , not by the certain understandings that the framers of that instrument may be supposed to have had of each other, and which never transpired. In a word, sir, I think it a very poor compliment to that convention, to suppose they couched the idea of an African slave under the term person; and at any rate, the constitution was in degree obligatory until ratified by a certain

number of state conventions, who I presume cannot be supposed to be acquainted with this understanding in the national convention, and consequently must have ratified it upon its own merits, as apparent on its face." *New-York Daily Gazette,* 26 March 1796, DHFFC, 12:819, 820. *the implication, quiet, New-York Daily Gazette,* 27 March 1790, DHFFC, 12:841–842. *Intemperate,* Madison to Benjamin Rush, 20 March 1790, PJM, 13:109.

21. For example of later filled blank spaces, see, b.1, b.6. The space between the heading and the first line was also often used. See, for example, b.1-2 (28 May). The DHC does not show these revisions as insertions. See, for example, DHC, 3:12–13 (28 May) (revision from Journal Copy), 13 (29 May) (the words before "M^r. C." were likely revisions), 14 (end of 29 May entry was a revision). The DHC is not completely reliable in showing inserts. The editors assumed that small writing was inserted and missed insertions in ample space and, alternatively, mischaracterized words as later insertions. For slips, see the Evidence, Catalogue; Charles R. Keller and George W. Pierson, "A New Madison Manuscript Relating to the Federal Convention of 1787," *American Historical Review* 36 (October 1930): 26–28 (counting 22 slips). For example of slip designed to cover, see DHC, 3:24, Slip 2, b.3-3. For discussion of Jefferson's use of wax, see Summary Description, Thomas Jefferson Papers: An Electronic Archive, Massachusetts Historical Society, http://www.masshist.org/thomasjeffersonpapers/notes/about.php. For description of pin, see Eppes to Madison, 1 November 1810, PJM (PS), 2:609–611 (describing that Hamilton's plan was "fastened with a pin to one of the leaves of the original"). For later slips (Slip 1, b.21-4 (15 June); Slip 1, b.73-4 (25 July)), see Keller and Pierson, "A New Madison," 20, 28.

22. For names, see DHC, 3:8; MJC, 25 May, Journal (Convention), DHC, 1:48–49. *total neglect,* DHFFC, 10:598–599 (11 May 1789). For revisions of names, see 25 May, 28 May, 29 May, 30 May, 31 May, 1 June, 2 June (b.6-2). Madison may have first copied the May 28 rules onto a paper (likely "note B") and later to a large slip. DHC, 3:11–12, Slip 1, b.1-2. The additional rules on May 29 were copied in the blank space on the last page of the first sheet. DHC, 3:14–15, b.1-4.

23. *Other clauses,* DHC, 3:33 (31 May). *Clauses relating,* DHC, 3:29 (31 May). For proposition to resolution, see DHC, 3:29 (31 May). For revised entry endings, see DHC, 3:26 (30 May), 34 (31 May), 62 (4 June), 79–80 (6 June).

24. DHC, 3:9 (25 May), 177 (20 June), b.1-1, b.29-4. Madison may have also added "than from Delaware" on May 30. DHC, 3:26.

25. *At length,* DHC, 3:24, Slip 2, b.3-3 (30 May). For related motions, see Slip 1, b.49-1 (5 July), Slip 1, b.56-2 (12 July), Slip 1, b.57-1 (13 July), Slip 1, b.59-4 (16 July). On judiciary, see Slip 1, b.10-3 (5 June), Slip 1, b.19-3 (12 June), Slip 2, b.19-3 (13 June). For supremacy, see Slip 1, b.61-2 (17 July). For executive, see Slip 1, b.74-2 (26 July). *&c,* DHC, 3:574, Slip 2, b.96-4 (21 August). For British statute, see DHC, 3:571, Slip 1, b.96-2 (20 August).

26. *Insert,* DHC, 3:14 (29 May). For powers, see DHC, 3:555–556, Slip 1, b.93-4 (18 August). For rights, see DHC, 3:565–566, Slip 1, b.95-2 (20 August).

27. DHC, 3:8 (25 May), 38–39, Slip 1, b.5-4 (1 June).

28. For General Pinckney speeches, see DHC, 3:193, b.32-4 (22 June), 212 (25 June). For Ellsworth, see DHC, 3:255 (30 June). For examples of Madison speeches, see DHC, 3:116 (12 June), 352 (July 17). A search for "illegible word" in the DHC transcript will reveal other examples of heavily scored words. A search for "stricken out" will reveal the alterations observed by the DHC editors, as will viewing almost any page of the manuscript in microfilm or digital image.

29. DHC, 8–9, b.1-1.

30. *Rather cautious,* DHC, 3:21 (30 May). *brought,* DHC, 3:33 (31 May). *at different,* DHC, 3:252 (30 June) ("well" followed by an illegible word stricken out). *These,* DHC, 3:273 (5 July). *This,* DHC, 3:173 (20 June).

31. *Civil,* DHC, 3:100 (9 June). *Constitution,* DHC, 3:338 (14 July). *no salary,* DHC, 3:117 (12 June). *equality,* DHC, 3:23 (30 May). *misdeeds,* DHC, 3:89 (8 June) (revision of replaced sheet). *election,* DHC, 3:63 (5 June). *electing,* DHC, 3:96 (9 June). *freeholders,* DHC, 3:427 (25 July). *fixing,* DHC, 3:460 (7 August). *existing,* DHC, 3:32 (31 May). *demagogue,* DHC, 3:26 (31 May), 49 (2 June) (shown as illegible in DHC).

32. *The words,* DHC, 3:23 (30 May). *slaves,* DHC, 3:297 (9 July). *slaves,* DHC, 3:309 (revision), 308 (motion) (11 July).

33. *Rebellion,* DHC, 3:171–172 (20 June). *they were,* DHC, 3:174 (20 June). *the inconveniency,* DHC, 3:437 (26 July). *the subject,* DHC, 3:376 (19 July). *Public,* DHC, 3:363 (18 July). *principle,* DHC, 3:27 (31 May).

34. *The Rich,* DHC, 3:265 (2 July). *We cannot,* DHC, 3:275 (5 July).

35. *Reduced,* DHC, 3:318 (11 July). *Domestic,* DHC, 3:477 (8 August). *Here then,* DHC, 3:134 (16 June).

36. *Be stable,* DHC, 3:29 (31 May). *would,* DHC, 3:57 (4 June). *the two,* DHC, 3:232 (28 June). *was reduced,* DHC, 3:272 (5 July). *evil mentioned,* DHC, 3:436 (26 July). *obnoxious,* DHC, 3:496 (10 August). *the word,* DHC, 3:517 (13 August).

37. *He illustrated,* DHC, 3:160 (19 June). *during,* DHC, 3:159 (19 June). *He thought,* DHC, 3:161 (19 June). *Let them,* DHC, 3:162 (19 June). *no superstructure,* DHC, 3:338 (14 July). *the perpetuity,* DHC, 3:341 (14 July).

38. For insertions, see the DHC. For Franklyn and Gherry, see, e.g., DHC, 3:42–43 (2 June). For added "c," see Slip 1, b.1-1 (delegates names). For example of "C," see DHC, 3:35 (1 June). *certain,* DHC, 3:228 (28 June). *communicate,* DHC, 3:267 (2 July). *partly, equality,* DHC, 3:245–247 (29 June). *Revision,* DHC, 3:133 (16 June). *He is,* DHC, 3:42 (2 June).

39. *The deputies,* DHC, 3:24 (30 May). *For instruction,* DHC, 3:9, b.1-1 (25 May). On Randolph, see DHC, 3:53 (Wilson), 54 (Gerry) (4 June). *favor,* DHC,

3:52 (2 June). *family,* DHC, 3:85 (June 7). *family,* DHC, 3:84. *money bills,* DHC, 3:118 (13 June); for Madison comment, see DHC, 3:119. *rash,* DHC, 3:268 (2 July). *we have,* DHC, 3:261 (30 June). *by y^e, fixed,* DHC, 3:460 (7 August).

40. 5 July footnote, DHC, 3:270; 13 July footnote, DHC, 3:326. 29 August footnote, DHC, 3:647; 5 September footnote, DHC, 3:683; 9 September footnote, DHC, 3:708.

41. For 28 May footnote, see DHC, 3:10, Slip b.1-1.2. For footnotes, see DHC, 3:83 (7 June), 117 (12 June), 212 (25 June). The style of the footnotes differs, for example, between an X and a dotted X. For N.B. example, see DHC, 3:124 (15 June), 422 (24 July). *this hint,* DHC, 3:66–67 (5 June).

42. For 5 June speech, see DHC, 3:67, b.20-4 (original sheet to "Republic with"), b.21-1 (replaced sheet). For motion, see DHC, 3:68. Madison scratched out a now illegible word and wrote "establishing." For debates, see *Debates on the Federal Judiciary: A Documentary History* (Washington, D.C.: Federal Judicial Center, 2013), 1:53–66; Maeva Marcus and Natalie Wexler, "The Judiciary Act of 1789," in *Origins of the Federal Judiciary: Essays on the Judiciary Act of 1789,* ed. Maeva Marcus (New York: Oxford University Press, 1992), 13–39; Charlene Bangs Bickford and Kenneth R. Bowling, *Birth of the Nation: The First Federal Congress, 1789–1791* (Madison, WI: Madison House, 1989), 45–49; Wythe Holt; "'To Establish Justice'" Politics, The Judiciary Act of 1789, and the Invention of the Federal Courts," *Duke Law Journal* (1990) 40:1421–1531.

43. For speech, see DHC, 3:72–74, b.11-4, b.12-1 (6 June). For discussion of October 1787 letter and Federalist 10, see Chapter 8. For helpful discussion of idiosyncratic nature of Madisonian federalism, see Max M. Edling, *A Revolution in Favor of Government: Origins of the U.S. Constitution and the Making of the American State* (New York: Oxford University Press, 2003), 3–10.

44. *We have,* DHC, 3:74, b.12-1. *distinction of color,* Petition from the Pennsylvania Abolition Society, 3 February 1790 (15 February 1790), DHFFC, 8:324–326. *the abominable practice,* 17 March 1790, *Daily Advertiser,* 20 March 1790, DHFFC, 749, 752–753.

45. *Co-ordinate,* DHC, 3:78 (6 June); see "coordinate," Federalist 48 (1 February 1788), DHRC, 16:3, 5 ("the co-ordinate departments"), Federalist 49 (2 February 1788), DHRC, 16:16 ("departments being perfectly co-ordinate"). *rights,* DHC, 3:78; see Madison's Speech on Amendments, 8 June 1789, PJM, 12:196, 207.

46. DHC, 3:85–86, b.14-1 (7 June); DHC, 3:88–89, b.14-3 (8 June). For versions, see SRFC, 61 (8 June) (Butler: "No Line can be drawn between the State Governments and the General Government"); 60 (Lansing: "Madison—wished the precise Line of Power could be ascertained—But totally impracticable"); RFC, 1:169 (Yates: "Mr Madison wished that the line of jurisprudence could be drawn—he would be for it—but upon reflection he finds it impossible"). *the impossibility,* Madison to Jefferson, 24 October 1787, PJM, 10:205, 211. For

Federalist 37, see DHRC, 15:343, 345 ("Not less arduous must have been the task of marking the proper line of partition, between the authority of the general, and that of the State Governments."). For Judiciary Act, see An Act to establish the Judicial Courts of the United States, 24 September 1789, Statute 1, Statutes at Large, 1st Congress, 1st Session, ch. 20, 73–93.

47. *A ride,* Madison to Washington, 4 January 1790, PJM, 12:466, 467. *forgot,* Jefferson to Madison, 9 January 1790, PJM, 12:469. *domestic,* Madison to Washington, 4 January 1790, PJM, 12:466, 467. *very,* Washington to Jefferson, 21 January 1790, PTJ, 16:116–117. *remain,* Madison to Eliza Trist, 31 January 1790, PJM, 13:11; see also Madison to Jefferson, 24 January 1790, PJM, 13:3–4.

48. *Slight,* Madison to Washington, 4 January 1790, PJM, 12:467; see also Madison to Madison, Sr., 21 January 1790, PJM, 13:1; Madison to Jefferson, 24 January 1790, PJM, 13:3. For attendance, see PJM, 13:xxvii. On secretary of state, see Jefferson to Madison, 14 February 1790, PJM, 13:41. On Jefferson's arrival, see PTJ, 16:3.

10. The Influence of Mr. Jefferson

1. On Jefferson's return to Norfolk, Virginia, November 23, 1789, see PTJ, 15:2; 16:vii–ix.

2. Jefferson to Madison, 6 September 1789, PTJ, 15:384, 396; see also ibid., 389; PTJ, 16:146, 147.

3. Madison to Jefferson, 4 February 1790, PJM, 13:18–21; PTJ, 16:147. For a discussion of Madison's revisions to letter and revised copy (1799 watermark), see PJM, 13:25 n.; PTJ, 16:146–147.

4. For collaboration, see Jefferson to Madison, [ca. 30 March 1790], PJM, 13:130 (mode of communication to Congress); Queries concerning Jefferson's Report on Weights and Measures [ca. 20 May 1790], PJM, 13:226–227. For general discussion, see Adrienne Koch, *Jefferson and Madison: The Great Collaboration* (New York: Knopf, 1950), 97–108. *duplicate,* Randolph to Madison, 23 March 1790, PJM, 13:116 [*sic*]. *expeditious,* Madison to Jefferson, 30 June 1789, PJM, 12:267, 272. *very,* Jefferson to Short, 7 May 1790, PTJ, 16:443–444.

5. *Executive,* PTJ, 16:380 n.; Stuart Leibiger, *Founding Friendship: George Washington, James Madison, and the Creation of the American Republic* (Charlottesville: University of Virginia Press, 1999), 112. For Jefferson's opinion, see Jefferson's Opinion on the Powers of the Senate Respecting Diplomatic Appointments, 24 April 1790, PTJ, 16:378–382. On controversy and dinner, see PJM, 13:244–246; Koch, *Jefferson and Madison,* 103–108; Andrew Burstein and Nancy Isenberg, *Madison and Jefferson* (New York, Random House, 2010), 218–219. *the votes,* Madison to Pendleton, 22 June 1790, PJM, 13:252. *had lost,* Jefferson, Memorandum on the Compromise of 1790, *Liberty and Order,* 64–65.

6. For law study, see Jefferson to John Garland Jefferson, 11 June 1790, PTJ, 16:480–482. For weights and measures, see PTJ, 16:602–617, 623–675. For arrearage opinion, see PTJ, 16:455–462, 468–470. For Jefferson's analysis of residence bill, see 17:163–183, 194, 195, 197.

7. On visits, see Madison to Washington, 17 November 1790, PJM, 13:297. For list, see PJM, 13:286–89. The list included "Jefferson's Notes" (perhaps the *Notes on the State of Virginia*).

8. For invitation, see Jefferson to Francis Eppes, 8 October 1790, PTJ, 17:581. For response, Francis Eppes to Jefferson, 14 October 1790, PTJ, 17:592. On the family, see Annette Gordon-Reed, *The Hemingses of Monticello: An American Family* (New York: W. W. Norton, 2008), 163.

9. *The desire*, Jefferson to Washington, 27 October 1790, PTJ, 17:643. *Negroes*, Instructions for the Montpelier Overseer and Laborers, [ca. 8] November 1790, PJM, 13:302–304. On Philadelphia, see PJM, 13:xxvii.

10. *Bank*, Jefferson to Mason, 4 February 1791, PTJ, 19:241–242. On national bank, see *Legislative and Documentary History of the Bank of the United States*, eds. M. St. Clair Clarke & D. A. Hall (1832; New York: Augustus M. Kelley, 1967), 39; H. Jefferson Powell, *A Community Built on Words: The Constitution in History and Politics* (Chicago: University of Chicago Press, 2002), 21–29; Benjamin B. Klubes, "The First Federal Congress and the First National Bank: A Case Study in Constitutional Interpretation," *Journal of the Early Republic* 10 (1990): 19, 21–22; Colleen A. Sheehan, "Madison v. Hamilton: The Battle over Republicanism and the Role of Public Opinion," *American Political Science Review* 98 (2004): 405–406. For Hamilton's opinion, 13 December 1790, see PAH, 7:236–342. On congressional debates, see *Legislative and Documentary History of the Bank*.

11. *Well recollected*, Madison, 2 February 1791, PJM, 13:372, 374; see DHFFC, 14:366–381. For Sherman, Memorandum from Sherman to Madison [ca. 4 February] 1791, PJM, 13:382. *proceeded to*, Boudinot, 5 February 1791, DHFFC, 14:437. *If Congress*, Ames, 3 February 1791, ibid., 14:392. *that the power*, Sedgwick, 4 February 1791, ibid., 14:398–399.

12. Opinion on the Constitutionality of the Bill for Establishing a National Bank, 15 February 1791, PTJ, 19:275, 277–278. For Notes, DHC, 3:745.

13. *One*, PTJ, 19:277–278. For Notes, see DHC, 3:744–745.

14. For Journal, see DHC, 1:196–197, 228; in general, see Mary Sarah Bilder, "How Bad Were the Official Records of the Federal Convention?" *George Washington Law Review* 80, no.6 (2012):1671–1674. Madison's anti-incorporation stance seemed to differ from his inclinations during the Convention. On August 18, Madison had proposed a general congressional incorporation power. Its absence in the final draft as plausibly indicated the delegates' belief that the power was already in Congress, as that the power was explicitly rejected. For August 18 list, see Journal, DHC, 1:130–132; RFC, 2:324–325.

15. *Multiplication,* Jefferson to Ebenezer Hazard, 18 February 1791, PTJ, 19:287–289. *double,* Madison to Jefferson, 17 July 1810, PJM (RS), 2:418–419. *the sooner,* Jefferson to Francis Eppes, 14 March 1791, PTJ, 19:554.

16. *Anti-monarchical,* Jefferson to Washington, 8 May 1791, PTJ, 20:291–292; *Halfway-house,* Jefferson to Mason, 4 February 1791, PTJ, 19:241–242. On edition, see PTJ, 20:268–290. *the political heresies,* Jefferson to Jonathan B. Smith, 26 April 1791, PTJ, 20:290 n.1. *views,* Jefferson to Washington, 8 May 1791, PTJ, 20:291–292. The politics of 1791 are controversial. Julian Boyd cast Jefferson in the starring role, already opposed by the "intrigue and deception" of Hamilton. PTJ, 18:282.

17. *Great hopes,* Jefferson to Washington, 20 June 1791, PTJ, 20:558–559. On trip, see PTJ, 20:434–453; *The Tour to the Northern Lakes of James Madison & Thomas Jefferson, May–June 1791,* ed. J. Robert Maguire (Ticonderoga, NY: Fort Ticonderoga, 1995); Gordon Wood, *Empire of Liberty: A History of the Early Republic, 1789–1815* (New York: Oxford University Press, 2009), 146–147. On Freneau, see PTJ, 20:453; Burstein, *Madison and Jefferson,* 232; Koch, *Jefferson and Madison,* 120; Ralph Ketcham, *James Madison: A Biography* (Charlottesville: University of Virginia Press, 1990), 332.

18. *Fox,* Richard Peters to Jefferson, 26 June 1791, PTJ, 20:590. *a bad,* Jefferson to Peters, 30 June 1791, PTJ, 20:573. *I have,* Charles Pinckney to Madison, 6 August 1791, PJM, 14:66, 68.

19. On Eppes's arrival, Jefferson to Mary Jefferson, 24 April 1791, PTJ, 20:250. *write,* Jefferson to Francis Eppes, 15 May 1791, PTJ, 20:412–413. *I fear, the badness,* John Wayles Eppes to Jefferson, 1 May 1793, PTJ, 25:632–633.

20. The Madison Papers, volume 1, Edward Everett Papers, 1675–1910, Ms. N-1201, vol. 229 (MHS).

21. See discussion in the Evidence, the Manuscripts, Jefferson's Copy.

22. See discussion in the Evidence, the Manuscripts, Jefferson's Copy.

23. *I am, papers,* Madison to Jefferson, [13 March] 1791, PJM, 13:405. *come,* Jefferson to Madison, 13 March 1791, PJM, 13:404. On possible task, see PTJ, 19:544–552; PJM, 10:7–8.

24. Eppes to Madison, 1 November 1810, PJM (PS), 2:609–611.

25. Eppes to Madison, 1 November 1810, PJM (PS), 2:609–611.

26. The extent of the *Anas* is debated. The *Jefferson Papers* editors argue that Jefferson intended in 1818 only to compile the documents from 1791 through December 1793. PTJ, 22:33–38. For one version, see *The Writings of Thomas Jefferson,* ed. H. A. Washington (Washington, DC: Taylor & Maury, 1854), 9:87–211. For an edition in supposed order, see *The Complete Anas of Thomas Jefferson,* ed. Franklin B. Sawvel (New York: Round Table Press, 1903). On the *Anas,* see Joanne Freeman, "Slander, Poison, Whispers, and Fame: Jefferson's 'Anas' and Political Gossip in the Early Republic," *Journal of the Early Republic* 15 (1995): 25–57; Joanne B. Freeman, *Affairs of Honor: National Politics in the*

New Republic (New Haven: Yale University Press, 2001), 62–104. On charges against Hamilton, see Merrill D. Peterson, *The Jefferson Image in the American Mind* (1960; Charlottesville: University of Virginia Press,1998), 33–34. On toning down, see Freeman, *Affairs,* 101–102. *nearly as,* Jefferson, 29 February (1 March 1792), PTJ, 23:184, 187. *calm revisal,* PTJ, 22:34.

27. *British,* Notes, 13 August 1791, PTJ, 22:38–39. *a high,* Memorandum, 12 March 1792, PTJ, 23:258–230. *treasury,* Memorandum, 28 February (1 March) 1792, PTJ, 23:184. *such,* Memorandum, 29 February (1 March) 1792, PTJ, 23:186. For Agenda [ca. 11 July 1792], see PTJ, 24:215–217.

28. *Internal,* Washington to Jefferson, 23 August 1792, PTJ, 24:315–318. *undermine,* Jefferson to Washington, 9 September 1792, PTJ, 24:351–360.

29. Notes, 30 September 1792, PTJ, 24:428–429. For discussion of Mason's imperfect reflection, see ibid., 428–429 n. On September 30, 1792 visit, see RFC, 3:367.

30. *Numerous,* Notes, 1 October 1792, PTJ, 24:433–436. On dinner, see Notes, 11 November 1792, PTJ, 24:607. On rumor, see Notes, 19 November 1792, PTJ, 24:638. *fact,* Notes, 7 June 1793, PTJ, 26:219–221. On document (2 February 1793), see PTJ, 25:155n.

31. *Paper-men,* Notes, 23 March 1793, PTJ 25:432–435. *cleansed,* Notes, 7 February 1793, PTJ, 25:153–155. *affair,* Notes, 17 December 1792, PTJ, 24:751. *were,* Notes, 6 May 1793 (regarding 18 April meeting), PTJ, 25:665–667. For 1793 end, see *The Complete Anas,* 187.

32. *Certainly,* Notes, 23 May 1793, PTJ, 26:101–102. *the Minister,* Notes, 21 July 1793, PTJ, 26:545. *Republican,* Jefferson to Madison, 11 August 1793, PTJ, 26:651–654. *by accident,* Notes, 28 November 1793, PTJ, 27:453–456.

33. *There were,* Notes, 10 July 1792, PTJ, 24:210–212. *ten,* Notes, 1 October 1792, PTJ, 24:433–436. *believed,* Notes, 6 August 1793, PTJ, 26:627–630. On the pivotal nature of July 1792, see Jack Rakove, *Revolutionaries: A New History of the Invention of America* (Boston: Houghton Mifflin Harcourt, 2011), 435–441.

34. *Too republican, National Gazette,* 8 September 1792, [1:359]. *highest,* [Hamilton], Amicus, *National Gazette,* 11 September 1792, [1:362]; PAH, 12:354–357. For discussion of Hamilton's reference to the Convention, see John C. Hamilton, *The Life of Alexander Hamilton* (New York: D. Appleton & Co., 1841), 2:465. For references to related accusations in the *New-York Journal,* see James Watson to Hamilton, 30 August 1793, PAH, 15:311–312; DHC, 5:249–250. In July, Freneau published "Rules for changing a limited Republican Government into an unlimited hereditary one," *National Gazette,* 4 and 7 July 1792, [1:281, 285]; *Liberty and Order,* 111–115. On Hamilton-Jefferson-Freneau conflict, see Stanley M. Elkins with Eric L. McKitrick, *The Age of Federalism* (New York: Oxford University Press, 1993), 282–292. On press, see Jerry W.

Knudson, *Jefferson and the Press: Crucible of Liberty* (Columbia: University of South Carolina Press, 2006).

35. *Briefly,* Madison to Pendleton, 4 April 1790, PJM, 13:138–139. For response, see Pendleton to Madison, 21 April 1790, PJM, 13:154–157. *knowing,* see Madison to Pendleton, 2 May 1790, PJM, 13:184–185.

36. On essays, see PJM, 14:110–112; Colleen Sheehan, "The Politics of Public Opinion: James Madison's 'Notes on Government,'" *William and Mary Quarterly* 49 (Oct. 1992): 609–627. *consolidation,* Government of the United States, 4 February 1792, PJM, 14:217, 218. For Notes on Federal Government, see Madison Papers (DLC); PJM, 14:157–169. *influence,* PJM, 14:158. Madison discussed the effect of slavery and freehold property requirements on politics. He described the "Southern States" as "aristocracies." Madison noted that government would operate differently if "the slaves [were] freed and the right of suffrage extended to all." Ibid., 163.

37. *Openly,* A Candid State of Parties, 22 September 1792, PJM, 14:370–372. The sentence is oddly reminiscent of the Yates's version of Madison's June 26 speech. *Who are,* Who are the Best Keepers . . . , 20 December 1790, PJM, 14:426–427. The overlap between these essays and the seemingly missing sentences from Madison's original speeches raises the possibility that he was writing by criticizing his former positions.

38. Notes on William Loughton Smith's *Politicks and Views,* [ca. 4 November 1792], PJM, 14:396–402. For pamphlet, see [William Loughton Smith], *The Politicks and Views of a Certain Party, Displayed* (1792).

39. For five sheets, see the Evidence, the Manuscripts, Five Replaced Sheets. For general discussion of Madison during these years, see Colleen A. Sheehan, *James Madison and the Spirit of Republican Self-Government* (Cambridge: Cambridge University Press, 2009).

40. For "Republican Govern[men]t," see DHC, 3:216 (June 26), DHC, 3:361, 362 (July 17). For other example, see DHC, 3:28, 31 May (Wilson) ("republican Government").

41. *Not to be,* footnote, 17 July, b.62; DHC, 3:358–359. *in case,* Madison to Jefferson, 24 October 1787, PJM, 10:205, 207–215. It was part of the text (although also marked with brackets to be moved to a footnote). Madison may have drawn on material in the original pages, although the attenuated phrasing would have been unusual for the Notes' style. Madison then added a now partially illegible sentence referring to the number of "avowed friends" of the executive on good behavior and those who "privately" favored the tenure.

42. For August 7 speech, see Notes, b.80; DHC, 3:467–468; RFC, 2:204. For comment in appendix, see Payne Copy, page 807 (DLC). For two other versions, see Papers (Gilpin), 3:Appendix, No. 4, viii–xiv; *Writings* (Hunt), 4:121–127, n.1. For *National Gazette* essay, Property, 27 March 1792, see PJM, 14:266–268. King recorded Madison arguing that the right of election should be "confin[e]d

to Freeholders." RFC, 2:208. McHenry noted that Madison had supported Mason's arguments that if the process was open to all freemen it would be an aristocracy. Ibid., 2:209–210. The lengthy speech began nearly the same way—discussing the various permutations available by which freeholders, property holders, and those without property might be represented. Although far too long to replace the original speech, its existence suggests that Madison wanted to revise it. A note later stated that Madison had "felt too much at the time the example of Virginia." Papers (Gilpin), 3:Appendix, ix.

43. *Even after,* Jefferson to Madison, 1 October 1792, PTJ, 24:432; Fawn M. Brodie, *Thomas Jefferson: An Intimate History* (New York: W.W. Norton, 1974), 276–286. For farewell address draft, see Madison's Draft, 20 June 1792, PGW (PS), 10:480–484. *from 1793,* Jefferson to Mary Jefferson Eppes, 3 March 1802, PTJ, 36:676–677.

44. On Trist, see Ketcham, *Madison,* 88; Burstein and Isenberg, *Madison & Jefferson,* 272. On marriage to Dolley Payne, see Note, PJM, 15:341–342. On Virginia visit, see Jones to Madison, 14 August 1794, 15:350.

45. For September 7 and 8, see b.121 and b.122. The September 15 entry is not extant in the Jefferson Copy. Notes, b.129 and b.130.

46. For Washington's notions, Journal, DHC, 1:178–179 (September 4); RFC, 2:493 n.1. Madison had copied these notations into his Journal Copy. Journal Copy, September 4 ("of the whole number," "appointed," "except treaties of peace"). On "immediately," see RFC, 2:498 n.12. For Eppes's note, see Jefferson Copy, September 8, [page 120]. For possibly related note, see RFC, 4:58 (1937) (discussing memo on treaty of peace).

47. *For god's sake, my,* Jefferson to Madison, 7 July 1793, PJM, 15:43. On 1793 essays, see *The Pacificus-Helvidius Debates of 1793–1794: Toward the Completion of the American Founding,* ed. Morton J. Frisch (Indianapolis: Liberty Fund, 2007). For Camillus essays, see PAH, volume 18; *Liberty and Order,* 197–202. *for god's sake take,* Jefferson to Madison, 21 September 1795, PJM, 16:88–89. On Jay treaty, see Jerald A. Combs, *The Jay Treaty: Political Battleground of the Founding* Fathers (Berkeley: University of California Press, 1970); Todd Estes, *The Jay Treaty Debate, Public Opinion, and the Evolution of Early American Political Culture* (Amherst: University of Massachusetts Press, 2006); Mary Sarah Bilder, "How Bad Were the Official Records of the Federal Convention?" *George Washington Law Review* 80, no.6 (2012): 1674–1679. For visit, see PJM, 16:xxvi; Madison to Jefferson, 18 October 1795, PJM, 16:104–105. Madison later wrote that he left a "packet of papers promised to you." The Madison Papers editors suggest that these papers were the Notes. Madison to Jefferson, 8 November 1795, PJM, 16:121–122 n.1.

48. *To suppose, intent* [Hamilton], The Defence No. XXXVIII [Camillus 38], [9 January 1796], PAH, 20:22–34. On Washington's response, see Bilder, "How Bad," 1677–1678. On deposit, see RFC, 3:370. For message, see George

Washington to the House of Representatives (30 March 1796), *A Compilation of the Messages and Papers of the Presidents*, ed. James D. Richardson (New York: Bureau of National Literature and Art, 1896), 1:94–196. For further discussion, see Bilder, "How Bad," 1674–1676.

49. For Madison's letter to Jefferson, see Madison to Jefferson, 4 April 1796, PJM, 16:286–287. For Madison's speech, see Speech, 6 April 1796, PJM, 16:290–301. For more extensive discussion of the episode and speech, see Bilder, "How Bad," 1676–1679. Madison's paragraph on the ratification debates is often quoted (as it underlies certain modern constitutional originalist theories) but almost always without the larger context in which the argument was discussed. For discussion of modern use, see Jack Rakove, *Original Meanings: Politics and Ideas in the Making of the Constitution* (New York: Random House, 1997), 17–18.

50. For sheets, see b.129–b.130 (September 15); b.131–b.132 (September 17). These sheets are on Budgen paper. The replaced sheet for September 7 (b.121) is Budgen paper. In addition, slip b.1-2 (May 28) with the additional rules is on Budgen paper. The last sheet for September 7–8 (b.122) bears the countermark, Taylor. The sheets for September 17 appear to match Jefferson's transcription of them in 1796 and are also similar to the Jefferson Copy. See Jefferson to Madison, 17 April 1796, PJM, 16:328–330.

51. On missing letters, see PTJ, 29:186 n. On marriage, see Eppes to Jefferson, 25 September 1796, PTJ, 29:186.

52. On return, see PJM, 16:xxvii. For last sheet inserted in the Notes, see b.122. On announcement, see PJM, 16:xxviii.

53. On return to Virginia, see PJM, 16:xxviii.

54. Stanhope Smith to Madison, 4 January 1795, PJM, 15:436–437.

55. Jefferson to Madison, 16 January 1799, PJM, 17:208–211; PTJ, 30:622–625.

56. Madison to Jefferson, 8 February 1799, PJM, 17:229–230.

57. Madison to Jefferson, 8 February 1799, PJM, 17:229–230.

58. Madison to Jefferson, 8 February 1799, PJM, 17:229–230. Jefferson continued to urge Madison to write. Jefferson to Madison, 5 February 1799, PTJ, 31:9–11. Historians disagree over whether Madison complied by writing two additional anonymous essays in the *Aurora General Advertiser* in January and February 1799. PJM, 17:211–214. On delegates: a chronological list of death dates appears in Charles Warren, *The Making of the Constitution* (Boston: Little, Brown and Co., 1937), 813–814.

59. On the Kentucky Resolutions (10 November 1798), see PTJ, 30:529–556. On the Virginia resolutions (21 December 1798), see PJM, 17:185–191. *a compact*, Jefferson's Fair Copy, PTJ, 30:543. Madison's Virginia Resolutions employed the compact language but seemed less emphatic. For apparent wavering,

see Madison to Jefferson, 29 December 1798, PJM, 17: 191–192. *palpable violations,* Jefferson to Madison, 23 August 1799, PTJ, 31:172–174.

Conclusion

1. Jefferson to Adams, 10–[11] August 1815, *The Adams-Jefferson Letters: The Complete Correspondence between Thomas Jefferson and Abigail and John Adams,* ed. Lester J. Capon (Chapel Hill: University of North Carolina Press, 1959), 2:452, 453; Adams to Jefferson (Aug. 24, 1815), ibid. 2:454, 455. Adams worried that published material on the Revolution diverged from his memory. A printed speech "appeared to me very different from that, which you, and I heard." Jefferson agreed that the Revolution posed a problem because the "councils, designs and discussions" were "conducted by Congress with closed doors, and no member, as far as I know, having even made notes of them." Jefferson had taken a few notes, but found them unsatisfactory. The speeches were "the heads of arguments," or in "one mass, without ascribing to the speakers their respective arguments." Adams to Jefferson and Thomas McKean, July 30, 1815, ibid., 2:451; Jefferson to Adams, 10–[11] August 1815, ibid., 2:452–453 [*sic*].

2. Adams to Jefferson (24 August 1815), *Adams-Jefferson Letters,* 2:454, 455.

3. *Memoirs and Letters of Dolly Madison,* ed. Lucia B. Cutts (Boston: Houghton, Mifflin and Company, 1886), 198.

4. Jefferson to Judge William Johnson, 4 March 1823, *The Works of Thomas Jefferson,* ed. Paul L. Ford (New York: G.P. Putnam's Sons, 1904–1905), 12:277.

5. For letter, see Hamilton to Timothy Pickering, 16 September 1803, PAH, 26:147–149; see also Timothy Pickering to Hamilton, 5 April 1803, ibid. 26:102–104. For 1812 printing, see "Gen. Alexander Hamilton," *The Weekly Register,* ed. H. Niles, 7 November 1812, 3:148–149. On 1798 printing in the *Aurora,* 13 January 1798, see Louise Burnham Dunbar, *A Study of "Monarchical" Tendencies in the United States, from 1776 to 1801* (1923; New York: Johnson Reprint Corp, 1970), 125–126. For 1801 printing, see John Franklin Jameson, "Studies in the History of the Federal Convention of 1787," *Annual Report of the American Historical Association* (1902), 1:148 (describing William Cobbett's publication in *Porcupine's Works,* volume 1).

6. John Wayles Eppes to Madison, 1 November 1810, PJM (PS), 2:609–611; *your Original,* Jefferson to Madison, 26 July 1810, ibid., 2:440–441. Madison sent an extract from his June 18 notes for use in a biography. See Madison to John Mitchell Mason, 12 January 12 1810, ibid., 2:174; see William Lewis to Madison, 30 December 1809, ibid., 2:152. For Madison's suggestion of the "fallibility of Mr. H's memory," see "Madison's Detached Memoranda," ca. 31 January 1820, PJM (RS), 1:598, 618–619. For discussion by son, see John C.

Hamilton, *History of the Republic of the United States* (New York: D. Appleton & Co., 1857–1865), 3:340–347.

7. Madison to Gales and Seaton, 2 February 1818, PJM (RS), 1:213–214. On Gideon edition, see *The Federalist, on the new Constitution,* ed. Jacob Gideon (Washington: Jacob Gideon, Jr., 1818), 3; Irving Brant, *James Madison, Commander in Chief, 1812–1836* (Indianapolis: Bobbs-Merrill, 1961), 426–428. For review of controversy, see *The Federalist,* ed. J. R. Pole (Indianapolis: Hackett Publishing Co., 2005), xxiii; *The Federalist, a Commentary,* ed. Robert Scigliano (New York: Modern Library, 2000), xvi–xxiv.

8. *Journal, acts and proceedings of the convention, assembled at Philadelphia, Monday, May 14, and dissolved Monday, September 17, 1787, which formed the Constitution of the United States* . . . (Boston: Thomas B. Wait, 1819), 9. On project, see Adams to Madison, 22 October 1818, PJM (RS) 1:367–370; Madison to Adams, 2 November 1818, ibid. 1:372 (PJM editors could not find letter in 2008); Madison to Adams, 7 June 1819, ibid. 1:465; Madison to Adams, 27 June 1819, ibid. 1:476; Mary Sarah Bilder, "How Bad Were the Official Records of the Federal Convention?" *George Washington Law Review* 80, no.6 (2012): 1626, 1646, 1680. On missing list of ayes and nays, see Bilder, "How Bad," 1646 n.211.

9. For plans and documents, see *Journal, acts and proceedings,* 123–134. On credentials, see *Journal, acts and proceedings,* 3–58; Bilder, "How Bad," 1666–1667. For Pinckney's plan, see *Journal, acts and proceedings,* 71–81. *not find,* Madison to Adams, 2 November 1818, PJM (RS), 1:367–369; see Adams to William Jackson, 16 October 1818, SRFC, 307–308; William Jackson to Adams, 19 October 1818, ibid., 309. For Pinckney's letter to Adams and Pinckney draft, see DHC, 1:309–321. For review of controversy over Pinckney plan, see Richard Beeman, *Plain, Honest Men: The Making of the American Constitution* (New York: Random House, 2009), 93–98; Christopher Collier and James Lincoln Collier, *Decision in Philadelphia: The Constitutional Convention of 1787* (New York: Ballantine Books, 1987) 87–101; S. Sidney Ulmer, "James Madison and the Pinckney Plan," *South Carolina Law Quarterly* 9 (1957): 416–443. The Notes collection contains comparisons of the *Journal* and an earlier publication, see Observation on Pinckney's Plan, GR 142, A–F.

10. Madison to John Quincy Adams, 13 June 1820, PJM (RS), 2:67–68.

11. See, for example, DHC 3:42, 51 (June 2), 64, 69 (June 5), 101, 107 (June 11), 110 (June 12).

12. *Secret Proceedings and Debates of the Convention* . . . (Albany: Websters and Skinners, 1821). For excerpts ending July 3, see *American Citizen,* 25 November 1808, p. 9; *Alexandria Gazette,* 12 January 1809, p. 9. For 1813 reprint, see *American Law Journal* 4 (1813): 563–570. For Martin, see *Secret Proceedings,* 9–94 (quotation is at p. 20). On relationship to anti-Madison campaigns, see RFC, 1:xiv; James H. Hutson, "The Creation of the Constitu-

tion: The Integrity of the Documentary Record," *Texas Law Review* 65 (1986): 9–12.

13. Madison to Joseph Gales Jr., 26 August 1821, PJM (RS), 2:378.

14. *American Citizen*, 25 November 1808, p. 9. On controversy, see James H. Hutson, "Robert Yates's Notes on the Constitutional Convention of 1787: Citizen Genet's Edition," *Quarterly Journal of the Library of Congress* 35 (1978): 173; SRFC, xxv–xxvi; Arnold A. Rogow, "The Federal Convention: Madison and Yates," *American Historical Review* 60 (1955): 323–335. For Lansing pages, see Hutson, "Creation," 12, 14–17; compare ibid., 16–17 with RFC, 1:535.

15. RFC, 1:xviii; Max Farrand, "The Records of the Federal Convention," *American Historical Review* 13 (1907): 44, 56–59. For Delaware instruction, see RFC, 1:4 (May 25), 38 (May 30). For June 11, compare *Secret Proceedings*, 115–116 and DHC, 3:107.

16. For motions, see RFC, 1:104 (June 4), 202 (June 11), 217 (June 12). For speakers, see ibid., 1:373–376, 386, 389–390, 407–408, 425, 463, 464, 467, 484–485, 487, 489–493, 510, 515, 527 (relying on Farrand's identifications). Farrand overlooked some likely additions. See, e.g., RFC, 1:488 (30 June, "planks do not fit"), 499. For margin note, see DHC, 3:177.

17. RFC, 1:378; DHC, 3:189.

18. *Secret Proceedings*, 7.

19. John G. Jackson to Madison, 9 December 1821, PJM (RS), 2:434–435; Madison to John G. Jackson, 28 December 1821, ibid., 2:441–442.

20. Madison to Thomas Ritchie, 15 September 1821, PJM (RS), 2:381. For inquiry about "Sketch of the Proceeding of the Federal Convention," see Thomas Ritchie to Madison, 8 September 1821, PJM (RS), 2:379.

21. "Debates in the Federal Convention of 1787 by James Madison, a member," John C. Payne's Copy of James Madison's Original Notes on Debates in the Federal Convention of 1787, JMP, Series 5f (DLC). For evidence of post-Yates copying, see ibid., 333 (June 22 speech included). For May 29 plan, see Payne Copy, 22–38; DHC, 3:14. For June 19 instruction, see DHC, 3:162; Payne Copy, 278.

22. Payne Copy, 1230; *Journal*, 494. On controversy that arose over Adams's printing of the clause, see John Quincy Adams: Memoirs, RFC, 3:456–458 (referencing "errors of punctuation"). Like Eppes, Payne had difficulty with September 7. He left a page blank (1125 verso).

23. See, e.g., Payne Copy, 1152 (divergence between Notes and printed *Journal*), 1153 (footnote).

24. Payne Copy, 1222–1223, [1246]; DHC, 3:769–771. The final page is missing the lower third.

25. Payne Copy, 257–258; RFC, 1:293 n.9. The first two sentences are in Payne's hand; an addition discussing Yates was written by a hand signed

"Editor." For appendix, see ibid., Appendix, 28, 48 (Payne editorial note), 48–49 ("Editor" note); *Papers* (Gilpin), 3:Appendix, xvi (reprinting note).

26. John C. Payne Copy . . . Debates in the Confederation Congress—and copies of letters, 1780–1788, series 5c, JMP; *Papers* (Gilpin), 3 volumes. On "consolidate," see Madison to Henry Lee (25 June 1824), Founders Online, NA, http://founders.archives.gov/documents/Madison/99-02-02-0247 (ver. 2014-05-09). Alternative readings appeared in John Taylor's *New Views of the Constitution,* which cited printed sources to advance a constitutional interpretation based on "state nations." John Taylor, *New Views of the Constitution* (Washington, DC: Way and Gideon, 1823). 9. On "consolidate," see Jack N. Rakove, *Original Meanings: Politics and Ideas in the Making of the Constitution* (New York: Vintage, 1997), 161–202.

27. Jonathan Elliot to Madison, 11 November 1826, Founders Online, NA, http://founders.archives.gov/documents/Madison/99-02-02-0789 (ver. 2014-05-0); Madison to Elliot, 15 November 1826, Founders Online, NA, http://founders.archives.gov/documents/Madison/99-02-02-0793 (ver. 2014-05-09); Elliot to Madison, 21 November 1826, Founders Online, NA, http://founders.archives.gov/documents/Madison/99-02-02-0798 (ver. 2014-05-09); Madison to Elliot, 25 November 1826, Founders Online, NA, http://founders.archives.gov/documents/Madison/99-02-02-0804 (ver. 2014-05-09); Elliot to Madison, 12 February 1827, Founders Online, NA, http://founders.archives.gov/documents/Madison/99-02-02-0911 (ver. 2014-05-09); Madison to Elliot, 14 February 1827, Founders Online, NA, http://founders.archives.gov/documents/Madison/99-02-02-0912 (ver. 2014-05-09). On deaths, see Charles Warren, *The Making of the Constitution* (Boston: Little, Brown, 1937), 813–814.

28. Madison to Elliott, 1 November 1827, WJM, 9:291–292; Founders Online, NA, http://founders.archives.gov/documents/Madison/99-02-02-1160 (ver. 2014-05-09). In the original, the sentence on confounding is followed by an explanation that has been struck, stating in part "and thus by improving the exactness . . . ," JMP, series 1, General Correspondence.

29. *Invited,* Elizabeth Gregory McPherson, "Reporting the Debates of Congress," *Quarterly Journal of Speech* 28 (1942): 141, 144; see Richard J. McKinney, "An Overview of the Congressional Record and its Predecessor Publications," *Law Library Lights* 46 (2002): 16–22. On Pitman, see Edward H. Butler, *The Story of British Shorthand* (London: Sir Isaac Pitman & Sons, 1951), 93–94, 100. *substantially,* 44 U.S.C. sec. 901 (2006); Michelle M. Springer, "The Congressional Record: 'Substantially a Verbatim Report?,'" Government Publications Review 13 (1986): 371–378; Mildred L. Amer, *The Congressional Record: Content, History and Issues* (1993), CRS-93-90; Amy Atchison and Jennifer Lentz, "Questions and Answers," *Legal Reference Services Quarterly* 18 (2001): 97, 99.

30. *Most,* Madison to S. H. Smith, 2 February 1827, RFC 3:475; see also Madison to James Robertson, 27 March 1831, ibid. 3:497 (suggesting publica-

tion of "at least of a posthumous date"). King's comments are reported in T. H. Benton, *Thirty Years View* (New York: D. Appleton and Company, 1854), 1:58; RFC, 3:466. On deaths, see Warren, *Making,* 813.

31. *Matter,* Madison to Israel Keech Tefft (3 December 1830), Founders Online (NA), http://founders.archives.gov/documents/Madison/99-02-02-2234 (ver. 2014-05-09). *consolidate,* "Notes of Major William Pierce on the Federal Convention of 1787," ed. J. Franklin Jameson, *American Historical Review* 3 (1898): 310, 314, 317 (reprinting *Georgia Gazette* and *Savannah Georgian*).

32. *Proposition,* Madison to Jared Sparks, 8 April 1831, Founders Online (NA), http://founders.archives.gov/documents/Madison/99-02-02-2323 (ver. 2014-05-09). *irresistible,* Madison to Sparks, 25 November 1831, Founders Online (NA), http://founders.archives.gov/documents/Madison/99-02-02-2476 (ver. 2014-05-09). For comparisons, see RFC, 3:505–513. On 1830, see Jared Sparks, "Journal," RFC, 3:478–481.

33. On Convention, see Madison to Andrew Stevenson, 17 November 1830, RFC, 3:483–490 (general welfare clause); Madison to Reynolds Chapman, 6 January 1831, ibid., 3:494–495 (canals); Madison to Professor Davis (1832), ibid. 3:518–521 (domestic manufactures). On Madison during retirement, see Ralph L. Ketcham, *James Madison: A Biography* (New York: Macmillan, 1971) 613–617; Drew R. McCoy, *The Last of the Fathers: James Madison and the Republican Legacy* (Cambridge: Cambridge University Press, 1989), chapters 2–4; *Letters and Writings of James Madison,* vol. 4 (Philadelphia: J. B. Lippincott & Co., 1865). On views on slavery and American Colonization Society, see Ketcham, *James Madison,* 625–630; McCoy, *Last,* 260–286, 308–322; Scott J. Kester, *The Haunted Philosophe: James Madison, Republicanism, and Slavery* (Lanham, MD: Rowman & Littlefield, 2008), 99–118; Susan Dunn, *Dominion of Memories: Jefferson, Madison, and the Decline of Virginia* (New York: Basic Books, 2007), 31–60. On will, see Will and Codicil, 15 April & 19 April 1835, WJM, 9:548–552; Ketcham, *James Madison,* 629; McCoy, *Last,* 318–323.

34. *The only,* Madison to Sparks, 1 June 1831, WJM, 9:459, 460. *A proposition,* Madison to Rives, 21 October 1833, DHC, 5:390–395. On Hamilton's speech, see N. P. Trist, Memoranda, 27 September 1834, RFC 3:533–534 (describing two speeches). *The finish,* Madison to Jared Sparks, 8 April 1831, Founders Online (NA), http://founders.archives.gov/documents/Madison/99-02-02-2323 (ver. 2014-05-09). *too often,* see Madison to Edward Everett, 23 June 1835, Founders Online (NA), http://founders.archives.gov/documents/Madison/99-02-02-3145 (ver. 2014-05-09). John C. Hamilton's claims appeared in print after Madison's death in John C. Hamilton, *Life of Alexander Hamilton,* vol. 2 (New York: D. Appleton & Co., 1840), 464–466, 474–475, 486 n., 490–492 n.

35. Note of Mr. Madison to the Plan of Charles Pinckney, *Papers* (Gilpin), 3:Appendix, v–vi; see Madison to William Duer, 5 May 1835, Founders Online (NA), http://founders.archives.gov/documents/Madison/99-02-02-3123 (ver.

2014-05-09) (similar sentiments). On controversy, see Sparks to Madison, 14 November 1831, Founders Online (NA), http://founders.archives.gov/documents /Madison/99-02-02-2472 (ver. 2014-05-09); Madison to Jared Sparks, 25 November 1831, Founders Online (NA), http://founders.archives.gov/documents /Madison/99-02-02-2476 (ver. 2014-05-09); "Observations on Mr. Pinckney's plan &c, Notes, A–F (DLC); reprinted as James Madison on the Pinckney Plan, RFC, 3:506–513. The editorial note is not in Madison's hand. James Madison, Notes, 147b (DLC); RFC, 3:505; *Papers* (Gilpin), 3:Appendix vii n.*.

36. Will and Codicil, 15 April & 19 April 1835, WJM, 9:548–552. For description, see Catherine Allgor, *A Perfect Union: Dolley Madison and the Creation of the American Republic* (New York: Henry Holt and Co., 2006), 402–403, 411; Paul M. Zall, *Dolley Madison* (New York: Nova History Publications, 2001), 101; see also *The Selected Letters of Dolley Payne Madison,* eds. David B. Mattern and Holly C. Shulman (Charlottesville: University of Virginia Press, 2003), 4–5.

37. For an example of deletion, see Payne Copy, 378 (June 25) (material crossed out darkly and Notes' sentences crossed out). For example of additions, see notes to Paterson and Hamilton plans in what appears to be Madison's hand. Payne Copy, 213–214, 257–258. *The few,* b.132-4; DHC, 3:771. For appendix, see Payne Copy, Appendix, 1–49. For similar approach to revision, see Notes on Nullification, December 1835, WJM, 9:573 n.1 ("These *notes* were written almost entirely in Madison's own hand and revised by him with the aid of Mrs. Madison and his brother-in-law, John C. Payne."). For multiple hands, see Payne Copy, Appendix, 48–49 (Editor notes). *found,* Note to speech of J. Madison of August 7 1787, found among his papers, No. 2, Payne Copy, Appendix, 14. For discussion of Payne's notes for Hamilton plan, see John C. Payne to William C. Rives, 28 July 1836, DMDE, DPM 2843; Rives to Payne, 3 August 1836, DMDE, DPM 3025 (recommending citation to Pitkins added to note); Payne to Rives, 6 August 1836, DMDE, DPM 2849; Rives to Payne, 10 August 1836, DMDE, DPM 3027.

38. For discussion, see, e.g., John C. Payne to Edward Coles, 3 August 1836, DMDE, DPM 2845; Payne to Coles, 25 September 1836, DMDE, DPM 2954; Madison to Catherine E. M. Rush, 6 September 1836, DMDE, DPM 3072. Payne describes forwarding a copy to Andrew Stevenson to consider foreign publication. Payne to Stevenson, 21 August 1836, DMDE, DPM 2952. On copying, see Anna C. Payne Causten to Frances Dandridge Henley Lear, 16 July 1836, DMDE, DPM 2975; Payne to Coles, 18 July 1836, DMDE, DPM 2842 ("inexpert aids doing their best"); Anna C. Payne Causten to John P. Todd, September 14, 1836, DMDE, DPM 2812 (Anna and Mary completing Eppes copy). On "very great inaccuracies" in Eppes copy, see Payne to Albert Gallatin, 30 September 1836, DMDE, DPM 2817. The date of the return of the Jefferson Copy is not currently known. After Jefferson's death, Madison had letters returned. See

Henry S. Randall, *The Life of Thomas Jefferson* (New York: Derby & Jackson, 1858), 3:604.

39. See Rives to Martin Van Buren, 29 August 1836, DMDE, DPM 2978; Payne to Henry Clay, 16 December 1836, DMDE, DPM 2967A; Payne to Rives, 24 December 1836, DMDE, DPM 2970. On transfer, see John C. Payne to Richard Smith, 21 November 1836, DMDE, DPM 2964; Dolley Payne Todd Madison to Smith, 1 April 1837, DMDE, DPM 1005. On sale, Dolley P. T. Madison to Rives, 15 January 1837, DMDE, DPM 0985; Act of March 3, 1837 (authorizing amount); Act of July 9, 1838 (printing the Madison papers). Extensive correspondence in the Dolley Madison papers for 1836–1837 relates to publication; see PJM, 1:xvi–xxiv.

40. *The original,* Rives to Dolley P. T. Madison, 20 February 1837, DMDE, DPM 0989. *grave,* Senate Debate, 20 February 1837, Gales and Seaton, *Register of Debates in Congress* (1837), 24th Cong., 2d Sess., 13:870. *an accurate,* William C. Rives, *The History of the Life and Times of James Madison* (Boston: Little, Brown and Co., 1859–1868), 2:309. On Rives, see McCoy, *Last,* 323–369. On notes, see Rives to Payne, 3 August 1836, DMDE, DPM 3025. On Rives's wife, see John C. Payne to William C. Rives, 28 July 1836, DMDE, DPM 2843; Payne to Rives, 4 August 1836, DMDE, DPM 2846. On borrowing, see Rives to Dolley P. T. Madison, 31 March [1838], DMDE, DPM 1103; Brant, *James Madison: Commander,* 524; Dorothy S. Eaton, Introduction, *Index to the Madison Papers* (Washington, D.C.: Library of Congress, 1965).

41. *Original,* Dolley P. T. Madison to Rives, 27 February 1837, DMDE, DPM 0993. *intimates,* George William Featherstonhaugh to Rives, 10 April 1837, (enclosure), DMDE, DPM 1010A. *the money,* Dolley P. T. Madison to John Payne Todd, 23 March [1837], DMDE, DPM 0998. *copy,* Dolley P. T. Madison to John Forsyth, 1 April 1837 (draft), DMDE, DPM 1004. On trunk, see "Nation's Rare Documents Unprotected against Fire," *New York Times,* 28 May 1911; Allen Culling Clark, *Life and Letters of Dolly Madison* (Washington: W. F. Roberts, 1914), 504 (describing trunk in State Department, Bureau of Rolls and Library); see email and digital image from Lisa Kathleen Graddy, deputy chair, Division of Political History, National Museum of American History (Smithsonian), June 7, 2010 (on file with author).

42. *Papers* (Gilpin), 1:xxvi. For facsimile, see "Fac-similes of the Manuscripts of Mr. Madison carefully copied from the originals . . . ," ibid., 3:[backmatter]; see Eric T. Slauter, *The State as a Work of Art* (Chicago: University of Chicago, 2009), 1–8. For reprint, see *The Debates on the Adoption of the Federal Constitution . . . with a diary of the debates of the Congress of the Confederation as reported by James Madison,* vol. 5, ed. Jonathan Elliot (Washington: Printed by the Editor, 1845), Advertisement.

43. *To seclude, Library Journal* 19 (January 1894): 23–24. A teaching guide stated that "the inquiring visitor" could see the "original manuscript in

Mr. Madison's fine handwriting." James Woodburn, *The Making of the Constitution* (Chicago: Scott, Foresman and Co., 1898), iv. For Allen's description of restoration and mounting, see Letter from the Secretary of State reporting the results of an examination of the revolutionary archives . . . (January 1895), *Executive Documents of the Senate,* U.S. Cong. Serial Set, 53d Cong., 3d Sess., Ex. Doc. 22, 11; Andrew Hussey Allen, "The Historical Archives of the Department of State," in *Annual Report of the American Historical Association for 1894* (Washington: Government Printing Office, 1895), 281–298. For image, see WJM, 3: photograph after page 2 (hinge at top). For evidence of restoration, see Notes, b.41.

44. Introductory Note, DHC, 3:iii–iv. The Madison Notes were also described as the Appendix, *Bulletin of the Bureau of Rolls and Library* (dated 1897; issued 1900), no. 9; Gaillard Hunt, *The Department of State of the United States* (New Haven: Yale University Press, 1914), 315. On Weissenhagen, see Ages, Etc. of Employees, Department of State, 57 Cong., 1st Sess. (Dec. 1901), Doc. 65.

45. "Minor Notices," *American Historical Review* 5 (1900): 795–96; see also J. Franklin Jameson, "Reviews of Books: The Writings of James Madison," *American Historical Review* 8 (1903): 559–561. On sets, see "Adverse Report from Printing Committee," *Monthly Catalogue, United States Public Documents,* no. 223–234 (Washington: G.P.O., February 1914), 388–389.

46. *Original,* WJM, 3:xii. *The Debates in the Federal Convention of 1787 which framed the Constitution of the United States,* eds. Gaillard Hunt and James Brown Scott (New York: Oxford University Press, 1920), 17 n.1. *constantly,* F. W. Coker, "Book Reviews," *Yale Law Journal* 30 (1921): 645–647. *significance,* RFC, 1:xix. *sometimes,* RFC, 1:xviii n.23. *more radical,* RFC, 1:xviii n.20. On efforts to show revisions, see Farrand to Byrne Hackett, 10 March 1910, Yale University Press Records, 1907–1955, RG 554, YRG 34, Accn. 19ND-A-148, Box 2, folder 6; Yale University Press to Farrand, 10 March 1910, ibid.; Yale University Press to Farrand, 11 March 1910, ibid. *distinction,* RFC, 4:12 (1937); see Farrand to George Day, 19 December 1934, Yale University Press Records, ca. 1919–1970, RG 554, YRG 34, Accn. 1990-A-058, Box 83, folder "Farrand-Records." On Farrand's discussion of editions, see RFC, 4:x–xii (1937). For editions based on the Hunt edition, see *Documents Illustrative of the Formation of the Union of the American* States, ed. Charles C. Tansill (Washington, DC: Government Printing Office, 1927); *Notes of Debates in the Federal Convention of 1787 Reported by James Madison,* ed. Adrienne Koch (New York: W. W. Norton, 1987); *The Debates in the Federal Convention of 1787,* ed. Robert S. Alley (Amherst, NY: Prometheus Books, 2007) and multiple web versions.

47. On transfer, see *Annual Report of the Librarian of Congress* (Washington, D.C., Library of Congress, 1922), 44. For first page and attached slip, see *James Madison and the American Nation, 1751–1836: An Encyclopedia,* ed. Robert A. Rutland (New York: Simon & Schuster, 1994), 134.

48. *In pursuance, Debates* (Gilpin), 1:xv–v; *Debates on the Adoption,* 5:109, 121–122 (1845). The description appeared prior to Gilpin. See "Madison, and the Madison Papers," *United States Democratic Review* 5 (March 1839): 248– 249. *paper,* Dolley P. T. Madison to Andrew Jackson, 15 November 1836, DMDE, DPM 0942; Circular from John C. Payne to Prospective Publishers, 24 September 1836, DMDE, DPM 0934A.

49. *A sketch,* DHC, 3:1; Notes, 2a. For description, see DHC, 3:796o (the DHC does not reprint the Dolley Madison paragraph); Notes, 1m (first paragraph), 7a–b (Dolley Madison's hand?). For dating , see reference to James Barton Longacre and James Herring, *The National Portrait Gallery of Distinguished Americans,* vol. 2 (life of Webster) (Philadelphia: Henry Perkins, 1835). Using roman typeface to show Madison's handwriting and italics for the other handwriting, the draft reads: I was enabled to write out ~~during the intervals~~ my daily notes ~~in the extent & form~~ [*see page 18 during the session or within a few finishing days after its close—see pa. 18*."

On another sheet of paper, the sentence and additional paragraph appear with some revisions. Notes, 1m. Farrand does not mention the incomplete description. RFC 3:540 n.1, 550. Hunt states that the "original notes appear to have been lost since Gilpin's edition." Hunt, *Debates,* 15 n.5, 16 n.1. For similar description in Jefferson's papers, see *Memoir, Correspondence, and Miscellanies from the Papers of Thomas Jefferson,* ed. Thomas Jefferson Randolph (1829), 1:21 ("I took my notes in my place while these things were going on, and at their close wrote them out in form and with correctness").

The Evidence

1. James Madison, Vices of the Political System of the U. States, April 1787, JMP, Series 1 (DLC).

2. Although the Library is in the process of removing the Madison Papers from large volumes, I examined the manuscript attached by hinges in the reading room. The Library was not comfortable removing the sheets for examination on a light table. Further examination may ascertain whether the Whatman paper matches that used at the Convention. The fourteen pages are arranged as follows: pp. 1–4 (bifolium, GR inside the crown and J DeBus[sscher]); pp. 5–8 (bifolium, J DeBusscher); pp. 9–10 (folio, J DeBussche[r]); pp. 11–12 (folio, lower part, Whatman W cypher); pp. 13–14 (folio, top part, Whatman W cypher). The eleventh vice begins on page 10.

3. On puzzle, see PJM, 9:358 n.10; see also Jack Rakove, "James Madison and the Constitution," *History Now,* September 2007 (Gilder Lehrman Institute for American History), at www.gilderlehrman.org/historynow/09_2007/historian2.php. In April, Madison wrote, "The great desideratum which has not yet been found for Republican Governments, seems to be some disinterested &

dispassionate umpire in disputes between different passions & interests in the State." He suggested the negative as a possible solution. Madison to Washington, 16 April 1787, PJM, 9:382, 384. The eleventh vice similarly states, "The great desideratum in Government is such a modification of the Sovereignty as will render it sufficiently neutral between the different interests and factions. . . ." The "extensive Republic" is the apparent solution.

4. For b.12, see DHC, 3:76; MJC (6 June). For b.14, see DHC, 3:87–88; MJC (7 June). On b.11, Madison abruptly refers to "Resol: 9"; he previously favored "clause." DHC, 3:68. The Journal described "the 9th resolution." MJC (5 June). Intriguingly, Madison included the word "institute," instead of "appoint," the word used in the journal and the Journal Copy. DHC, 3:68–69; MJC (5 June).

5. For discussion of Madison's name, see RFC, 1:xviii n.23. For formal ending, see DHC, 3:69, 88. For original and revised closing on b.13, see DHC, 3:79–80.

6. DHC, 3:68–71, 74–75, 89–91 (noninclusive listing). Madison needed the transitions from the surrounding sheets to match the replaced sheets. The speeches on b.12 could not run over, and the last speeches are each one sentence occupying only two lines. The transition from b.14 to b.15 was difficult because Wilson's speech carried over, and the final words—particularly, *Federal liberty*—were squished.

7. The strongest evidence dating Madison's insight about the extended republic to June is an undated note by Hamilton. Under the heading, "Principles," Hamilton wrote "Madisson's Theory," and lists two principles. The first is that republics should "have such extent as to render combinations on the groups of interest difficult"; the second refers to refining representation through the election process. RFC, 1:146. Farrand placed the note in the records for June 6; however, he acknowledged the sheet contains no date and it was "impossible to assign them satisfactorily." RFC, 1:145 n.10, 146 n.13. For other arrangements in *The Papers of Alexander Hamilton* and the Hamilton Papers, see Constitutional Convention, Notes Taken in the Federal Convention, PAH, 4:161–176; Constitutional Convention (1787), Speeches and Writings File, 1778–1804, Alexander Hamilton Papers, 1708–1903, Box 23, Reel 20–21(DLC) (microfilm) (marked pg. 106 and (75)). Ford initially assumed the notes related to the *Federalist* essays but changed his mind. See Worthington C. Ford, "Alexander Hamilton's Notes on the Federal Convention of 1787," *Proceedings of the Massachusetts Historical Society,* 2d Series, 18 (June 1904): 848, 849, 851; Worthington C. Ford, "Alexander Hamilton's Notes in the Federal Convention of 1787," *American Historical Review* 10 (Oct. 1904): 97–109. Hamilton's notes contain another comment on an enlarged sphere on June 1. RFC, 1:72 ("The way to prevent a majority from having an interest to oppress the minority is to enlarge the sphere."); Constitutional Convention (1787), Speeches and Writings File, 1778–1804 (marked pg. 104 and (75)). The PAH editors add "[Madison]" to the comment. PAH, 4:161.

8. For b.30, compare DHC, 3:177 with MJC (21 June), 3:181, 183 (the first resembling the Journal Copy). The end of June 23 is similar but not identical to the Journal Copy. See DHC, 3:198 with MJC (23 June). Nonetheless, there are aspects that may the product of copying. On June 21 (b.30), Madison omitted NJ in the vote. DHC, 3:181. On b.33, Madison erred in writing "eligible" instead of "illegible." DHC, 3:198. He made an odd error, "On the 2d member of the sentence"—as if confused because he had copied "member" too many times. Ibid. The catchwords between sheets and original sheets are awkward. On b.30-4, Madison ends with "but is content with $_{plan}$" (the first word on the original sheet) instead of "the plan." The catchword on b.37-4 is unusual: "this subj."—the first word on the following page is "subject." On b.42-4, Madison omitted the catchword.

9. For Pinckney's speech in his hand, see Notes, vol. 2, GR 142, I–O (GR 142, 600–606). For Madison's version, see b.33 (first paragraph), b.34–b.36; DHC, 3:199–207. For speech in final form, see RFC, 1:397–404.

10. For margin note, see b.30-1 (June 21); DHC, 3:177. Madison later added a margin note on b.43-1 (June 29) that Hamilton had left the Convention. Madison planned to insert the return date but never did. Notes, b.43-1, DHC, 242.

11. For examples of superfluous words, see DHC, 3:592 (instant), 612 (at the instance), 616 (entered on), 628 (to whom). Madison relied on the journal for the order and most motions, interspersing material taken from his rough notes. On August 22, he included the comment, "See Report in the Journal of the Convention of this date"—later altering it to make it appear as if it was an instruction regarding insertion of material. DHC, 3:592. Eppes found it sufficiently confusing that he copied it as "vid the report in the Journals of Congress of this date." EJC (Payne copyist note added); Press Copy EJC (showing original Eppes text). For error, see MJC (23 August), Notes, b.100; DHC, 3:592 (ex post facto law). For reversal, see MJC (September 13), DHC, 1:195–196; DHC, 3:737–747. The journal page was loose and reversed. See Charles R. Keller and George W. Pierson, "A New Madison Manuscript Relating to the Federal Convention of 1787," *American Historical Review* 36 (October 1930): 18; Formal Journal of the Proceedings of the Convention, Records of the Continental and Confederation Congresses and the Constitutional Convention, Record Group 360 (NA) (microfilm), [151]. The sheets for September 15 and 17 cannot be analyzed using the journal because it was not kept on these dates.

12. For McClurg letters, see PJM, 10:157, 161. The September 15 receipt to Blair was not located (Virginia State Library). See PJM, 10:168; see email correspondence with Kelly Sizemore, Archives Research Services, in 2010 and May 5, 2014 on file with author. For letters, see Madison to Madison, Sr., 4 September 1787, JMP, series 1(DLC), PJM, 10:161; Madison to Jefferson, 6 September 1787, JMP, series 1 (DLC), DHC, 3:163–165. Although Hutson described the September 4 letter as matching the Notes, the study was not aware of the Whatman

variations. James H. Hutson, "The Creation of the Constitution: The Integrity of the Documentary Record," *Texas Law Review* 65 (1986): 27–30. The Notes for September 3 and 4 contain long verbatim selections of the journal. The integration includes Madison's loss of place and miscopying "The Remainder of the" on b.116–3, DHC, 3:674. The end of September 4 reflects Madison's decision to place a motion apparently in his rough notes, but not in the journal, relating a clause on judging privileges. Similarly, the September 5 proceedings (b.117–b.118) follow and integrate the journal. The September 6 proceedings also follow and integrate the journal (b.119–b.120). Again Madison's effort to copy the journal is seen as in the errant line "It was moved to insert." DHC, 3:689. If the September letters were ever discovered to match this section, then Madison secretly copied the journal during the Convention. While overturning these conclusions, it would even more significantly overturn conventional understandings about the journal and the Convention.

13. b.133–b.136. Hamilton was in New York from August 20 to September 2 and returned to the Convention in time to serve on the Committee of Style. For letter, see Madison to Pendleton, 20 September 1787, JMP (DLC) (watermark of CB inside a heart). On Bauman and Ephrata Cloister, see Thomas L. Gravell, George Miller, and Elizabeth Walsh, *American Watermarks, 1690–1835* (New Castle, DE: Oak Knoll Press, 2002), 238.

14. For speech, see b.131; DHC, 3:761–764. For anecdote, see b.132-4; DHC, 3:770. In the appendix to the Jefferson Copy, Eppes wrote at the bottom of the second page of Randolph's July plan, "For Dr. Franklin's speech inserted here ["with" or "vid"] the end of part the 3d of the debate of the convention." The comment may indicate that the Franklin speech appeared as a separate document at the time of the Jefferson Copy.

15. For Franklin speech, see *American Museum* (Philadelphia: Matthew Carey, December 1787), 2:558–559 (including "viz"). The speech was reprinted in 1793. *Works of the late Doctor Benjamin Franklin* (Dublin: P. Wogan, 1793), 290–292. Farrand asserted that Madison's version was the one delivered, but offered no evidence. RFC, 2:641 n.1. For other description, see Letter to Jefferson [?], 11 October 1787, RFC, 3:104–105. One difference between the Notes and the printed speech is a parenthetical in the Notes, "(if approved by Congress & confirmed by the Conventions)." The parenthetical does not appear in "Speech in the Convention," *Writings of Benjamin Franklin,* ed. Albert H. Smyth (New York: Macmillan, 1907), 9:607–609. The *Documentary History* printed another transcript. DHC, 4:278. For Madison's comment on another depiction of the speech, see James Madison to George Washington, 20 December 1787, PJM, 10:334–335 and n.2. The source for the print publication seems more likely to have been Franklin than Madison. For McHenry's version, see RFC, 2:649.

16. *The American Jest Book: containing a curious variety of jests, anecdotes, bon mots, stories* (Philadelphia: Printed [by Henry Taylor] for M. Carey and W.

Spotswood, 1789), 18; *Ben Franklin Laughing: Anecdotes from Original Sources by and about Benjamin Franklin,* ed. P. M. Zall (Berkeley: University of California Press, 1980), 96, 148. *I have; observed,* Notes, b.132-4; DHC, 3:770 ("said" written over "often").

17. "'Journal' of the Federal Convention of 1787," United States Presidents Collection, General Collection, Beinecke Rare Book and Manuscript Library, Gen. Mss. 271, Box 1, f.49; Keller and Pierson, "A New Madison," 17–30. For dating, see ibid., 20–24.

18. MJC, [1]. The 1892 sale catalog stated that the header included the date 1787; however, the catalog compilers may have simply assumed it was 1787 as they did not precisely copy the heading. *The Washington-Madison Papers Collected and Preserved by James Madison, Estate of J. C. McGuire,* Cat. No. 694, (The Bicking Print, 1892), 179. The provenance was Payne Todd, ibid., vi. For paper, see Keller and Pierson, *A New Madison,* 22 n.18. For example of letter, see Madison to Tench Coxe, 18 September 1787 [1789], PJM, 12:409–410 n.1.

19. On secretary's records, see Mary Sarah Bilder, "How Bad Were the Official Records of the Federal Convention?" *George Washington Law Review* 80, no.6 (2012): 1620–1682. *loose,* Major Jackson to General Washington, 17 September 1787, DHC, 4:281; also Washington's Diary (September 17), ibid. *retain,* b.132; DHC, 3:770. *those very,* Luther Martin, "Reply to the Landholder," 3 March 1788, *The Maryland Journal,* 7 March 1788, Records, 3:276, 278.

20. *I am,* Washington to Madison, ca. 23 September 1789, PJM, 12:420. On absence of diary, see *The Diaries of George Washington,* eds. Donald Jackson and Dorothy Twohig (Charlottesville: University of Virginia, 1976–), 1:xlv–xlvi; 5:445, 448.

21. Compare MJC, 20 August, with first page (May).

22. MJC, 25 May, 28 May, 30 May, 31 May, 1 June. For Journal of Convention and for Journal of the Committee of the Whole House, see DHC, vol. 1; Records of the Continental and Confederation Congresses and the Constitutional Convention, Record Group 360 (National Archives). Keller and Pierson suggested that the ink change indicated that the rules were copied from another source. Keller and Pierson, *A New Madison,* 25 n.26. Although there are minor changes (e.g., Madison's common substitution of *that* for *which* and alterations in capitalization), the rules match the May 28 rules.

23. MJC, 23 August, 31 August, 7 September. The September 7 section dealt with the treaties of peace issue. See DHC, 1:188. For skipped page, see MJC, 7 August (end), 8 August; Keller and Pierson, *A New Madison,* 18. For reversed order, see MJC, 13 September; DHC, 1:195–196; Keller and Pierson, *A New Madison,* 18. There are many small marks throughout the manuscript, for example, small hatch marks to mark end of propositions to committee on August 20 and August 22, small "x" on August 24. MJC; Keller and Pierson, *A New Madison,* 23 n.22.

24. MJC, August 29 (later added "in the original Journal"), June 2, June 9. The June 9 matter related to the executive, Journal, DHC, 1:217. On July 17, the secretary placed two unanimous votes in the margin relating to the executive being a single person and chosen by the national legislature. He placed printer's hands in the proceedings; however, he inadvertently reversed the order of the two votes in the margin. The DHC and Farrand place the two motions in the apparent correct order. Journal (Convention), DHC, 1:97–98; RFC, 2:22. When Madison copied the Journal, he wrote these in the incorrect order. MJC, 17 July. In the Notes, however, Madison retained them in his original correct order. DHC, 3:353; Notes, b.61.

25. MJC, 4 September ("of the whole number," "appointed," "except treaties of peace"). Journal, DHC, 1:178–179 (4 September); RFC, 2:507. Madison did not include "immediately" as an addition by Washington, although the DHC shows it as added. MJC, 4 September; Journal (Convention), DHC, 1:178. Keller and Pierson note that the word is not in Washington's handwriting. Keller and Pierson, *A New Madison,* 522 n.19. They identify "treaties of peace" as a complication. Ibid., 23 n.21.

26. Journal, DHC, 1:196–197. The secretary originally wrote "last clause," but it was altered to "first." Ibid. MJC, 14 September. He later added "Original" before "Journal."

27. For tallies, see DHC, 1:227–261; Voting Record of the Convention (Microform Publication M866 (NARA)), available online.

28. For Jefferson Copy, see The Madison Papers, vol. 1, Edward Everett Papers, 1675–1910, Ms. N-1201, vol. 229 (MHS). A microfilm copy is available. The MHS staff was exceptionally helpful to me in permitting it to be examined on a light table, and assisting with other technical expertise. In 2014, Peter Drummey re-examined the manuscript. *particular,* Eppes to Madison, 1 November 1810, PJM (PS), 2:609–611. For dating suggestions, see PJM, 10:7–8 (summer 1791); PTJ, 19:544–551 (1791–1793); Keller and Pierson, *A New Madison,* 25–26, 29 (1795–1796). For Jefferson's possession in 1796, see Jefferson to Madison, 17 April 1796, PJM, 16:328–329. On Maria Jefferson Eppes, see PTJ, 20:413 n. On Jefferson's retirement, see PTJ, 28:2.

29. For Press Copy, see Notes of the Federal Convention, James Madison Papers, 1781–1847, Ser. VI (NYPL). On provenance as part of Ford Collection, see email from Thomas Lannon, Manuscripts Division (NYPL) to author (May 9, 2008). The NYPL copy is discussed in PJM, 10:7–8 and in an excellent 1985 description by Richard Bernstein. Richard B. Bernstein, 1 February 1985, James Madison Papers Collection Dossier, Curator of the Manuscripts & Archives Division, emailed to author, May 9, 2008. Microfilm is available (missing a few images). My thanks to Thomas Lannon and the staff of the NYPL for generous assistance. On Jefferson's letterpress, see Silvio A. Bedini, *Jefferson and His Copying Machines* (Charlottesville: University of Virginia Press, 1984), 16–25;

Silvio A. Bedini, *Thomas Jefferson: Statesman of Science* (New York: Macmillan Publishing Co., 1990), 329–332. On letter press technology, see Barbara Rhode and William Wells Streeter, *Before Photocopying: The Art & History of Mechanical Copying, 1780–1938* (New Castle, DE: Oak Knoll Press & Heraldry Bindery, 1999), 7–48, 84, 91; Pamela Clemit, "William Godwin and James Watt's Copying Machine: Wet-Transfer Copies in the Abinger Papers," *Bodleian Library Record* 18 (2005): 532–650; Jonathan Shectman, *Groundbreaking Scientific Experiments, Inventions and Discoveries of the 18th Century* (Westport, CT: Greenwood Press, 2003), 276–280. My thanks to Martha J. King, associate editor, *Papers of Thomas Jefferson* (Princeton) for assistance. Madison was sent a copying machine by Jefferson just before the Convention but may not have used it. Jefferson to Madison, 30 January 1787, PJM, 9:247, 251–252 (describing machine); Madison to Jefferson, 23 April 1787, PJM, 9:398. For other press copies by Eppes, see Seneca Nation to George Washington, with copies, 1 December 1790, Thomas Jefferson Papers, Series 1, General Correspondence. The Press Copy is largely extant for Part 1 of the Jefferson Copy (May 14–June 20), although some pages are missing, usually corresponding to Madison's speeches. The Jefferson Copy and Press Copy do not exist for June 21 to July 17. No Press Copy exists for Part 2 of the Jefferson Copy, except for the final twelve pages for August 20–21 (beginning partway down on Notes, 96–1, PC, Part 2, pp. 190–201). The Press Copy includes many pages of the Jefferson Copy beginning with August 22 and ending on September 17, but with many pages missing. The Press Copy includes the Hamilton plan and the July 10 Randolph proposal. The early provenance of the Press Copy is unknown. The dating of some revisions can be established with the Press Copy. For example, the change from "federal Constitution" to "federal system of government' occurred after the Jefferson Copy. EJC, Part 1, 1.

30. EJC, frontis (overwritten with note to translator). At the end of the Randolph plan, Eppes wrote: "For Dr. Franklin's speech inserted here vid the end of part the 3d of the debate of the convention." The word is either "vid" or "with."

31. For examples, see any page in the Jefferson Copy. These discrepancies were fixed by Payne and the copyediting team after Madison's death. Payne included a note to the printer to fix the style at the beginning of the delegates' comments. Note to Translator, EJC, Part 1, frontis.

32. EJC, Part 1, 1–6. For September 7 note, see EJC, Part 3, 120.

33. The sections of the Jefferson Copy are Part 1, May–June 20, section 1 (Notes, b.1–b.12) (EJC, pp. 1–74); section 2 (Notes, b.13–b.20); section 3 (Notes, b.21–b.29)); Part 2, 18 July–21 August (Notes, b.63–b.98); Part 3, 22 August–17 September (Notes, b.99–b.132); Appendix (Randolph plan and Hamilton plan). The Press Copy shows the page before August 22 with the original "Part 3^d." The Jefferson Copy shows the later alteration of the "3" to "last." Watermarks are consistent with papers made prior to the mid-1790s, for

example, Taverham, Sandy Run, Edmeads & Pine, J. Whatman, a simple posthorn, a W posthorn cypher, and a posthorn shield-GR watermark.

34. Replacement pages were inserted on wove paper with the raised stamp, Philadelphia / Amies / superfine or the Amies watermark of a dove. This paper was likely made by the Dove Mill, Pennsylvania after 1800. See Gravel, *American Watermarks*, 7–12, 236; John Bidwell, *American Paper Mills, 1609–1832* (Hanover, NH: Dartmouth College Press, 2013), 37–41. In the original second part of the Jefferson Copy, pages 63–141 are not extant. This missing section begins near the end of 25 July (Notes, b.73-3 (just before Madison's speech)). The Jefferson Copy begins again on August 13 at the end of the day (Notes, b.88-2 with McHenry's speech). A partial explanation may involve the need to insert the resolutions referred to the Committee of Detail. Throughout, the later copyists may have removed more pages because Eppes often started the day at the top of a page. The first section of the final part of the Jefferson Copy is extant (pp. 1–112) (Notes, b.99–b.119-1). Five pages (pp. 113–117) are not extant. Assuming the page number is accurate, it appears to be a missing sheet and a half sheet (which does appear on occasion), likely with one page blank. The missing material covers the end of September 6 and the beginning of September 7 (Notes, b.119-1 to b.121-2). Pages 118–121 are extant; however, Eppes noted on p. 120 that "part of a days debate" appeared to be missing. The copyists added seven pages to cover material on b.122 (Taylor). Pages 122–128 are not extant (Notes, b.123–b.124). The beginning of b.123 (8 September) was copied by Eppes, but September 10 and 11 are no longer extant. Pages 129–144 are extant. These pages began with September 12 (partway through Notes b.125) to near the end of September 14. The copyists added the Report of the Committee of Style. A final puzzle involves the last missing pages. Three pages (145–147) are not extant (Notes b.128-3 (Mr. Gerry 2^{ded} (September 14))–b.130 (September 15)). These pages must have included the end of September 14 and September 15, raising the possibility that only two pages in the Jefferson Copy covered September 15. The nineteenth-century copyists, however, required almost 19 pages. The discrepancy could suggest that the Notes' lengthy September 15 proceedings were composed after the Jefferson Copy. Alternatively, the page numbers on the Jefferson Copy could be inaccurate. The final pages are extant: pages 148–158 (17 September, Notes, b.131–b.132).

35. On watermarks, see A. H. Shorter, *Paper Making in the British Isles: An Historical and Geographical Study* (New York: Barnes & Noble, 1972); A. H. Shorter, *Paper Mills and Paper Makers in England, 1495–1800* (Hilversum, Holland: The Paper Publications Society, 1957); Richard L. Hills, *Papermaking in Britain, 1488–1988: A Short History* (London: Athlone Press, 1988); Thomas L. Gravell and George Miller, *A Catalogue of Foreign Watermarks Found on Paper Used in America, 1700–1835* (New York: Garland Publishing, Inc. 1983); Gravel, *American Watermarks;* B. J. McMullin, "Watermarks and the Determination of

Format in British Paper, 1794–circa 1830," *Studies in Bibliography 56* (2003–2004): 295–315; Philip Gaskell, *A New Introduction to Bibliography* (1972; reprint, Winchester, U.K., St Paul's Bibliographies, 1995), 57–77. On the difficulty of distinguishing variations, see Peter Bower, "The White Art: The Importance of Interpretation in the Analysis of Paper," in *Looking at Paper: Evidence & Interpretation: Symposium Proceedings, Toronto 1999* (Ottawa: Minister of Public Works and Government Services, Canada, 2001), 5–16.

36. On the Whatmans, see Thomas Balston, *James Whatman, Father and Son* (London: Methuen & Co., 1957); John Balston, *The Whatmans and Wove Paper: Its Invention and Development in the West* (West Farleigh, Kent, U.K.: J. N. Balston, 1998); J. N. Balston, *The Elder James Whatman: England's Greatest Paper Maker (1702–1759)* (Bury St. Edmunds, UK: St. Edmundsbury Press, 1992), 2:270–72.

ACKNOWLEDGMENTS

I began working on Madison's Notes in 2008. Since then I have been helped by many people who offered to track down manuscripts, raised questions, offered suggestions, and provided encouragement. For those individuals not mentioned by name, please know that the omissions are inadvertent.

I am appreciative of the comments provided by colleagues who heard versions of this research at the University of Connecticut Law School Colloquium; the University of Maine; the University of Southern California Gould School of Law, Center for Law, History, and Culture; the University of Wisconsin Law School; Brigham Young University Law School; the University of Illinois Colloquium on Constitutional Theory, History, and Law; the University of Pennsylvania Law and History Consortium; Harvard University Humanities Center Seminar in the History of the Book; Harvard Law School, Legal History Workshop; Massachusetts Historical Society, Early American History Seminar; the University of Hawaii Law School; the Yale Alumni Association of Boston meeting, Faneuil Hall; the Boisi Center for Religion and American Public Life, Boston College; the Boston College Law School Summer Workshop; the Boston College Clough Center for the Study of Constitutional Democracy; Stanford Law School; and University of Chicago Law School.

Many people offered wise counsel, posed hard questions, and suggested avenues of research: Richard Bernstein, Warren Billings, Ann Blair, Peter Bower, Alfred Brophy, Antonio Cantu, Patrick Chase, the late Morris Cohen, Saul Cornell, Garrett Epps, Bill Ewald, Lisa Kathleen Graddy, David Hall, Paul Halliday, Charles Hobson, Todd Ito, John Kaminski, Bettye Kearse, Ralph Ketcham, Richard Leffler, Susan Lively, Maeva Marcus, Michael McConnell, Brian McMullin, Dan Mosser, Eric Nelson, Peter Onuf, David Pfeiffer, Grant Quertermous, Jack Rakove, John Reardon, John Reid, Robert Scigliano, Barbara Clark Smith, Lawrence Solum, Tomas Stohr, Judith Tankard, Kevin Van Anglen, Michael Vorenberg, Richard G. Wilson, and Conrad Wright.

Without the assistance of a wonderful group at the Library of Congress, the book would have never been possible: Julie Miller, L. Maria Nugent, Mary Haude, Barbara Bair, Fenella France, and Bonnie Coles. At the Massachusetts Historical Society, Peter Drummey, Conrad Wright, Nancy Heywood, and Sara Sikes helped with the Jefferson Copy. At Yale's Beinecke Library, Graham Sherriff, Moira Fitzgerald, and the late Morris Cohen provided indispensable access to Madison's Journal Copy. At the New York Public Library, Thomas Lannon and Laura Ruttum aided me with Madison's letters and the Press Copy. Jody Rapport searched her father's papers for me. Many other individuals and libraries answered inquiries and suggested leads. I am grateful for the assistance of librarians and archivists at the Yale University Archives, the Rosenbach Library, the Huntington Library, the Library of Virginia, Rauner Special Collections Library, and many individuals, including David Langbart and Patricia Anderson (NARA), Janie Morris (Duke University), Gwen Gosney (Guilford College), Elise Allison (Greensboro Historical Museum), Lita Garcia (Huntington Library), Martha King (Papers of Thomas Jefferson), Tammy Kiter (New York Historical Society), Regina Rush (University of Virginia), Amy Larrabee Cotz (Montpelier), Rebecca Hatcher and Daniel Hartwig (Yale University Archives), Joan Sherer (Bunche Library), Grant Quertermous (Montpelier), Olga Tsapina (Huntington Library), Jill Gage (Newberry Library), Heather Riser (University of Virginia), Charles Greene (Princeton), Jim Holmberg (Filson Historical Society), Kathie Ludwig (David Library), English Showalter and Ted O'Reilly (New York Historical Society), Carol Beales (Copley Library), Barbara Smith Clark (Smithsonian), Anne Covell (University of Iowa), David Connors (Haverford College), Earle Spamer (American Philosophical Society), David Langbart (National Archives), Dana Lamparello (Historical Society of Pennsylvania), Kelly Sizemore (Library of Virginia), Patricia Anderson (National Archives), and Anne Southwell (University of Virginia).

At the Boston College Law Library, I wish to thank Filippa Anzalone, Helen Lacouture, Deena Frazier, Laurel Davis, Katie Sosnoff, Hannah Clarke, Kelli Farrington, Mollie Hammond, Jason Liu, Michael Mitsukawa, Tuananh Truong, and the librarians at O'Neill Library. For assistance with administrative aspects of manuscripts, I thank Patrick Mahoney, Jeanne Stowe, Jonathan Hixon, and Laura Woodring at Boston College Law School. For excellent assistance with production, proofreading, and copyediting, I thank Katrina Vassallo, Edward Wade, Ashley Moore, Karen Woerner, and Jay Boggis; and Graciela Galup for the splendid cover design.

Research was supported by generous grants from the Cromwell Foundation, the Michael and Helen Lee Distinguished Scholar Endowment, the Clough Center for the Study of Constitutional Democracy, the Boston College Committee on Catholic Intellectual Traditions, and the Boston College Summer Research grant program. I thank the administration of the law school and, in particular, Dean Vincent Rougeau, Associate Deans Joseph Liu and John Stachniewicz, and Clough

Center Director Vlad Perju for support. The support of Michael and Helen Lee, John Gordan III, and the board of the Cromwell Foundation has been indispensable.

My thanks to the students in my constitutional history seminars and American Legal History classes for the past decade, with whom I have enjoyed discussing and learning about the Convention. Andrew Golden was indispensable early in this project. In addition, William Lacy, Jacqueline Beatty, Alyssa Russell, Michael Palmisciano, Justin DeRosa, and Michael Samuel compared sources and helped to check notes. My thanks to my many teachers, in particular, those in the English Department of the University of Wisconsin–Madison, where I learned to read texts carefully.

Among my many wonderful colleagues at Boston College Law School, two groups have kept me particular company during this book—my legal history colleagues (James Rogers, Daniel Coquillette, Francis Herrmann) and my lunch table colleagues (Renee Jones, Ray Madoff, Judith McMorrow, Mark Spiegel, George Brown, Hugh Ault, Sanford Katz, Norah Wylie). Sharon O'Connor, my coauthor on another project, watched over various drafts, and her organizational advice was invaluable.

Since the inception of the project, Bernard Bailyn repeatedly discussed and read parts of the manuscript. Without his wise counsel, the book would be incompletely imagined and completely unfinished. Kent Newmyer generously read an early draft of the manuscript when I was stuck, and his sage advice helped me regain focus. The late Pauline Maier offered helpful comments on a chapter at a workshop at the Massachusetts Historical Society, and her enthusiasm sustained significant redrafting. Jack Rakove read with an extraordinary and careful eye, and his probing questions and insights significantly improved and clarified important arguments. Avi Soifer, David Mattern, and the anonymous readers for the Press read the manuscript, and their thoughtful comments have resulted in a far better book. My editor, Kathleen McDermott, supportively shepherded the manuscript during the long writing process. The interest of Dana and Lizzie Mackey, my three siblings (Anne, David, and Debbie Bilder), Larry and Veronica Bilder, and my entire extended family has been greatly appreciated. For the last several years, Eleanor and Lucy generously embraced a kitchen table covered with drafts and a mom sometimes distracted by revising a manuscript. Above all, I have been carried through the low points along the way by the conviction of David Mackey and my mother and father, Sally and Richard, that this book was worth writing.

INDEX

Adams, John, 38, 41; correspondence of, 223; monarchy, 210; notetaking by, 26

Adams, John Quincy, 225, 230

"Address to the inhabitants of Great Britain," 21

Allen, Andrew H., 237

Almon, John, 23

Amendments. *See* Bill of Rights

American Colonization Society, 233

American Philosophical Society, 221

Ames, Fisher, 172, 206

"Ancient & Modern Confederacies," 38, 94–95, 159

Annapolis Convention, 13; attendees, 39; in Madison's legislative diary, 32; Madison's role, 38–40; report, 40; subsequent working notes, 35

Apportionment, 162

Appropriations. *See* Money bills

Articles of Confederation, 3, 12; Constitutional Convention to revise, 52; correspondence on constitutional interpretation, 37; failure of revenue amendment, 29; *Federalist* comments on, 160, 163; New Jersey Plan, 91; notes blaming failure on state legislatures, 35; reform of, 10, 41

Asgill, Charles, 28

Bailyn, Bernard, 3

Baldwin, Abraham, 42

Banning, Lance, 6

Bassett, Richard, 40

Beckley, John, correspondence of, 56

Bedford, Gunning, 104; notetaking at Constitutional Convention, 58

Beeman, Richard, 4

Benson, Egbert, Annapolis Convention, 39

Billey (enslaved man), 30–31

Bill of Rights, 14, 132–134, 155, 170, 174–176

Blair, John, 42; Virginia plan, 77

Bland, Theodorick, 172; Continental Congress revenue debate, 29

Blount, William, 42, 152

Boudinot, Elias, 22

Bradford, William, 20

Brant, Irving, 2, 8, 41, 271n14

Brearley, David, 79, 290n21

British influence, 101–103, 113, 135, 208, 210, 213

Bullard, Patrick, 23

Burnett, Edmund, 22

Butler, Pierce, 42, 109, 193; notetaking at Constitutional Convention, 76, 82, 103, 165; proportional representation or equal state suffrage, 61

Caldwell, James, 25

Carey, Mathew, 23–24

Carrington, Edward, 41, 50, 55; correspondence of, 56